Helen Gurley Brown's

Having It All

Shows You How to Have It All.

The famous, sexy, hard-working lady who made The *Cosmo* Woman a celebrity and a success, gives you the lowdown on everything (and we do mean *everything*) from love to having a better body and a better job, from what to wear to how to get married and *stay* married, from your diet to your face (and how to make the most of it), everything, men, money, fame . . . including, among 200 other important topics, such gems as:

Places to Love

• Standing up in the Tower of Pisa • On the chairlift at Vail • In the New York Jets locker room • Every Saturday in a sauna • On a bed of pine needles in a pine forest • In a canoe • In a marble bathtub—*without* water • On the Cyclone roller coaster at Coney Island • In the john of a 747 en route to Europe • Inside a sleeping bag while waiting in line for the Kentucky Derby

(And much, much more.)

Most Pocket Books are available at special quantity discounts for bulk purchases for sales promotions, premiums or fund raising. Special books or book excerpts can also be created to fit specific needs.

For details write the office of the Vice President of Special Markets, Pocket Books, 1230 Avenue of the Americas, New York, New York 10020.

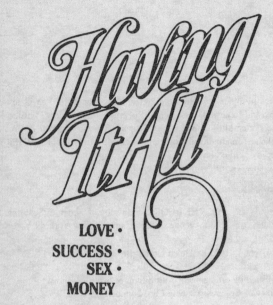

Having It All

LOVE ·
SUCCESS ·
SEX ·
MONEY

EVEN IF
YOU'RE STARTING
WITH
NOTHING

Helen Gurley Brown

PUBLISHED BY POCKET BOOKS NEW YORK

Lyrics from *Can Can* by Cole Porter. Copyright © 1953 by Cole Porter.
Copyright Renewed. Assigned to Robert H. Montgomery, Trustee of the
Cole Porter Musical & Literary Property Trusts. Chappell & Co., Inc.,
Publisher. International Copyright Secured. ALL RIGHTS RESERVED.
Used by permission.

POCKET BOOKS, a division of Simon & Schuster, Inc.
1230 Avenue of the Americas, New York, N.Y. 10020

Copyright © 1982 by Helen Gurley Brown

Published by arrangement with Simon & Schuster, Inc.
Library of Congress Catalog Card Number: 82-16823

All rights reserved, including the right to reproduce
this book or portions thereof in any form whatsoever.
For information address Simon & Schuster, Inc., 1230
Avenue of the Americas, New York, New York 10020

ISBN: 0-671-60545-3

First Pocket Books printing November, 1983

10 9 8 7 6 5 4

POCKET and colophon are registered trademarks
of Simon & Schuster, Inc.

Printed in the U.S.A.

For Cleo and David

Contents

Chapter One

WHO *ARE* YOU?

It is after "The Tonight Show" and I have been awful! I wonder for the 3,578th time—the approximate number of times I've been on the show, multiplied by the number of times I brood about it afterward—why I *subject* myself to this torture . . . does anybody *need* self-flagellation? Riding back from the NBC studios in Burbank to the Bel-Air Hotel in West Los Angeles, tummy allowed to pooch out for the first time in five hours, bravely smiling little face finally free to crumple, I consider asking the driver to try entering the Hollywood Freeway southbound from the southbound *off* ramp; if we make it, this would have us moving north when everybody else was coming *south* and take care of future "Tonight Show" appearances, as well as all life's other problems, very nicely.

Slumped in the seat, I am in pain and, for once in my life, it has nothing to do with looks (a bit of hang-up for me, as it seems to be for so many—more later if you're still reading). With a "Tonight Show" hairdresser working on your hair for twenty minutes, your hairpiece for twenty minutes, and the two of them *together* for twenty minutes, and one of their makeup wizards working on your face for close to an hour, how are you going to look—*ugly?*

Tucked into Calvin Klein's beautiful new silk pajamas—I am al-

1

ways tucked into *somebody's* beautiful new silk pajamas for "The Tonight Show"—and starved to one hundred and five pounds, how are you going to feel—*frumpy?*

No, looks aren't the problem at the moment; performance *is*. This evening, as usual, I have been a babbling, chattery, jittery, just-barely-passable panel member. The jokes between guest-host Don Rickles and fellow guest Fernando Lamas have been bouncing around me like fresh fluffy tennis balls, getting enormous laughs from the studio audience, while my *own* dear little attempts at humor—"There are three kinds of kissers: the fire extinguisher, the mummy and the vacuum cleaner . . . the vacuum cleaner sucks up everything but your eyebrows"—get barely a gurgle of response.

Not hard to understand—I am basically about as funny as a glob of mayonnaise on the sleeve of your new chiffon blouse. So, I ask myself yet one more time, *Why* don't I use my basic brain, stay home and edit *Cosmopolitan*—something, by God, I *can* do better than these jokers, and avoid all this *pain!* Why, indeed? Because, as we are pulling into the Bel-Air driveway, forty minutes from the end of the show, the slow, inexorable cheering up begins. I'm here, at this lovely hotel, in this lovely city, doing "The Tonight Show," I remind myself, because they asked *me*, I didn't ask *them*. Through a long, slow, painstaking process, I have earned the right to be a "Tonight Show" guest, and I'm no better, no worse than most of the other non-entertainer guests they book. If I were *really* terrible, they wouldn't ask me back, would they?

So what, my dear young friend, has any of this to do with *you?* Well, it's just that mouseburgers—people who are not prepossessing, not pretty, don't have a particularly high I.Q., a decent education, good family background or other noticeable assets—can come a long *way* in life if they apply themselves. I am a mouseburger and I have applied. From a problem-ripe youth spent in Little Rock, Osage and Green Forest, Arkansas (the last two are small Ozark Mountain villages), through seventeen secretarial jobs in Los Angeles to my present job at *Cosmo* in New York, I have applied almost *daily*. It occurs to me that if you are *also* a mouseburger (complete test in a moment) who would like to apply, perhaps I can help. Being on "The Tonight Show" is not a very good example (though it *does* reach seventeen million people a night, and I've been guesting for twenty years!) of what can happen to a hardworking mouseburger but there are others: you can have deep love, true friends, money, fame, satisfying days and nights—anything you *want* when you apply *seriously*. And the rewards *grow* through the years. In my fifty-ninth year (as I write these words), I must tell you there are days that are the most exciting and exhilarating I've ever known . . . love with a man that seems the newest, sexiest and most passionate I've *also* ever known (and sexy love was always my specialty . . . you don't have to look like a Playmate to enjoy *that*—more later). Some days I feel genuine *power* in my hands and it feels *good*. And the joys seem to be increasing rather than decreasing at a time when many women my age feel dumped and useless. Some mornings I'm actually euphoric. There are still the *other* mornings, of course, when I wonder if I could do it with an overdose of Pyribenzamine, the only drug in my medicine cabinet (it calms down hives), but those mornings are *few!* So, in this special time of my life, I would like to share some of my joy and some of my "craft" (I *am* crafty, but who ever really believed only the Cream-of-Wheat-hearted inherit the earth?) with *you*. If you hunger for better things, as I have hungered for them, and if you have *guts*—maybe I can help.

Of course we have to determine if you want the same things I have wanted for my book, my craft, to be useful to you. Can we do a little check? Do you, by any chance, *also* want:

To love and be loved by a desirable man or men?

To enjoy sex?

To be happy in your work—and maybe even famous?

To make money—possibly a lot?

To look great?

To have wonderful, loyal friends?

To help your family?

To be free from *most* anxiety?

Never to be bored and maybe leave the world a better place?

Okay, then possibly I *am* your guru, but here's the next test. Since I can only help *mouseburgers*, we now need to find out if you *are* one. (Of course I realize the term "mouseburger" is not quite accurate and should never be visualized—but it *is* the word I've grown accustomed to.) Please answer True or False to these statements:

1. *You're smart.* You may not be an intellectual or a scholar, but you *are* "street smart." Like a little forest animal, you are quick and adaptable. You "know" things. You have what people call good common sense and, because it's so natural for you, you think everybody has it.

2. *Technically smart people intimidate you, but you* know, *in*

3

your way, you are as "smart" as they are. First you're *scared* when you're in over your head with the brilliant, famous, successful, rich, but if you have a chance to hang in for another visit, or if *this* one goes on long enough, you may find yourself questioning whether they're *that* much smarter than you are.

3. *You are sensitive (intuitive) to the point of near craziness.* You can tell *instantly* whether or not you are sinking into a man, and whether other people are sinking into other people. When somebody is making a fool of himself, *you* suffer, not so much because you are a warm, tenderhearted person (though you are), but because you can't help feeling what that other person is *feeling.* . . . Temporarily, you *are* that other person! When a man is falling in love with a woman—not you—you know *that* (and it usually *hurts!*). You sense when a party isn't getting off the ground, when a sales pitch is failing, when you're going to get fired, when somebody likes or doesn't like you at first sight, when the audience hates a nightclub comic, when a person does or does *not* want to discuss his tragedy or triumph. . . . Let's just say if you were any *more* sensitive, your fuzz would always be getting blown away, just like a dandelion's!

4. *You get instant telephone vibes.* About one sentence into a conversation and you *know* you have somebody on the other end of the phone who is an idiot and who will never be able to help you. Other people would figure this out in a few *minutes,* but you know it *instantly.*

5. *While being intuitive, you are also impatient.* You've pulled into a service station and there's a car at each of the two islands, an attendant at each island. The hood is already up on one car, not on the other, so the hood-up one ought, logically, to be finished first. You "know" better. Something about the way the three men— attendant, father and young boy—are strolling around the hood-up car gives you the feeling they're into a Baltimore Colts discussion and you're better off behind the unopened car. Other people are barely aware they ought to *choose* a car to pull in behind, whereas to you, wasted time behind the wrong car would be almost unendurable.

6. *You're modest.* Though you don't deny you have a certain amount of charm and even talent, nobody is apt to hear it from *you;* you tend to downplay rather than stress your assets. Bragging would make you nervous.

7. *Envy is not unknown to you.* Put it this way. In everybody under ninety who isn't in jail, terminally diseased or under indictment

by the Federal Government, you can probably find something admirable they *have* and you *haven't* (and wish you did). As for the really golden people, words haven't yet been invented to describe the disparity you think exists between you and them.

8. *You're more selfish than altruistic.* Idealistic would not exactly describe you—you are not mad to move to India to push birth control or to Riyadh to hasten civil rights until you get something together for *yourself.*

9. *You have a sweet natural sex drive that brings you enormous pleasure.* This deep gut sexuality may not be discernible to others *immediately* as it may have been placed in the "wrong" *body* (nobody is ever going to mistake you for Jackie Bisset), but it's *there.*

10. *You're eccentric and not un-proud of being "different!"* Maybe you sleep in a Pittsburgh Steelers sweatshirt, do your vacuuming at 4:00 A.M. and eat salad with your fingers. You don't conform or *want* to conform to a peer group. It's not that you have your *own* cult following, God knows; you just don't want to be anybody's clone.

11. *You can keep a lot of things going at once.* You can cope with more than one job, one love affair, love affair *plus* marriage (if that's what you want), one close friendship, etc. Your mind is always racing ahead to see what must be done *later* in that hour, that day, that week. Sometimes you rest—*totally*—but in the nonrest time you are getting it all together. You may be deep into *one* activity, but you're always thinking ahead to the next one. The thinking ahead is called being "well organized" and you *are*, even *now.*

12. *You have drive.* You *look* tame, but there is this fierceness, the never quite giving *up* on a project, the willingness to put more *in.* Physically you are not stronger than other people. Your drive comes from your brain. You sometimes hear people who *aren't* making it say they don't have the physical strength to be driven, but "physical" isn't where drive comes from. If you eat properly, sleep enough and exercise, you have the energy. The non-drive person just isn't emotionally set up to *use* it. You may not be either, early in your life, but gradually this funny, gusty drive grows on you.

13. *While being impatient almost to the point of insanity about day-to-day trivia, you have patience for the long haul.* You don't *expect* instant success. You may have worked eight straight weeks on a television script, but you aren't *really* shocked when nobody buys it. You will absorb the disappointment and get on with the next project. You will wear the bastards *down!*

5

14. *You sometimes hurt.* You are capable of sustaining almost indescribable pain! You can be so affected by seeing "him" with another woman that you're certain you will not only never *smile* again, you may not even be able to get your mouth open to *talk* (except to your shrink). Your getting-hurt-by-a-man capacity is *boundless* (topless, bottomless, sideless and backless!) but you're also pretty good at other kinds of being hurt. You may sometimes wonder if you wouldn't be better off *without* some of this capacity to suffer, but it's just one side of the coin; the other, *good* side is your responsiveness and capacity for love.

15. *It's hard for you to be casual about anything.* "It doesn't really *matter,* not REALLY!" you keep muttering to yourself when the job, the soufflé, the weekend plans are falling apart. You ought to be more selective in your grief, but to you, *everything* matters.

16. *Peculiar (to put it mildly!) as you are, you can't think of anybody you'd rather be.* Actually you feel kind of extraordinary at times . . . different from the others, yes, but somehow, well—don't laugh—*better!* You don't want to change skins—you just want to "improve" the skin you're in. Mousy as you are, on certain days you even feel a sense of *power,* probably based on having done something well. Then after a brief-lived feeling of "superiority," you are *apt* to slink back into your mousecage and say, Who, *me,* superior?!—I must be mad! No, you are *not* mad! You are a "mouseburger," and it is quite a wonderful thing to be.

17. *You want it all, and are "willing to pay the price."* You want material blessings as well as deep emotional satisfaction. You want life to be rich and thick rather than thin and watery, but—and this separates you from the dreamers and rationalizers—you simply do not kid yourself that what you want is "inexpensive," let alone free. You know the price for the kind of life you want is work—hard work! You know you can't *hope* yourself to a better life—you must *take* yourself there. Let's put it this way: Your basic mouseburger qualities—brains (though you're not an intellectual), sensitivity and youth—are the cake mix. Add the hard work and you get *cake*.

If you answered "True" to at least ten of these seventeen possibilities, I think you and I are alike. If you answered "True" to even five, I may be able to help you.

Shall we begin?

Chapter Two

HOW TO "MOUSEBURGER" YOUR WAY TO THE TOP

The crux of the Mouseburger Plan—the plan to get all those things you want—is, yes, your *job*. That's where the money, success and clout come from. Also, the kind of job you have can seriously affect what kind of men you meet, and more importantly, whether these men are going to be interested in you.

Could we talk for a moment? A beautiful secretary will be asked *out;* a beautiful account executive will have more impact on a man when *she's* asked out and, if you *aren't* beautiful, a serious job will bring you to more (good) men's attention. Secure, attractive (what I call "good") men are more impressed when your job equals *theirs,* or is at least a serious one. In fact, overall, fewer and fewer men find a woman's success anything but a turn-on.

Oh, vestigial male chauvinists still lurk in the woodwork but most men have learned to enjoy loving a doer rather than a dodo. Am I putting down secretaries? Good God, no! I *was* one for thirteen years, and it's still the best way to get started in many companies; it's just that the big rewards and the big men come when you have moved to another plateau.

This is how it works: You get to a man by dealing with him on his professional level, then stay around to charm and sexually zonk him. Yes, I know sex exists for us to feel good and enjoy ourselves, but you can feel *very* good and enjoy yourself like a sea otter and zonk him as well. More later.

Okay, I'm obviously not going to push a "heavy" job at you just because of the men you will meet or what you'll mean to them after you meet them. The best reason for a great job is the kind of life it can bring and the soul-happiness it supplies—but before we go another step, I must warn you that the Mouseburger Plan and the rest of this book are about equally divided between work (and its pleasures) and love (and its pleasures)—the big two in any sane person's life. Children are something else—we'll discuss them later. Well, I believe life and love are better with an aspiring, achieving man than with a drone, and that kind of man is more apt to be yours if you *also* are not a drone.

Getting There the Other Way

But isn't there an easier way, the traditional way to have a wonderful life? Any nubile girl should be able to attract a "decent" man simply because *all* youth is sexy and desirable. Why can't you acquire, through a "good" marriage, all the wantable things in life, then serve on a hospital committee, fund-raise for charity, devote one day a week to the museum while being the Good-Person-Adored-Wife of this gorgeous man?

For many women, I think that is still the goal. Despite every gain of the Women's Liberation movement, lots of women still prefer their man to have the important job, while they nurture and support him emotionally and occasionally dip into the professional world to stave off ennui. I think many women *still* consider Jacqueline Onassis, Jackie's sister, Lee Radziwill, and Princess Grace the kind of people they'd like to be.

Oh, my poor benighted darlings, even Jackie, at age forty-six, found that being a rich, beautiful Adored Person was not necessarily The Answer. Jackie reentered the work world as an editor at Viking Press seven years ago and is now an editor at Doubleday. We *know* she didn't need the money. Her sister, Lee Radziwill, went into decorating. Charlotte Ford, to add to the list of rich, adored darlings who tried or are trying for a career, got up to her hubcaps in women's clothes (Charlotte Ford for Don Sophisticates). Christie Hefner and Christina Onassis run or help run their fathers' empires. Gloria Vanderbilt long ago took on a heavy career, writing, painting, and subsequently designing linens, dishes, dresses, and now jeans. As for Grace Kelly, she never could have been Princess Grace of Monaco but for her job; being a movie star *(that's* a job) brought her to the Prince's attention. Since their marriage, Grace is said to have wanted to continue to act, but the Prince frowned, so she has poured all the drive into Monagasque industries. Six years ago she joined the board of directors of Twentieth Century-Fox (she left when the company went private); she has also given poetry readings in the U.S. and written a book.

So much for princesses being happy just begetting little princelings and playing palace. (We'll see how Princess Di makes it—she's still young.) And may I point out once again that men like John Kennedy and Prince Rainier aren't going to marry a dear little person, worthy but unknown, like you or me—they're mostly going to marry an actress, a model, a Jet Set dazzler, a daughter with a wealthy father, somebody with *money,* somebody whose family has money, and then—here's my point—those women aren't happy just being wives and mothers *anyway.*

Lauren Bacall said to David Hartman on "Good Morning America" recently, "People should tell your children what life is about . . . it's about *work!* . . ." And, as F. Scott Fitzgerald said to his daughter Scottie, "Your mother learned too late that work was dignity . . . the only dignity." Never mind dignity. Nothing is as much *fun* as achieving.

May we stay with the discussion of the men in your life one more minute? Suppose you agree you can't "get" the supermale unless you have some kind of glamorous package to offer him, but you don't want a supermale *anyway,* just a nice, beautiful male person. Well, my dear, the nice, beautiful male person you love and marry may get more and more successful until the time comes when you're boring him and he will leave you (or less and less successful until *he's* boring *you* with his mid-life crisis and occupational and other insecurities). Even lovely stay-homes, with incredible homes to stay in, closets full of Adolfos, and garages full of Mercedes-Benzes get left out in the garage *with* the Mercedes because they don't have an identity aside from being somebody's wife and mother. I've observed that the women who have as good jobs as their men get left less frequently (although they *do* get left or sometimes they leave *themselves);* and when they are left or leave, they are obviously better able to cope. Rich or poor, you have a better chance of keeping him—and keeping him *interested*—if you *belong* to something or someone besides him. Most men these days love your *paycheck,* incidentally.

What about your *sexuality* if you achieve? Let's talk about *that* for a minute.

Sex and Success

What *is* sexual? Sexual means loving your body, loving being a woman, loving *men,* loving *their* bodies and loving your bodies together. Well, not one of these activities is in any way antithetical to success, even to enormous success.

Does a *man* ever have to choose between being a totally sexual person and loving his work? Of course not, and neither do *you!* You can put love of men *and* love of work first. Can you also be a terrific mother? Thousands of women say yes, and we'll have some tips in a moment.

What about getting masculine and flinty as you climb? Well, being an executive or whatever high-powered person you become doesn't really change the *inner* you, nor how you present yourself. To direct others you don't have to raise your voice one decibel or look less than edible. You're apt to raise your voice a lot higher shrieking at your husband than at the men in the office, and I'm not sure it doesn't require *more* flint to get a falling-down house into shape than it does to run an office.

In other words, what's so feminine about staying home? As for your appeal to men, successful women *have* it . . . don't even entertain any other idea! Why else are stay-at-home wives terrified of their men "staying late at the office" and spending time "on the road" with their female associates? The sexiest women are the achievers, for they are the most interesting and exciting. They challenge a man by being as desirable, sought after and respected as he is.

I've already mentioned (I'm very big on this point!) that a smashing job puts you in touch with the kind of man you couldn't get to as a drone or nonworker unless you're nineteen, a great beauty, or both. As for the *act* of sex, I think passion for work and passion for a man are totally related—you do *everything* with energy and heat. So, yes: you can love deeply *and* be an enormous

10

success. In just a little while we'll talk about love and sex in spangly detail.

But now we must move from the interesting subject of loving men to the somewhat less interesting subject of loving a job. A job, you'll recall, is the means by which you are going to become a Big Winner and have life's riches. Yes, I know you probably *have* a job and expect to have a career, so this pep talk may be a little irritating. Whoever *supposed* you would merely be a man's appendage, the kind of woman who gets left in the garage with the Mercedes-Benzes or that your man would have any better job than *you?* Those days are *over.* Very well, what may *not* be over is your idea that you can have "my brilliant career" *quickly*, and *that* I want to talk to you about, plus I have a few ideas about how to make *this* job—*any* job—useful to your future.

Ready?

In the Beginning

We (you with me helping) are now going to begin the arduous task of mouseburgering your way to the top and, yes, that's what we're going to call it—mouseburgering: quietly, steadily *getting* there although at the moment you feel like nobody special, possibly even a *mouse.* I'll just say right here: The ones who feel *too* special, too gifted, endowed and smiled on by the gods are probably going to get there later than you, if at all. Their egos are too big.

So here we go! You have a job, any scruffy little job—it doesn't really matter what it is, and you don't have to like it. This first little job will probably not get you anywhere much, but what it can do is put you in the arena. Once in the arena, you can begin to grow and to grow *up.* Are we addressing women who are going to become architects, lawyers, doctors? Perhaps. Though they're in a different world, many of these ideas couldn't *hurt.* Still, I'm probably addressing women who aren't *sure* where they're headed.

How old are you? Twenty-one? Thirty? It doesn't matter—you need only to have some kind of job somewhere. Then, from the most unillustrious beginning, however young or old you are, you move ever so gradually *up*, and, if you stay *with* it, the gradual moving up takes you to the top. It's true. It doesn't matter where you start, or with what company; what matters is starting—and hanging in.

May I tell you about *my* early jobs? They were pitiful, and I was pitiful *in* them. In my first, as secretary to an announcer at radio station KHJ in Los Angeles (pay six dollars a week while I learned shorthand and typing as fast as I could in secretarial school), I can still hear the man *screaming* over some newly discovered secretarial "idiocy." There were those who thought he might burst something with all that screaming, and I was one of the people who thought it! Then, having started that job at age eighteen, *sixteen* subsequent secretarial jobs followed, all tiny, scruffy ones, and I was twenty-five years old before a really good secretarial job came along, or before I got any good *at* it—that's seven years of scruffing! Well, scruffing is *okay*. In your early jobs, how *can* you be inspired? How much inspiration *is* there in something for which you get paid five dollars an hour (all you're worth at that point, but who wants to hear *that?*) and which is probably pure drudgery. But one job takes you to another and another, and somewhere along the line, your talent—everybody has *some*—begins to emerge.

Let's talk about talent.

There Is *Something* You Can Do Better Than Other People—That Will Eventually Be the Basis of Your Career

In each of us "specialties" exist. There are only tiny signs of them in your youth (you write poems, make doll clothes, win from grownups at bridge); the specialties may not surface strongly or take shape as career possibilities until your thirties. At *that* point, you're able to talk people into things on the telephone, predict stock-market trends, do good research. Maybe you can look at a room and see it a different way, are a sensational cook, can design, organize, are persuasive with animals, children. Maybe you love oceans, rocks, trees, theater. I can only tell you about the business world, since it's *my* world, but your own specialties will begin to surface sometime after you take a job, or jobs, and then they can be honed. You do *not* have to know early in life what you want to do in terms of career. Should you try going to a career counselor to see what you might be good at? I'm not sure it helps much. You can probe and theorize until you are a bundle of nerve endings, whereas being *in* a job, testing yourself, makes the decision about your life work so much *easier*. I feel talent emerges only when you're already *in* the work world, getting paid for what you do. More in a moment.

What kind of talent *is* there? Which is yours? I tried to figure out categories like "hard thinkers" (engineers, bankers, astronomers); "soft thinkers" (lawyers, university professors, biologists); "people who need people" (salesmen, politicians, clergymen); "creative mavens" (writers, photographers, composers); but they all overlap, so categorizing talent doesn't work! Doctors can be very creative (all that diagnosing!) and photographers have to be "hard thinkers" to understand camera speeds and lenses. Let's just say that somewhere in the melange of job and talent possibilities is *you*, with subtle little predilections that will keep cropping up until one day they become your *thing*.

My thing, honestly, is *feeling!* How I ever got a career out of feeling I don't know. Can you see *that* written down on a job application? Nevertheless, "feeling" made me write "good" letters to my advertising-executive boss when he was out of town. I could "feel" what he wanted to hear—how much we missed him, would he come home *soon*, and then I threw in a little office gossip! His wife said, "Don, that girl can write—you ought to let her write copy," and one day, after I'd worked for him for three years as a secretary, he *did!* For the next *two* years, I wrote Sunkist radio commercials at Christmas, again sort of *feeling* what to say to a housewife about a Sunkist navel orange that would keep her hand off the dial. Immediately afterward, I scampered back to my secretarial post. At the end of my *fifth* year secretarying for this man, the last two writing ad copy once a year at Christmas (by feeling!), I finally got to write copy full time.

I was thirty-one, finished, finally, with my seventeenth secretarial job—and that was thirteen years after I started working. In the new copywriting post, I still "felt" my way along about what to say in the ads I worked on—but to get to the present moment, the editing of *Cosmo* is nearly *all* feeling. I assume *you* hurt like I hurt, and so I know what articles to assign to help us *both* "get through the night." When the articles are turned in by the writers, I can "feel" whether they *"work!"* (If *I* like them, so will you—we're alike.) It's such a *small* talent, really, "feeling" one's way through a piece of writing, but it began when I was young. That specialty— feeling—isn't much, is it? But it was enough.

You, *too*, will begin to have your own little specialties. I am *still* uneducated and not a heavy thinker. I remember a press conference with Jimmy Carter during which I couldn't understand a lot of what he was saying and not just because he is a colorless speaker; it was because my brain turns off at complex subjects! It happens again and again when I'm with people in other worlds than mine. Sometimes when my husband (hereinafter referred to as David) and I are going to dinner with a tycoon, I wonder what *I* am going to talk about! They are in finance, running corporations, analyzing news. Yes, there is quite a lot about magazine publishing to discuss—printing, production, distribution—but I don't really know those aspects of publishing, you see. I concentrate on *Cosmo*'s *writing,* so what I really know is "feel"! Well, surely you have a talent as good as that.

Gradually you find out what it is.

Get Your Nose Out of the Air About Secretarial Work

"Starting as a secretary is a shrewd course for any ambitious young woman," says Joan Manley, group vice president of Time Inc., in charge of all book activities (secretarying is how *she* started, of course). "It plugs you in at a higher level than most entry-level jobs. You can eavesdrop and learn a lot."

Stephanie Phillips, Robert Redford's agent for many years and producer of the Broadway hit *The Best Little Whorehouse in Texas,* went from "floating secretary" to associate producer at ABC in one year because "I was willing to work at ten or eleven at night and when a production job came up, I could go back to all the men I'd worked for and they gave me a terrific recommendation."

Secretarying *is* a great position in which to learn and look around. And if you've tried to get one in a classy company recently, you may find even *that* job isn't so easy to get. I recommend you *try* to get one. Many secretaries don't have to take shorthand these days; they type from tape-recorded dictation. So just get *in.*

Specialties you may not even have noticed in college will begin to surface. Four of my secretaries have moved on to editorial jobs at *Cosmo. Thousands* of potential dynamos start their job climb *yearly* from secretarial work. Lynn Nesbit, senior vice president of International Creative Management, who handles such clients as Tom Wolfe, Michael Crichton, Adam Smith, Michael Korda and a dozen others, began *her* career as a receptionist for the Sterling

Lord Agency. Admittedly, there are secretarial jobs and secretarial jobs. . . . Some are so sensational you may want to stay *in* one. Barbara Seabrook, secretary to Norton Simon Industries chairman of the board David Mahoney, has her own secretary and describes herself as Mahoney's "ambassador to the outside world." Jean Ansel, administrative assistant to Robert Tisch, president of Loew's Corporation, for the past thirty-two years, says, "I got into the secretarial world because I didn't have any alternative and stayed because this job has been my college education, my entree into politics, society, the world of big business. I have no wish to go out and open a boutique or run a travel agency because I just wouldn't be dealing with the same echelon of people I now am." Nancy Finn, administrative assistant for twenty-six years to Arthur Sulzberger, publisher of *The New York Times*, says, "On this level you *do* operate on your own, initiate, follow through . . . I have an assistant now. Of the two hundred members of the Seraphic Society I belong to—secretaries and administrative assistants to the top officials in New York—I don't know any who isn't content with her job."

Not *bad*, you see, being at the center of power, courted by upward-mobile, top-secret-hunting young executives with only *you* knowing who's out front. As a young actor, Marlon Brando dated studio secretaries almost exclusively. F. Lee Bailey, Yousuf Karsh, Allen Funt and dozens of other gifted men *married* their secretaries. I could go *on!*

A College Degree Isn't
That Important

Of course, you need a degree to become a doctor, lawyer, professor, or serve one of the sciences, and personnel managers of the world *love* to see B.A., M.A. or even Ph.D. on your job application, but those degrees don't necessarily get you even the *beginner's* job you want.

Go to college to get an education, to learn how to think, to grow *up*, but you have to work in a job to learn anything and move to a better one. Your college degree won't even make you a whiz *in* your first job. You think you're too good for *them?* Hah, *they* think—rightly—the job is probably too good for *you!* What can you *really* do for a company until you've had a chance to work there?

Some of us didn't go to college at *all* . . . me, for one. Robin Duke, wife of U.S. Chief of Protocol Angier Biddle Duke, and herself national cochairman of the Population Crisis Committee, consultant on population to the United Nations, member of four boards of directors of giant corporations, president of the National Abortion Rights Action League—whew!—didn't attend college. Margaret Thatcher, first woman Prime Minister of Great Britain, who *did,* says "self-education counts for much more than the education you receive at school." Harold MacMillan, former British Prime Minister, quotes his professor at Oxford: "If you work hard and intelligently, you should be able to detect when a man is talking rot. And that, in my view, is the main, if not the sole, purpose of education."

Fate Has *Something* to Do with Your Success— But Not Much

You really needn't think much about luck. *Everybody* is lucky —as well as *unlucky.* I was luckier than my sister, who had polio at age nineteen that left her crippled—can there be any *comparison?*—but *not* so lucky as, say, Katharine Graham's daughter, Lally Weymouth, born rich, brainy and beautiful. "Lucky" people are simply the ones who grab the good fortune that comes to them and run with it.

John McGraw, owner/manager of the New York Giants baseball team, used to say, " 'Lucky' teams win ball games." And the more you do with your good fortune, or luck (of which we all have *some),* the more you have. Example: I was married to a man who thought up the idea for *Sex and the Single Girl* and encouraged me to write it. Being married to a "book man" was luck. Would I have written the book without him? Probably not. But then, David also tried to help another important lady in his life (before me) write a book and nothing *happened.* I'm told she had all the encouragement *I* had (David is very *persistent* about women getting the best out of themselves) and may even have been a better writer—not so hard to imagine—but all the pushing and coaxing and "luck" didn't "take" in her case. And if I hadn't been so "lucky" as to have David around to get a book out of me, well, I like to think I would have written another book for somebody else *some* day or maybe *not* written a book but achieved another kind of success. I had become *reasonably* successful, with "luck" and work, before meeting David, so maybe I would have been another Shirley Polikoff and thought up a "Does She or Doesn't She?" campaign, or started my own agency like Jane Trahey and Mary Wells Lawrence. Somehow, mouseburgers know what to *do* with the luck in whatever form it arrives, but they get it in the first place by *pushing*.

Don't Worry If You *Aren't* Smart or Ambitious Very Early

It's all *right* to be awful in your first jobs, though I hope you'll start being bright sooner than *I* was. Although there was never any question that I had to work—my sister Mary telephoned people from her wheelchair for C. E. Hooper Rating Service, predecessor of the Nielsen Company, to see what radio show they were listening to (pay: forty cents an hour); Mother pinned tickets on merchandise in the marking room of Sears Roebuck; and we couldn't have managed without my eighteen-dollar-a-week salary—I was awful for *years!*

All that financial insecurity may have left me permanently scarred (I tend, still, to be rather anal about money), but it didn't make me prematurely smart or ambitious! In my twenties, six jobs into my subsequent twenty, and working on the Abbott and Costello radio show as a script girl (this was before the ad agency job), I had *yet* to show the teeniest amount of initiative—*nothing!* I was far more interested in sneaking across the corridor at NBC to watch the Bing Crosby show rehearse than in getting *our* script changes up to the mimeograph room. One day my producer-boss asked me to list props we were going to need for sound effects and I left out the big three—gravel crunch, squeaky door, nail being hammered into wood. Once I asked a number of guests on the show to appear for rehearsal at NBC; when the rehearsal was called off, I forgot to notify the guest *star!* Do you *know* how serious it is to have somebody famous show up at a studio for rehearsal when there isn't one?

On Pearl Harbor day, December 7, 1941, the other secretary in my department at radio station KHJ heard the horrendous news, jumped out of bed like a little greased mosquito and went straight to the station. *I* heard the news, hadn't a notion what Pearl Harbor meant to the world *or* radio station KHJ and went back to sleep. (They gave Mary Ellen a raise and sent her around town in a limousine for a month.) I also did my share of sneaking to the beach or mountains on a workday, calling in sick with "poison ivy" and showing up the *next* day with arms and legs slathered in milk of magnesia in order to look "diseased." Thank God I *did* those things . . . I'm so blinders-on *work*-oriented now! I'm just saying, regardless of financial need, it's okay to feel no real sense of responsibility in your early work life, and I think you have to be about twenty-eight or thirty even *now,* with all those opened-up opportunities for women, before you can get to be really valuable to a company and be highly paid.

You don't *like* hearing that and you think I'm a dinosaur not to say you can get there *fast*—once you make up your mind? Sorry . . . I'm being *realistic.* You just keep working away, and *gradually* a career begins to happen.

To Succeed, You Don't Have to Talk Anybody into Doing Anything Flashy for You— or Have Chutzpah

We've all seen Thirties movies in which the office boy mesmerizes the producer into letting him and the producer's secretary star in his Broadway musical, or in which the billionaire is persuaded to back a loony invention powered by aardvarks. Well, that isn't the way it happens in real life. You don't *brazen* your way to the spoils; you know by now that you *inch* your way there. Stalking a boss in his office (or sleeping with him at his summer place) while you are still a baby worker in order to ask for the Big Chance is probably the *last* thing you ought to do, because very likely you aren't ready for the B.C. Nag for the *little* things; don't let them overlook anything you are ready to do, but don't pester for the inappropriate.

When I was a secretary at the William Morris Agency, a call went out for actresses to try out for the lead on the Corliss Archer radio show. An actress! Lights! Fame! So I tortured myself for two straight days, threw up both nights and, finally, could *not* get up the nerve to ask anybody about an audition. What I saved myself from was total, ignominious humiliation! I could barely deliver *phone* messages, let alone a dramatic line. I think the only way you can become an enormous success is by not doing anything *false* to your character, anything that doesn't "feel right," like pushing friends, bosses, strangers to give you the big chance too soon.

18

Of course, it is absolutely okay to use family or other connections to *get* a job (there's no use being stuffy), possibly some place above the bottom—then you'll have to fake it for a while as you learn the job you aren't yet actually qualified for. You may be *fine* and can skip early slavery jobs altogether—I just never had the connections to *get* a job by pull, so let me address other mouseburgers now in lowly posts: Work at the job you're *in*. Do more than your share in that job. Study. Inch along. Pile up "goodness" until you are *so* good everybody can see it and not ignore you . . . if not in this present job, then in the next one.

Don't *Worry* About Challenge and Fulfillment in Your First Few Jobs, *Please!*

Whenever you take a new job, I'm sure you always ask, Is this the right job for me? Will I be happy? Is there enough challenge?

My dear, nobody wants you to waste your time, but you can soul-search yourself to pieces and it isn't *necessary*.

You are very likely *not* going to be glorious, gutsy Veronica Hamel, public defender of "Hill Street Blues," in *this* job, nor real-life Jessica Savitch, no matter *how* much you preinvestigate, so just jump in! If you try out six jobs in two years and leave them all, your record and your life won't be smirched; if you stay in a dull little job "too long," that won't destroy you either. If you keep working and growing and getting better, you *will* get to the job where you can blossom.

Mine was at the ad agency I mentioned a moment ago, sixteen secretarial jobs and nine years after I began. When I arrived on their doorstep to apply and had a feeling "this might be the place!" I simply eliminated eight jobs on my application form so they wouldn't think I was a drifter! Fortunately, nobody checked the employers *left* on the form to see how long I'd stayed.

In your thirties, with lots of job experience behind you, you can think carefully about whether a new job has enough to offer; for now, would you just please dip your little footsies in the water and get them *wet?*

Don't Worry About Starting Late
(Should You Have *Got* Sidetracked)

Although it takes more energy and guts to get into the job world when you've been out of it, or never got *into* it in the first place, a beaver can do it. I'm going to cite just one example: My friend Madelon Talley, recently director of investing for New York State, had been housewife and mother for sixteen years and had *never* held a job when she persuaded one of the partners of the Dreyfus Corporation to let her work for him as an unpaid helper. "First all I did was go out for coffee and do errands," says Madelon, "but I read a lot, got interested in investments and turned out to be—you know—kind of *good* at it." "Good at it" had Madelon, within a year—*one year*—handling two Dreyfus funds totaling more than sixty-five million, with an annual income for herself of over fifty thousand dollars. While at the New York State Common Retirement Fund she managed sixteen *billion* dollars. She's now in private practice where she heads up New Court Capital Management.

There are so many late starters and late bloomers in the job world, we could write a book just about *them.* You already know my thoughts about not having to have a "challenging" job to begin with. Just get into a place and start doing *something.* Once there, if you've got the yearning, needing, longing to be one of the "haves," pretty soon you'll *have.*

A Certain Amount of "Alone" Time or Actual Loneliness Is an Integral Part of Your Growth

At about age twelve, I used to sit out on the porch of my grandmother's house in Osage, Arkansas (population forty), on summer nights watching stars as big as cotton blossoms and dream about life in Hollywood. My sister Mary and I read *Photoplay, Movie Mirror, Silver Screen* like love letters and saved every picture we could find of Jean Harlow, Joan Crawford and Clark Gable. Hollywood was as far off as *Mars,* of course, but I'm *certain* that longing-lonely time was, in an odd way, the beginning of my "drive." There was a Saturday night—age thirteen—when I had some terrible things called "the itch"—where did they *get* those diseases?!—when I got washed down with Lysol while everybody

20

else in my junior high school class was at a party. . . . Talk about *lonesome* . . . and *longing!*

Later, at seventeen, riding on a Santa Fe Trailways bus from Harrison, Arkansas, to Los Angeles to enroll in business school with two thousand (bottom-numbing) miles to do not very much else *but* think—and worry—*that* was a lonely, yearning time that probably "powered" *my* need to succeed after I got through my slothful, baby workdays. Gail Sheehey writes of Gloria Steinem's adolescence, "Alone with the scratch of rats in the walls of a ramshackle house where water froze in the glass before morning because the furnace was always being condemned, shunned by the Polish and Hungarian working people who looked upon hers as the only family in the neighborhood on its way *down.*" *That* must have done something to help create a future leader of the feminist movement.

Says Carolyn Wyeth, sister of Andrew, Jamie's aunt and a gifted painter herself, "When I was maybe seven, my sisters would run down into the woods and play by themselves and not include me. I don't remember being bothered by it especially . . . I think all great stuff comes out of being alone. At the time you may feel lonely, but it's doing something wonderful to you. If you have that till you're twelve or fourteen, boy, you're all right."

In order to "power" yourself to achievement, perhaps you, too, may need some lonesomeness and dreaming-of-the-good-life-out-there-somewhere that isn't anyplace near your neighborhood at the *moment*.

If You Have Daily Anguish from Things that Aren't Your Fault, the News Isn't All Bad

Says New York City's former commissioner of the Department of Ports and Terminals Susan Heilbron (at thirty-four, Susan was the first *woman* commissioner and she dealt with all those tough waterfront people), "When your friends are on teen tours in Europe and you're working the local bakery for the summer, nobody would opt for that, but that's what *created* me . . . having to work constantly through school."

Have *you* a rotten family, bad health, nowhere looks, serious money problems, a minority background, nobody to help you? Early-in-life problems can be the yeast that makes you rise into *bread!* Some of us—Barbara Walters and talent agent Sue Meng-

21

ers, to name *two*—think you can't even *get* all the way if you aren't underprivileged and frequently unhappy as a young person. In a series of articles on women leaders in *The New York Times*, Gail Sheehey said that each of her interviewees "confronted a crisis in childhood, the death or abandonment of a parent or chronic insecurity due to the failings of a father." Examples: Jane Fonda's father left the family for what was described to Jane as "a trial separation." Soon the father she loved was seen keeping company with a girl barely out of her teens and asked his wife for a divorce. Mrs. Fonda entered a mental institution. The cause of her death shortly thereafter was kept from Jane until she read that her mother had slit her own throat. Robin Duke, president of the National Abortion Rights Action League, says her father "was a great golfer but he never really worked. That chronic insecurity has stayed with me always and is certainly a key in my strong sense of responsibility." In her very direct way, Joan Rivers sums it all up by saying, "Any child who is totally happy and totally secure is going to be a nice easy person to like when he grows up, but he or she isn't going to get to be the head of General Electric."

About looks, God *knows* one would rather be programmed to become gorgeous, but you know what? Gorgeous girls used *always* to get sidetracked from a career and can even *now*. They are still grabbed most quickly by the rich, famous, important men their looks attract, are married and impregnated, then are kept home being mamas and matrons until the divorce, after which a serious career is harder to get started. A woman can surely *have* a career with young children in her life, but it's easier if you get the career solidly launched first.

Now here comes the most important thing I will ever say to you—are you ready?

You Must Put the Hours In

There is no *way* to succeed and have the lovely spoils—money, recognition, *deep* satisfaction in your work—except to put in the hours, do the drudgery. If you give, you get. If you work hard, the hard work rewards you. Restless young people (*you?*) tend to think other people do it some other way than through child slavery—that the others are not only luckier and cleverer but that "it" somehow just falls on them and presto they are in the "big time." Almost *never* does that happen. Nearly every glamorous, wealthy, successful career woman you might envy *now* started as some kind of shlep.

Diane von Furstenberg used to lug a bunch of sample dresses around in heavy suitcases to stores where nobody wanted her *or* her dresses. Julia Phillips, Academy Award-winning producer of *The Sting* and *Close Encounters of the Third Kind*, was once a novice fiction reader at the *Ladies' Home Journal*. Composer Stephen Sondheim (to mention a *man* for a change) persuaded a carefully cultivated friend, Oscar Hammerstein, to look at his compositions and say *why* they needed more work, then tried again and again for *years* until he got better. Gloria Steinem, pretty enough to go through life as a goddess, got a job as a Playboy bunny (waitress), wrote about her experience, kept writing until she became an editor of *Glamour* and *New York* magazines, then became a leading figure in one of the most important revolutionary movements of our lifetime—the Women's Liberation movement. Mary Wells Lawrence, owner of Wells, Rich, Greene Advertising agency (billing: four hundred million), says "I was born typing . . . I don't remember learning. My ability to type when I left college earned my first job for me—in the advertising department of the basement floor of a department store. When I was fourteen I sold hats at a hat bar in a department store after school and on Saturdays." My dear friend Sue Mengers, the highest-paid woman executive in the world (she represents Barry Manilow, Gene Hackman, Ryan O'Neal, Sidney Lumet, etc.) was a secretary in the William Morris Agency for five years before becoming a press agent, then a talent agent. "Did you know you were going to become who you became?" I asked Sue recently. "Are you insane??!!" she said. "I thought if I were *lucky,* I was going to marry a dentist and be able to quit work!" Even Farrah Fawcett and Ali McGraw put in years of modeling before they were tapped for television and movie roles. Gradually, *gradually,* specialties—*your* specialty—begin to surface.

I'll be quite blunt; the baby worker who thinks *she* can do it without experience is a *jerk!* My friend Walter Meade, vice president, publisher and editor-in-chief of Avon Books, calls all this experience that separates the pro from the amateur "being able to put the *ass* behind it." John Chancellor, of the prestigious NBC evening news, says that to become a news mogul you have to "put the time in . . . work in the field . . . file stories, file stories, file stories."

Barbara Walters says, "No matter how much things have changed, my advice is, get your foot in the door—especially broadcasting where there is so much competition—get your foot in the door and then just work your fanny off."

Don't Be Your Own Best Friend!

I think unconditional love is what a mother feels for her baby, and not what you should feel for yourself. Author Margaret Halsey said in a *Newsweek* editorial: "The [false] idea is that inside every human being, however unprepossessing, there is a glorious, talented, and overwhelmingly attractive personality. Nonsense. Inside each of us is a mess of unruly, primitive impulses, and these can sometimes, under the strenuous self-discipline and dedication of art, result in notable creativity."

I couldn't agree more. If we're too approving of ourselves too early, we may never be motivated to move onward. Yes, of *course* you should feel pleased at the day's job well done, the face and body exercised and well-groomed, but heavy self-love must be *earned*.

Be Encouraged—There Are Only a Few Good *Anythings* in Life

Does there seem to be such a chasm between you and the achievers—all those people making so much money already and you there in your little drone's job that you think you'll never cross the gap?

My dear, let's look ahead one second—people will *need* you in big jobs, so just give yourself time to *get* there. There is nothing, *nothing* but room at the top. . . . Headhunters charge large companies thousands of dollars merely to try to *find* good people for top jobs. The few people who *are* good in any field can dictate where they'll work and what they'll earn. You can one day be one of them. You move to the big time from having been promising in the small time long enough to have somebody give you the chance.

Being successful in a big job, staying there, isn't much of a problem either—the challenge is moving up from your small job *to* the big one and caring enough to inch along and *arrive*. . . . And that is what I am going to try to help you do. More specifics about getting from one job to another *soon*.

Rule Out of Your Mind Forever
that Competition Is Bad

Competition may be bad for *lazy* people or dumbbells, but all "competing" *really* is is being "your best self."

Does anyone *really* say to herself, "Aha! I will make this sale because it will just *kill* old Ralph, or I will design this great dress because Daphne, my rival, will be furious!" You sell and design because it's what you *do* in life and you do it the best you can; you're not even *thinking* about anybody else most of the time when you work. You are simply "getting on with it."

Diane Sawyer, co-anchor of the CBS "Morning News" show, says, "Competition is easier to accept if you realize it is not an act of aggression or abrasion. It's a 'given' in the broadcast industry. Whatever news story I'm working on, two other networks are automatically after the same story. . . . I've worked with my best friends in direct competition. Whatever you want in life, other people are going to want, too, and you have to believe in yourself enough to accept the idea that you have an equal right to it."

Linda Wachner, president and chief operating officer of Max Factor, says, "You're really never competing against anyone but *yourself* . . . trying to get the very finest performance out of *you*. There are endless rewards for *all* of us. You are not taking anything away from anybody else when you are good."

It's Okay to Separate Yourself from the People
Who Aren't Going Your Way

I *never* liked the looks of the life that was programmed for me—ordinary, hillbilly and poor—and I repudiated it from the time I was seven years old, though I didn't have many means of repudiation. I didn't like my little-girl cousin who peed in the creek in front of a lot of other people. I didn't like all my cousins saying "ain't" and "cain't" and "she give five dollars for that hat."

They were, and are, dear, lovely people who lead honorable lives in the Ozark Mountains, but I wanted something else. And so I began to feel and be "separate." Later in life, you can rejoin the ones you left—for periods of time, at least. After all, you *are* they, but early on you have to quietly separate yourself in your head from those people (friends, family, colleagues) you don't want to be like. You can also have *work*mates who don't want what you want, and you mustn't let them hold you back because they repudiate your zeal and ambition.

Be one of the girls, but also *don't* be one of the girls!

Try to Make Life Thick and Lush, Not Thin and Skimpy

I know an accountant who has just *enough* to do every day. She's been in the same job for eight years, her first and only job. She watches a little television, checks in with a few rabbity friends, occasionally has a rabbity friend to dinner, plenty of time to do *everything*, but virtually nothing to do in the *time!* Then there's my friend Penny, whom people are always clucking over because "the poor girl is driving herself *crazy* with all that activity!" Penny is taking five Latvian exchange students in for Sunday dinner, getting one kid off on a ski trip, the other into his Halloween costume, attending her weekly disco dance class, finding jobs for several unemployed friends, giving her mom a perm, and *trying* to write an article for one of the airline magazines while working as a secretary to a movie producer. Doesn't she *ever* let up?! Never. And Penny is one of the most loved, least depressed women I've ever known. If you want a bit more professional recognition than Penny, a lot of the "thickening" in life should have to do with your *work*, but that will come when you have a job which *deserves* the investment of time. In the meanwhile, while you're still a baby worker, life's thickening should come from *anything* that interests you. If you *aren't* "overbooked" and "overcommitted," there's a very good chance you aren't getting half enough out of life or out of *you*.

For a Long Time, Maybe Years, Your Bodytime Must Be Geared to Other People's—Later You'll Have the Joy of Working to *Your* Bodytime

Most bosses need you to work from 8:30 or 9:00 A.M. to 4:30 or 5:00 P.M. Later, when you're *successful*, you can do what feels best to *you*.

I now get to *Cosmo* at 10:30 or 11:00 A.M. and work until nine, ten, or whenever I feel like stopping (if David's in California, I stay until after midnight). That seems self-indulgent when forty-four other people are asked to arrive at nine or ten, but I get away with it because I'm the boss and because, being an owl, I *accomplish* more arriving late and working late. Doing what *your* body likes is one of the perks of success!

What Makes Us Do What We Do?

I hope I've convinced you—the only thing that separates successful people from the ones who aren't is the willingness to work very, very hard.

Where does drive *come* from? We don't know for sure, although it can come from deprivation, as we mentioned earlier. I think if you are still reading, you may have it, even if it's buried pretty far inside you just for the moment. Some people refer to this carrying-on as the Puritan Work Ethic—working hard because we feel guilty if we *don't*. That's okay. Of course no boss, shrink, parent, husband, or *I* can get you to work cravenly and go the distance if you don't feel like it. The willingness has to come from inside you because you are scared, needy and ambitious. . . .

Mildred Arnold, vice president in charge of merchandising for the Los Angeles Thrifty Drug Stores' five hundred and twenty outlets (and about two hundred fifty million dollars' worth of merchandise a year), says, "You don't *need* drive . . . you just have to see that a job needs doing, want to see that a *good* job is done and *do* it!" Mildred walked into Thrifty a few years ago in response to a "Help Wanted" sign in the window. That's about as low as you can *start!* (I think she had/has *secret* drive.)

Aside from causing her to work prodigiously, drive also probably saved the life of Twentieth Century-Fox Films president Sherry

Lansing, about whom one never hears anything but the most extravagant praise. Struck by a car going forty miles an hour through a crosswalk, Sherry's skull was cracked open, her leg shattered, and she wasn't expected to live. Says Dr. Harvard Ellman, the surgeon who treated her, "Her leg was broken in so many pieces that if she lost the circulation in any of them, she'd lose her leg. Her will, her determination had a lot to do with her recovery. In my twenty-five years of practice, I've never had a patient more positive."

And this is my all-time favorite "drive" story, although it's about a *man:* As recalled in *Reader's Digest* by an assistant coach at Ohio State, "Two of us were looking out the window one day and saw Woody [Woody Hayes, Ohio State's long-time brilliant coach] slowly easing into the last empty space in the parking lot, barely wide enough for a car. But he couldn't get out of the car; there weren't more than four inches alongside and he couldn't open either door. A moment passed, and then he backed the car out. Now, as we stared in disbelief, he got out of the car, walked to the rear, planted his hands on the trunk and slowly, grimly, pushed the car back into the space."

I would try to do that, wouldn't you?

Success Is Almost Inevitable
for the Mouseburger

Once you decide to apply drive (and *don't* let the word frighten you . . . it just means doing whatever there is to do that day *that day*) to your work, go this "try harder" route, "pull out all the stops," few, if any, *grisly* disappointments actually befall you—you get to be too valuable, even in your modest little post. Also, the plan begins to work *immediately;* you don't necessarily make visible progress each hour, day or week, but it's there, happening, and you'll start feeling the satisfaction and small rewards (head pats, more money, more responsibility) right away.

Starting gradually, the plan begins to deliver more and more—professionally and personally—and pretty soon you go like *crazy.* As successful as I was in my late thirties, and then in my forties, the *most* successful I've been is in my fifties, when everything that was *going* to take hold has had a chance to *take* hold! Once in a while you have a setback—lost job, company politics you couldn't get out of the way of, horrendous personal problems—men, love, health, money—but as you get older, you get *stronger*. Your skin will be slightly less peach-fuzzy, but you will become more beautiful, sexier. You will be in full bloom when other women are losing their husbands, children and confidence.

Remember, this quiet little plan *only* calls for you to try to be excellent in whatever small thing you do—nothing alien or beyond you. Start when you feel like starting, inch your way along, but it will never let you down; you will never go backward if you keep at it. Okay, but what should you be doing *now* to get ahead? What daily stuff?

Here are some ideas.

Getting There Means *Not* Being Stingy

Could you come in on Saturday? Could you take anything home? Can your boss think of anything that would be helpful to *him* personally (those denigrated "personal chores!") *or* the project? . . . You don't care if it's menial, you just want to *help!* Turn in work nobody asked for—it may not be accepted, but there's almost no way people can't be impressed that you *did* it.

So un-Women's Lib, you say . . . so beneath you, fooling around with the *little* stuff when you were meant for big, beautiful achievement. Bullshit! You want to get on with your life and make real money, and the way to do *that* is to extend yourself. God knows you aren't taking the work home for *them*, it's for *you*. And that goes for helping the other girls, too, including that bitch Angela, who would have done us a favor *not* to have pulled through her last bout with mononucleosis.

Not helping simply means you are dumb. Your head is wrong. "Nice" girls finish *first*.

Let me go on: Being too niggardly and selective about what assignments you'll accept—"but I'm not getting *paid* to do that!" —is like being too skimpy with how much *love* you are going to give out in life: it may be better to *over*invest. It may seem that people are "using you" but actually it's the other way around— you are using *them*. Do get *credit* if you can—no use coming in on Saturday to straighten the files if no one ever knows you were *there*. Just don't be too stingy with your "free labor" for bosses or co-workers.

Do It This *Minute,* or at Least This Day

The best way to get noticed and loved before you're brilliant at your job is to do everything *instantly.*

A boss may give you five "instantlies" and you have to decide which to do first, second, etc., but get *on* with it all. One of my helpers whisks off to the store the same day she hears my *need* for two-pound dumbbells, taupe eye-liner, plant fertilizer and Woolite, even though *Cosmopolitan* would surely not be in peril if she waited and God *knows* all that errand running isn't what her mother sent her to college for. You'll be relieved to know the dear child also evaluates manuscripts, does research, handles just about everything that doesn't absolutely require *me;* but the point is she not only does the grubby stuff—cheerfully—she also does it *fast*—and I can't live without her.

Your Ability to Make Good Decisions About *Little* Things Will Become an Important Asset

When I was a young copywriter, I would write about twenty versions of the same piece of copy, mostly all terrible. Out of the entire mess, perhaps *two* would be worth turning in. Somehow my little brain told me which the two *were,* and in those two, which words and phrases to cross out and *try* to make better. I think it was more a matter of deciding what to leave in and what to toss than being able to *write* well that kept me my job.

Suzanne de Passe Lemat, the glamorous black executive in charge of motion-picture development at Motown Records, says, "I've always been connected with my soul . . . felt and known things that helped me move in the right direction." Small *personal* decisions can begin to contribute right away to your success—deciding *not* to slither away from extra work they just handed you, *not* to call in "sick" when you *could* stay on your feet and go to work, *not* to spend every possible moment hanging out with your pals, *not* to badmouth the people who employ you, even though you think they're idiots. We're really talking about the decision to do what's good for your *job* rather than what might be more personally pleasurable. Anyway, I can assure you that what's *there* in that squirrely little job of yours, plus the "right decisions," will be *enough* to get you to the next plateau.

Although You're Aggressive on the Inside, It Doesn't Necessarily Show

A woman who now makes over one hundred thousand dollars a year told me recently, "I used to despair of ever amounting to anything because I thought you had to stride around like Joan Crawford and be dynamic and aggressive and I knew I'd never make it!"

A few women do still literally pace forcefully, speak dramatically, act important, making the rest of us feel meek and ineffectual. I've seen the pacers, the dramatic speakers clamber right up there—for a little while—but usually they clamber right back down because aggressiveness is about *all* they have. You see, there is *no* substitute for brains plus charm plus *hard work*. You should be "privately aggressive"—just quietly firm up on the job, make the "good decisions," keep your shiny eyes open for places to go. Need, yearn and *work*—that is the kind of aggression that brings success, not acting dramatic.

The Way to Dress for an Office Is *Pretty*

There just isn't any reason to hack your way up in tweed or gray flannel if they bore you. Blending in with the furniture is *one* way to "dress for success" but not the *only* way. Whatever you feel you look nice in is what you probably ought to be wearing, provided it isn't slashed to the navel or dripping with lace. Even *fluffy* is okay! *Cosmo*'s fashion coordinator, Gretchen Parks, wears a white voile summer dress that turns us *all* on—boys, girls, typewriter repairmen, everybody. . . . It's great!

Maybe it's different in *your* world and you ought to wear all that dull businessy stuff, but I've never seen a woman held back in a job because of what she wore if her brain and drive and devotion were okay.

Getting Along with Other People Is 50
(Maybe Even 60, 70!) Percent of Your Success—
But that Doesn't Necessarily Mean Being
Gregarious or Funny or Even "Popular"

They may never say you are a budding Carol Burnett, slap their
knees and declare, "My God, that Adeline is *funny!*" but it doesn't
matter. If you are kind and trustworthy, some people will *love* you,
most others will at least *like* you. All it takes is not being a pain in
the ass. You see, you can't *succeed* and be a pain.

Let me tell you about a royal pain in *my* office. She has yet to
smile or say hello when you meet her in the hall. She works *reasonably* hard and is smart, but she is unpleasant. One night I was
working late and around 11 P.M. I had a *food* fit. I couldn't find
anything in the refrigerator where we all store food, and this particular night I started going through people's *desks. Shameless,* but
hungry is *hungry,* and I planned to make full confession and resti-
tution the next morning. In Lydia's desk I found the last of a box of
raisins and ate the whole thing—twenty-six raisins, stale and dry,
and nothing ever tasted so good! The next morning, Lydia was
waiting for me as I came through the reception room. "Mrs.
Brown," she said, "did you eat my raisins?" "Oh, my God,
Lydia," I said, "I did and I meant to bring some in with me on the
way to work. I'll get them at lunchtime." She skulked away.
Later, when I saw her again, she still looked angry. "Lydia," I
said, "did you have special plans for those raisins?" "Yes," she
said, "I'm dieting and that was my eleven o'clock snack."

My Bonnie instantly went out to the market, got a big box of raisins for Lydia (for which she never said thank you), and the subject
of raisins never came up again. On pain of *death* would I ever have
robbed that girl's desk again, but what a goose she was! For one
thing, a boss, right or wrong, is nobody to humiliate, even though
desk-scavengering is pretty tacky. She could without *too* much effort have gone across the street for more raisins, or stolen bond paper to assuage her pique, or whatever!

I was not planning to become this girl's biggest life problem,
and, more importantly, this was a chance for her and me to have a
"guilty secret." "Had any more food fits, Mrs. Brown?" she
could have asked, or, "I left fudge brownies this week and they
weren't touched!"—and become a special favorite. Not that *that's*

such a big deal, either, but it doesn't *hurt* your career to have people think you are adorable and charming. To be a pleaser and a charmer is *not* selling out; it is investing in happiness (yours!) through the process of making other people glad to be around you.

Okay, you have your *own* atrocity stories, but just let me quote Boston psychologist Harry Levinson, who says, "Abrasive personality is the single most frequent cause for the failure of bright men and women in the executive ranks of business and industry." Some *entertainers*—actors, singers—behave badly and survive, but they are different from you and me—we simply *can't* be stuffy, snippy, selfish, snapping-turtle little bitches and succeed.

Don't Tell *Everybody* Your Personal Problems

Share personal grief with one or two office friends you like, but don't burden your employer. He should probably know about any serious problems in your life, but don't use him for a daily confessional. I once had a helper who deeply saddened (as well as *bored!*) me with the continuing saga of her husband's aged father having come to live with them, disrupting the household, being a pain in the neck, etc., etc., sandwiched in with her grief about a face-lift she felt had gone wrong (it looked fine to *me*).

An office *is* a home, to some extent; it's where you live every day, so why *shouldn't* people know something about your personal life? Just don't bog *everybody* down with your grief; pick listeners selectively.

Sexual Harassment Isn't
What It's Cracked Up to Be

My assessment is *totally* personal, *totally* prejudiced, but I think if an employer or boss is giving you a bad time with his unwanted sexual attentions and absolutely won't stop though you've reasoned with him and complained to management, then you have to *leave*. Did no one every change jobs because of *other* unpleasant working conditions? This is simply *one* of them.

Thinking back to the Forties—will you allow me?—when jobs were *not* easy to get, when you did *not* do anything to rebuff or offend a boss, even a horny one, lest he fire you, a lot of passes were surely made but, Jesus, I can't remember anything really heavy or bad coming out of it. One of my bosses at dear, staid Music Corporation of America used to ask me to come in on Sundays to "get rid of this extra work," and he would chase me around his beautiful quiet office with all those fabulous antiques and sometimes *catch* me, but only for a few hugs and kisses. . . . Was that so terrible? No, it shouldn't have been part of the job, but how much trouble was I *in?* Of the millions of naughty suggestions made by millions of male employers to their "defenseless" female employees yearly, I'd say half cheered the girls *up,* half brought the girls *down,* but probably nothing bad has come out of *most* of them.

I watch television interviews with women who are suing an employer because of some unacceptable sexual conduct which took place five years previously. . . . I'm sure they are justified, but I can only think of the *better* things I would do with the five years than be bogged down with hate, litigation and legal fees . . . like change companies and get on with one's professional *life!*

Forget Trying *Not* to be a Woman (Whatever That Means) in Business

We said earlier that successful women remain sexual beings. What you also need to remain—or become if you already aren't—is *charming.* You'll need all the charm you can muster to be persuasive and comfortable to be around, and charm isn't masculine or feminine. If you can make a man (boss, client, employee) feel more masculine and confident because of the way you look at him when he talks, then *do*—you'll listen just as attentively to other women. Rapt attention between the opposite sexes *does* tend to have a sexual quality, however, and so, to some extent, one could accuse you of "using sex" in business when you gaze straight into his eyes. That's okay. The sexual you is part of the *whole* you and doesn't snap off—God, we *hope* not, anyway!—between nine and six. At any rate, you can *think* sex and still do business—I've done it for *years!* The *garbage* one reads about keeping sex out of your work! Sex is *there* because he's a man and you're a woman, but that knowledge doesn't make you jump on each other in the conference room or get each other fired.

I've seen one or two cases of a man getting so nutty about a female co-worker, usually his employee, that he went berserk and really *did* screw up his career (with her help, of course!) but I have never seen it happen the other way around, *never!* Maybe that's because until recently we didn't have any high-powered careers to screw *up!*

Let me ask you something. When you meet a man, don't you *always* idly wonder what he'd be like in bed? *I* do—even with garage mechanics and maitre d's of Moroccan restaurants. Nobody *knows* you're wondering that—and it's only sexual curiosity (we'll get to sex in another chapter). A lot of the time you're going to be concentrating too hard on your work to think about what sex you or anybody else is. As for sex impeding the workload, I think sexual tension and electricity between men and women in an office *help* get the job done. Trying to please somebody you're nutty about can be productive.

The late, gifted Kay Daley, Creative Director of Revlon and inventor of the first and subsequent fabulous shade promotions (Fire and Ice, Cherries in the Snow, etc.), believed that a sexual bond between creative people—art director and copywriter, account executive and copy chief—was productive. We both felt we'd had that productive association with men we never went to bed with and it was *great*. You may have it, *too*. (Of course, sex isn't always *just* in the air—sometimes you get *on* with it.)

Okay, being "crazy in love" is a confusing, often work-interrupting state, whomever you're in it with, but being in it with somebody at work is no more confusing or work-interrupting than if the somebody is across town. With the exception of my present job at *Cosmo,* may I say I have never worked *anywhere*—and I've worked a lot of anywheres—without being sexually involved with *somebody* in the office. What else are office friends *for?!* It can be a bit depressing to be dropped by the office Don Juan as he works his way through the secretarial staff and you discover you were number eleven, but this situation need not deprive anybody of employment.

As for not sleeping with the boss, why discriminate against *him?* It's like sleeping with anybody else; there are the good times, the bad times, and the affair probably won't go on forever, but the liaison doesn't necessarily affect the P and L—yours or the company's. Sleeping with somebody influential isn't the way to get to the top, we all know *that,* because, no matter what exalted position somebody crazy about you puts you in, you can only stay there with talent and brains. . . . I just think you can sleep with whom you want to—quietly and discreetly (do you really need to tell *anybody?)* without disaster.

Success Is Cumulative

Okay, have we established that you don't *ever* have to do one spectacular splashy thing that has everybody "oh-my-Godding"? Success is the day-to-day goodness you keep turning in.

Let me give you a non-people example. To celebrate *Cosmo*'s selling more copies than any other women's magazine at the newsstand, we decided, a couple of years ago, to reprint our "blockbuster" articles in a tenth anniversary issue and started looking through ten years of back issues for the "spectaculars." We couldn't *find* any! *Nothing* was outstanding—no blockbusters. They all folded into each other like egg whites into a soufflé. The only semiwild thing we had was Burt Reynolds nude in the centerfold, but looking back at that photo in retrospect, *it* wasn't that spectacular (and, since we didn't print up any extra copies, *that* issue was actually no more "successful" than others).

Okay, "cumulative success" is how it is going to be for you, too—success sneaking in on little cat feet simply because you gave the best you could day after day, week after week, year after year. My book *Sex and the Single Girl* was not *my* big push—not the one big important thing. It was just the next effort . . . to sit down and put together a few book chapters because I was in trouble with my advertising job and was doing something to keep busy. Truth. I was thirty-nine by then and had already been working twenty-one years!

You get in the habit of working diligently, and one day that puts you in "scoring position."

Always Be Working Out

Although I've suggested you do just about *anything* that keeps your motor tuned, work-oriented or not, the working out is *best* applied to your job, and gradually, you will begin to undertake little projects that contribute to it.

May I tell you two of mine?

As a baby copywriter, I used to pass the Statler Hilton Beauty Shop every day on my way to work and notice their terrible windows, all fly-specked and boring. Miss Busybody went to her typewriter and did up twelve "special offers" for the shop to put in its windows to lure working girls like me in to have their hair done. "We'll have you out in fifty minutes," "Haircut five dollars on Tuesdays," "Bring us a picture, we'll copy it," etc. I really didn't know what I was talking about and I was a very shy mouse, but the shop printed them up, reported good business and invited me in for a free hairstyling. Any busybody could do *that*.

Second brainstorm: One of our accounts at the ad agency was a reducing salon. I got the addresses of twenty wealthy women—wives of movie producers, business tycoons, etc., wrote each woman a letter containing personal information about *her*—her kids, charity work, etc. (gleaned from gossip and news clips), and suggested the salon mail the letters inviting the women in. Out of the twenty contacted, five called and made appointments—not bad for a neophyte copywriter. Nobody asked me to hustle customers—the salon never really thanked me, not even with a free ride on one of their motorized couches—it just occurred to me that my letters frequently moved people and I could "work out" on behalf of this client.

I entered a thousand contests in which you wrote a testimonial slogan and *nothing* happened until finally I won *Glamour* magazine's Ten Girls with Taste Contest (the prize was a wardrobe from Joseph Magnin and trip to Hawaii). My taste was terrible, but I wrote good letters! To use a somewhat "heavier" example of "getting on with it," when *Sex and the Single Girl* was published, I got lots of mail from women who wanted advice about their love lives. Reading it, David said, "You ought to have a magazine," and one Saturday night we sat down and wrote up a format. David did the rationale for there *being* such a magazine. I jotted down several dozen article ideas and possible advertisers, nothing very brilliant. Without going much further than that, David took our prospectus to several publishers, all of whom turned it down; finally the Hearst Corporation said they didn't want to *start* a magazine, but had a failing one—*Cosmopolitan*—on which we could, perhaps, superimpose our ideas. That's what we did. I'd never set foot in a magazine office except for a few minutes at *Glamour* when I won the contest, but seventeen years later, I'm still at *Cosmo* and I could not imagine a better job—all the result of "working out."

David and I already had *some* successes behind us; I'd written a book and been an advertising copywriter; he'd edited a magazine and been a movie executive. We knew how to write a proposal somebody might *read*, and David had enough friends to get appointments with publishers. Still, we'd both had failures. We'd both been fired two or three times. I'd entered (but not won) those dozens of contests, written (and had rejected) stories and articles, tried for a dozen jobs I never got. The magazine prospectus, along with the outline for *Sex and the Single Girl* were simply two *successful* efforts in a long line of projects that didn't automatically work. The point I want to make is that we *did* our magazine outline immediately—the minute we thought of it—without the slightest prospect of anybody *wanting* it. I think if we sat around and planned and discussed and philosophized endlessly, *Cosmo* would never have happened.

Okay, is that clear? *Don't* screw around contemplating; get your rejection so you can get on with the *next* project!

P.S. I don't recommend workshops, seminars, night school, even college courses—at least they never got *me* anywhere. Listening to experts and working out in *school* are simply delaying tactics; you need to be working on the real *stuff*.

Moving Up

Okay, how long are you to carry *on* like a craven little nit, doing all that "pleasing" and all those grubby chores in whatever job you're in?

Not forever. Let's say you're doing okay in your job but the big stuff isn't happening. Very well, I think you must now realize strongly in your gut the need to be something better than you currently are, and then you must have *enough* needing, yearning and quiet gall to get *on* with it.

How? Well, it may just *happen!* Companies need to move along anyone who is movable and it's happening more and more to women since Women's Lib got after everybody. Still, selfish and maddening as it is, people are not always looking for opportunities *for* you. They need you doing what you're doing and are also too busy trying to be successful themselves to worry much about *you*.

When I was a copywriter on the Max Factor account at Kenyon and Eckhardt, Factor needed a new advertising director and I asked my boss if I could apply. He said absolutely no and practically fell in a heap laughing. Actually, he was probably right—budgets and marketing strategy are *still* beyond me and I would have been unsuccessful in the job. *You* may ask, however, and receive.

If not, then you will eventually have to go job-hunting. Don't do that until you've got the good out of where you *are,* however. A young lady who was my secretary for four years began to write some of the full-page *Cosmopolitan* ads we ran in *The New York Times* during year three. Joining me when she was eighteen, Peggy sort of got "dry behind the ears" for three years and grew *into* writing. I don't think I asked her to write those ads—perhaps because *I* have always written them and was rather proud of my own efforts. Peggy subsequently became promotion coordinator for *Cosmo's* publisher.

You can't *just* have your eye on the next rung. You have to do what you were hired for efficiently and expand ever so gradually so that you don't upset the rhythm of the people you're working with. And you can't be too brassy. You must have a very careful sense of what you can ask a boss to let you do that is not within your present work frame. A secretary who came to work for me asked instantly if she could attend all our *Cosmo* editorial meetings—those usually attended only by senior editors. I'm sure she felt she was just being enthusiastic, showing a willingness to learn, but it didn't come off quite that way. Secretaries are *not* yet editors—you work *up* to that—and it had a slightly jarring effect (one is put in a position of saying No, which makes a boss feel funny). You may make some mistakes in this business of asking and not receiving—that's almost inevitable. My advice is to volunteer like crazy and also turn in work that nobody asked for—but make it easy and comfortable for your boss to ignore that extra work or say No to your requests. Don't be *irritating.*

Okay, if there *is* no better job in your company (school, hospital, bank, library, TV station, store, doctor's office), then it's time to go to another place. You will need to make phone calls, pin down appointments to *get* the next better job—to arrive at a place where you can *blossom.*

PHASE II—*Very well, let's say you are now, at last,* in *that blossoming job. Maybe you have a secretary of your own, are in charge of a department. Here are some* new *rules to use now that you're somewhat further along.*

Don't Be Afraid that Success Will Defeminize You

We've already said that you remain a sexual person no matter how successful you are, that man-woman awareness continues to exist in offices even *with* all parties working hard and making big contributions.

Okay, you could accept that idea as long as you were in a minor job, but now, having been offered a new spot that will send you soaring, you are scared to death to be tampering with traditional man/woman hierarchy . . . i.e., men must be big, strong, superior (as in *he* boss, *you* underling), women sweet little girls (as in adoring secretary). As even a *minor* executive, you're afraid you'll screw up how men feel about you.

I understand that fear but it is totally unwarranted. Joan Ganz Cooney, president of Children's Television Workshop, who created "Sesame Street" and is one of the most admired women in the country, says, "I tell young women to think about the strong mothers of this world . . . do they not function in a role of complete authority during the most important learning years of a man's life? Does a man think of his *mother* as masculine? In my office, many men have cried with me, and I think they rather enjoy it . . . they couldn't let down the emotional barriers with a male boss. The women don't cry as much. I am an earth mother perhaps, but there's a sort of collegial atmosphere here. . . . We talk everything over, we *all* participate, then I make the final decisions. Does making decisions defeminize anybody? No!"

Robin Smith, former president and general manager of the Book Club Division of Doubleday and Company, now president of Publishers Clearing House, largest magazine subscription agency in the world, says, "When you become an executive, you do not raise your voice or get loud or masculine. You got where you got and continue to become more successful by using logic, reasoning—by being rational. These qualities are where your strengths lie and what got you to the boss-position in the first place. . . . There is nothing masculine about them. You also get what you want by being stubborn—a very *feminine* trait!"

When Juanita Kreps was Secretary of Commerce, undersecretary Dr. Sidney Harmon said, "She was always female . . . not exactly flirtatious but I never forgot she was a woman."

Well, one could go on and on with testimonials, but the bigger job can only make you more desirable to *most* men. . . . That is God's truth.

Now let's talk about how to *do* it.

Get Back to Them in a Hurry

You're more important now. People are asking you for ideas rather than an extra set of Xeroxes. Give answers and ideas quickly and it will save you from having to give terrific ones! The longer you wait, after somebody has asked for an opinion, the better your answers have to *be*. By coming to some conclusion quickly, they will always feel that from you they get *action*. It may take a *little* time to collect material you need, but don't take too long.

If You Don't Know What Somebody Is Talking About, *Ask!*

Obviously you have to be a *little* careful about being ignorant of something you're already supposed to know. Also, you may not want to ask the person who gave you the assignment *or* the most important person involved in it, but if you're adrift, get *help!* Bungling along as though you understand when you *don't* is insane and can get you into *big* trouble.

Don't worry about knowing everything in your new job *instantly*, however. Lois Korey, formerly executive vice president and creative director at Needham Harper and Steers Advertising, now head of her own agency, says, "There's something to be said for *not* knowing too much. You don't know all the dont's, so you dare to try where others who know more won't try at all!"

It's Okay to "Borrow" Ideas from a Friend
When You're Stuck

Before we were married, I would take my Max Factor television and print-ad assignments to David and get "contributions." (Translation: he would bail me out with a lot of concrete suggestions.)

I'm *still* borrowing, from David and everyone else, material for "The Tonight Show," *Cosmo* ads, little speeches I have to make, plus anything I can get my hands on for the magazine. Speaking of borrowing talent, David has written the cover blurbs for *Cosmopolitan* for the past seventeen years, and the article ideas *he* likes are the ones we assign. When my friend Charlotte Kelly became public relations director at *Ladies' Home Journal,* she used to borrow from both David and me. Now she's senior vice president/director of corporate communications at the giant ad agency D'Arcy-MacManus & Masius and people borrow from *her.* It is idiotic *not* to use all the resources you have. Call it research, call it talking things over, but do call!

Getting other people to generate ideas helps generate your *own.*

Make Your Boss Look Good

Though you're up the ladder a rung, you probably still have a boss and always *will* unless you go into business for yourself; even presidents and chairmen of corporations have bosses (boards of directors). Your job, always, is to make that person above you look good at the same time that you get what *you* need from the job. You try to "lighten the load" for him or her—and I'm not just talking about secretaries lightening the load, but about executives working for other executives. Actually, the better job *you* do, the better it is for the person above you. Don't worry about your boss getting the credit for what *you* do. He or she usually *will* but that isn't as bad as it sounds. People who are good are *good,* and though the boss may not give you public credit, the word gets around. And there are many enlightened bosses who *do* give credit and will help you move ahead. Professor Eugene Jennings, graduate professor of management at Michigan State University, after conducting extensive research on people who get ahead, says, "Corporate success comes fastest to the person who becomes a crucial subordinate to an already mobile superior, complementing or supplementing the superior's skills.''

We'd better say a word here about bosses who will not *let* you make them look good or, it seems, let you do much of anything else . . . you and they are just not clicking. We've all had one or two of those and you go crazy. How can you *get* anywhere when they are your direct conduit to success? Well, they will either leave the company—finally—or *you* do. Doing every mouseburger thing you can for their good and yours is the only way you can play it for the moment. Maybe they'll get uncrazy.

Try to Do the Difficult Things First Each Day, But If You Can't—Don't

For some reason, the column I write for *Cosmo,* "Step Into My Parlor," always gives me fits, but the first Saturday morning of each month I sit down fresh and frisky at my typewriter to *try.* If, after a half hour of fussing, I can't put ten decent words together, I abandon the column and do something *easier*—like editing somebody *else's* work. As I gain momentum with the editing and feel "success" setting in, I go *back* to the typewriter and my column again. Don't do small stuff early in your energy cycle or you'll blow your "golden hours," but occasionally you have to do the "possible" to develop the momentum for the killer task.

Double Up on the Mundane Stuff

Don't suppose you can do only one thing at a time! A man I know commutes to New York from his country place every Monday morning dry-shaving with an electric razor while he drives; he listens to the news, skims *The New York Times* on the seat beside him, takes in the Westchester countryside and manages not to run his XKE into the road divider. This is a sensuous man who loves nature, but is also a self-employed millionaire who says he can't *afford* to do only one thing at a time.

I am never *anywhere* without manuscripts and sharpened pencils; they go with me in the cab, to the dentist's office, waiting for a lunch date, or even to the theater if we're early. I read by flashlight in David's screening room when guests arrive late for the movie. If I can't get somebody off the phone, I am inching through a newspaper or magazine while we talk, making lists or at *least* pushing back my cuticles!

Is it *crazy* and life-destroying to be so busy? *I* don't think so. I decided long ago that time was too precious *not* to fit a lot in! It's okay to "squander" time on vacation, in bed, or just *"thinking,"* but do double up on chores. What we're really talking about is being organized, and that merely means you fit it *all* in. . . . Nothing ever comes at you as much of a surprise! You think *ahead* of the moment.

In the midst of whatever you're doing, you are lightly in touch with the fifteen things still to do that day, night or week. Your kitchen cabinets are always stocked with staples. You don't run out of Tampax or pantyhose. Christmas-present buying starts in *January*. You hardly ever have only *one* item to buy in the drugstore, department store or market—you've got a little *list* for each place. You know what can be done on the phone instead of in person, what can be handled by a six-line letter that will save a phone call (conversations escalate), what you can do this weekend to get ready for your trip in two weeks, what you can do on the *airplane*. For that matter, you know what you can do on the *way* to the airport—I usually have breakfast (mozzarella cheese), read, put on nail polish in the car. You certainly know how to cut short luncheons, meetings or phone calls that are taking too long. "Organized" sounds revolting, doesn't it? But it *isn't!* The more you fit in, the more you *can* fit in. And organized people are usually the ones other people want to be around because we don't screw up and cause everybody pain.

Telephone Tricks

A lot of your business life is conducted by phone. These are things I have learned about *that*.

—Even though somebody has accepted your call, always ask if he is *busy*. *Always*. "Is this a good time to talk to you?" You may be babbling on and he may be loathing your (necessary) long explanation of the project, whereas letting him call back at his convenience would get you a receptive audience.

—Thank people who are "bigger than you" for calling back. Nothing says they *had* to return your phone call, and the first thing you should do is thank them for calling.

—When *you* call, leave your *number* with your name—even if you think people already know it.

—Don't try to handle two subjects on the same phone call if one of those subjects is "gratitude." Don't call up to thank somebody for whatever wonderful thing he did and then, on the same call, ask for another favor. Sometimes you have to make two separate calls, one of them *only* to express gratitude.

—Use your own judgment about whether to tell a secretary what you want or to try to get through to the boss. If it's somebody you don't know, you may need to tell *her* what you want. P.S. Tell your *own* secretary charm and compassion are the big two telephone watchwords. She should always act as though she'd *love* to put the person through but can't right now, and should ask if she can do anything to help.

—Be ruthless with the time-wasters—the ladies at home who have nothing to do but gossip, the friends at their offices who are having a slow day. Wind down from the conversation—"Gerry, I have some people waiting." "Tom, you were so good to call. I'll ring up *soon.*" Learn to use cutoff maneuvers.

—Also learn *not* to answer the telephone. You can have cutoffs on your phone at home. If you're working late at the office, don't answer the phone *there* after five o'clock. It takes courage to ignore a ringing phone, but if you weren't *there* you wouldn't be answering. Just pretend you aren't there.

Don't Forget to Write

If you have a secretary and can dictate, write instead of telephoning people *outside* your company. A letter can take a minute or less to dictate; phone calls require chitchat and tend to expand. Keep your letters *short,* especially to important people. Liz Smith, the syndicated columnist, keeps up with a network of friends through short notes. We all think we're on her mind constantly, and maybe we *are,* but she doesn't squander time on phone calls.

Write *few* office memos, however. They tend to bore everybody and the long ones are usually written by time-wasting, defensive people. Write to corroborate instructions, to say that you're working on a project that's due (the small interim report) or to submit original ideas so you have a record. Keep whatever you write *short,* with lots of paragraphs and white space.

Cardinal rule of business and social life: Never say bad, cruel, crummy, unhappy, unpleasant, critical things in a letter. If they must be said, try to say them in person or at least by *telephone*. Put the good things in writing.

This is an important rule I *never* deviate from. If you *do* have to say something unpleasant in writing, couch it in the *most* reasonable, conciliatory, understanding terms. Compliment while you complain. *Cosmo* has a valued contributor who writes four- (six-? eight-?) page handwritten letters, full of diatribe and criticism. She is a fabulous human being, but who wants to destroy one's morning or entire day by *reading* this hate stuff? Some of her letters I have never read; others I tuck underneath the phone book for several days until I get the courage.

Do you want people doing that with *your* letters?

As You Succeed, Keep a Low Profile

Some people can hardly get their dear little sweaters and T-shirts buttoned after their first little success—their *chests* are all puffed up, you see. Well, we *all* love attention and the limelight, but I think how successful you can become is probably in direct proportion to how much you shut *up* about it.

A film actress I know—whom my husband feels it would be mean-spirited of me to name—told a reporter in the *National Star*, "I know I'm beautiful, talented and will eventually be a big star." That was 1975, and though she *is* beautiful and talented, I don't see the "big star" thing *yet*. Well, bragging is a different no-no; what we're talking about now is not needing to get *stroked* too much. It's true most of us are spurred on by the *need* for recognition; in fact, I'm not sure that isn't how most of us "*get* there," needing to be loved for *something*—if not for our beautiful *selves*, then for our beautiful *work*. But, you see, you have to be rather sneaky about it—you just *can't* go about saying "Stroke me, flatter me, tell me I'm *wonderful*," even when you are getting pretty good.

I think you keep two sets of books. In one set, you record the *truth*—how well you are *really* doing. This is the secret set—just for you and loved ones. In the other set are more modest entries and statements, and these are for *public* consumption! That's just the opposite of how you might think the game would be played. Many people *do* play it the other way; they say all the braggy things publicly, knowing privately that they're not in such hot shape—but if you're good you don't *need* to brag. People usually *know* how well you are doing because they hear it from other people, or they just kind of glean it by how *busy* you are. If they don't know how well you are doing, you can *quietly* tell them, but no hollering and *demanding* praise.

It Is Hard for People to Be Happy
About Your Success: Don't Expect It

How happy are *you* when your best friend gets a book contract or a five-thousand-dollar raise? You are and you *aren't* happy. It's not so much that you truly *resent* the friend's success or would snatch it from her, but when somebody *near* you gets fame and money, you *have* to think, What about *me?*

Success happening to people you don't know is much easier to bear! Just accept that, aside from your husband, lover, mother or other *very* special (about three to a thousand) people, most of your friends are going to get that sinking feeling when you are doing better than they are. Some of *my* old friends are still trying to get me "not to work so hard," ostensibly to save my health, but actually because my success makes them nervous. I understand, but am not about to be "saved."

Get Rid of Your Guilt About Dropping Old Friends
You No Longer Feel Comfortable With

People's lives change. To keep all your old friends is like keeping all your old clothes—pretty soon your closet is so jammed and everything so crushed you can't find anything to wear. Help these friends when they need you; bless the years and happy times when you meant a lot to each other; but try *not* to have the guilts if new people mean more to you now.

Be Terrific with the People Who Work *Under* You

"Apple polishing," flattering, charming, being darling to *superiors* probably makes sense to you and, of course, you must do *that*, but you absolutely cannot make it if you aren't also good to the mailroom boys, switchboard operators, elevator men, *anybody* in a lesser job than yours.

Praise, praise, praise. I know a glamorous magazine editor who was always wonderful to her overlings, rotten to her underlings. Alice rose in the company—and rose and rose—but finally got fired, both from lack of talent and also from having climbed up on top of everybody else's smashed fingers. Well, usually people *help* people who are out of a job, but in this case, everybody just stood back and let Alice tumble.

Being snotty with people under you is *idiocy*. They won't do anything right for you *while* you work together and will eventually help get you fired! Denigrating, deprecating, undermining people on the same level with you is equally dumb—it doesn't hold back *their* success but it can *yours*.

Never Lose Your Temper at Work

You must *not* let it all hang out. The more visibly angry you are and the *oftener,* the less people respect you. They don't get afraid of you; they know that out of control by *you* means *in* control by *them!* You do yourself irreparable harm by having temper tantrums. Confront people, yes, but quietly and with dignity. Out of control is a luxury you can't afford.

Success *Doesn't* Make You Invulnerable

The most successful women in the world are still totally, crushingly vulnerable. So are most successful men. So what *else* is new? Superstar entertainers are viciously attacked by reviewers and the criticism wounds them. Presidents read vilifications in *The New York Times* and *The Washington Post* and recoil. If you can feel passion for *anything*—children, family, a beloved man, your work—you can also experience *hurt* from these people and things. Don't worry about vulnerability. You can and will hurt many times, but the hurt can't really *hurt* you. Getting behind the hurt, using it to "power" you to your next project can even make you more successful.

Don't Be Destroyed When They Don't "Love You Anymore"

All love isn't romantic; you can love *many* people. I love the captains at "21," the elevator men in the Argonaut Building, where I work, the switchboard girls at the Bel-Air Hotel, several dogs and cats (some of them *passionately*), a few teachers, house-keepers, hairdressers, not to mention loving one's *heroes*—writers, painters, singers, actors—along with "standard" loves—family, husband, friends. Love is good wherever you can find it and you can find yourself loving an *office*. . . . *I* surely have.

The thing *not* to do is think the office loves you back unequivocally, the way a mother loves you. They love you as a teammate and worker as long as you're there. Once you leave, nobody may even want to *talk* to you when you show up again for a friendly visit, and if you were *fired*, the chill is palpable.

Office love is for people who are still *in* the office, and who make each other's days more exciting. I can think of no relationship in the world quite like that of copywriter and art director, or editor and writer, when they're getting the best out of each other. Love your office and your office mates. Just don't try to have office love make *up* for the other kinds, or expect it to survive separation.

Don't Worry If Your Early Specialty Takes Over Until You Can *Do* Only One Thing Well . . . It Is Enough!

I'm so bad now—worse than in my youth—at cooking, decorating, and *anything* involving numbers or machines, that I can barely cope, but I can *pay* somebody to do those things while I do what *I* do best—edit. A *few* multifaceted people have *more* than one specialty and can switch from field to field: Gloria Vanderbilt moved from writing to designing, Bess Myerson from television panel shows to consumer advocacy and politics, Diana Vreeland from editing to museum consultant, Sherry Lansing from modeling to story editor (and later studio head), but not *many* people can do this. Sometimes the switching is done after nobody will let you *do* the previous thing any longer. The late Wilhelmina, too old to model (though still gorgeous), started a fabulously successful model agency; George Balanchine, once a gifted dancer, now choreographs and directs. Bill Bradley, former New York Knicks center, is Democratic Senator from New Jersey.

I think the "best" people never get bored with their specialty, however. Marvin Mitchelson and F. Lee Bailey are still lawyers, Katharine Graham is still a newspaperwoman, Virginia Masters goes on being a sexologist, Carol Bayer Sager composes, Joan Didion writes, Robert de Niro acts. . . . Why grow disenchanted just because you are "still" doing something you're good at and enjoy? You don't have to be queen of the world in six different professional queendoms.

You Will Possibly Always Work *Harder* than Other People—and Spend More Hours Working Than They Do

How can you *not* accomplish more and be more successful if you put the hours in? Yes, you can get stale and dreary if you *never* leave your work; but I have always found that working intensely at something you love simply breeds more success; I believe people who must get away often and lengthily from their work life simply haven't been lucky enough to find the thing they ought to be doing! I can't *imagine* job burnout if you love your work. At any rate, I have never known a really successful person who didn't work harder (Mike Wallace, Jane Fonda, Clint Eastwood, Mikhail Baryshnikov, Ann Landers, Steven Spielberg, Chris Evert Lloyd, Phil Donahue, Norman Lear . . . I could go on forever) than other people, or who got very far *away* from his or her work for very long.

When I was a copywriter at Foote, Cone and Belding—*that* again but it was my breakthrough job—my six *male* co-workers used to growl when they saw me curved over my typewriter at 5:30 P.M. when they went home to Pasadena, Altadena, and Alhambra to spend the evening with their families. One of them even complained to our boss that I was taking advantage of the rest of them because I wasn't married and didn't have to go home. Too *bad* about him! I saw him recently and he's *still* going home at five-thirty to Altadena to be a daddy and family man, though his kids are now thirty-five years old.

Give Credit to Fellow Employees *Always,* Whether You Are Boss or Employee

Many people warn you not to get your ideas stolen. In Jane Trahey's book *Women and Power: Who's Got It and How to Get It,* a chapter, "How to Defend Against Idea Thieves," *implores* you to get all the credit you can for what's *yours.* Stealing does occur, but in forty-two years of working (Jesus God!) I have found people usually know who is turning in the good stuff, regardless of who grabs the credit. As a boss, I know I am impressed when I compliment somebody on an idea or piece of work and they say, "Well, Barbara Ann did that," or "Myra pulled it together." It just makes you think more of the person doing the crediting. God forbid you should take credit for something that *isn't* yours! That is really dumb.

Don't Be Crooked

We all cheat (a little or a lot) on expense accounts, steal a few supplies, etc. I'm not going to give you guidelines about *that,* but do show a little judgment! My beloved accountant, Herbert H. Meyer—he was my wedding present to David—says: "When you get red in the face, stop!"

That seems wise.

Speak *Up* About Money—When It's Time

I'm now ready to face the fact of your needing and deserving more money.

If you feel you're due, *ask.* Waiting for them to "recognize your worth" and reward you may take too long (they *recognize* your worth all right, but may not do a thing about it until you ask). Ask only when you know you're doing a fabulous job and they wouldn't want to do without you (this can be in some of your earlier jobs, of course; I really don't mean you to *starve).* When you ask, don't stress how much you *need* the money—family responsibilities, car payments, etc. Mention these in passing, but stress how much you love your job, love the company and want to contribute even more. Outline what you've already done and what else you'll be doing to justify the raise. Don't try for the crazy top dollar, because even if you *get* it, people will be looking at you funny every time you make a mistake and saying, "My God, we're paying *her* this salary?!" They should feel *they* made a good deal. You should feel *you* have a good deal. A salary is only okay if it works for *both* of you. Getting another job offer is frequently the *best* way to get a significant raise but—a crucial "but"—use this device only if you're prepared to accept the other offer. You can't say you're *going* to go without actually being ready to leave. Also, upping a salary by threat of leaving can work only once or twice—after that the company gets tired of the blackmail and may say *Go*. It's okay to tell your boss about job offers even if you *don't* plan to leave, or aren't pushing at the moment for a raise. It doesn't hurt them to know you're sought after!

What to Do When You Get Fired

Getting fired is horrible—don't expect to feel good! I have been fired five or six times. Twice it was my fault. The other times I was doing the "right things" and still got the ax. Once, the ad agency kept two other copywriters and sacked *me!* I spent the entire weekend with two *different* shrinks and cried nonstop for forty-eight hours (talk about looking like a *raccoon!*). Recently, when I was dropped from my regular segment on "Good Morning America," after being on the show for two and a half years, I handled things a lot better—I cried every *day* for fourteen straight days and *still* have fits of melancholia when I think about it!

Since I can't imagine anything better than working, may I respectfully suggest you *not* use your severance pay to take a trip to see the Inca ruins but to start looking for another job right away. Blues and problems go *with* you, you know, and a vacation when you've just been fired (always an ego blow) and you don't know what's in your future *can't* be as pleasurable as trip-taking on a full stomach. Sign up for unemployment insurance, of course, but since that can take as long as six weeks from the time you leave a company, maybe you'll have *another* job by then. You know what to do: call prospects, send résumés, answer ads, pester friends, see employment agencies. . . . Your job now is getting a job.

Writing a Résumé

Put vital statistics first—name, address, phone, age, marital status. Put job experience next—start with your present or last job and go back chronologically. Education comes after that, also starting with the latest schooling; list extracurricular activities last.

I've never seen this done, but *I* think it's a good idea to add some ideas on how you might fit into the company you're sending a résumé to. I read a dozen résumés a week and can rarely find anything that their authors might do for *me*. Why not do your homework and come up with a few ideas of jobs you could handle in the company? If you look nice, send along a snapshot—preferably full-length—to the hottest prospects. Even if you have an appointment, always send a résumé beforehand to save everybody's time.

PHASE III—*Okay, you're into high gear . . . you have now been working five, ten or fifteen years. Let us say you have now got into work that defines and strengthens you, satisfies you deeply most of the time, while sometimes driving you wild with its problems. Here are the rules I worked out after finally putting babyhood and puppydom behind me. They serve me now and I hope may possibly serve you.*

Insist on Knowing What They Want to See You About
Before You Make an Appointment

People always want something. It's okay to ask them what it *is* before they come in. Frequently they ought to be seeing somebody else. *More* frequently you can handle whatever it is on the phone instead of taking time for a person-to-person visit. Usually people *prefer* to stop by, feeling they can be more forceful in person. You must be firm—at *least* get the gist of their project first. It's hard to get somebody out of your office in less than half an hour, or even an hour, without being rude. How many half-hours do you *have?*

Don't Answer Your Own Phone

Answering your own telephone is friendly. After you get to be a big executive, it is also dumb. Once people get you on the phone, you can't be rude, and you can get stuck with a lot of people you shouldn't be talking to in the first place. What then is happening to the important stuff you *should* be doing? Down the old drain!

A good assistant will put through everybody who *ought* to get through to you and be cordial to those who shouldn't. She should be just as polite to callers—even the dumb ones—as she is to *you.*

Give Quick Decisions

We already talked about getting back to them quickly, as an *employee*. As boss, you'll have to think decisions over for a little while, but not *that* long. Thinking for a couple of weeks won't necessarily make the decision any more "correct" than if you'd decided within one day.

The worst bosses I've ever had, and the ones I hear other people complain about most, are those who can't seem to get back to you with anything, even answers you don't want to hear. Don't leave anybody dangling. The things you can decide quickly, *decide!*

Don't Worry About Being a Good Executive

There aren't that many good books to guide a young executive, but you might try *The Managerial Woman* by Margaret Hennig and Anne Jardim (Anchor Press, Doubleday), *Men and Women of the Corporation* by Rosabeth Moss Kanter (Basic Books, Inc.), *On Women and Power* by Jane Trahey (Rawson Associates).

If you have a bona fide talent other than administration that's got you where you are, you'll be okay *without* guidance. Just using the general intelligence you use to get along with friends, beaux, plumbers, waiters, fathers, brothers, veterinarians, etc., will give you the *feel* of how to "boss." My first "executive assignment" was handling David's housekeeper when we got married. I thought she'd like me better if I helped with the dinner dishes—little things like that—but she didn't like me better at all. . . . She thought I was the jerkiest person she'd ever met.

When I arrived at *Cosmo,* I knew *nothing* about handling other people, having never even had my own secretary before, and here were thirty-four people looking to *me* for leadership. . . . The night after my first day at *Cosmo* I slipped out of bed around midnight and curled up in a little ball under David's desk! David found me around 4:00 A.M. and got me back to bed.

I'm still not the *best* executive, but I try. Anyway, it doesn't matter if you start badly because you pick up experience, as in any other activity, and you get better. It also doesn't matter that you're female. Nobody cares what sex you are if you're fair, decisive, spread a little cheer, and run whatever you're running well.

These are good basic rules that I've picked up for being an executive. I wish somebody had told *me* them the night I was under the desk:

1. Hire the best people you can get for a job.
2. Give them a little time to sink *into* their jobs and encourage them like mad.
3. Let them do what they were hired for, plus new things you figure out as you go along. Don't do *anything* somebody else can do instead of you, even if you can do it better. Delegate, delegate, *delegate!* That's where I fell down for *years*—I thought only *I* could do a lot of stuff and nearly expired from overwork. Guilt is one of the worst flaws in young-executive-esses. We're so damn used to *serving* that we keep pitching in and helping out. Control yourself!
4. Give clear instructions. Say exactly what you want and when you want it.
5. Don't pit employees against each other.
6. Reward good work with kindness, appreciation and money.
7. If you haven't got the person who can do the job, fire him or her and hire somebody else.

Most bosses can summon the courage to fire a real dumbbell but rationalize that somebody so-so is at least in there doing something and he's *trying*, so kindhearted (lazy!) you will just let him stay. God knows firing is painful not to mention the heartache for the fire-ee (though I have less sympathy than I should because first-rate people don't *get* fired all that often and first-rate people, if fired wrongly, wind up okay again someplace else). What's maybe *worse* than firing (to be honest) is the pain of hunting for a new person . . . all that interviewing . . . all that lost momentum! Employee searches are *grueling*, and I have found headhunters, in the magazine business at least, no help whatever. Well, let me just point this out: People have to have a chance to *learn* their jobs, but once you determine they are *never* going to be first-rate, they should go. A half-good person is dragging down the whole shop and it is rarely charity to keep him and penalize everybody else. You will sometime need to *make* yourself go through the agony of replacing lameness with goodness.

To rev up your courage when firing, keep reminding yourself

that "right is on your side" after you've concluded that it *is*. This comes in handy in *any* rough situation in which you're going to make somebody mad. Right is on your side and you've *got* to do what you're doing, okay?

Now for some auxiliary rules.

With all employees, search out ways to give credit and give all the credit *away*. President Reagan has a sign on his desk: "There is no end to the good that can be accomplished if you don't care who gets the credit." As we've said, a smart boss surrounds herself with geniuses (so as *not* to have to do the work herself). Well, the geniuses need public as well as private stroking. On the other hand, when the time comes to correct or criticize, maybe merely *suggest* to, you will notice, no matter how carefully you do it, *some* of your people will go into the sulks or worse—a full-fledged tantrum! "Well, if that's the way you feel, I'd be happy to leave!" or "*I* don't think my expense account is too high!"—cool, deadly hate leveled at their obviously crazed, ungrateful boss! It's awful, *they* are awful but very valuable so you dare not say what you *might* as they carry on like gorillas. Unpleasant as it is, you have to speak up for the good of the company or the product or because they are lousing up you and their co-workers, so forget *their* not being manly or womanly, *you* will have to be the grownup. Say what must be said as tactfully as possible, then stand back and wait for the fallout; they will calm back down. I do find this about the ugliest of all executive chores—dealing with valuable people who cannot take any *form* of criticism, who make you the heavy, them the "wrong-ee." If someone is *always* too difficult, then they will finally have to go, but I have clung to gifted recalcitrants for *years* because of their enormous talent. Incidentally, if you think an employee is mad at you, don't fight the urge to go and make up, even though you feel you *ought* to stay in your top-person office until he cools off, sees how wrong he is and comes to *you!* Even if he's wrong, it's okay to go to him rather than waiting it out and worrying yourself into a *fit!*

To sum up, theoretically you will long for *all* employees to have high morals, not cheat on their expense accounts, love one another, be utterly loyal to *you*, not cause any trouble, work their tails off and help your company or product succeed. Of that little list, best concentrate on item seven, working your way back up the list with emphasis in that order. Of course, if they are *impossible* to deal with or flagrantly *dishonest,* no matter what their contribution, they may have to go, but the smartest employers in *this* era have stopped expecting paragons and are willing to accept quite a lot of "nonsense" in order to keep key people. What you'd *like* to do when they want six months' leave of absence "to finish my book," a big raise for "my assistant who is otherwise going to leave," "Please send me to Honolulu for that conference," is blast them out of the room and say, "Don't *ask* me for that . . . don't *hit* me with this!" but what you usually do instead is smile and say, "I'll try to get it for you" and hope they don't come back with another haymaker soon. It's called Dealing with Reality. We already said there are only a few good anythings; if you've got some, you *pay!* One more point: You can't take *away* perks once given. It's okay to withhold the corner office, a personal secretary, the Christmas bonus, a month's vacation—but once you have proffered these gifts, nobody ever wants to get along without them.

Stay in the Channel

There are *channels*—a boring, bureaucratic word that means people have their own territory and you don't mess with it even if you're the boss. You don't give orders to somebody else's secretary, and an underling doesn't come directly to you, passing up her own boss, to get approval for an idea. If she skips past her boss and shows up on your doorstep, send her *home!*

Are you too stuck-up to talk to and encourage the "help"? Never! But even the most informal office has a *structure*—an "organization chart." You have to stay with it or nobody knows exactly who does what or who reports to whom and you wind up with outraged people, hurt feelings and nobody doing a good job because dear friendly you has failed to provide a real *work* plan and to stay *with* it until time to change.

Don't Be Cheap

A rather important editor was leaving *Cosmopolitan* to take a new job for a lot more money. I decided to combine her going-away party with a rum-tasting being offered us by one of *Cosmo*'s big liquor advertisers. Instead of buying all that champagne just for Yvette, why not get the party *free,* I reasoned—and taste a little rum in the bargain! Sure, we would all have to fill out a tiny questionnaire saying which rum we liked best, but did it really matter how one achieved effervescence?! *Cosmo*'s smart managing editor saved me from my penuriousness and may have saved the departing editor from remembering me and her previous association as cheap and unsatisfactory. We brought in the champagne, threw the appropriate party and I made a note to show a little more class next time.

Let me give you another example of cheap. A girl I know thought of an idea for a book her boss could write, oversaw his writing of it and eventually got him a publisher. She didn't want a percentage of the book—it wasn't *that* time-consuming a project— but the idea was hers and she was always *there,* in the wings. On publication day, he sent her a one-hundred-dollar savings bond— capital outlay: eighty-seven dollars and fifty cents. A thousand-dollar bond would have been *minimal.*

"Cheap" is almost worse than nothing. Praise, praise, praise— publicly when possible—and give appropriate presents. Yes, a lot of things are part of a person's job, but there are only a *few* good people in your work world and you want those people loyal to *you.*

Do the something extra.

Spread the Spoils Around

You can't be the *only* one who gets the goodies from management. It seems silly to mention it, but some bosses are so greedy (for *themselves* only) they forget underlings are *not* thirteenth-century peasants who can be satisfied with a glass of mead and three festivals a year. Fulgencio Batista of Cuba and, more recently, the Shah of Iran, apparently forgot that rule. They took 95 percent of the spoils for themselves and plowed back into their countries only 5 percent. That sort of thing *aggravates* people!

If everything's coming up orchids—perks and money—for *you,* you'd better figure on getting some of this stuff for your key people, too—the ones you couldn't look so good *without.*

The Number One Secret of Success

While sensibly dumping everything that you can on other people, how do you best occupy *yourself*? You observe—and this word is so stuffy and overused I'm afraid it will turn you off, but here goes—*priorities.*

Please understand we're not talking about shopping expeditions and gossip calls to friends going on the back burner. That's understood! We're talking about *work* choices.

Think carefully what your company hired you for, which activity of yours will most favorably affect the P and L and therefore means most to *you,* in terms of your rise in the world. Whatever you decide that activity *is,* it should be up front in your head at all times—number one priority every single day. Alan Lakein, the time-management expert, suggests literally keeping a reminder of your A priority thing in front of you on the desk. The number one activity of *my* work is the *product* for *Cosmopolitan,* and I keep a copy of the magazine on my desk, just in case I should ever forget. Some people think that just because they are busy, they're giving their best shot. They devote equal attention to each task as it comes in. At the day's end, exhausted, they may even be self-congratulatory about all the work they've done, while the important stuff goes further in arrears. I still see important executives—men mostly!—carrying on this way, devoting as much time to a minor employee's hardship story or decorating the reception room as they do to the company *product.* The hardship story should be listened to by somebody down the line and the couch refurbished by another somebody else.

Alan Lakein suggests putting letters and memos in piles on your desk or in desk drawers marked A, B and C priorities. By the time you get to C, he says, you may find you don't even have to *do* it!

At any rate, you've got to do your number one thing as much as you can.

Though You Play Hard and Well, Once You "Get to the Top" You May Not Enjoy Play *More* than Work

Activities connected with love and sex you don't stint on. They are your blood and oxygen, the very life of life. Sports, hobbies and parties—well, while these will be *satisfying,* they may never give you that insanely wonderful "flow-feeling" that comes from work. In your world now, you are never looking at a watch or clock to see whether it's time to go home or anywhere else, but only to see if you *must* be torn away from your beloved thing because you're supposed to be across town for an appointment. When you have worked hard, the tennis, handball, dancing, museum visit, movie and play feel marvelous but, at least for me, during the play-time there is always something missing—a feeling of contentment and peace, some silent power over life and adversity, that continuing thrill of achievement, all of which comes when I get back to my typewriter, to my dictating machine and manuscripts, back to the office to assign and check on projects.

I don't know whether that's quite normal. What we're describing here is a workaholic, and people tend to lump workaholism with alcoholism, runaway gambling, compulsive eating and other naughty habits. We are not *lumpable!* Work brings such fantastic rewards, how could you *not* do it a lot, and joyously?!

In describing a year of bone-crushing work ahead, Beverly Sills says, "I know that anybody who does all this and doesn't have to, everybody thinks she's very driven. The truth is, I *enjoy* it all so! Can't it be that simple? I think it is! I don't feel overworked. I get a constant kick out of being heavily committed. Is that sick or something? God, what would I *do* sitting still?"

Workaholism is different from other "isms." Don't let people badmouth it to you! As Mae West said, "Too much of a good thing can be wonderful."

As You Succeed, You Will Continue to Be a Fan. Great! Never Lose that Sense of Wonder and Adulation for Other People with Talent

I used literally to sit at the feet of Dorothy Schiff when she was editor and publisher of the *New York Post*. Dolly would invite me to tea and I would sit on this beautiful rug she had needle-pointed herself and listen to her talk about presidents and kings. I still have the wildest crush on Rupert Murdoch, who now owns the *Post*, Estee Lauder, David Mahoney, chairman of Norton Simon, Inc., Charles Bluhdorn, chairman of Gulf & Western, Steve Ross, chairman of Warner Communications, Herb Siegel, chairman of Chris-Craft, Michel Bergerac, chairman of Revlon, and a dozen others. The joy is that when you *get* there, you can get these people on the phone—they respect you back (and they talk to you at parties).

It isn't the *least* reward for all that hard work!

Run Scared! You're Good and You Know You're Good but as Somebody Once Said, "Nothing Recedes Like Success"

Fred Silverman said, at the time he was president of NBC, "There is a philosophy that is good no matter what you are doing. That is to always act as if you're in last place. You shouldn't take success for granted because you can turn around one day and say, 'My Lord, it is all gone.' "

Jane Pauley, co-host of NBC's "The Today Show," says, "Every Monday morning after a weekend away from the job I wake up shivering in fear at the prospect of another show. It's been three years and every Monday morning I forget how to do it. The prospect of coast-to-coast humiliation gets the adrenaline pumping again, but I've always suspected that the essence of Jane Pauley is that small scared girl who wakes up shivering every Monday morning." Comedian Joan Rivers says, "Any form of complacency is the kiss of death for any professional."

I believe that totally. *Run scared* . . . and they'll never catch you.

PHASE IV—At the Top . . . *And now you're at the pinnacle . . . one of those rare (female) creatures who have earned the right to be called . . . a mogul!*

The Board Room

Let's talk for one moment now about jobs at the highest level of management . . . senior vice president, merchandise director, chief executive officer.

Are the rules different there? Not really. The hard work, talent and common sense that got you from the bottom to the top in the first place will also keep you there. But what about all the skullduggery you have to cope with . . . people jockeying for power . . . office politics?

Some people "believe in" office politics, but I love Florence Skelly's (she is president of the research firm Yankelovich, Skelly and White) comment: "Office politics are just the natural selection of people who want to be with other people they can get along with . . . people they feel comfortable with. It's the normal way any group—even a woman's charity group—functions. It's why new U.S. Presidents always change staff and change cabinets . . . they want people on *their* team. Now every young man working his way up the hierarchy is not immediately accepted into the inner circle any more than a woman will be. You gain people's confidence. If somebody is kept out, it may not be 'political' but simply that that person is a big pain in the A. Women are so good at appropriate behavior . . . a female characteristic nurtured since the world began. We do it socially all the time. We haven't been in mid-management long enough for many of us to be picked for the C.E.O. jobs but office politics will not keep us out."

What about male chauvinism? "Of *course* it still exists," says Polly Langbort, senior vice president and director of communications planning at Young and Rubicam, largest U.S.-owned advertising agency in the world, "but it's better now; it really is. I recently spoke at a Westinghouse Radio sales-promotion meeting and was amazed to find the audience was two-thirds women—*young* women in their early thirties. Not very long ago that audience would all have been men."

Mardie McKim, vice president, public affairs, at Dart and Kraft, Inc., says, "This is a relatively new thing men are dealing with . . . female executives. We've got to give them a chance to 'assimilate' us. I used constantly to be in meetings where they addressed everyone as 'gentlemen.' Now they've finally got around to 'Mardie and gentlemen.' ''

Pamela Nelson, national merchandise manager of Sears Roebuck, says, ''Sometimes I talk to a group made up principally of men and tell them, 'I realize you all refer to me as the house broad'—since they *do* refer to me that way behind my back. That amuses them.''

What does one *do* about the chauvinism that still ranges from scheduling business lunches at a male bastion women can't get into to open, unabashed hostility? Pamela Nelson says, ''What matters most is the bottom line. They can't be too prejudiced against women with the figures to talk *for* you.'' (Her $225,000,000 annual volume talks loudly.) ''With men who are visibly uncomfortable with women, you try to get them to explain something in their area of expertise, then get into *your* area. We're all after the same customer. She buys a refrigerator from them and slacks from me, maybe I know something that can *help* them.''

Jane Evans, executive vice president of General Mills, says, ''Never lose your sense of humor, and if you don't have one, develop one! Never take yourself too seriously or lose your temper. So many women are so intense they make men feel uncomfortable in their presence. I've seen women trained in assertiveness somehow manage to find the one ranking male chauvinist in the room, walk up and *attack* him! It embarrasses everybody and sets back her own cause irreparably. You have to try to use your *own* sensitivity to understand what they're going through and help. Shake hands. Smile. *You* aren't going to be the one they have trouble with!''

Pamela Nelson adds, ''Debate is absurd. You can debate with your friends, but, for the most part, the haters hate secretly behind your back. Them you finally get the better of with friendliness, kindness and compassion, a sense of humor plus the brains and hard work that got you there in the first place!''

When are there going to be more women *chief* executives? Jane Nelson says, ''Boards of directors select presidents. So far, very few women sit on boards and those who do didn't come up through the business ranks but were chosen for having held political office or were simply well known in the community. As more female *executives* make it to the board room, they will be in a position to select female chief executives.'' Florence Skelly adds, ''Up until recently there has been such a small pool of women from which chief officers could be trolled. When you've got *two* women in mid-management jobs and fifty men, naturally the top job isn't going to go to one of the two women. When you have as many women as men to pick *from*, more women are going to wind up in the top spot."

All over the country I hear about "support groups"—women with big jobs who hold meetings—officially and unofficially—to offer each other and younger women support and counsel. Yes, we *are* gaining on Mount Everest!

Expect to Continue to Have *Some* General Pain and Trouble, Nearly Every Day of Your Life

Why would anybody hammer you so hard to try for a thing that possibly won't make you "happy"—not all the *time* anyway? Because it's *better* up there in almost every way, more exciting and rich and soul-satisfying. You're more *respected*—you can *buy* whatever you want, get people on the phone, and people will come to your parties! There's also this: If you don't try, you will never know what you *might* have been, will you? I believe so much that I have tears in my eyes as I tell you this—it is simply a better life to reach out, to take the baby steps toward a small success on your own rather than live through even the most marvelous man or children, never mind whether there are still blue days and neuroses when you get there!

When you *have* the blue days, it's easier to cope with them from a base of wide, rich experience. For whatever it's worth, work success allows you to *pay* for help—from shrinks, attorneys, accountants and the *best* doctors. Every other Thursday morning I visit a shrink for forty-five minutes (cost: one hundred dollars) who helps me sort out business and personal problems. Does it seem odd for somebody to give *you* advice who is still being shrunk?! I'll bet it does, but this isn't psychoanalysis—just a friendly chat with somebody very shrewd, who *listens*. Weekly, my tense little body is delivered to a sorceress for shiatsu massage. It's heaven, it costs sixty dollars, and I can afford it! I don't mean to brag about these price tags. I'm just saying that hiding out and underachieving don't necessarily make you happy, from what *I* observe, and, though dedication to a career doesn't free you from life's problems, it brings a heady pleasure to know that you've used *most* of your potential and that you can pay for luxuries, one of which is body-and-soul helpers.

Children—Part of Having It All

Now it's time to mention *children*—which a lot of people feel are a serious part of having it all (I don't agree and never wanted any but you have your own ideas about *that*). *Can* you successfully raise children and hold a big job? Without any question, yes. You just have to have incredible amounts of energy and a need to do both—plus help at home. Most present-day authorities agree you don't stay home because the child needs *you* but because you have a great, primordial need to be *with* the child. Actually, any warm, loving, attentive adult, related or not related to the family, will do just as well as a mommy (did Queen Elizabeth *personally* diaper Charles, Anne and Andrew and play hopscotch with her little heirs?). In an experiment conducted with monkeys at the University of Wisconsin at Madison in 1958, Dr. Harry F. Harlow found that monkeys placed in proximity with terry-cloth-covered "surrogate mother" dolls achieved considerable contact-comfort from *them*, also security and trust. This led the monkeys to a future based on a healthy exploration of the environment.

Employers cannot now refuse to *hire* you if you say you want children; they can't refuse to hire you even if you are pregnant, and they also have to give you a pregnancy leave and take you back after the baby arrives.

How do the children feel? "Children are comfortable having mothers do what other mothers do," says Evelyne Prouvost, publisher of French *Cosmopolitan,* mother of five, ages two to twenty-two, "and since so many mothers now work, the children find it acceptable, just as it's now much less difficult to be the child of divorce since they've got so many friends with divorced parents, not to mention extra sets of grownups who dote on them." "They're *proud* of your job," says Kathie Berlin, senior vice president of the public relations firm Rogers and Cowan. "Through my work, Kimberly has visited the White House, held hands with Paul Newman, chatted it up with the 'Today Show' panel. I don't think she *wants* me at home!"

Whether everybody *should* be a mother and also succeed in the marketplace is something else. Betty Friedan feels we are all being pushed to do one thing only (achieve outside the home) as we were all once pushed to do the *other* thing (stay home and be mommies), and both kinds of pressure are unacceptable. The point is, if you're so *inclined,* and willing to "pay your dues," you *can* have both—job success and well-raised children. These are ground rules, gleaned from successful working mothers:

1. Forget guilt over wanting to work. "Guilt is hopelessly unnecessary and debilitating," says Lynn Nesbit, senior vice president of International Creative Management. "I had three miscarriages, major surgery of the uterus, and two cesareans within five years in order to bring children into the world. I couldn't live without them but I also never contemplated life without a career. Both pursuits are honorable."

2. "Don't agonize too much," says Ellen Salzman, corporate fashion director of Saks. "You can drive yourself mad if you think of all the terrors and pitfalls of a 'double life.' Renny and I had David and Elizabeth before I was twenty-five and I just figured I'd muddle through." (Ellen has muddled through nicely, now responsible for the overall look for women's ready-to-wear and accessories for Saks' thirty-two stores.)

3. You must have help at home. "In the beginning, a lot of your salary may go for household help," says Penny Hawkey, senior vice president and creative group head of McCann-Erickson. "At the time of the birth of my first baby, we were paying child support for two children by my husband's first wife; he had decided to leave his advertising job and become an anthropologist-philosopher-writer-farmer-Hudson River boat pilot, and *still* I'd say a third of my salary went for a baby helper. Gradually you get ahead of the game." Says *Cosmo* executive editor Roberta Ashley, "It costs about the same whether a housekeeper lives in or lives out and you have a lot of advantages when they live in—you can stay out at night, you don't have to rush home from the office after work, you know somebody is there in the morning. With a day helper you're less spontaneous because you have to work out hours if you want to be away in the evenings." "The way you *keep* somebody is to overpay and undercriticize," says Gretchen. "You also let things go. My Loretta can't (won't!) clean very well, so on Saturday and Sunday you might say I *do* do windows!" "Whether a man will help in the kitchen depends on his mother," says Carol. "Mine *doesn't.* You also can't send him to market . . . he comes back with tiny ears of corn vinaigrette, olives and pâté—but it's no good banging your head against the stove because he hasn't got a cassoulet simmering on *top* of it. Usually they do something to make up for household imbecility . . . like love you and pay a lot of bills."

4. Know that you are going to have to give *up* some things with children plus job. "Your social life is very different with children," says Juliette Boisriveaud, editor of French *Cosmopolitan*, mother of Mathieu Renard, twelve. "You may be able to do justice to your job, justice to your child and, hopefully, to a husband, but you can't also have a big social life. You stick close to home, have people in, go to other people's houses where they have children and you can bring yours along. You also leave the party early and hope they'll do the same at your house." "It all happens on weekends," says Bobbie. "No dinners in the middle of the week for eight people and no gourmet dinners *ever.*" "You're off the cocktail party circuit," says Ellen, "even when it's connected with your work."

5. Work for a company that *understands* the needs of working mothers. The Estee Lauder factory in Melville, Long Island, allows mothers to arrive early in the morning at the same time the children will have left for school, get home when the children do. The Connecticut General Corporation in Bloomfield, Connecticut, is one of a handful of big corporations with a day care center at headquarters. The Continental Illinois Corporation of Chicago has flexible work hours for mothers and has installed a computer terminal at home for one of its Denver bankers who recently had a baby. Says Lynn Nesbit, "In the early years I had a tie line in my apartment. People would call the office; my secretary would put them through to my house, and they never knew they were talking to me at home." Lynn's boss, I.C.M. mogul Marvin Josephson says, "People are stupidly shortsighted who do not accommodate gifted female employees who want to be mothers."

6. Don't live in the country or the suburbs if you work in the city. "Commuting two or three hours a day is going to take a gigantic hunk of energy along with the *time,*" says *Cosmo*'s head art director Linda Cox, whose husband drives her to work in twelve to fifteen minutes. "Work close to where you live or move closer to where you work." (Linda, husband and child, like many other working mothers and fathers, go to the country on weekends.)

7. Be realistic about what kind of job you can *handle.* Mallen De Santis, *Cosmo*'s beauty and health editor, recommends, "You can't go on the road for three or four weeks at a time or attend sales conventions. You may have to forgo business travel altogether and only work nine to five." (Other mothers don't agree and *do* fit in *travel.*)

8. "You must be *available* to your children," continues Mal-

len. "They have to be able to get you on the phone, visit you at the office, and somebody needs to be there when they get home from school. Yes, it's *still* important." As for the "quality of time" spent with the kids making up for the quantity, "You need *both,*" says Bobbie, "but if you rule out a drink after work, shopping the sales and a few other time-wasters, you can manage. During Robin's early years, I made it home from the office at five-thirty, gave her her bath and dinner, put her to bed. That was an hour and a half for her every night. The housekeeper got her up in the morning."

9. Find "helpers" who will accommodate *your* schedule. "I've got a dentist who will take me at seven in the morning," says Ellen Salzman. "He's *this* year's find, also a hairdresser who works until nine at night. Your children can be sick. You *cannot*. You have to take extraordinary care of your body so you can stand the strain."

Well, now, isn't all that inspiring . . . if somewhat exhausting?! It doesn't seem to matter to the child at what *moment* you decide to return to work, though most of these mothers felt sooner was better than later because (a) the company won't have got used to doing without you; (b) you can tuck babies in, kiss them good night and forget about them. *Older* is when they need you more for consultation and friendship. Evelyn Lauder, vice president of Estee Lauder, says, "I worked Friday night, delivered Gary Saturday morning, was back at work three weeks later." Listen, those girls are *busy!* And as far as one can detect, *happy.*

Making It

Okay, we're coming across the finish line. Why, really, should you listen to or do what I say? I was trying to find an answer for this one several years ago when I was visiting David in Martha's Vineyard while they were filming the original *Jaws.* (God, I have been working on this book *forever!*) We were out on the wharf visiting the *Orca* (before the shark sank it) and I saw a rather pretty girl— twenty-two perhaps—sitting in a canvas chair out on the dock. She had a nice body, long legs, which she was toasting in the sun. I studied her—the face isn't as good as the body, I decided . . . nose a little big, eyes a little small, mouth a bit thin. Nice girl, nothing special. What if she ran into a desirable man up here in Martha's Vineyard? I asked myself—the young director on this picture, Steven Spielberg, the actor Richard Dreyfuss? Would she have a chance with, say, Woody Allen, Jack Nicholson, Mick Jagger, Warren Beatty, Al Pacino, Cary Grant, Jerzy Kosinsky or any other—at that time—well-known bachelor? She would have a chance as a hanger-*on*, I decided . . . a little cookieburger that one of these men might take on for an evening, for, after all, she is nubile and pleasant-looking and probably not unintelligent. But unless she turns out to be the millionaire dock-owner's daughter (millionaires' daughters frequently do okay) or had some other illustrious family member to help her (people tend rather to like to collect famous politicians' children) there probably would be no *way* she could appeal to these men on her own—there's just nothing that accomplished to *listen* to. Yet I know as I walk past her with David and the *Jaws* production man that if that girl *wants* to . . . if she craves everything out of life as much as I have craved it—longs as much as *I* have longed—she can have her man—a good and "heavy" one . . . as well as a place in the sunshine which will make people listen to *her* and not reject her because she looks only okay but not great. Drive and need and longing can get her to that place and that point—*any* intelligent woman can get there. It does take intelligence and a non-assy quality and yearning and needing and *drive*. Drive is *not* doing something unfitting or uncomfortable like getting on the phone and trying to sell parcels of land in Haiti or freezer plans at home (though that might be appropriate in your case). Drive is not *chutzpah*, because some people (certainly me) don't *have* that. Drive is *need*, that need that is *always*, inexorably, connected by the anklebone to self-discipline and work! Good old self-discipline . . . where you make the unpleasant choice instead of the pleasant one. Drive is frequently deciding *not* to do something—not eating nine hundred calories at lunch, not mucking around wasting your day—as much as it is *doing* something not so pleasant that's tough on your brain or body. My girl in the canvas chair at Martha's Vineyard can make it if she wants. She can finish her article instead of going to the beach; she can turn a job into a career. She can pass up the pecan pie à la mode. She can go to the gym. It's up to her . . . I hope she decides yes.

Now let's move into the area of looking and feeling good. I know a lot about the latter, a little about the former—both good places to start a life-enhancing campaign.

Chapter Three

DIET

The most basic thing to get on with after your job—or during it—is how you look and feel. It is unthinkable that a woman bent on "having it all" would want to be fat, or even plump, so I am now going to give you my diet rules. I'm not a doctor, but a long-time, hardened-criminal-case dieter like me possibly knows as much about diet as many people, including doctors, who write books and magazine articles on the subject. Many doctors don't know *any-thing* about nutrition, incidentally. You're supposed to check with a doctor before you begin a diet. Okay, *check*. He won't have any magic to get you *through* the diet, but he can give you his blessing.

There is really only *one* diet rule you need to remember. Here it comes: To lose weight you can't *eat* as much as you have been eat-ing. To keep it off, you *still* can't eat as much as you have been eating. It is *that* simple . . . and that simply awful! How you go about not eating as much is what all those hundreds of thousands of written words are about. On some diets, protein is the star—everything up to and including rattlesnake meat is okay if it's protein—while others declare that that much protein will *kill* you! Certain diet mavens recommend grains and cereals (that's the stave-off-your-first-heart-attack-with-roughage crowd), while *my* diet guru, Dr. Robert Atkins, believes all those carbohydrates in grains would do *in* hypoglycemic (low blood sugar) people like me. There are banana evangelists and banana haters, egg promoters and egg detractors, dairy-food enthusiasts and dairy-food denigrators. . . . Well you know all about the controversy, so how do you work out a diet and lifetime eating plan for *you?*

Let's do the basics first.

Virtually *Everybody* Has to Diet, So Stop Thinking of Yourself as Special

A few metabolically peculiar people can shovel in an entire Javanese pig and it doesn't show, and a few others actually *crave* only celery root and olives (they're disgusting!), but almost everybody over the age of thirty (maybe even younger) will have to deprive her body of food she loves in amounts she craves in order to stay skinny. That's *dieting:* eating less than you'd really like to for the rest of your life! To be specific, by the age of forty we need only about three-quarters as much food as we took in at nineteen to maintain our weight, and at fifty we need exactly half as much . . . *half!* So, my darling, you are part of a huge, nonexclusive mass . . . if you'll pardon the expression.

The way you are going to be exclusive is by *succeeding* on your diet. Now, many women say they don't *want* to look cadaverous, like a model. Well, models don't happen to look cadaverous. They look *great.* The right *parts* of them are round and pretty, and they are mostly *healthy* from taking such good care of themselves. They sacrifice. The truth is that few "civilians" will eat as little as a model eats in order to stay as slender as she does. You may *not* have her gazelle legs or elongated torso, but slenderness is within your (our) total control. It's your very own body and it's up to *you!*

Nevertheless . . .

Nobody Ever Really Tells You
How Rotten Dieting Is

Lots of diet writers promise that dieting is easy. They lie! Actual dieting—getting your weight *down*, not just sustaining it—is the *pits!* *Terror* is the word for facing a day with only eight hundred calories—black, ugly terror. Never mind that a day without wine is like a day without sunshine; a day with that few calories (or even a few *more*, say one thousand) is not worth getting *up* for. You wish you could sleep, zombielike, right through it. Losing one measly pound is hard *work*. You deprive yourself, suffer and abstain, and that's all you've lost . . . one measly pound. After all, thirty-five hundred calories (the equivalent of one pound) is a lot of calories not to take in! Even "sustaining," after you've reached your ideal weight, is no fun because the second you start to eat comfortably again, the weight sneaks right back on you. Like giving up smoking, which I understand is the *most* difficult thing to give up, giving up food is *not* nice. You have to stop *kidding* yourself that there is a special diet—*any* diet—on which you won't feel deprived.

Singer Peggy Lee once said in an interview in the *Los Angeles Times* how delicious an apple was for dessert now that she'd given *up* pie and cake. Hah! One year later our abstainer had zoomed back up to one hundred fifty pounds! I reckon the apple didn't quite *do* it over the long haul (she's down again now).

Dr. Robert Atkins (*The Diet Revolution*) is almost psychotic on the subject of avoiding carbohydrates, especially refined sugar, but people who have summered with him in Southampton tell me he succumbs occasionally to sweets.

Nobody has it easy. Okay, *that* (the grisliness of dieting) is out of my system.

Despite All the Controversy About How to Go *About* It and How Terribly Tough It Is, Dieting Really *Is* Moral, Sexy and Healthy

Let's talk about looks first. Do you like fat *men?* Of course not. You may "forgive" fatness in certain darling men, but their fat is a turn-off. Okay, you ought to be suspicious of men who say they like fat *women.* Those men want *mothers,* or at least a comfy, cushiony, sofa-pillow girl to sink into and hide out in. Never mind what *any* man says he likes in terms of your body weight *anyway*—you want to weigh in slender because your body and your brain *feel* best on a low-calorie, low-carbohydrate diet. . . . They really do. You simply have more energy. God *knows*, not carrying twenty or ten or even *five* extra pounds has to make it easier to get around, right? Think how exhausting it is to lug a ten-pound bag of kitty litter up the stairs. Well, ten pounds around your *middle* is just as big a drag.

Dr. Myron Winnick, director of Columbia University's Institute of Human Nutrition, says, "It's almost impossible for a healthy person to be too thin. There are very few medical problems associated with thinness." Good, nutritious, skinny eating can change your life. It changed *mine*.

May I give you a testimonial? I was a sick little thing in my teens, twenties and even thirties, and spent crazy amounts of time in doctors' offices, not to mention in *bed* (alone). Then I got healthy. At the age of thirty-six I started to "eat right," to take vitamins, then in my forties to exercise, and now, in my fifties, I am *ridiculously* healthy. I haven't missed a day at work at *Cosmo* because of illness in *twelve years,* and in the five years before that only five days with one bout of Asian flu. Though doctors swear everybody gets two a year, I don't *have* colds. Anyway, from "decent" skinny eating (no salt, no sugar, minimal starch), exercising an hour a day, taking vitamins (sixty a day now), no smoking, no drinking, no caffeine, no drugs and being *motivated* to stay. well, your life can change utterly. Mine did.

I seem to have taken on *two* subjects here—not being *fat* (losing weight if necessary) and healthy eating. Well, they are very much connected. To lose weight you have to give up carbohydrates (sugar and starch, as in corn muffins, chocolate chip cookies, fettuccine Alfredo and five thousand other things), and to *stay* slender and healthy you have to keep on avoiding them. So—good nutrition makes you slender as well as feel good. But can't you weigh a *little* more than "ideal" and still be healthy? Yes, a *little* more perhaps—five or ten pounds—but now we come to pride. If you want a flat stomach, huggable hips, round but slender arms, you've probably got to be at the "ideal" weight or less, because those extra five or ten pounds *never* go to the throat, breasts or shoulders where we'd *like* them, but always to the stomach and hips.

To give you an example of a skinny (but sensational) woman, there's Cheryl Tiegs—one hundred two pounds, and she's five feet ten inches! Well, the *price* for the ideal weight is, yes, semistarvation! Your body isn't actually *starving*, of course, it's fine and healthy, but your brain is possibly "starved" for those lovely treats you had at nineteen when your figure briefly became its ideal size—if it did. *Insurance* companies say you can weigh a lot *more* than you did at nineteen. *They* say you can carry around the most fantastic amounts, like one hundred twenty-eight pounds when you're five feet three inches! (How about *that*, Cheryl Tiegs?) Those weights are mythical if you want to be cute and sexy. Those weights allow you to be pudgy.

What *Should* You Eat?

If you want to lose weight, it doesn't matter *what* you eat less of as long as you eat *less*. No foods are more "dietary" than others. A calorie is a calorie, whether it's in strawberry waffles or bibb lettuce. If you're dieting, however, you can simply eat *more* bibb lettuce . . . tons and tons more for the same calorie count, so that's why certain foods are said to be "dietetic." The reason people try to help you *select* food to diet with is because some have more value—protein, vitamins, minerals—as well as more *satiety* value than others, and so make the dieting easier. Yes, nine hundred calories of pecan ripple ice cream is *just* as "slimming" as nine hundred calories of veggies, broiled fish and eggs, but you won't feel *satisfied;* in fact, you probably won't even be able to continue with your ice-cream diet for two reasons: the *quantities* will be meager—just five little one-half cup dishes of ice cream, quickly slurped, for a whole day, and there go the nine hundred cals—whereas veggies, fish, eggs mound *up* and you can have them in several courses. More important, your body will not be getting nourished with ice cream, and you will eventually feel too rotten to continue dieting. *Cosmo* diet writer Catherine Houck explains it this way: "Different foods are absorbed in the body at different rates, leaving you feeling either pleasantly full or gnawingly hungry, depending on what you've eaten. Pure sugar is absorbed most quickly; complex carbohydrates (potatoes, rice, grains, etc.) somewhat less quickly. Proteins and fats are digested at the most leisurely pace of all, causing blood to rise slowly and steadily and remain at this level for a longer period, so you don't get as hungry. In other words, a high-carb diet tends to stimulate appetite; a high-protein diet helps contain it. Also, a great number of calories are required to break *down* protein for use as energy in the body. Carbohydrates use very few calories to produce energy. Since protein uses about thirty percent of its caloric value while converting to energy, you can eat thirty percent *more* protein than carbohydrates or fat and still stay within your caloric limit."

There are a lot of diets to choose from. My husband, who is now slender—God knows how with his dieting *system*—picks his favorite item from *each* diet and does a melange. Loving Scotch, he's on the "drinking man's diet." Dr. Atkins says butter and cream are okay so he's into hollandaise. Linus Pauling recommends massive quantities of vitamin C so David has fresh grapefruit juice squeezed *hourly* at the Bel-Air Hotel (only one hundred calories, but twenty-two carbs per cup). And "I need *energy!*" announcement presages his eating a Hershey bar. Since Nathan Pritikin is death on alcohol, David doesn't feel really comfortable with Nathan's grains and cereals, still he *does* embrace Pritikin's vegetables, etc. etc.

Well, whether you follow a diet somebody else worked out or do your own, what is *painfully* clear is that to lose weight you cannot eat as much as you have been eating. To maintain, you have to continue to eat less. The amount of time you decide to spend eating "less" will obviously influence your diet plan. If you plan to get the weight off in six days, you'll have to cut to the *bone*.

Suppose you're working out your own diet. Well, you just pick a daily calorie count—nine hundred, one thousand, twelve hundred, fifteen hundred or whatever—and decide what foods within that count you will eat daily. If you're not too overweight, probably just cutting out bread, butter, desserts and alcohol will get most of the weight off over a few weeks. If you want to move faster, or you've already cut out those things and are still a few pounds too heavy, stick to a specific calorie count each day. *Calories and Carbohydrates* by Barbara Kraus (Grosset and Dunlap, $7.95) gives a calorie and carbohydrate count for seventy-five hundred brand names and basic foods. I find it invaluable.

Whether you plan to move fast or slow, count or not count calories, most *weight*-losing diets suggest a protein base for each meal, plus green veggies without butter, a little fruit, no cream, *no* alcohol, *no* sauces or gravies. I embrace Dr. Atkins' lifetime diet plan, which leans heavily on protein and a few veggies and virtually *eschews* fruit. No matter *what* diet you're on, if you cut carbohydrates and don't even eat all the meat, eggs, fowl and fish you want, I think you'll get there faster.

When they get to their lifetime sustaining diet, most people work out their "staples"—things they have nearly every day that work for *them*. Example: Margaux Hemingway says, "I stick with fresh organic vegetables, fruit and fish, sunflower seeds, soybeans, fresh carrot and parsley juice." Photographer Francesco Scavullo cooks vegetables in a wok—"onions and peppers, then I throw in zucchini, bamboo shoots and mushrooms, along with distilled water, and let everything steam for ten minutes." Model Maud Adams has a boiled egg and plain yogurt with bran and honey for breakfast, raw vegetables and a piece of cheese for lunch, fish, a large salad and one steamed vegetable for dinner. Lynda Carter always has salad for lunch, "my one big meal . . . with Jerusalem artichokes, string beans and cucumbers or whatever vegetables I'm in the mood for." Billie Jean King's diet program consists almost exclusively of fish, fresh fruit and vegetables. Lauren Hutton concentrates on *breakfast*.

Listen, these people's diets are not any more interesting than yours or mine. I'm just suggesting that after you get into the nutrition business—to be skinny *and* healthy—you usually "specialize." At home or bringing my lunch to the office I subsist on just five things: tuna salad made with half mayonnaise, half plain yogurt with fresh veggies on top *or* the HGB salad (recipes follow), diet Jell-O, warm cottage cheese with crisp apple and mozzarella cheese chopped in, plus four protein tablets for dessert. It sounds pitiful, I know, but I *adore* these things and I'm *healthy*. You do get enormously fond of your staples—you *trust* them. I eat mine in four separate courses per meal, which takes about forty minutes because, when I'm alone, I eat and read at the same time . . . two of life's greatest pleasures *combined*.

My husband doesn't eat *any* of these things. For him we fix "regular" food, and I am usually its fixer. Anyway, when *you're* at home, you may want to stick to staples, too. You get all the variety you need at other people's houses, at home when you entertain (can't feed *them* tuna salad and warm cottage cheese!) and in restaurants. (I "specialize" in restaurants, too. More in a moment.)

Listen, you'll work out *your* own plan, but here are recipes for my staples in *case* you'd like to try them.

Anna's Tuna Salad

½ small onion, grated
2 medium-sized dill pickles, chopped fine
2 medium (or one big) stalks celery, chopped fine
2 fairly heaping tablespoons mayonnaise
2 fairly heaping tablespoons plain yogurt
1 7-ounce can tuna (non-dietetic, dump in the oil)
1 hard-boiled egg, grated

Add onion, pickles and celery to mayonnaise and yogurt. Let stand ten minutes. Shred tuna very fine and add to yogurt/mayonnaise mixture. Add grated egg last. On top of the salad I always pile more chopped onion, sliced green or red pepper, cucumber, undercooked green beans cut in pieces, cherry tomatoes and sliced mushrooms. *Very* satisfying. (Don't gobble this whole recipe all at once!)

HGB Tossed Salad

(Use as many of these ingredients as you like in the amounts you like—you don't have to have them all.)

iceberg lettuce
raw spinach leaves
chopped cabbage, red or white
green beans (cooked al dente)
cherry tomatoes (cut in thirds)
1 tablespoon or so tuna salad
diced breast of chicken or turkey
grated Swiss cheese
grated hard-boiled egg
crumbled bacon (from a can)
shrimp (very optional)

Chop everything rather fine. Toss with one tablespoon *only* homemade oil-vinegar-herb dressing or diet dressing not to exceed one hundred calories. One tablespoon will cover a *mass* of ingredients if you keep tossing.

Now for a few *more* diet and nutrition thoughts.

Slender People Who Say They Don't Count Calories Don't Have to Because from Long Diet Experience They Can Pick out the Right Amount of Food to Eat Every Day—Without Counting

Most of us lifetime dieters have given *up* desserts, bread, butter, pasta. These things just go out of our lives forever, so we don't need to tot up *their* calories any longer. For that matter, we are so used to small portions of un-rich food that we don't need to tot up calories on just about *anything* we eat. We know *instinctively* if it is over or under our count.

A novice dieter *does* need to get acquainted with calorie counts, however. An egg is seventy, a small apple eighty, four ounces of broiled fish two hundred, four ounces of lean hamburger two hundred fifty, chili con carne one hundred thousand (I'm kidding but not *much!*) etc., etc., etc.

You should know that thirty-five hundred calories equals one pound, so to get a pound *off* you have to deprive your body—slowly or quickly—of that many calories, and if you *add* that many—quickly or slowly—you will *gain* a pound. When you are working out your *sustaining*-weight diet, you'll figure out how many calories your body can take in each day and *sustain*. (I sustain at about eighteen hundred because I *exercise* an hour a day; otherwise the count would only be fifteen hundred.)

"Forgetting calories" can happen after you have been watching your weight for about a year, I'd say, or maybe only six months if you're dedicated.

Crashing for a Specific Event Is Tough

Deadline dieting for the assignation with *him*, the job interview, a vacation is no different from being told you've *got* to do *anything*. Your natural response is "Oh, *do* I?" and you *don't!* As alcoholics have to give up booze *totally* and reformed smokers must not start smoking even one cigarette if they want to stay safe, *you* have to do more or less *permanent* slender-eating if you don't want to fall back into that wretched, debilitating, demoralizing lose-and-gain-it-right-back syndrome.

If you succeed only for an "occasion," you'll probably start eating again when the "occasion" is past. While we're into what doesn't work—*I* find that pictures of skinny girls in bikinis pasted on the frig door, hanging one's own bikini there, or putting up a photo of you *in* it at a tinier weight only cause one to get belligerent. You soon tear the photos to shreds and eat what you were going to eat *anyway*. Forget reminders and special events. When it's "time" to diet, you will.

Exercise Is *Good* for You— But It Won't Make You Skinny

Heavy exercise uses up about three hundred calories per hour, but we're talking *heavy*. . . . Are you really going to jog, swim, bicycle, or canoe right after that pasta orgy? I used to run up and down four flights of stairs at the Carlton Hotel in Cannes—up and down, up and down, up and down—to try to undo the damage of those South of France three-star restaurants, but twenty flights up and down *possibly* took care of *one* plate of *soupe de poisson*. Yes, members of the Detroit Lions and Chicago Bears eat five-thousand-calorie meals and burn them off in play but remember they *weigh* from one hundred ninety to two hundred thirty-five pounds to begin with and so can tolerate more calories than you, never mind the football. Olympic figure skater Linda Fratianne's coach says she watches her weight at all *times* and diets even when she skates twelve *hours* a day! Exercise because it makes you feel good, keeps your body taut and young, helps *especially* when you've "lost weight in the wrong places," but *not* because it's much help in using up calories.

Exhaustion and Tension Are
the (Bitter) Enemies of Diet

You think you ought to *lose* your appetite when you're worried and tense. The exact opposite is true. You really can't *diet* when you're strung out, sleepless or fatigued. Personal problems, business crises only seem get-*throughable* with a food fix. So, start your diet when you are calm. You may be depressed about *being* overweight, but not facing a monster day for any other reason. Don't try to give up smoking and eating at the same time. Smoking is worse for you than being overweight, and if you go up a few pounds after stopping, not to worry. . . . *Later* you can diet.

Tiny Tastes—Just to Keep in Touch
With Forbidden Delicacies—Are Dangerous

In an article in *Cosmo,* famed food critic Gael Greene suggests, "a *forkful* of fettuccine, the peak of a chicken croquette, one sugar-coated bourbon ball, a heaping teaspoonful of butter-pecan ice cream. Amazing [says Gael] how just one taste buffers up the willpower."

Not anybody's willpower *I* know. One tiny taste of chocolate soufflé or a little dab of Napoleon can open a whole Pandora's box of need and greed.

I agree with that adorable diet maven Richard Simmons who says, "A sliver leads to a slab, a slab leads to a slob!"

When You Eat Might Not Be
as Important as People Say

"They" are always telling us to eat a big breakfast, a light lunch and a tiny dinner. Well, late-day abstinence is all very well for *morning* people who peak early, but how about us owls who only really get going about four in the afternoon? Nothing but an apple and glass of milk after six o'clock at night would leave us starving during our *golden* period—four to midnight! I do it the other way around—a tiny breakfast, if *any*, medium lunch and never a night if

I can *help* it that I dine before nine—plus a snack at bedtime! People with low blood sugar—hypoglycemics—have to eat more often, and five small meals a day *may* allow you to eat a tiny bit more—Shirley MacLaine and Carol Channing eat five a day—but I don't really think it matters *when* you eat. . . . All that matters is how much.

Self-Induced Throwing Up After an Orgy Is Brave, But Not Good for You

Never mind that the ancient Romans did it, some determined young ladies (a couple of famous ones) keep to skin and bones *now* by eating and whoopsing. Well, it's not only *unpleasant* but *unhealthy.* One of *Cosmo's* medical columnists, Dr. Elizabeth Morgan, says, "The stomach begins to empty fifteen minutes after a meal and to lose any calories at all by vomiting, you must do so right away. Do that and you *will* lose most of what the stomach has absorbed. Along with the calories, however, you'll lose gallons of valuable digestive fluid, a loss that can cause serious salt and water imbalance in the body. Stomach acids that come up during vomiting also irritate the esophagus (food pipe) and can eventually cause it to bleed and 'rupture.' " *Another* "solution" shot down!

Skipping Meals Mostly Doesn't Work— Postponing them *Does*

Some people eat only twice or even *once* a day and, yes, that qualifies as skipped meals, but skipping meals for *most* of us simply guarantees that we will eat the skipped meal's calories at the *next* meal. Suppose you skip your usual breakfast: two eggs, protein toast with diet margarine and coffee—two hundred fifty calories. The body keeps track and says, "You *owe* me that food. I didn't have it for breakfast, but I want it now for *lunch, plus* what you were going to give me anyway for lunch, *plus* some *extra!*" You'll take in far more than the two hundred fifty breakfast calories saved.

A tiny meal at its proper time is usually a better way to keep one's calorie count down than "doing without." Stretching the times out *between* meals can be effective, i.e., letting at least five hours lapse before you eat again. Let's say, on Saturday, even though you've been up three hours, you don't eat breakfast *or* lunch until *noon,* then have something else at 5 P.M., then real dinner at 10 P.M. Or, on a workday when you're going to a party or on a date, you have a small breakfast at 8 A.M., a small lunch at one o'clock and maybe nothing to eat between lunch and dinner at nine. Some people can hack this waiting and some can't. I know *I* can only go five hours without food. The moral is: Don't try to kid your body. It *knows* how much food it needs to "sustain" for a day and *you* know how many calories you've planned to *give* it. Space the meals so you take in *only* that much.

There Are *Secret* Dieters in this World
—A Disgusting Group!

We all know secret *eaters* who eat just little snippets of food in public ("I never touch dessert," she says, repugnance and pity written all over her face as you reach for a macaroon), but have a quart of Haagen-Dazs ice cream every night *before* dinner (and the hips to show for it). These people we pity, but they only harm themselves. The *lowest*-grade sneaks are the secret *dieters*. They harm *us* because they set a bad example. There she is, all ninety-eight pounds of her, seemingly going berserk—"Yes, I *will* have another Rob Roy, and some of those wonderful cottage fries, and onion rings!"—giving the impression of having this *superior* metabolism while everything *you* eat is going straight into fat.

What you *don't* know, because she isn't saying, is that this is the first solid food she's had for two days. Yesterday morning she had ten string beans and some herb tea, and nothing since. Never mind what this restaurant showoff is putting away; *you* have to stick to what's proper for *you!*

People Are Rotten About Helping
You with Your Diet

Only a near and *very* dear one—husband, lover, maybe a close friend, rarely a mother—will help you stay on a diet. "You're such a skinny little thing," people say, if you're *already* thin. "Don't you *ever* eat?" (Yes!) Or "*You* certainly don't have to diet, why are you passing up dessert?" (How many desserts do they suppose you've passed up to *look* this way?) Some go so far as to suggest, "You'd look better with a little *meat* on your bones." (It doesn't *go* to my bones, dearie, it goes to my tush!) How proprietory they are about *your* flesh! If still plump, you're supposed to eat to cheer up the ones who aren't eating. . . . You are their *surrogate* eater.

Some hostesses and hosts—not all, but some—still heap food on your plate, get their wounded-owl look when you refuse the peanut-butter torte with shortbread cookie *plus* Irish coffee. One aggravated hostess put chocolate chips in my Sanka out in the kitchen one day, then gleefully told me what she'd done after I drank. Bitch!

Restaurant personnel *defy* you to diet on the premises. . . . People not eating isn't how they make money or a reputation. Having never been *known* to send you a shrimp cocktail "on the house," they will magnanimously send over a slab of Black Forest cake "compliments of Luigi." Girlfriends who *love* you leave salted almonds on the coffee table when you visit. Husbands who love you skinny want you to diet on other people's time.

What all this pushing does to some of us is simply create the will to *resist*. They'd have to get my jaws open with a *crowbar* now to get dessert down me. These are things I long to say (but haven't yet) when badgered by the dum-dums: "No, I do not have a wasting disease. Yes, I love good food. Yes, my taste buds are as normal as yours. Yes, I could get through that plate of spaghetti carbonara like the garbage scow working Madison Avenue if I took a notion. No, I am not out of my mind or even particularly neurotic (about food anyway). Staying slender is a deliberate act of will and I do it not so much for health reasons but because five extra pounds or three or *two* go straight to my stomach and it becomes distended as though a whole watermelon were in there. I have *always* had a stomach problem, and heavy exercising—I do an hour a day—does no good whatever unless I also keep the weight down. My mother was pear-shaped. I am *potentially* pear-shaped. Two reputable, conservative doctors have *both* recommended I stay at this small weight. It takes a great act of willpower to eat little enough to keep my stomach flat and my hips from expanding, *despite* all the exercising, so please get your beady eyes off my clam broth and go jump into your own potage Saint-Germain with cheese croutons, you creep!"

Everybody thinks skinnies have some special metabolism (and some perverse skinnies *encourage* them to think that). This idea is reassuring to fatties because how could anybody *expect* them to stay slim without that old special trick metabolism. Sadly there *is* no trick metabolism—just self-discipline, which is maybe the neatest trick of all.

Nevertheless, You Can't Blame *Them*
if You Fall Off the Wagon

Fantastic food is *everywhere* . . . in restaurants, the deli, supermarket, other people's houses, your house, and we all know all the excuses . . . it's Christmas, it's Thanksgiving, I'm in love, I can't diet when I'm with *him,* it's my birthday, my mother forces me to eat, I have to have stuff in the house for the kids, I'm going on vacation, I have to take clients to lunch, I go to lots of parties, we eat in restaurants four nights a week, blah blah blah. We're *all* in eat-situations all the time and not *one* of the excuses for eating is valid . . . not *one!*

The most dangerous place of all in terms of giving in to food is probably *your* house, where there aren't any distractions to keep you from tripping to the frig. But *wherever* you are dieting—a little disapproval (and no help at all!) from loved ones, friends, restaurant personnel and all the others notwithstanding—you *can* manage not to eat much; it just takes guts. It hurts me to see people I care about cave in. One of my dear friends gained eight pounds— eight!—on a one-week trip to Atlanta to meet her beloved's family. Marsha said it was wall-to-wall gravy, biscuits with honey, hush puppies and grits, Karo-pecan pie and pinto beans with salt pork, but she *could* have resisted. She might have said, "I've got a stomach bug (*everybody* respects stomach bugs) and have to eat just plain chicken . . . I'm so sorry!" or have told the *truth:* "I have painfully lost twenty pounds and dare not start back up again . . . will you forgive me?" and begged for something simple.

The family and the beloved wouldn't have *liked* it but they wouldn't have packed her off to the airport either. One is *looking* for excuses not to be good, *n'est-ce pas?* To get rid of calories at parties and outfox a determined host, I have dumped champagne (which I adore) into other people's glasses when they weren't looking or, in a real emergency, into a split-leaf philodendron, wrapped eclairs in a hanky and put them in my purse, *once* in an emergency, sequestered one behind the cushion of an upholstered chair—in a napkin of course. At a restaurant one day, the host kept piling raspberries on my plate. "Raspberries can't hurt you," this fool kept babbling. Well, it was after a night when I'd overeaten and *everything* "hurt me," so, when he left to make a phone call, I put all the raspberries in a napkin and left it on the banquette seat. How did I know he would sit down on the napkin in his beige gabardine suit? He had it coming, right?

But let's say once in a while even *you* decide to hell with it, you're going to be a gracious guest, make the hostess happy and *have* the frozen lemon mousse. Well, right next to you will be a guest who says, "No, thanks, Camilla—looks wonderful but I'll pass," and *he* doesn't get thrown out of the house or even frowned at. You *wanted* the mousse and it wasn't the hostess's using the electric prod that made you have it, right? To get myself to abstain, I help other people fill and refill their plates, have passed a hundred thousand brownies and whipped cream in my time without having *any*. . . . The activity takes your mind off eating. Gradually, when you get into lifetime skinny-eating and carefully let yourself *remember* the trouble you were in after the *last* splurge, what you had to suffer to get back to where you were, you *do* get to be ruthless enough to stare down every beckoning batch of garlic toast, hot hors d'oeuvres, petit-fours, no matter *how* much you want them.

Oh, dear, such heavy lecturing. Let's get back to what to do when you are about to start to try to lose a few pounds.

Go Easy on Salt

You already know this, but salt causes water retention and bloating so you'll look puffier and weigh more when you get on the scale. More seriously, salt contributes to hardening of the arteries and senility, which you don't ever want to happen to *you*. When cooking for you and loved ones at home, cook *without* salt, even if recipes call for it. Never add salt to restaurant food. You get enough natural salt in food to stay healthy without adding your own, and pretty soon you get used to the taste of food without extra salt.

Substitute Sugar Is Better Than No Sugar

The Food and Drug Administration tells us that saccharine and sucaryl, even the amounts contained in two bottles of diet soda a day, may be carcinogenic. Occasionally a headline announces that they aren't *sure* this is so and a denial is issued, but whatever they are currently saying, I have chosen to *ignore* the warnings. Having given up every *other* kind of naughtiness in food and drink, this one I'm not repudiating because it makes the other give-ups *possible!* I am addicted to sweets and there is no such thing for me as a "reasonable" amount. A taste of somebody's chocolate fondue sends me ravening for the whole plate . . . you might as well give Dracula just a *whiff* of blood. Okay, if saccharine and sucaryl suffice for sugar in my life, I think they're worth the risk. One could get natural sugar in fruit, of course, but bananas, oranges, pears have calories *and* carbohydrates galore, and even the natural sugar in fruit doesn't make me feel too wonderful. I try to keep the fruit to one piece a day.

As I write this, a new artificial sweetener, aspartame, is being test-marketed. I've used it and it's sensational. Put out by G. D. Searle & Co. under the brand name Equal, it should be available for all of us soon.

Diet Desserts Are Dubious Friends

Either the diet stuff doesn't make up for *real* dessert (you still feel deprived) or you eat so much you're back up to a thousand calories. A so-called "diet" candy bar has two hundred fifty cals— *not* inconsiderable; a diet cookie has one hundred cals, and who wants just one cookie? The candy bar is more apt to be made from "healthful" ingredients—carob instead of chocolate, honey instead of sugar—than it is to be low in calories. The famous diet caramel candy you're supposed to eat three pieces of before a meal to cut your appetite—I went through a whole box (a month's supply) in a day and a half just like regular candy.

You probably have your own thoughts about diet desserts . . . certainly strawberries, raspberries and melon are *on* limits if you don't eat too many, though I lie low with fruit because it's loaded with sugar, albeit "natural." I use *cases* of D-Zerta (strawberry, raspberry, cherry, orange, lemon, lime) at thirty-two calories a bowl. Use one fourth the water directions call for so that one envelope makes only one serving, not four, of nice chewy jelly. Make two envelopes at a time.

If you *do* like diet dessert, here's a good recipe:

Rich Chocolate Mousse

1 envelope D-Zerta chocolate pudding
2 envelopes Sweet 'n Low, Sugar Twin or other artificial
* sweetener*
1 rounded tablespoon instant Sanka, Brim, or
* regular coffee*
2 cups skim milk
2 tablespoons (2 ounces) Hershey chocolate syrup
2 tablespoons (1 ounce) brandy

Empty chocolate pudding mix, sweetener and regular or caffeine-free coffee into saucepan. Add milk. Stir vigorously with a fork until pudding dissolves. Add chocolate syrup. Place on fire and stir constantly until pudding comes to a boil (about 10 minutes). Add brandy. Remove from fire and pour into dishes. Serve warm or chilled. Package instructions say one envelope serves four but those are very skimpy portions. This recipe serves *three*. One hundred forty calories per serving and quite delicious.

A Skinny Can Invest Her Calories in Food *Or* Drink—But Not *Both*

Just by cutting out liquor and wine, some people can take off a dozen or so pounds in a few weeks. . . . Of course, these are people who drink quite a *lot*. Whatever diet you follow, you virtually *can't* drink during the losing period—maybe one glass of wine or one highball a day. After you get to "sustaining," you more or less have to choose between "gracious" amounts of liquor *or* food. Several skinnies I know *do* drink several highballs or glasses of wine a day, but they eat very *little*. It's absolutely up to you. What few calories *I'm* allotted, I prefer in food, except in sexy moments.

(P.S. You *know* which is *healthier*.)

Old Reliables

1. Eat very slowly so that it takes longer to finish your tiny portions. Chew each mouthful of chewy things thirty times.

2. Interrupt yourself when eating. In restaurants you are frequently with people—men especially—who (a) have ordered a lot more food than you; (b) do most of the talking so they won't even eat what they've ordered very *fast*. To make the little portions last longer, put your fork down—you won't *want* to put your fork down, but do it—every so often, and count to a hundred before picking it up again. If you hold your stomach in for that hundred count—keep breathing!—you get double the good out of the eating hiatus.

3. Don't drink water while eating. Dr. Neil Solomon, author of *High Health Diet and Exercise Plan* (Putnam, $9.95), says, "Liquids dilute digestive juices and also wash food down so easily you may eat *more.*"

4. Eat only when you're *hungry*. You can sit with people who are eating and not eat *with* them, you know, if you aren't "due." (As you know, I think a good plan is to let five hours go by between meals, unless you're on five *small* meals a day.)

5. Stop eating before you feel quite satisfied. This is the hardest diet rule of all—not to let yourself feel really full; but if you *do* stop just short of satiety and wait a bit, fullness catches up with you. It's good to leave something on your plate—only I can't *do* that! If it's there, it's mine, by God, and I'm going to *have* it. I find it better not to let the food get put on the plate in the first place. If you order small, eat slowly and stop between bites (as just suggested), you'll finish up about the same time as the other diners and *won't* be reaching for the rolls and butter.

6. Give away any naughty food present received—cookies, candy, cake—immediately. Don't screw around.

7. Weigh once a day (the old lie-detector test!) at the same time. Before breakfast, after eliminating, puts you at your slimmest.

8. Remember that eating less or eating *more* on a particular day may not show on the scale the next morning. Whichever you did *will* register soon enough . . . don't get discouraged or elated too soon.

9. Accept once and for all that dieting is *hell* and stop getting depressed about it! The more you do it the better you get at it, like anything else hard that you learn to do. That's the *truth*.

Finally Comes the Business of Not Being
Able to Eat All You Want—
﹐Even of the "Good" Stuff

You think because you have forsworn English muffins oozing with butter and drowning in marmalade that you are home *free*. Look at *me*, you chortle as you slurp down papaya slathered only in lime juice, lump crab meat with only a little mustard-mayonnaise, yogurt, bananas and wheat germ—me, enjoying *this* stuff, who only used to turn on for rice pudding and peanut butter-and-jelly sandwiches.

Don't dislocate your arm patting yourself on the back! Just because it's *healthy* doesn't mean it's *innocent*. The best chef salad in the world (at the Russian Tea Room on West Fifty-seventh Street in New York), with only *honorable* ingredients like lettuce, tomatoes, breast of turkey, Swiss cheese, eggs, etc., must have *easily* nine hundred calories, even with vinaigrette dressing instead of blue cheese, double the mushrooms and hold the tongue! Cheese—beautiful, high-protein Bel Paese, Cheddar, Swiss, Port Salut, Gouda—is one hundred calories per *inch*, never mind cholesterol, which isn't your problem yet. Even cottage cheese with satisfying amounts of fresh raspberries, banana, pineapple and peaches, topped with plain yogurt and sunflower seeds, can total five hundred calories—nearly one third of *this* dieter's total daily calorie allotment.

A friend once got to maintaining on *vanilla*—poured it on everything from scrambled eggs to glazed carrots and gobs in coffee figuring, could it *hurt?!* Vanilla has eight calories per teaspoon and he was soon mounding up a couple of hundred extra calories a day.

No, it isn't nice, no, it isn't fair, after you've given up your "bad old companions," that this *friendly* stuff could hurt you! Well, the (somewhat!) good news is that binge-ing on the "good stuff"—wall-to-wall chicken salad, sea bass in white wine sauce, deviled crab—is a *little* easier to eradicate the results from with a quick crash diet or a fast—possibly because the base *is* protein—than binge-ing on starch and sugar, at least I find it so. And gradually, *gradually* you learn never to let yourself *get* more than a pound or two up before you start knocking it off. Incidentally, the minute you leave your starvation diet, whatever kind you're on, to return to normal "sustaining" (not fat) eating, you will instantly put on a pound or two. *That* is aggravating, but it happens. You probably need to get down about a pound *below* where you wanted to be so you can use that minus-pound to start eating normal rations again.

On "Heavy" Diet Days, You Must Not Let a Morsel of Food Past Your Lips that Hasn't Been *Planned* For

When you're into big-time serious dieting, you must *plan* what you're going to eat that day—seven hundred cals, one thousand cals—and not eating another *thing*. How easy it is to screw up the day. You go to the kitchen for a glass of water—we all *know* why you can't get one from the bathroom tap: the bathroom isn't where that smidge of corned-beef hash is resting in the skillet from your husband's breakfast which, for some reason (and we all *know* the reason), you *didn't* throw out with the garbage after breakfast!

Or you tell yourself lettuce doesn't count—a whole *pound* of iceberg is only fifty-six calories for God's sake, so you grab the lettuce, but first thing you know you are "doctoring" it with a tablespoon of oil and some bacon bits and a tomato wedge. How bad can a tablespoon of cottage cheese be? Pure protein, but then you have a quarter of a pear, those seven cherries, eighteen seedless grapes, a tablespoon of yogurt to accompany the cheese, gobble gobble gobble. Actually, there aren't many calories in the hash or salad or cheese and fruit, and you aren't into Big Time Sinning like half a jar of marshmallow fluff spooned down while you stand at the sink, but, my friend, it's a snippy-poo here and a snippy-poo there and by early evening you've snippy-pooed yourself right off your diet! Those bites have broken your willpower. When you get to the last meal of your diet day, instead of your three-ounce hamburger patty and a sliced tomato, you're apt to say, What the hell, I've already blown my plan and I *am* starving, so it's gobble gobble gobble some more. . . . *La diète, c'est finie!*

After eating *any* meal, especially your last of the day, you must let the factory close down. Get yourself away from where food is. Have nothing until your next planned meal.

When You Cook for Company
Don't Worry About *Their* Calories

You may not usually cook with butter, cream, sugar, salt or a *lot* of tasty things, but you shouldn't deny *company* these ingredients. Even dieters don't like pristine pickings when they come to visit. If you serve skimpy on the theory you want to *help* guests diet, a determined eater will go straight for the breadsticks, every shrimp on the platter, your entire veggie collection with *all* the dip plus lemon-fluff dessert intended for six other guests, and look hungrily toward the kitchen. Don't *push* food at anybody, of course, and you can provide a choice of melon or a richer dessert. Don't wince if they leave half their food on the plate, but serve "regular" delicious stuff and serve *enough*.

Let *them* do the skimping, never you.

Restaurant Dieting Is Not that Big a Deal

Restaurants aren't so hard to diet in. You've got friends and gaiety to distract you and only prescribed little portions placed in front of *you* if you order right. In a French, Italian or almost *any* ethnic restaurant, they can come up with plain roast chicken or a piece of fish. I had turbot and plain spinach three times a day four days in a row in Italy last year to make up for a previous three-day pasta-freak and the restaurants were very nice about it.

What a passionless, prissy way to see Italy—I know!—but not letting your weight really start mounding up is a bigger passion for *some* of us. At a Japanese place you can scrape the batter off the tempura, skip the rice, eat small portions. You can *plan* your restaurant fare before you *get* there. I unswervingly order either of two things: Perrier to start, mixed green salad for first course, broiled fish for an entree, Sanka (with sweetener) for dessert; *or* consommé for a first course, broiled fish and *one* vegetable—*sans* butter—for an entree, Sanka for dessert. I have *gallons* of Sanka with Sweet 'n Low from the table or Equal from my purse while other people finish the meal grandly.

I must say restaurants are sometimes hateful about the Sanka-instead-of-dessert business. They *want* you to have dessert, of course, so will not always bring Sanka or coffee while the others are *having* dessert, and you sit there with *nothing* to pour down you but *air*. When they *do* bring the coffee, they pour one cup, then put the pot across the room where you have to call the waiter for a second cup. I'm (nearly!) always screaming at them to at least fill the cup to the *brim!* One of my three favorite restaurants in the world brings a scant cup of hot (actually tepid) water and a Sanka package so you make your own at table. . . . I've made and finished mine by the time the waiter leaves. The darling White Elephant Club in London does bring you an enormous pot of hot water, a big cup and a whole *jar* of Caffee Hag, God bless.

As for food, you can actually eat nothing at *all* in a restaurant. I have had *only* plates of bouillon after some horrible binge earlier in the day. Listen, as long as your friends and loved ones get to eat, they don't mind *too* much if you don't. They just think you're a little peculiar but, after a few cluckings, leave you alone.

When one-hundred-and-two-pound Cheryl Tiegs gets up to one hundred five, she says she *stops* eating and maybe you, *too*, will have to stop eating occasionally.

Take *Your* Kind of Food *With* You

How can anybody feel safe in a *hotel* room when you can order from room service like a pasha and some hotels keep it available all *night?* I never leave for *any* trip without mozzie or Swiss cheese in a brown paper bag and some protein tablets (my candy). These "staples" keep one from *calling* room service, can even be breakfast in the morning if you're in a hurry. These *good* rations also get you through airport waits or for meal service to begin on the plane. On long shopping trips, I take along half a banana, hard-boiled egg or *tiny* wedge of cheese.

The point is never to get so hungry you'll be tempted to stop for a bad old snack when just the tiniest amount of "friendly" food would get you by to mealtime. You can even take club soda or a diet drink to houses where you think people may not stock these things.

Don't Expect to Be Good the Rest of Your Life

There is almost no such thing as a bingeless human being, and it's okay to get off the wagon and get back on. Expecting never to eat anything bad again or not to eat too much of the *good* stuff is like expecting never to be unhappy again . . . unrealistic. Once "upon you," the binge is almost impossible to stop, wouldn't you say? A slipping dieter or binge-er will get dressed in the middle of the night to go to the deli, will *kill* the loved one who tries to keep her from opening the refrigerator door. On the pretense of "helping the hostess," a "slipper" will take guests' plates from the table, rush them to the sink and gobble what's left on each one before anybody else makes it to the kitchen. A binge has to be gone *through*, like a fit! Heavy and *frequent* binge-ing usually comes *before* you have decided to "go straight" (get to your wanted weight and stay there forever).

That was the case with me (the case history I know most about). I have never *been* fat because I always made myself pay for binges (thirty-six hours without *any* food . . . ghastly!) immediately, but just because you put yourself on the rack the next day doesn't mean you aren't one of the world's "best" compulsive eaters. Dear little good-person me has binged until I looked like the snake in the Frank Buck (late, great wild-animal collector) movie who crawled through the slats of a cage to reach a young pig, swallowed the pig whole (as is the wont of snakes) and, with the pig in his tummy, couldn't get out of the cage again . . . disgusting! On my birthday binge a few years ago a friend sent a Candygram—one pound of fairly good chocolate delivered by Western Union. As soon as the Western Union boy departed, I sat down by the front door and ate the whole thing. Incredible what the human tummy will *hold* . . . it just stretches and stretches!

Why do we do that to ourselves—eat until we're ill? A thousand books and magazine articles have been written about motives: low tolerance for frustration, anger and depression (opposite sides of the coin) compensated for with food, needing to be fat so you can "hide out" from job and/or sex success . . . if you're frightened of either of these Big Two, fatness will pretty much guarantee you won't *get* them. A load of self-hate may cause us to try to *destroy* ourselves with food . . . *all* these hang-ups are reasons to gobble, but I think we may also do it just because the food is *there* . . . all of those fabulous (worthless) yummies mother and other authority figures never trained us *not* to eat. Only recently have people become anything but *derelict* about nutrition . . . and now, all grown up, we simply don't *believe* the bad stuff should be out of our lives forever. Well, one Hershey kiss leads to another Hershey kiss and one Toll House cookie calls for fifteen, and you're off and gaining. I *think* my binge-ing days are over. Not slippage—I still have too much of my "staples": tuna salad, cottage cheese, mozzie cheese, things like that, but *heavy* sinning is in the past.

Two Christmases ago somebody sent David (poor darling never even *saw* his present) some Greek pastry and I ruthlessly (attack dogs chewing on my calves couldn't have stopped me) went through the whole thing—two pounds—from midnight to six o'clock the next morning . . . I just kept tripping to the frig for another fix. When it was all gone, even the crumbs, something clicked off—or on—in my head and I said, You know you can't *do* this anymore—this insane gobbling and then the equally insane compensatory starving. Dr. Atkins had for several *years* been coaxing me to give up sugar, and the day of the pastry fit— December 11, 1978—I went cold turkey off sugar. Since then— four years ago—I've had just one encounter—preplanned. I promised myself that on my first anniversary of abstinence I would have something wicked, and, since the same Greek pastry had arrived for Christmas from the same innocent friends, I sat down and ate about half a pound. It was the best thing I'd ever tasted and I could feel myself slipping down down down back into the old morass . . . binge-ing having to be followed by remorse and starvation. It was like falling once more into the hands of a cruel but devastating lover you thought you'd got *free* of. I closed the tin, gave the rest to the housekeeper (I can't seem to put *anything* in the garbage or flush it down the john), and now my fourth anniversary has passed. *You* don't have to give up sugar totally, my love, as I seem to have had to, but I'm just describing how one binge-er *sort* of broke the habit. Even with sugar out of my life—to *finish* this interminable saga—I still weighed, at five feet four, one hundred ten or twelve pounds, still had a poochy stomach . . . I've *always* had it and, yes, I do exercise like a maniac (exercise in next chapter). So I went to see one of those gifted doctors that maybe you can only *find* in New York, who confirmed that one hundred five would indeed be a much better weight in my case and gave me a product called Optifast to get off the five pounds. To get from one hundred ten to one hundred five, where I now stay, I had three Optifasts a day plus one small meal for six days. Even *with* a meal a day—not giving up food totally—the routine was terribly unpleasant. I would tell myself, "You are Juliet, taking the poison now so you will be able to see your lover (solid food!) a little later . . . *swallow!*" Eating less than you'd like to is *always* unpleasant but I find doing it in one swoop—Optifast actually tastes okay—better than months of semistarvation to get to the low mark.

Okay, that's one person's "How I got the weight off—with crashing—and kept it off" story. Could we talk about crashes and fasts for a moment?

Crashing Is Okay, So Is Fasting

If you have *lots* of pounds to lose and would like to see *instant* progress—say five to ten pounds off in a hurry—*before* you go on the long-term slog, or if you, like me, have only two to five pounds *total* to lose, but you're tiny and the daily calorie count for your frame is already so low you can't stand the torture of cutting *that* by a third for several weeks to get off the two pounds, you may want to do something more drastic than the *slow* torture, and crash a few pounds away quickly.

Isn't crashing bad for you?

No, not a little crash. Dr. Irwin Stillman, author of *The Doctor's Quick Weight Loss Diet*, says, "In my experience there's no question that quick-action dieting which alters radically and suddenly your ways of eating is the best way to reduce . . . the too-prevalent viewpoint that a fast take-off of weight is linked inevitably with a fast put-on . . . is not true. I have seen too many people struggle with slow-take-off diets, then slip and put on weight quickly—and give up. They don't know how to take off those added pounds in a hurry so they're discouraged from trying again."

Dr. Stillman is pushing *his* diet, of course (high protein), and it's a very efficacious plan. Whatever crash plan you embrace, you can probably only stay on for a week or two if you're *big*, a day or two if you're *small*, then go on to normal, slower dieting if you still have some distance to go. Even total fasting for a couple of days can't hurt physically though you're uncomfortable. The important thing is *not* to return to normal fat-eating that got you into trouble in the *first* place the very moment you're off the crash or the fast, but go to your regular slim-eating "life plan" if you're now where you want to be, or to a less horrendous *diet* if you have more pounds to lose.

There are many ways to crash or fast for one or two days. With a *juice* fast you simply pick a calorie count—say five hundred *calories*—and divide these among whatever liquids—tomato, orange, grapefruit, cranberry, grape—you plan to consume. Liquids have *calories* like everything else, so you have to count. Muscat, Malaga, Tokay, Thompson seedless grapes have two hundred and seventy calories per pound, so you could get in a bunch of grapes—two, three or four pounds—and have nothing but *grapes* all day. As for crashes with other food, Dr. Stillman's *Quick Weight Loss Diet* allows lean meat, chicken, turkey, fish and seafood, eggs, skim-milk cottage cheese—enough of all these to fill you up—for anywhere from a four- to seven-pound loss per week. Not bad. The Grapefruit Diet suggests one-half grapefruit or four-ounce glass of unsweetened grapefruit juice at the start of *every* meal, all protein foods mentioned on the Stillman diet plus vegetables without butter for as much as a fourteen-pound loss in ten days. The Amazing *Egg* Diet, said to have been developed at the Mayo Clinic, suggests an egg and half grapefruit for *every* breakfast, eggs plus veggies for most lunches and dinners—twelve pounds off in fourteen days. There are so *many* ways to diet. If you'd like a selection, I suggest *The Dieter's Companion: A Guide to Nutritional Self-sufficiency* by Nikki and David Goldbeck (McGraw-Hill); *Consumer Guide Rating the Diets* by Theodore Berland and the editors of *Consumer Guide; The Diet Book* by Carol Guilford (Drake Publishers).

This is one of *my* favorite crashes—to be followed for two days, preferably Saturday and Sunday (with someone you love?) for a loss of two pounds. Breakfast: one egg cooked without butter, one glass of white wine. Lunch: two eggs cooked without butter, two glasses of white wine. Dinner: medium steak, all fat trimmed, broiled, and finish the bottle of wine. You'll need one bottle of white wine per person per day. Cold-turkey fasting—*no* calories for the day—is the most dramatic of all. As I've told you, I used to do that about once a month after a hideous binge, but that twenty-four to thirty-six hours is really a lost day from your life because you're so *uncomfortable*—you certainly can't *think* straight or get anything done. A milder semifast or a crash of only five hundred to eight hundred calories seems preferable to me. Even a preferred *crash* diet is so individual, such a matter of personal taste, you should choose the least painful way for *you*. My own crash diet, as

I mentioned, is done with Optifast, though I never get more than two pounds up any more because I can barely stand the torture of getting *that* much off. If you're interested, your doctor may be able to prescribe Optifast or another diet helper. Even though skinny —or maybe *especially* though skinny—one is nearly always *thinking* about food! As my friend Jackie Lehman says, "I am either guilty or hungry at all times! If I go straight, I'm hungry; if I eat enough to be comfortable, I'm guilty." Ah yes, we all know the syndrome. Some dieters claim to have "shrunk" their stomachs to the point that a lot of food revolts them. *Quel* joy! There is some question as to whether a stomach (the inside stomach, holding the food) can *be* shrunk but, if it can, I am not among the *shrinkees*. I think you may have to have a tiny touch of anorexia nervosa to maintain an ideal weight . . . not a *heavy* case, just a little one! Can you make yourself get almost *sick* at the sight of anything floating in gravy? Become nauseous sitting next to a person pouring ketchup on his spareribs? Can you viciously clamp your jaws shut and keep teeth clenched if they try to force-feed you even a *bite* of sautéed soft-shelled crab? Can you admire your utterly outstanding pelvic bones the way other people admire Bo Derek's bosom, take *endless* pleasure in patting your stomach because it (still) isn't there, thank God!, go into *deep* depression at the gain of even *half* a pound? Good! I've got *two* of those down pat—the jaw clamping and the depression—and am working on the others. There are *worse* preoccupations than good nutrition and staying slim. Now I think I'll go get a plate of tuna salad, after which we are going to discuss exercise, but only for a few pages because all this self-discipline is driving *me* buggy and could drive *you* to stop reading or give up mouseburgering. Here we go.

Chapter Four

EXERCISE

You already know what everybody says about exercise. It makes you look better, breathe better, think better, sleep better. . . . Probably you *already* are exercising. If you aren't, you may not want to hear one more word on the subject. Nevertheless, I have a few thoughts about it that *nothing* is going to keep me from telling you!

History first. I was forty-seven—forty-*seven!*—before I even got started, let alone got hopelessly *hooked* on exercise. At Belmont High School in Los Angeles in my fourteenth year I used to take "rest" while the other kids took gym. While *they* were out on the hockey field, lining up at the baseball diamond, choosing sides for volleyball, about twenty of us scrawnies were given a glass of milk and two graham crackers and put to bed for an hour. At my next Los Angeles high school, John H. Francis Polytechnic, I once again took "rest" while the other children played, then in my senior year, I was finally strong enough for regular gym. Bliss . . . for a very brief moment. The one and only time I ever got my hands on the basketball and started to throw—you don't *forget* these things—the whole team was screaming at me to stop. It seems I was in the wrong court aiming at *their* basket. They could have saved themselves the screams. No ball of mine ever got anywhere *near* a basket. I couldn't get a volleyball over the net, throw a softball anywhere close to the person at bat, hit even a *strike* . . . not once, not ever. In a social game or two of tennis (Poly High had no court) I was *rigid* with shame at never being able to get a serve into the opponent's court, return any but the *gentlest* ball. I could swim just a few yards, thumping and panting; diving meant bellyflopping and getting water in your sinuses. . . . You do get the picture?

In the years between high school and *Cosmo* (twenty-six to be exact!), except for social dancing and an occasional *walk,* exercise and sports had about as much to do with *my* life as tea dancing has to with an aborigine's. In my late thirties, through good nutrition, I did get healthier but still had only the briefest, tiniest skirmishes with exercise. About the time *Sex and the Single Girl* was published—I was then forty—I remember reading a book by Bonnie Prudden, a well-known exercise expert of the day, suggesting we each set aside one hour a day to get our bodies into shape. Is this woman *deranged?* I asked myself. Even if the idea remotely appealed to one, which it didn't to *me,* where would one get the *hour?*

Six *more* years went by and then one day, after a few more tiny unsuccessful run-ins with exercise (one humiliating one at a Fifty-seventh Street gym where the instructress was a *nazi!* "*Nein, nein,* Mrs. Brown, the knee comes up when the ankle goes down. . . . Please, Mrs. Brown, you're holding up the class!"), I just quietly, stealthily, secretly began to exercise at home.

I don't know what triggered the beginning. I can't remember the hour or day or moment or even the motive for beginning something to which I am now so dedicated I'd sooner be parted from my telephone (or maybe my *hands*) than give up—but some time in the spring of 1969 (were you *waiting* for this soul-searching pin-down of the date?) it happened.

That was thirteen years ago, and since then I have managed to exercise one hour a day every day, missing only two days (to have a D and C in the hospital, but I exercised the day I went in and the day I got home and the day my mother died) in that entire time.

Now, that is a little extreme, yes? Maybe even crazy. When I had my eyes done (more later), I was hard at it the morning I went to New York Hospital Day Surgery, started exercising again—just a few routines—the day *after* surgery (since I was home), though I couldn't see the floor. The doctor had forbade

100

all exercise for two weeks so my energy could go into *healing*, but I was certain he meant me to be an exception. Well, you don't have to be that crazy and dedicated to get the good out of exercise, but let me give you, unemotionally if possible, some reasons you might want to fit a "formal" exercise plan into your life.

Exercise Makes You Feel Better

Any regular exerciser will tell you his/her body feels different (better) with than without. You have more energy, get sick less. Exercise protects you from illness.

Example: A man runs for the train. If he has not been exercising, his cardiovascular system can't pump enough blood to the heart and the respiratory system can't supply enough oxygen to meet the sudden demands, and he can have a heart attack. If the same man has been exercising and giving both systems a workout all along, he can run for the train every day and both systems can take it.

Anxiety—asking for a raise or putting your grandmother in a nursing home—can produce the same kind of stress, and the body's equipment (those same two systems), underexercised, can barely handle the load.

There is even stress in pleasure . . . making love or climbing the stadium stairs to watch a football game.

The purpose of regular exercise is to *maintain* the body's highest level of performance for the cardiovascular and respiratory systems, got it? Yes, even a young person can be in abysmal shape. A few years ago the U.S. Army rejected over 50 percent of its applicants because they couldn't meet the physical requirements—slobby, shapeless, falling apart at twenty-one!

Two more testimonials to exercise: A 1979 study of one hundred New York longshoremen showed that, although all were about twenty pounds overweight, with bulging stomachs and plenty of life problems, all were in good health and rarely got sick, because of their continuous outdoor physical work. And this: recent Duke University research, reported in *The New York Times*, indicates that "regular, vigorous exercise improves a person's ability to dissolve blood clots . . . findings that add to the growing body of evidence that physical fitness can reduce the risk of developing and dying of heart and blood-vessel diseases."

Okay, these are not *your* problems—not *yet* anyway—but don't you want to know what you're staving off? In *your* age group, my pretty friend Judi Drogin says, "Exercise just seems to energize you. You can be so tired you can't move your tail to the coat closet, but once you work out you wind up feeling good . . . I have no idea why." Says Barbara Ann: "It's done so much for me that when I *don't* exercise I'm a caged animal."

The testimonials could go on and on, but let's try a few more facts.

Yes, You Can Eat a *Little* More,
But Not Much

Nonkiller calisthenics—the kind I do—use up three hundred calories an hour. That's a baked potato with butter, Parmesan cheese and chives—*not* an orgy, just a little treat. You can figure out your *own* three-hundred-calorie special, but most of us hour-a-day exercisers don't eat up an *extra* three hundred calories—we find the exercise just *about* "keeps back the jungle." With it you can eat enough to feel *comfortable;* without it, meals would have to be skimpier. I'm not sure exercise doesn't make you hungrier (people keep claiming it doesn't), but if it does, you're only a *little* bit hungrier and you don't actually eat beyond what you were going to eat anyway.

Exercise Has Sex Benefits

Some exercises actually produce horniness—there's a recipe for one on page 166. More important—because *you* probably feel horny anyway—you *look* better to your bed partner and to yourself (of the two, being pleased with your body is more important, because how *you* feel about your looks affects your ability to enjoy sex). Third sex benefit of exercise: You can get into *any* position ever invented without dislocating a *thing*. It seems to me a man used to an agile girl could hardly put *up* with one whose bones kept cracking or who said things like, "Oh, God, Henry, I think my back went out." I suppose being in love with the woman *helps*.

Exercise Vanquishes Depression

Medically proved *fact:* Exercise lifts the spirits of moody, melancholy people. In a University of Wisconsin study of depression with three control groups, one group was sent jogging, another took antidepressants, a third visited shrinks. The joggers came off by far the least depressed. I can absolutely vouch for exercise's efficacy in *that* department. No matter how yucky I feel on getting up in the morning—and sometimes I am mildly depressed then—an hour of exercise miraculously lifts the gloom. Your body, loosened up, seems to detoxify your *brain.*

You Look Better in Your Clothes

A firm body does it for everything from T-shirt and shorts to jersey cocktail dresses. People looking at you may think you're cute and trim from "nature," but *you* know it's from exercise and exercise's soul mate, diet. The diet gets you slender; exercise makes you firm, so that when somebody pokes his finger in your tummy or arm, it (the finger) doesn't *disappear.* Exercised people enjoy getting dressed in the morning, especially if you love clothes as much as I do. You look, well, *cute,* and you don't have trouble getting anything zipped or buttoned.

Meeting the Challenge Feels Good

Okay, we hard-core, nut-case exercisers do it for all those reasons, and they are *big* reasons, but there is possibly a *bigger* one: Exercise, after you become an addict, gets to be a test of will . . . you against failure, against defeat, even against death. Your chosen routine is a standard you set yourself to live *up* to.

Am I getting too intense? You get to feeling that as long as you exercise *every* day, life cannot ever really do you in; you are no longer vulnerable but, like breathing, if you *stopped,* you might die! Yes, I *am* intense! Whereas *mind* improvement requires heavy, serious commitment, exercise is something you can do with relative simplicity in order to have control over your life, to change it for the better. Exercise is work, too, of course, requiring a commitment, but there is no comparison, for me anyway, in the willpower needed to get your *body* to alter its course and getting your mind to do so. My mind won't cooperate with *anything* I tell it to do, usually. There are also *degrees* of commitment to exercise whereas a new mental discipline presupposes going the whole hog or you won't get it.

Exercise staves off age, and let me say this about *that*. I don't fear death but I do fear the loss of femininity, of attraction between me and a man. If I could die f——g, that would be the way I would want to go, and if the moment came a little sooner than I'd hoped, that would be a small price to pay for having stayed female all my life—not that your *brain* doesn't have something to do with femininity also.

Heavens, I'd better get back to *you*, little friend. You *aren't* aging yet or thinking of dying. Let me try to tell you what else I know about exercise.

You Do the Exercising for *You*, Not for Them

Despite what I said about exercise keeping your body attractive to the man you're in bed with, in bed isn't where you *are* most of the time and, with your clothes on, even *men* can't necessarily *tell* that you're exercised; weight loss is far more dramatic and noticeable. Also, people are usually, thank God, listening to what we say and *forgiving* us our flab, so this exercising business is really for *you*—don't expect big back pats and congratulations because you've pushed your pushups to forty-five and can, lying down, hold your legs off the floor for three and a half minutes. Friends and loved ones can even be exasperated that you're into something which takes you away from them, also Something Admirable they haven't embraced. You don't *need* their approval. *You* know how wonderful your body feels and looks undressed, and then there *are* those (lucky) other people who get to see you clothesless.

The Man in Your Life May Never Join the Cause

One morning when I was writhing on the floor with stomach cramps after a thirty-six hour fast *plus* my usual hour of huff-puff, David said disgustedly, "You and Dick Zanuck (his partner) are going to *kill* yourselves and I will have to attend *both* your funerals!"

Poor nonaddicted darling, getting the propaganda from his partner—Dick runs five miles a day and is a tennis ace—and me you *know* about. The best you can hope is that a nonexerciser will be tolerant. Mine climbs uncomplainingly over my prone body to get to his shirts every day. Of course, your special man may *also* be an exercise nut, and that gives you a terrific bond.

How to Start

If you aren't exercising already, how to begin? Well, on little pussycat feet you just pad *into* it. As with dieting, one day, after you've been thinking about it a *lot,* something clicks on in your head and you begin. For your first exercise foray you may go to a gym or dance class. Maybe you'll learn what they do and do it at home. You won't have their machines to work out on, but you can do plenty of things by yourself. Perhaps you and a friend start exercising together, though you'll eventually go it alone. Study a *book. The Royal Canadian Air Force Exercise Plan for Physical Fitness* (Pocket Books, $1.75) has a *very* good twelve-minute-a-day program with simple instructions; the exercises get progressively harder, and gradually you do each one more time, but never for more than twelve minutes a day. *Jane Fonda's Workout Book* (Simon and Schuster, $18.95) has a complete exercise program for beginners or the advanced designed to burn calories and improve your shape. She and others also offer exercise records or cassettes.

A professional or civilian friend who knows more about exercise than you do might work out a little routine for you, or you could collect exercises from various friends. That was my system for years. I did two from actor Roy Scheider, one each from Paul Newman and Robert Redford (they never knew they contributed, but friends told me what they did and I did it, too), one from screenwriter Stirling Silliphant (he I sometimes wished had never been born . . . Stirling's was a *killer*) and a few from exercise books. Last year Barbara Pearlman (*Barbara Pearlman's Dance Exercises* and *Barbara Pearlman's Slendercises,* $6.95 and $9.95 from Dolphin Books) came to my house and gave me some super new routines to replace old ones. This year nearly *everything* got replaced as I took on a new guru, Michael Abrums, an ex-Marine with a studio in Beverly Hills. People I respected with good bodies told me he was the best in the world and that I had to try. I am crazy about what he has taught me, similar to things I've done in the past but tougher—accent *heavily* on posture—and am devoted, so far.

I think you *should* keep trying new exercises as soon as you get too comfy with the old ones. I'm still struggling with Dr. Norman Orentreich's double-chin remover: lift base of tongue up into roof of mouth and swallow, says Norman, who has got to be *crazy* . . . the base of your tongue is nailed down and won't *do* that!

Calisthenics, isometrics, yoga, dancercises, ballet, Mensendieck, aerobic exercising, gym workouts—they're *all* good if you do them, yes, religiously! Would that somebody could tell us different from religiously, but that *is* what's required.

You also know to start modestly and work up. A few heavy crash sessions will only discourage you because your body isn't ready for so much abuse, and you'll stop after exhausting yourself a couple of times. Begin little and move on.

Exercise Doesn't Give You a Gorgeous Body Unless That's the Kind You *Started* With

If they'd only let us *choose* . . . I'd have traded my swan neck and pretty ears (who needs great *ears?*) for a bosom and long legs *any* time, but it's all fixed at birth, you see. Your basic body is where your bones are and trying to get any of *them* rearranged . . . well, you might as well try to get your typewriter to eat *grass*—but wait, there's hope. Exercise *can* make some things a little smaller—inch loss it's called. My hips came down from forty to thirty-six inches . . . not bad . . . but I must point out again that "smaller" *mostly* comes from weight loss, which comes from diet; exercise makes you firm.

Good Posture Is the Best Thing
You Can Do to Look Better

Posture has to be *part* of your exercise regime: shoulders back and down (like a West Point plebe), fanny scooched in and up can make an *enormous* difference in your looks. It's hard to remember to *do* that with your body. Some lucky kids had parents who kept after them to sit up and stand up straight but most of us grew up stoopy. The only way to get good posture *now* is to think about it *practically all the time.* You have to keep after and *keep* after yourself. Michael Abrums is a fiend about posture; we clients go around terrorized of letting down, and that kind of fear is just about what it *takes* to eradicate years of slumping. Push your fanny into the back of the chair when you sit, shoulders back and down. (You'll be the only person in the room resembling a *statue!*) Back your body up against a door, thumbs hooked at nose height, heels one inch from door, small of back pushed flat against it, tummy in. That is *perfect* posture; try to walk around that way. Further discipline: hook your elbows around a twenty-eight-inch broomstick, cane or umbrella placed across shoulder blades, hands positioned a little wider than shoulders, wrists straight. Walk around *that* way.

In all these years I have *never* got the posture thing licked, but I'm *determined* to. I work on it now all the time.

Finding a Gym

A big city has dozens of gyms, all with different instruction and machines to work out on. Ask friends where *they* go or just call up gyms from the phone book and ask what they offer. Some give a free first session. Nearly *every* exercise maven thinks *his* system is the only way to salvation and says the others will *kill* you. They're wrong, of course! Anything you do regularly is good. For two years I visited a terrific little gym on Fifty-eighth Street in Manhattan (Carola Trier) to work specifically on inner thighs and underarm flab (the terrible two!). Carola is terrific but I finally decided I couldn't spare the time to get there, get undressed, leotarded, exercised, showered, dressed again and back to the office when I could just as well work on my trouble spots at home.

Home does provide certain "luxuries": you can watch television for one. I see the "Today" show every weekday, "Face the Nation," "Meet the Press," "Issues and Answers" on Sunday. You can also listen to music. *That* is a nice experience—one hour of soaring music while you banish lumps. You can answer the phone or door if you *must*, plus you don't have to get dressed or *go* anywhere. Some women, having found a good gym, are more faithful to it than a lover. It seems to me gyms *and* outdoor exercise ought to augment your home routine but not to replace it, but about half the young women who work at *Cosmo* go to a gym. Exercise where you're happiest, but *exercise*.

What Equipment Do You Need at Home?

Some home exercisers have sophisticated home gyms. I use three-pound dumbbells for one chest exercise and one arm exercise—that's all. Dick Zanuck gave me an exercise wheel I was fond of but I kept falling *off* and had to abandon it. In our old apartment we were a little short of space so I kept my slant board under the living-room table. I used to feel like Dracula getting back in his coffin when I crawled under there at night, gazing up at a wooden slab (the underside of the table) only inches above my nose; we didn't move the slant board to the new apartment.

Your body and willpower are really all the equipment you *need*, of course. Another advantage to "home" exercise is that "home" can be anywhere. I recently totted up fifty-one different away-from-home locations where I have flailed about—on a tatami mat in the two-hundred-eighty-year-old Tawaraya Inn in Kyoto, in my tiny cubicle at the Hotel du Cap d'Antibes (furniture stacked on the bed to get enough *room*), head under the *desk* at the Inter-Continental in Bangkok (again to make room), on the deck of William Levitt's yacht, *La Belle Simone* (*mildly* green and seasick), in my office, in my psychiatrist's office (he wasn't there), in lodges, summer houses, chalets, in the ladies' lounge at Teterboro Airport, on a 747 (the standing-up stuff), etc., etc., etc.

Once, in Los Angeles, after a fourteen-hour flight from Sydney and before a five-hour flight to New York, I figured in my addled brain that by the time I got to New York with the sixteen-hour time difference from Sydney, it would have to have been more than twenty-four hours since I'd last exercised and I'd better do it *then*—never should twenty-four hours go by *without*. The TWA Ambassador Club gave me a little room, I locked the door, stripped down, went right to it—talk about *bleary*-eyed. At my sister's house in Shawnee, Oklahoma, where there are no rugs to trip up her wheelchair, I put my foam-rubber mat down on the bare floor for the rites. In friends' houses on weekends, strange animals and children peer in at you and try to "help." I don't mind the children and I love animals but do dread that awful canine *sniffing*. At home I exercise in my bedroom on a big pink terry mat made by stitching four bath towels together. Had enough?

Jogging and Other Active Sports

Says writer Lewis Frumkes in a recent *Cosmo* article, "Jogging is the most popular physical activity in America today, with its passionate (an estimated 25 million!) adherents testifying that their favorite pastime elevates the spirit (euphoria is promised to the constant runner) even as it makes the body skinny and strong. Experienced women joggers usually run in spurts of four to six miles, but even a one-to-two mile daily stint (easily accomplished in under half an hour) can do wonders for your complexion, circulatory system and state of mind."

This is all very well but I find jogging *loathsome!* The three times I tried I said to myself, If *that's* what you have to do to stay healthy, I will just have to go to pieces. But then, exercise *is* so individual. Lynda Carter, Dyan Cannon, Jackie Onassis, Jill Clayburgh, so many other women you admire, are mad for jogging. If you're just beginning, get Jim Fixx's *The Complete Book of Running* (Random House, $10.00) for guidelines. As for tennis, golf, handball, squash, swimming, *avanti!* You'll need equipment, of course, and, except for swimming, a playmate, but all are available for the search. A nurse I know who jogs four miles a day tells me she never has to worry about meeting men. Between the ones who come to her doctor boss for hair transplants and the ones who jog, she has a great pick. Herb Goldberg, author of *The New Male* (William Morrow, $10.95, and New American Library, $2.95), says a woman who concentrates on health instead of hair and clothes can run with a man, play tennis with men, go skating, boating, river-rafting, that being sports-minded is the new attraction available to *all* women. It's a *thought*.

Don't Forget to Walk

If walking is *all* the exercise you get, that's *enough,* though you will have to walk several miles a day to burn many calories (about one hundred calories per mile or three hundred to four hundred per hour for *brisk* walking), and it can never reshape anything but your legs. Still, walking *does* get your body moving. I'm now trying to walk twenty minutes a day—another of those things one has heard for a *lifetime* one ought to do, but you only listen when you hear it at the right time from the "right" instructor. *Family Health* magazine suggests these ways to incorporate walking into your everyday routine:

"1. Walk the extra foot, the extra yard . . . to the distant extension phone, rather than the one right next to you. To the reception room to greet the guest rather than waiting for him to reach your office. To the far bank of elevators, the last water cooler, the copy machine in another department.

"2. Walk someplace you regularly ride. Take the stairs instead of the elevator. Walk home from work or from the station or from your Tuesday manicure.

"3. Stop napping. Believe it or not, a half-hour walk is more refreshing and restorative than a half-hour nap in the afternoon.

"4. Invent a daily errand that requires walking. Walk to a small grocery store in your neighborhood for your yogurt. Walk the dog one extra time each day. Walk to a mailbox five streets away and send a daily postcard to a friend.

"5. Walk whenever the urge to eat comes over you. Steal away for a short stroll around the block at your accustomed hour to snack. No matter how leisurely a pace you set for yourself, you *will* burn calories."

There!

Exercise Escalates

The more you do the more you do. You see your body looking better, you feel the sap rising in your veins and so you up the amounts. That's okay. There is almost no such thing as too much exercise if you can carve out the time. The most dedicated exerciser among *my* friends is Eleanor Revson, wife of cosmetics tycoon Martin Revson. Eleanor exercises two hours a day, (*two!*) at the Lotte Berk salon (their routines are *killers*), then swims one hundred eighty—one hundred *eighty!*—laps in her pool. She also doesn't *eat*. Well, seeing this paragon with her dear, perfect little arms and legs sticking out of her newest Scaasi is enough to make you want to do just one thing—push her out the window—but she is so sweet and nice you restrain yourself (and think maybe someday you'll try to do what Eleanor *does* and look like Eleanor *looks*).

Exercise Never Gets Easy . . . If It *Seems* To, You Are Doing It Wrong!

You get more skilled and less clumsy, but if you are doing enough exercise to do any good, some of your routines will *hurt*—forever! Twenty percent of the ones I do are pleasant, 40 percent tolerable, 40 percent I'd just as soon get into a tub of ice, but, fortunately, no one thing goes on too long. As you get friendlier with your exercises, although they don't get "easier," you can fit more into the same time slot: ten sit-ups grow to twenty, thirty leg-overs become sixty. You always exercise against "resistance"—nothing must be lah-de-dah casual. And don't forget to *breathe*. We shallow breathers have to make a special effort to get air into us and that is done by gasping. As somebody (who?) once wisely said, there *is* no free lunch.

It's Okay to Exercise When You Are Menstruating or Sick

Could we agree that getting dysentery from eating unpeeled vegetables in a foreign country doesn't count as sick? Good, because I'm so fond of saying I'm *never* sick, and last year, coming back from Egypt eight pounds lighter and weak as watercress from Pharaoh's Revenge, I *was* sick, but the exercising never went (everything *else* did, of course!). For an exerciser there is no exhaustion, fatigue, home or office crisis, too-late night, too-early morning *or* illness extreme enough to keep you from your accustomed workout! We are stalwart! Besides, whatever has hold of you, the exercise generally makes you feel *better*. I'm just going to recommend one little *non*exercise to help with a problem. If your back and shoulders are tense, roll around on a tennis ball. Place it under small of back, neck, shoulders—wherever there's tension—and squirm hard.

How Long, O Lord, Does Exercise Take
to Do Any *Good?*

How you respond depends on your age. In your twenties, with regular exercise, you can feel, maybe even *see,* differences in your body in just three weeks; within three months of working out every day, you'll be in quite good shape; six *months* of daily workouts will have you almost a "ten." As you get older, you revise the amounts of time *upward.* For a woman in her forties, six months of steady daily work will bring improvement; a year will make her body firm and photographable. In your fifties, give yourself a year or *two* to get to looking really terrific.

You were hoping for something like "The Three Weeks' Summer Shape-Up" I recently saw outlined in a woman's magazine (not *Cosmo*)? No, angel, changing your body takes at *least* as long as getting a baby cypress to grow—or making a human baby. Like diet, exercise has to be stuck *with* or you wind up back where you started—flabby. Why worry about how long it takes? You've got the rest of your life to make good and the results are all that matter.

Pick a Time and Stay Faithful

I exercise the minute my little feet hit the floor in the morning. I'm afraid if I *don't* do it then, I never will. Other people prefer late night, lunch hour, after work. When you exercise doesn't make any difference, as long as you *do.* A workout every day seems preferable to me to two or three times a week because that way you can never just accidentally let a week or month slither by without. Can you stop for a while and start again? Of course, but it's dangerous! Like being an arrested alcoholic, I feel that missing a day of exercise would get me "off the wagon" and I might never get back on. Unless you're felled with a hysterectomy or lockjaw, it seems to me you'd best *continue,* without pause, once you begin, and every *day* is best.

When to Start

Starting to exercise late, on a "formal" daily basis, seems just as good to me as starting early, since when you are in your twenties and thirties your life style and vacations probably include swimming, dancing, bike riding; but in your forties and fifties you aren't dating and dancing and automatically getting shaken up as much. Then, I think, you need a *discipline*, a routine. Your young body will respond much faster. You don't have to be true to any one routine or type of exercise unless that's the one that pleases you forever and ever. "Spot exercise"—to attack certain problem areas —is surely advisable. Sometimes you finally do something you were told to do *years* ago by a different instructor, but it just didn't "take" at the time.

Have I convinced you at *all* that exercise is your *friend*, that it will never let you down if you are a friend back . . . loyal and faithful and true? Good. Now let's talk about a subject I get the jaw-wobbles about just *contemplating* what I'm going to say . . . beauty (the facial kind)!

Chapter Five

YOUR FACE
AND BODY

Would you agree that all of us—including mouseburgers—are just about *obsessed* with beauty? We worship beautiful women, bestow on them our wildest admiration—and our virulent envy! There are times when we non-beauties think nothing in the *world* matters except being "gorgeous," and since we *aren't*, we might as well zip ourselves into big zip-lock Baggies and go get into the freezer. As for women who *are* (technically) beautiful, nobody will *let* them forget they are *different* . . . different as razorbacks are from Miss Piggy. We're all homo sapiens, yes, but beautiful is, well . . . *different!* Maybe beauty criteria change a *little* from century to century, country to country, but usually when somebody is declared beautiful in *any* age, in *any* country, we can see exactly what they are talking about and it's no use hoping *our* style will come up when styles change . . . if you've got (technical) beauty, you've got it, if you don't, you don't, and you can't *get* it, no matter *what* magazines tell you. I'm not talking about beautiful on the inside . . . that we can aspire to, but *outside* is where they frequently judge! It starts early, our getting the idea—possibly because it's true!—that we aren't pretty. What *should* a mother tell a child who isn't pretty? Tell her she *is,* of course, and act as though she *were.* Many unpretty women seem to have grown up not *knowing* they weren't. A non-beautiful friend of mine's mother told her she had the cutest knees, the loveliest smile, the nicest complexion, to the point that my friend, right this minute thinks she *is* beautiful. "I was always told I was *perfect*," she says. "Who was I not to go along?!" A lawyer I know, a *troglodyte* . . . bald, face like a bloodhound, somebody it almost *hurts* you to look at . . . squires the *most* beautiful women as well as all *other* kinds and seems totally at ease with himself, them and life.

All I can say is lucky *them!* My mother, who had terrible hangups about beauty because of being compared to a ravishing younger sister, dutifully passed on all her beauty anxieties to *me*. Poor darling, she didn't *know* what she was doing. Her *family* apparently never let her forget how beautiful her *sister* was, even if they didn't actually say *she* was *plain* (she wasn't). Subsequently *she* never failed to point out to *me* (with big sighs) that pretty is better, while not ever suggesting that I *was!*

The subject of pretty didn't ever *not* come up in our house along with "men make fools of themselves over pretty [sigh] girls," with the unspoken suggestion that I wasn't likely to run *into* such foolishness! Sometimes my mother would peer closely at me and say, "I really do think you're getting better-looking every day," meaning, unmistakably, "You've got a long way to go, baby!" Quickly let me say she was a great mother—the *best*, supportive, generous, always encouraging me to use my *brain*, which mothers *didn't* in those days. I loved her and she me—it's just that she had this terrible thing about looks that helped create a baby neurotic—*me!*

Well, living with her beauty preoccupation, plus wall-to-wall acne at sixteen (I spent my entire senior year in high school going to the doctor twice a week to have pustules opened, Saturdays under an X-ray machine), almost guaranteed I would not grow up carefree or confident about my looks or *ever* stop trying to improve them. Did anything like that happen to *you?*

The Loving Enemy

You know who *else* contributes to beauty hang-ups? *Them.* The other sex! Can there be any question that straight from little-girl-hood on right up to, alas, this minute, men convey the idea that looks, if not *everything* in a woman, are surely the most *important* thing. *Playboy,* in my opinion, doesn't denigrate *women,* only women who are not *beautiful.* In *The Hite Report on Male Sexual-*

ity, in answer to the question "What things in general about women do you admire?" almost every man in the study responded in strictly anatomical terms—breasts, legs, buttocks, etc.

One's best *friends* can be partisans. My friend movie producer Robert Evans (*Urban Cowboy, Popeye*) has married *four* beauties—Camilla Sparv, Ali MacGraw, Phyllis George and Sharon Hugueny—and never in his whole life dated any but the beautiful (they line up). Warren Beatty, adored by female millions of *all* kinds, only has liaisons with the gorgeous. John Derek is a classic beauty-worshipper (has married three) as are Ryan O'Neal, Roger Vadim, Mark Goodson, Woody Allen, Louis Malle, super-agent Irving Lazar, and so many other men that one grows dizzy with the count. These men *acknowledge* us less-than-breath-stopping others, they talk to us politely, but I always get the feeling they think of us as plaster and mortar holding the buildings together—or something like that—never anybody to write poetry to. There he is, my friend Armando Orsini, *himself* a sloe-eyed, lynx-like beauty, sitting with me in his Italian restaurant on West Fifty-sixth Street as I wait for a guest. "That girl over by the window," says Armando. "That *nose* . . . that *classic* beauty. . . . You could *sculpt* a girl like that!" (Why do I feel he has something in mind other than sculpting?)

I know we make *our* mistakes, but I *swear* our sex would *never* sit with the other sex in a restaurant and say, "That man over by the window . . . that mouth, those shoulders. . . . You could *sculpt* him!"

One afternoon at NBC in Burbank, grips, associate producers, cameramen, talent coordinators, makeup men were all rushing from Studio A to Studio B in a kind of *stampede.* I thought they'd either gone mad or discovered typhus in *our* studio. "Bob Hope is auditioning 'perfect tens' for his special" was the explanation for the exodus. Watching a male *loved* one watch the Miss Universe Pageant on television is not a lot of laughs, though I suppose the activity ranks as "innocent" (he can't get *to* them!). Mostly you smile, wince occasionally, but it's hard, honestly, not to want to *be* a "ten," just once in your life to have someone see you across a crowded room and knock over chairs getting to you.

Do men worry about *their* beauty? Of course they do. What they worry about *most,* however, is height and penis size and they worry so deeply about these things, they are not even *discussed.*

Good, let them worry! They're too dumb to know we don't *care* about height and penis size and maybe that worry compensates *slightly* for what they do to non-pretty girls to make us feel rotten.

What about the raving beauties themselves and *their* relationship to us? I want to get this *all* out of my system! Well, for one thing, beauties are not very *honest.* "Who, *me* beautiful?" She gives you that cool gray stare that fells grocery-checkout boys and maharajas. "I don't know what you're *talking* about!" Like money for children of the rich, I guess beauty is no big deal if you've never been *without.* It's not that you don't love your beautiful friends, you *do,* and you know their beauty is to be *enjoyed,* but every so often the old wistfulness backs up on you again.

Sophia, Raquel, Farrah, Cheryl, Bo we will never be. So does that mean we shouldn't *try?* Oh, God, no, not ever! And here comes the message you knew would be coming along. Even though we will mostly wind up the way we came, stuck with the bones, skin, hair, fingernail structure and figure God (genes) gave us, *trying* for "beautiful" is not only one of life's pain-assuagers, it is one of life's ritualistic *pleasures.* At least it is for *me.* Trying to be beautiful is sensuous, feminine and reassuring. To use a cat analogy, for eighteen years my Siamese, Samantha, was such a pain in the tail I frequently wondered if life would not be better if she were to get enteritis like other cats and go to cat heaven. From babyhood she ate like a ninety-year-old dowager duchess. *Forget* cat food—she wouldn't touch liver, tuna, ground sirloin, and what she *did* eat had to be just *born*—one day in the frig was too old! You got the old sniff-and-stalk routine. To clip her toenails (with which she destroyed a whole roomful of white linen furniture as well as hunted field mice and lizards), she had to be held down by *two* people whom she didn't forgive for *hours.* . . . Half my life for eighteen years was spent arranging "baby sitters" for Sam when David and I were going to be away. In the last three years of her life she yowled constantly—favorite time: 5 A.M. Nothing wrong with her, the vet said, just expressing herself.

Then one day she waited for us to get back from a trip to Europe so she could say goodbye and she died. Was I relieved, after the expected period of mourning, to be *rid* of all that vexation and responsibility? Of course not! I thought I was going to die! Two years later I *still* miss her and look for her on radiators, kitchen windows, chaise longue.

Well, beauty routines are something like that . . . endless trouble, but they add *pleasure* to your life. When I had my eyes done and couldn't wear eye makeup for a month, I *missed* my pencils and crayons, not just because I looked different without them but because there wasn't this thing I *did* every day which was kind of sorcery-like and "improving." They say men enjoy *shaving*—it's the one time each day they get to look in the mirror and say, "Hey there, you handsome devil!" Us, too. Every day, but *more* than once, we get to study ourselves in the mirror, "play" a little, "improve" a little and admire, flaws and all! Maybe we can't be beautiful but we can be *better!* Truly, if they *"freed"* us (no more makeup ever) I would go get "back in my chains!"

As for being *born* beautiful—and I would opt for that with my first and last breath if the choice were offered—what we non-beauties never get through our heads is that beauty *isn't* "the answer"—not even with *men.* One beauty I know has been on hold with a homely, rich movie producer for five years—he *won't* marry her. Another haughtily divorced her husband, went through her *huge* divorce settlement, found it was cold out there, baby, wants him back now and he couldn't care *less.* Another well-known beauty's lover cheats like a cheetah—apparently the problem in beautiful Princess Caroline's failed marriage. "Happily *married"* beauties have *just* as many husband problems as we do.

As for careers, the women I know who are climbing the walls in their forties and fifties because of having no career, no interests outside the home, wanting a career—but it's *late,* are girls who got snapped up quickly because of their beauty and didn't really develop *themselves.* Plain girls also marry young, but who does it most frequently is the beauty. And a career *based* on beauty can run into trouble. She gets the job because she's beautiful but there's no there *there.* No career problems are worse than those of the beautiful "actress" who can't act. An insanely beautiful model I know was recently turned down for a Broadway role she wanted badly because the producer said she was "too beautiful." She wept just like a plain girl albeit her husband bought her a consolation diamond bracelet. Beauties drink. Beauties drug. Just like us, they are "insecure." In a recent letter from the lovely girl I grew up with in Little Rock, Arkansas (in our seventeenth summer Elizabeth was *triple*-dating some summer nights to get everybody fitted in), she had the gall to say, "Helen, I was terribly unsure of myself and felt inadequate in high school except maybe when conjugating a Latin verb." The *gall* of this person who nearly ruined my life by being beautiful to say she was "insecure"!

Beauties have *serious* depression. One of the most beautiful models in the business—twenty-one at the time—didn't show up for a booking one day and her agent, on a hunch, rushed to the girl's apartment, got the door beaten in, found her client beside an empty Nembutal bottle (forty-six pills missing). They got her to the hospital; she was close to death and nobody knew for several days whether there had been brain damage (there hadn't). Why did she do it? She later said, "I looked at myself in the mirror and said, Who *are* you? What have you accomplished? What is your real worth to anybody? And I didn't want to live."

Ordinary people get hooked on drugs, booze, men who beat them up, but I'm just saying beauty doesn't *save* anybody. And while beauty is of *incalculable* benefit in attracting a man, finally even *I* know it isn't required to get a man to like you, love you, even prefer you to a beauty! "I would always think you the most beautiful woman in the room," a man tells me who loved me a year before I met David, and I think he *meant* it. "You have your own wild-gypsy kind of beauty," another one said (I have about as much wild-gypsy beauty as an English muffin). They breathe beauty *into* us, endow us with whatever they need, get to thinking we *are* beautiful. I keep thinking Yoko Ono Yoko Ono—John Lennon loved Yoko Ono. . . . Interesting, yes, but not a beauty.

Even an *older* non-beauty (Yoko was older) can attract men if she is sexual, entertaining and good to them. Husbands get *used* to our looks, of course, ravishing *or* plain, because what really matters to them is being taken *care* of. He doesn't *mind* pretty but will accept nurturing from *anybody* (was Mother *gorgeous?*).

I swear my husband doesn't really *know* what I look like. Oh, he can tell me from Ann Landers waiting for him in the lobby at "21," but someone else had to point out that I'd cut all my hair off last summer. ("She *did?*") We non-beauties also find all *kinds* of men attractive, and don't miss out on some wonderful ones because our "standards" are too high. The beauty is afraid to settle. It's been so easy all her life, so many men paying court. Harry worships me, but maybe there's a *perfect* one out there I haven't *met*. Hah! We unpretty girls know you have to take a deep breath and *plunge*. Okay, nothing can replace beauty as the initial attraction but, well, our number comes up, *too*.

Now I want to point out something *important*—ready?

Brains Are Better than Beauty

Much of a mouseburger's life is spent achieving. Well, beauty doesn't help you *there* except as a model or an actress, and, in acting, beauty means less these days, as we've already said. Also, you spend a lot of your life *alone*. Beauty can't amuse you *then*, but brainwork—reading, writing, thinking—*can*. As for what your looks mean to others, friends and loved ones grow *used* to the way you look and care more about how much you sympathize with their life problems. Beauty can't cheer them much in a crisis; your help and understanding *can*. And you're interesting to talk to even when *not* helping. It seems to me a wildly beautiful woman *can't* cheer and encourage her friends as much—maybe we won't *let* her. As for being beautiful *and* brainy, I'm not sure I can handle that! Yes, I *know* such double-blessed paragons *do* exist—Polly Bergen, Gloria Steinem, Diane Sawyer—but I'm just saying if I had to choose beauty or brains, I'd take brains. Every time.

A Non-Beauty Needs Character

Character is a good thing for *everybody,* but people will swarm around a sensationally pretty woman even if she is a *lizard.* There is very little swarming around *ordinary*-looking lizards. So how do you *get* character—especially if you're starting a little *late?* How do *I* know?! This very morning I looked in the three-way mirror, observed this unsymmetrical face—not ugly or repelling, just totally *undistinguished,* and, what with the aging, I said to myself, My God, I've got to be *nicer* to people, got to endear myself to them with love pouring out of every *pore* of me to make up for this *face!* I've got to be Mother Teresa, Eleanor Roosevelt, Helen Keller, Scarlett O'Hara's *mother* and why, Lord, didn't I start *sooner?* I really don't *know* how you get character, but most mouseburgers—even me—seem to have *some.* Character just means being *responsible*—doing what you said you would do, defending a friend, raising money for causes, living up to what *they* (never mind *you* for the moment) need you to do in your job, friendship, family.

I'll bet you already have enough character to get *by.*

Not Being Pretty Doesn't Mean You Are Not Vain

How does an unpretty person get *off* being consumed with her looks when vanity should be for the likes of Lesley-Anne Down, Jacqueline Bisset, Catherine Deneuve? Well, you see, they didn't disconnect our vanity cord when they gave us a so-so face! Watch us so-so ones in the powder room as we fluff our hair, dust on blusher . . . not *one* of us gives it the throwaway treatment. We are as seriously vain as any ravishing beauty and that's *okay*. Caring, you see, is part of sexuality. I don't think a person unaware of her appearance—who just "throws it away"—can ever be as sensual or sexual as somebody who knows and *cares* how she looks. Self-awareness is *sexy,* and non-pretty girls, thank God, are *allowed!*

We Need Outside Corroboration

We are told to value ourselves *without* feedback, but if nobody is making a pass at you or trying to take you to Bermuda, how are you supposed to *feel?* Confident? And if you're so attractive, how come nobody has said a word about it in six weeks? Well, regarding the passes, it works out that if you *do* accept yourself pretty much *and* move away from total self-absorption to be concerned with other people and your *work* absorbs you, you *will* sexually catnip somebody—it's guaranteed. And if you take great pains with your looks, friends *do* notice and comment . . . that's what friends are *for*. That's also guaranteed. Don't feel "insecure" or vain because you sometimes need a fix.

Now let's move on to what we can *do* with whatever faces we have to make them look better. Lots of people think you shouldn't do *much,* that natural is best. Good God, nature can *destroy* you! As my beloved Dr. Orentreich says, "You can either let spinal meningitis and polio in their natural virulent form kill a little kid or you can fight back. You can let the body deteriorate, stop functioning, as in the aging process, or you can fight back."

I have been fighting back, mouseburger-fashion, with every shred of me all my life. Nature makes wrinkles, dark circles, scaly skin, dirt, illness, odors, bad dispositions, rages, hates; nature *tamed* makes for smoothness, wellness, sweet smells, smiles, beneficence, calm and love. Love is a cultivated state. So is beauty —or as close as un-beauties *get* to beauty, which is pretty close sometimes.

Okay, but are you going to take beauty advice from an avowed *non*-beauty like me? Well, my opinion has always been that taking advice from a beautiful woman is about as meaningful as Felix Rohatyn, the merger maven of Lazard Freres, telling us how to get the best premiums with S & W Green Stamps. . . . How would *he* know? What real beauty challenges does a beauty *have?* I am reading in a magazine that Livia, one of the great *Rumanian* beauties of the twentieth century, uses her "mother's nectar cream . . . the product of some thirty thousand bees." I daresay Livia *does* use her mother's nectar cream that all those bees gave up their lives for, but I'll bet Livia's flawless skin and bones come from her *mother* (genes), not mother's *nectar* cream.

Still ravishing in her seventies, another great beauty of our time, Dolores Del Rio, said in a *Women's Wear Daily* interview, "Take care of your inner beauty, your spiritual beauty, and that will reflect in your face. Every bad deed, every bad fault will show in your face. God can give us beauty and genes can give us our features but whether that beauty remains or changes is determined by our thoughts and deeds."

I have news for Ms. Del Rio. Thoughts and deeds do absolutely *nothing* for a forgettable face, but a little helping out—i.e., makeup and even plastic surgery (more later)—*can*. Sometimes I think we love to read what beauties are doing, or not doing, because, as long as we are reading, we don't have to do anything *ourselves!* Or maybe we actually think something they are trying and recommending will deliver up unto us a *smidge* of their incredible looks. Do, by all means, try anything Morgan Fairchild *tells* you to, but it's *possible* someone like me can advise better, or as *well,* at least, because our good looks, if we have them, have come from trying and self-discipline, not from Mother and God. Oh, dear!

Ready?

The Mouseburger and Makeup

First I'd like to discuss men's feelings about makeup. Men don't like you in makeup, right? Wrong. As we've already said, once a man is hooked on you, he doesn't care if you face is maggot white and your eyes sink into your skull like olives in a glass of grape juice. . . . The *smell* (pheromones), the *sex* of you are all that matters, but how do we *get* him hooked? Not with makeup, *that's* for sure. He does first have to *notice* you, however, and the made-up (even though lightly) face is one unmistakable signal that a woman is approachable.

Does that sound silly? Well, when feminists wanted to show their contempt for men and men's rules, they scrubbed their faces clean, let their hair hang straight and gray and wore black turtleneck sweaters. Men *got* the message.

The makeup worn by users may be subtle. You can't see those three shades of eyeshadow blended to one, may think the lip-glossed lips are from nature or the blushing cheeks from modesty (hah!) but even the *subtlest* makeup is a shorthand to the soul. It says, "I want to attract you so I have tried to perfect myself. I am wearing my badge. I am ready for a grown-up, exciting, full-fledged romantic man/woman relationship."

Somehow drab doesn't go with sexual. Yes, a girl in her twenties or younger gives off enough sex signals just by *existing* to attract men, but even *she* usually signals the opposite sex with artifice. Women who mostly eschew makeup still signal with their *hair*. Lightening, blonding, curling, streaking, highlighting—*those* are sex signals (if they aren't sex signals, what *are* they?), and that's okay. Vidal Sassoon says, "Hair is another *name* for sex!"

Forgetting men for the moment—and let's *do*—usually you *act* the way you look, and you *contribute* to that look as surely as nature does. Repeat: You *create* a "look," then *act* that way. Example: A sad-sacky little secretary runs around *Cosmo determined* to call no more attention to herself than a guppy in a swimming pool. She wears no makeup ever, hides out in little cotton sacks that look like her mother's housedresses, is twenty pounds overweight—naturally. She has a sweet face and perfect skin and is bright, but you can bet your new Carlos Falchi bag nobody pays any attention to her. . . . She *planned* it that way.

Another *Cosmo* assistant who has *utterly* forgettable bone structure and is hippy (the kind you can't fix with exercise or clothes) makes up carefully each day, wears pretty silk blouses, good skirts, perfume, and isn't an ounce overweight. She'll never be pretty but she says to us "Approach me . . . I'm here to be talked to" and we *do;* she has made the bid for attention.

Blusher, eye makeup and lipstick—the big three—add the *greatest* drama to a mouse-blonde with no eyelashes—she can get very definite-looking. Makeup makes less difference in a brunette who is *already* colorful, but she, too, can come alive. Makeup could make *more* of a difference in our faces except 90 percent of us still don't know how to *use* it. We have no more skill with makeup than we do with clothes.

Our taste is simply rotten and it shows up in what we put on our faces as well as on our bodies, or the combination of things we put on them. That lack of skill is fixable, of course; you have to plunge and keep practicing with makeup; clothes we'll get to in a minute. Never mind, however, whether you are doing it *right*—makeup delivers a message from the inner girl. It says, I want you to like and admire me. I have gone to trouble for you. I have dared to paint my eyelids jade green, turn my eyelashes sooty, clip on this red-red rose, tie my belt this new way.

Makeup says you have "joined up," have taken your life into your own hands and are making a bid for attention. *Avanti!* Bravo!

How to Do It

Now, there is every chance that, although you use cosmetics, you don't use *enough*. I'm not talking about *all* the time. Who needs to look like a Christmas pudding just to pick up a skirt at the dry cleaner's. Some days I never *do* get around to putting on makeup, though I hope that isn't the day the president of the Hearst Corporation picks for one of his little drop-ins. I mean, just possibly you are stingy with cosmetics even when *trying* to look glamorous. Do you still harbor residual guilt about their being "unnatural"? Do you resent spending the *money* for cosmetics? More likely, you still don't quite know what to *do* with them. For God's sake, learn! Pay for a professional makeup job and get the professional to show you how. Professional makeup artists don't *like* to teach, so you have to make a deal with them to give instructions as they work on your face. Practice as they show you. And practice and practice.

I've learned incredible things to do with an eyebrow pencil from my gifted friend Sebou of the Davir salon on Madison Avenue—he smudges it on as shadow over and under the eye. These books are good and can really teach you makeup if you'll study: *Mark Traynor's Beauty Book* (Doubleday, $11.95), *Instant Beauty* by Pablo Manzoni (Simon and Schuster, $9.95), *Designing Your Face* by Way Bandy (Random House, $8.95), *Adrien Arpel's Three Week Crash MakeOver/ShapeOver Beauty Program* (Pocket Books, $6.95).

Experiment. Practice. Keep *at* it. You'll want to *change* your makeup occasionally even if what you're doing is becoming. A woman can get addicted to a particular look, do it the same way for years and wind up looking time-warped as she ages. Besides, makeup styles change just as clothes fashions do. Have *fun!* Once in a while I *forget* the magic of makeup; then a *Cosmo* secretary walks into my office. I have gradually become aware that she is looking kind of special these days. Then I look a little closer and realize her glasses are different. "Tinted," she says, "they're pink halfway up." Well, just as blusher would, the pink casts a glow on this girl's face which is terribly becoming—it isn't love, it's plastic!

A week or so later a young art director brings me a layout and I am shocked. "What have you *done?*" I ask. "You look different!" (Her I'd always accepted as a little frumpy and here she is looking *sensational.*) "I've taken off twenty pounds," she says. "My hair is two shades lighter and it's *straight.*" Once again, whether I meant to be or not, I am *dazzled* by what you can *do* to look better with just "cosmetic changes"—lightening the hair, paring the figure—and I know all over again it is *worth* it. The "before and after" photos we take for *Cosmo* are the *most* dramatic proof of what makeup can do. Alas, I've never seen a "before" girl do her makeup ever again the dramatic way we did it for the photo—it's nearly always straight back to anonymity next day—but at least she knows how she *can* look.

Can you give too *much* for an image? Perhaps. A makeup artist at NBC, five feet two, wears three-inch heels at all times "to look better proportioned," although she stands on her feet six hours a day and is one day going to have a screaming sacroiliac. A pretty friend of mine can't get out of the restaurant ladies' room in less than twenty minutes though the rest of us make it back to the table in five to be with the men. Ilona has to stay in there combing, primping, lip-glossing until she gets it right.

Regardless of how much or how little you *usually* do, I hope sometimes you will do the big dramatic thing. My friend Ann Siegel recently got into her shoulder-length-with-bangs Cleopatra wig (yes, there *are* still wigs), a new striped chiffon Halston, Kohl-blackened her eyes and was simply to *die*. It wasn't Ann, but it was great! One night for a movie premiere I wore *two* hairpieces—so heavy I felt like somebody had a board on top of my head pushing me down—anchored with twenty horse-size hairpins that *seemed* to have been struck straight into the *scalp*.

Pain? Who cared! I never looked so good before or probably ever will again, with fairy-princess curls down the back, ringlets in the front, tiny gossamer silver bows perched everywhere like butterflies, plus full makeup by my genius friend Sebou.

You can *keep* your understated simplicity!

Which Cosmetics Should You Use— And How Much Should You Pay?

I'm going to take a deep breath now and say this: All cosmetics are virtually the same and, with few exceptions, all are equally *good*. That's my *opinion* based on years of using and lots of research. Nearly all cosmetics companies, large as well as small, have products supplied by outside laboratories. A few (Revlon for one) make their own cosmetics. There are hundreds of cosmetic laboratories in the United States. The formulas for cosmetics differ to *some* degree; one company may want its foundation greasier, drier, to have more slip or whatever. Expensive cosmetics usually contain classier *smells*. These cost a little more, but basic ingredients are about the same, so formulas vary only in the *smallest* way.

If cosmetics are "alike," why do they vary so in price? For one thing, *packaging* differs. A padded taffeta dusting-powder box runs the tab up higher than talcum in a can. Advertising costs no more for expensive than inexpensive products so don't blame the priciness on *that;* manufacturers of cheaper products may advertise *more*.

Frankly, I never ran into a really poor cosmetic in my life. Truth! Oh, some may get a little wilted if you keep them seven years; oil and pigment in deep smudgy eyecolors may go their separate ways; but for the most part, lipstick, blusher, mascara, foundation are *all* good and *stay* good. In the inexpensive lines I think Lip Quencher lipsticks are terrific; so are Noxell Cover Girl foundation and Maybelline eye products. (Nothing is as inexpensive as it once was *anyway!*) Less posh lines may not have the newest high-fashion colors quite as *fast,* but the high-fashioned taupes, smoky browns, plums will be available "cheap" soon enough.

Okay, since they're just as good, should you then always buy only the cheapest? God, no, I would never say *that!* Part of the sorcery of makeup is how it makes you feel as you apply it, as well as when you *wear* it. If you want the special subliminal good of using a lipstick or foundation with an ultraglamorous image (to create which, millions and millions of dollars have been lavished), *have* it! There is also the pleasure of owning these beautiful products, seeing them on your dressing table, having *other* people see them.

Cosmo's beauty editor Mallen De Santis sometimes takes a little of her beauty bounty to a friend in a government office, where the women definitely are not into the beauty world and are supposed to have "good common sense." They invariably swoon over the high-gloss, *glamorous* stuff, Mallen says—that packaging, those smells! Good common sense has nothing to *do* with our enjoying those products. . . . Long live the Revlons, Estee Lauders, Max Factors and friends. I use them all and am an addict.

The Perfume Fix

Is perfume all the same, too? No; perfume formulas differ considerably. A mouseburger on the rise can afford very little real *perfume* unless someone gives it to her. I sometimes wonder how *anybody* affords it. One hundred sixty dollars for an ounce of Joy! There is this vaguely reassuring "news," however: Fragrances come in so many *different* forms—perfume, eau de cologne, eau de toilette, bath oil—you can definitely smell nice by using *some* combination of them without cashing in your C.D.'s. Let's start at the beginning. Real perfume—extrait of perfume—usually contains *some* expensive ingredients: true flower oils (attar of roses, iris, narcissus, marigold, orange blossom, hyacinth, etc.) or other *natural* products (roots, grass, moss, beans, barks, fruits, leaves) and these *cost.* Most animal products like deer musk and ambergris that once went into the making of perfume have been replaced by synthetics. Now, perfume companies don't use nearly as *much* true flower oil or natural products as they used to—real French perfume of the thirties, forties, fifties was a different breed and *indescribably* wonderful—but they have developed astonishingly delicious-smelling synthetic components to take their place. Eau de cologne and toilet water duplicate the real fragrance; it's just that they're diluted so they'll *go* further. Perfume might contain, let's say, 30 percent "smell" (synthetic plus natural basic ingredients) and 70 percent "vehicle" (alcohol to carry the smell along). In cologne you might get 12 percent smell, 88 percent vehicle, or something like that; but considering how much cheaper cologne is, if you spray yourself often, you can still smell wonderful all day long . . . at a price. Bath oil, rubbed into dry skin, lasts exceedingly well, and for years that's all I used. To smell wonderful, then, it seems to me you pick a relatively inexpensive eau de cologne (cologne is stronger than toilet water)—Scoundrel, Jontue, Aliage, Tatiana, Narcisse Noir, Ambush, Sophia, Royal Secret, Indigo, are all good ones—or the cologne of a famous French name, use it after your shower, *before* dressing, keep replenishing from a spray flacon all day long. People who smell nice all the time have to *keep* replenishing; there *is* no other way. I buy empty crystal flacons—about five dollars—and fill them with a medicine dropper from a large bottle of cologne (or perfume if I have it) to carry in my purse. Filling flacons yourself is less expensive than buying the perfume or cologne already *in* them. You know fragrance *changes*, deteriorates if you keep it too long. Unopened, a year would be maximum. Once opened, six months is its life span.

Now, to smell ultimately wonderful, let me give you the whole routine. Though expensive, it's a plan to *aspire* to. Pick a fragrance, buy it in all its forms, to be used this way: Use bath oil in your bath or gel in the shower. Dry off. Dust *talc* on feet and body. Put *cologne* under arms (for many people, cologne makes a satisfactory deodorant) and over your whole body. Next you use *perfume* for accents after you dress at these pulse points: behind knees, crook of arm, wrist, cleavage, behind ears. Use a purse-size vial to refresh from all day long just as you would freshen lipstick.

Creams, Lotions and Salves

What about treatment products? How much can *they* do for you? Once more a deep breath: I think anyone who believes creams and lotions can keep her skin from aging might as well believe that Santa is coming down the chimney next Christmas with a floor-length sable coat. What treatment products *can* do—*probably!* (atmospheric conditions have something to do with it)—is keep your skin soft, more comfortable, *somewhat* moist and make dry skin less flaky. Dry skin isn't just that tight feeling your face has after being washed with soap and water—the famous late Dr. Erno Laszlo said skin *should* feel tight . . . that's a sign of *good* skin—but is parchment-paperlike, with minuscule pieces flaking off. For skin like that, or potentially like that if you don't care for it, moisturizer eradicates the flakiness just as hand lotion helps chapped hands.

As for what anything on the *outside* can do for or to anything on the *inside* of your skin, let me tell you I've had one fine (confusing!) time trying to find out the *truth* about the efficacy of moisturizers, night creams, spritzed-on or splashed-on water. It seems that water (moisture) *in* your skin is the big ingredient for making it beautiful. As skin ages, it *loses* moisture, which needs to be replaced. How do you do that? Well, skin gets moisture from hauling it up to the *top* layer from its *underneath* layers, also from your sweat glands and from the *atmosphere*. So the moistness of our skin, as I understand it, depends on the rate it comes up to the top from those underneath layers, how much water we get from our sweat glands, how fast the moisture leaves our skin by evaporation (on a hot dry day, it's goodbye moisture; on a *wet* day, moisture *stays,* etc., etc.), as well as the *condition* of our skin (older is drier) plus the *capacity* of the top layer of the skin to bind (keep) the water it gets *up* there. Whew!

So what *about* the products you put *on* your skin? Do they help? According to the dermatologists, lab people, beauty mavens I checked with, products that contain *humectants*—a combination of glycerine and glycotes (most moisturizers and other creams *do* contain these)—can indeed draw moisture in from the air and deliver it to your skin. Great! Catch 22: There has to be moisture *in* the air for the humectants to *absorb.* If the air is dry, as in an overheated room or in the desert, the humectants draw water *out* of your very own skin and release it to the air! Murder! The moisture can be sent either direction, you see, outward or inward toward the lowest humidity. The lowest humidity, as we said, could be in your skin *or* in the outside air, depending on atmospheric conditions. Just think about Irish women in all that mist and British women in their fog, with their beautiful skins (with or without moisturizing), while Arizona, Palm Springs or other sun-baked skins are frequently *parched,* and you'll get the picture.

Let's go through it again. If air is *damp,* moisturizers (with humectants) utilize that dampness from the outside to make your *skin* moist. Slap on the moisturizer. In *desert* heat, however, moisturizers would simply *steal* moisture from your skin and give it to the air. What desert-heat people want to do is seal moisture *in* their skin by using oil on their faces so what moisture is there *stays.* (The Bantus in South Africa use lots of oil.) Repeat: *Moist*-air people should use *moisturizers,* desert-air people *oil.*

Okay, suppose you want a moisturizer in your life, which brand should you use? Aha! Another deep breath. Just as with cosmetics, I don't think there's a great deal of *difference* in products. . . . They're mostly *all* good. According to the head of a medium-size cosmetics company, "No company has any product another company can't take to its lab and copy. If there's anything good around, it can be broken down and marketed by all." Are there daring, innovative products manufactured in Europe but, because of our strict FDA regulations, not available in the United States? My informant says no. There may be things to put down your throat which could make a difference *inside* you that are banned here but nothing for the *outside.* Okay, picking treatment products is your very own *choice.* There is no reason *not* to use expensive ones if you like them and can afford. Says my cosmetics-company friend, "My wife, who is *totally* knowledgeable about treatment products—she used to work in our lab and recognizes the ones made by our company are as good as any on the market—unerringly, meticulously passes by everything 'available at home' to buy the most expensive thing she can get her hands on." (Can't you see him wanting to strangle her?)

Use what pleases you. Having tried just about *everything*—manufacturers send me things, sometimes I buy and Mallen De Santis shares her treasure trove—I have to say that just like with cosmetics (a) I virtually never met a treatment product I didn't like; (b) I use them *all* and enjoy them tremendously; (c) if I were on the desert island people always talk about, and could take only a few items, they would be: Ponds cleansing cream, Mentholatum, Vaseline, and Lubriderm (an inexpensive lotion made by Warner-Lambert Company which can be used as hand lotion, body lotion or moisturizer). If I had more room, I'd take all of Georgette Klinger's line and dozens of others. P.S. Preparation H (for hemorrhoids) makes a great eye cream. Shrinks puffiness.

Skin Care

What about *care* of your skin? Well, regardless of how many *products* you use, *cleaning* your face thoroughly is the *Numero uno,* big-deal *most* important thing you can do to have a good complexion (except get born with it). According to *every* living expert, you must get *all* the makeup out of your pores every single day.

Soap and water, cream or liquid cleanser? Nobody agrees on *that* so *you're* the expert; use whichever feels comfortable. Some women get a deep-clean at a salon several times a year. *That* gives you baby skin for a day or so; the experience is sybaritic and marvelous, but salons are expensive and you can pretty much keep your own skin fresh and glowy with a daily scrub. Masques are pleasant and "freshen" your face but provide no residual good. You know about health affecting the skin. A booze-free, cigarette-free, junk-food-free diet definitely shows (advantageously) in your face provided you also keep it clean and *sleep* enough. Sleep is so pleasurable I think most of us *get* enough, but hitting the booze and cigarettes too heavily (by me, hitting them at *all* except to make love is too heavy!) are big temptations and they *aren't* your skin's friends.

Now, just because I've been at it so long (I don't think I've *ever* missed a night washing my face), because I used to have oily, angry, *terrible* skin during acne days and because, through slavery, I now have *nice* skin, may I tell you my skin-care routine?

1. *Wash your face daily,* probably at bedtime. Get off *all* the makeup. Use either soap and water or liquid cleanser. I use dermatologist Dr. Norman Orentreich's soap for dry skin with a Buf Puf (cellulose sponge to buff away dead skin; buy at drugstore).

2. *Rinse thoroughly.* Use your cupped hands or washcloth to scoop up at least twenty-five scoops of water. Dry with *clean* terry cloth.

3. If going to bed, use a *tiny* amount of moisturizer or eye cream around the eyes, on nose-to-mouth lines and throat—nothing on

rest of face. If going out, with or *without* makeup, use the tiniest amount of moisturizer on whole face, then put on makeup.

4. In summer, spritz your face many times a day with bottled water in a small plant-watering can. Spritzing *does* moisten skin like the Irish mists and London fogs, but water evaporates quickly and can't keep you dewy *unless* you keep *at* it. I use Mountain Valley bottled spritzer (on top of makeup); keep a bottle at home and office. Spritzing feels too cold in winter so I don't.

P.S. A humidifier at home and office is good but this kind of equipment is expensive and a pain in the neck to keep filling with water. A bowl of water placed on top of radiators in winter will keep air moist.

5. *Do face exercises.* Plastic surgeons do not believe in these; I do. Mine are from M. J. Saffon's *The Fifteen-Minutes-a-Day Natural Face Lift* (Warner Paperback, $3.95). I do twenty minutes in the morning, face creamed, *always*. Exercises *don't* help much with upper-eyelid folds and dark circles, are only moderately effective with turkey-gobbler chin folds (the platysma muscle) but they *definitely* help jawline, cheeks, mouth. Facial exercises are easier to get the hang of if somebody *shows* them to you. Maybe there is such a person in your city who can do that—or study Joe Saffon's book.

6. *Stroke.* With the most feathery touch (use little finger and fourth finger of both hands or *third* finger of each hand) stroke forehead and the area between eyes many times a day—no cream needed—to get rid of small frown lines, also to help you remember to relax and *not* frown. If you have time for a *total* stroking job, wear shower cap, cream face lavishly with cold cream (cream hands, too) and make tiny circles all over your face—gently, gently—using third and fourth fingers. Do this for ten minutes, then wipe every speck of cream off hands *and* face with a clean terry cloth. If you have time, repeat the process twice *more*—that's three creamings and strokings, three wipe-offs. Be sure wipe-off cloth is *clean*—don't reuse dirty portions. I learned this technique from Phyrrah Malouf, an exotic Lubbock, Texas, girl with lovely skin, and wish we had room to draw pictures of Phyrrah's suggested circle-and-stroke areas. *Very* effective.

7. *Use the ice treatment.* A number of movie stars do this. When you want baby-fresh skin, put two trays of ice cubes in a double plastic bag. Tie the end with a wire Baggie fastener, put bag with cubes into a basin of cold water. Cream your face and submerge in icy water but never let ice cubes (secure in their Baggie)

132

touch the face. Resubmerge and come up for air until you get bored—the longer the treatment, the fresher the face. This treatment tightens pores, *refines* skin. If you really like it—I do—buy a snorkel from a sports store—then you can breathe through your mouth under water and stay down twenty minutes at a time. I try to do this icy dip before a big-deal social or business date.

8. *Have silicone injections.* I have had tiny silicone injections in the lines between nose and mouth regularly for many years. They plump up the skin by causing your own skin cells to produce new collagen, which *replaces* lost tissue. Nearly everybody I know over the age of forty has these injections, too. It sometimes looks like a *sewing* bee up at my dermatologist's. How do you find a doctor to administer silicone? Thousands of doctors now work with it but not all are competent. If you will send a stamped, self-addressed envelope to Dr. Norman Orentreich (one of the doctors who pioneered the use of silicone cosmetically) at 900 Fifth Avenue, New York, New York 10021, he will suggest a qualified doctor in your area. Dr. Orentreich prefers silicone to collagen because many skins are allergic to collagen.

Now, just a few more skin-and-beauty thoughts and we're finished.

"You Got Some Color!"

You show up mahogany-color from vacation or from a weekend backyard sun-dabble and friends say so approvingly, "You got some color!" when what they *ought* to do—if they love you—is *weep!* You *know,* long bakes in the sun are the *dumbest* thing you can do to skin, that there's a direct link between skin cancer and sun exposure, that, as one dermatologist says, "hours of sun equal years of aging." Okay, you look sexy and sensational with a glow, but the *price!* I guess we can't keep you *out* of the sun totally, but you should use a sunscreen at all times—a sun*block* would be even better. With sunscreens and sunblocks, the higher the Sun Protection Factor (SPF), the greater the protection. A sunscreen will usually contain under ten SPF—a sunblock or superblock anything from ten to nineteen. Paraminobenzoic acid is the principal protective ingredient with both screens and blocks.

Glossy, Glowing Hair

Reading everything I know about hair care—and it isn't that brilliant—could get tedious, so I'll just mention the Big Five:

1. Shampoo as often as you like. Often won't hurt and, if it makes your hair look better, *do*. One soaping ought to be enough.

2. Get all the soap out. I do three choruses of *Guys and Dolls* and a couple of *Sonnets from the Portuguese*—just a silly little routine—under the blasting water before I let myself out of the shower. One *smidge* of left-in soap will ruin *everything*. If hair doesn't squeak, you aren't *there* yet.

3. At shampoo's end, stick your head under *totally* cold, rushing water for a minute for great final gloss. Dreadful shock to the old system so don't do it with a weak heart.

4. Conditioning seems to help. There are ninety-two hundred different kinds so you just have to fool around and see which you like.

5. *Change* hair products every so often. Your hair gets *used* to the old ones and doesn't respond anymore. Maybe it's like changing *men;* new ones challenge and bring out the best.

There, this ought to give you glossy hair. *You* have to figure out how to roll it up, comb it out. Now may I just give you one testimonial about professional hair care?

The Professional Fix

I have brain-damaged hair and, like *anything* brain-damaged, you don't always realize that it *is* until later. For years I thought my hair was like everybody else's—you know, just regular *hair*—and was about thirty-six (thirty-*six!*) before I figured out something was Terribly Wrong. There I was at the beauty shop with my clipping from *Vogue* of the style I wanted for the evening and there was this conscientious, perspiring operator *trying* with all her might to do what I wanted, and I am saying, "Dammit, why isn't it coming out like the *picture?!*" and she is saying, "I really *am* trying." Poor girl—people were so *kind* in those days—not to tell me I had exactly half enough hair for that style and what there *was* was too fine.

Well, just as a worried parent takes her child from one doctor to another hoping *somebody* will tell her he is only a slow starter (my hair also came *out* a lot with each shampoo), I began to take my hair *everywhere*—to the best dermatologists, scalp specialists, herbalists, begging to be told my hair was just "going through a phase," would one day come in bushy, brash and beautiful. Hah! One dermatologist had me save and *count* the hair which came out daily . . . one hundred twenty-two, one hundred twenty-three, one hundred twenty-four . . . I nearly went *blind* (did he stuff pillows with it at night?). A long-hair specialist recommended bending over, head between legs, and brushing a hundred strokes a day—the absolute *worst* thing you can do for fragile hair, I found out, hair in tatters, *later*. Another said I had an invisible fungus. This man has told *thousands* of thin-hair people they have an invisible fungus, which is very cheery until you realize invisible fungus isn't your problem at all—*genes* (them again!) are. Through the years, I stood on my head (not dangerous unless you fall *off*, which I occasionally did), upped my thyroid to three grains a day, had hormone shots along the hairline, used a slant board, drank everything healthful (and gagging and fattening) you could whirl in a Waring Blender—Brewer's yeast, bone meal, lecithin—got massaged, stroked, manipulated, conditioned. One morning I looked at myself in the mirror with Jhirmack's Nutri-pack peach cream hair reconstructor "with nucleic acids and electrolytes for severely damaged hair" on my *head*, Max Factor's Incredible Blue Mask on my *face*, and thought, Baskin-Robbins should make a *sundae* out of me.

Okay, so one day a year ago—listen, I'm *getting* to the point!—depressed about my hair, as usual, I said to myself, Very well, these are the jokes. You have fine, fragile hair which is *not* one day miraculously going to become fat, bushy and bountiful. You have done everything to get your face and figure to look better and succeeded a *little*. Now, finally, what *are* you going to do about your *hair* so it looks as good as it *can* look every day? After a shampoo it is just adequate, two days later *pitiful*. I was wearing it long—what you can't make up for in bushy I figured you make up for in *length*. I was shampooing only once a week because, with every shampoo, hair came out like needles from a six-month-old Christmas tree—and I presume one day I will totally run *out*. What *are* we to do? My hairdresser/makeup man on Madison Avenue can make me ravishing for a party by teasing the hair to its ultimate limit, but next day the hair is not only tattered but *collapsed*. Like many talented hairdressers, this one cares *passionately* how you look leaving his shop, not at all how you look between visits.

Okay, I talk everything over with *Cosmo's* smart, patient beauty editor, who senses that I am now desperate—*years* have gone into this silly pursuit of beautiful hair. "You must have your hair cut," Mallen says. "Cut?!" I scream. "They scalp you (sophisticated me said this) and you look worse than before." "Have it cut just a *little,*" she said. "It will give your hair a *lift.*" (I'd been cutting my own hair for years, not trusting—with reason, I felt—hairdressers not to Go Too Far.)

"Let me have somebody come to the office," Mallen suggested, and did. One day, doctor's satchel of brushes, combs and rollers in hand, this youngish person (Robert LaCourte) lopes into my office and says, "Go soak your head." I went to the ladies' room, got soaked, came dripping back, and he began to cut—"not shorter than an inch below the ears" he swore on his mortgaged salon and next credit in *Harper's Bazaar.* It took him about forty minutes to do this careful clip-clip, though I would have doubted I had enough hair to *take* that long. Then he just kept combing and fluffing with his hands and showed me what he was doing and how. When the hair was almost dry, he used the blow-dryer to finish up, said *I* must get a blow-dryer with brush attached so I could do the same thing. He said I was to wash my hair every *other* day, one soaping, dry it as he had, and he told me what products to use. I said the hair comes out *worse* with shampooing and, further, I don't have *time* what with exercising an hour before work, cooking David's breakfast, blah, blah, blah.

"The hair won't come out worse," he said. *"Make* time!" It doesn't and I *do* . . . I shampoo at midnight instead of early morning every other day and go to Leslie Blanchard—the best!—to have my hair colored every six weeks. Color doesn't make hair *stronger* but I don't think it hurts it much either. The cutting happened a year ago (we cut every two months) and my hair has looked better since then, at least 70 percent of the time.

So what is the moral of this *dreadfully* long story? This: (a) Sometimes even smart people can be rigid, dumb, blind about improvement, cling to prejudices they long since should have discarded. You'll allow *this* but don't touch *that.* You trust *this* expert but not *that* one. For years I totally trusted doctors but thought hairdressers were exploitive, money-grabbing, hair-health-destroying *creeps.* I was *wrong!* (b) There is undoubtedly *some* professional who can help you with hair, skin, nails, whatever your problem, as this gifted person helped me with mine (and he charged very little). (c) *Find* these people and then—big "and then"—do what they *say*.

Professional beauty people are like professional anything *else;* some are good, some are terrible. You have to try many, as I obviously did, to get the right *ones*. There is no *way* people who make their living from beauty can't tell you or show you something you don't know that will enhance your looks and your life.

Fingernails Are Helpable

Nails you *can* get results with—and it's thrilling! This year, for the first time, despite crummy "natural" nails from heredity, aging, poor circulation and typing all day long on my manual machine (the hum of an electric tells me the meter's running so I should produce something brilliant . . . it makes my mind dry up!), I've got *fingernails!* File in one direction, don't peel your nail polish off, wear rubber gloves in the kitchen, eat healthy . . . that's all kid stuff for me, but it never kept my nails from peeling, chipping, disintegrating before my *eyes*. I'm *already* on megavitamins, thyroid and protein supplements. This is what did it: just some silly cuticle cream—again from Dr. O.—faithfully rubbed into the nails at night; then I put on little cotton gloves to go to sleep. I also repeat the process as I do my face exercises in the morning. *That* has made my nails grow. If you have problem nails, I'm sure a dermatologist could give you a similar cuticle cream (the "growth" ingredient of the one I use is salicyclic acid, which basically firms up the keratin) to wear with little gloves, and probably you need to watch those other things—diet, kitchen chores, etc.—too.

Do we all agree? That cared-for nails with unchipped polish separate rich, glossy girls from the others more surely even than clothes or accessories? If you *care* to look rich and glossy, wear polish and keep it repaired.

Pretty Feet

Oh, God, have we *time* for feet? Usually they don't *show*, but here are some thoughts.

The worst enemy of pretty feet is rotten shoes. *Make* yourself buy shoes that are comfortable across the toes—never mind that the heels are skyscrapers. Throw *out* the ones that are giving you corns no matter what they cost! *Out!* The new ones you buy shouldn't pinch or rub. Wear your highest heels in short stretches, not to shop or stroll. (If fitted properly, skyscrapers don't hurt *feet*, just your *back!*) Take uncomfortable shoes *off* under the restaurant table, sitting in a movie, working at your desk, but the smarter thing is gradually to *own* no hurtful shoes. Fit in a pedicure when you can. Clean, toenail-clipped feet feel good, look sexy. Rub Vaseline or hand lotion generously around toes, then put on cotton socks or airplane slippers for a few hours to have baby-skin feet. Put *tired* feet under cold rushing water, then hot, then cold again for a few rounds to perk up your very *soul*.

Forget Shortcuts—Everything Takes the Time It Takes

Yes, it all takes time. Of course you can screw around for three and a half hours getting your makeup on for a party and nobody can see much difference between that and your twelve-minute morning office special that includes shower, makeup, hair *and* breakfast, but mostly you get out what you put in—like everything else in life—yah! Good grooming—what a dull expression but we've got to call it *something*—can't be totally slapdash or you won't *be* well groomed. The women you think look great do not look like that *just* because of their good bones and long legs. Their hair gets streaked, legs waxed, toes pedicured, fingers manicured, skin taken sometimes to the dermatologist, and that stuff takes money and *time*. When you're young, you can do nearly everything *yourself* (except possibly the good haircut) but later you need *helpers*. How much time you are willing to put in and how much money for the helpers only *you* can decide. For the exercised body and line-free face, I'm willing to spend one hour a day at home; I don't make many salon visits. (Now that money isn't the problem, *time* is . . . it's so ridiculous!) We know that a mouseburger's happiness depends on health, success in her work, success in love (that discussion is coming). For those big three you never count the cost. As for looking fabulous, you just have to see how much time is left *over*.

Plastic Surgery

Who *else* is going to tell you she's been under the knife to have her face fixed? Nobody, of course, and I was so careful not to tell *anybody* when it happened. Still, you've got to *know* about these things. Over the past eighteen years I've had rhinoplasty (nose bumps removed), dermabrasion (skin scraped) and my "eyes done." With all the face exercises I do and silicone injections, I hope to avoid a full face-lift altogether, but expect to get my neck tightened—part of the same procedure—one day. Should *you* do some of these major things "after the fall"? I would *hope* so. Anybody who cares how she looks should. How wonderful that these operations *exist*, have been perfected so much and can *help* so much. Most beautiful women (and men) that you think look terrific after fifty have had plastic surgery. These are a few things you should know about it.

1. The work is horrendously expensive and there are no cut-rates with good doctors. The best get so much business they don't *need* to give discounts even to people like me who could write articles about them or to society hostesses who could bring them more patients. These are the prices:

Nose repair	$ 750 to $3,500
Eyelid surgery	1,200 to 3,500
Face-and-neck lift	1,500 to 5,000
Breast reduction	1,500 to 4,000
Breast augmentation	1,500 to 2,800
Breast reconstruction	2,500 to 5,000
Abdominal lift	1,000 to 4,000
Buttocks-and-thigh lift	2,000 to 4,000

2. Average age for a (first!) face-lift is fifty-two. Eye, nose and breast surgery may be performed earlier. A face-lift or eye-lift should last from five to eight years, depending on the quality of

your skin and whether you stay in good health. A nose job and breast operation are "forever" unless you go back for alterations.

3. Most procedures are *utterly* unpleasant—nobody ever tells you *how* unpleasant—but the pain only lasts a day or two and you forget. Depending on *your* healing powers and which operation you have, recovery time varies. Although you can reappear in public and take up your regular life two to three weeks after a face-lift, six months is the *real* recovery period for every vestige of swelling to be gone. Numbness with eye/nose jobs, also face-lifts, can last up to six months but eventually goes. Body surgery—buttocks, thigh, stomach or upper-arm lifts—leaves noticeable scars. These operations are not encouraged by top doctors in the United States except in unusual cases.

4. Things can go wrong and *do*. Yes, you could be the one this happens to. Still, the incidence of calamities with a *good* surgeon is low. Banish the idea of hunting for a bargain—i.e., sign up with a doctor because he's cheap. To find a surgeon—the best are in the biggest cities—call your county medical society, the American Society of Plastic and Reconstructive Surgeons or consult the Directory of Medical Specialists (in most local or hospital libraries). This book lists background, training, and expertise of each specialist. Or you may prefer a more direct route: ask the most sophisticated women you know and doctors you're already going to. It is perfectly sensible to consult two or *three* surgeons before you pick one (they will charge for the consultation). Plastic surgery is paid for in advance. Many operations today are done on an out-patient basis in the doctor's office or a clinic. A local rather than a general anesthetic will be used in those places, but many doctors prefer the local anyway for all but major plastic surgery because it's less risky. Outpatient surgery usually cuts costs.

5. Surgery will not change your life, solve your problems, but it *can* give you a great emotional lift. Lose weight *before* the operation—then if there is sagginess in your face from weight loss, the sag can be snipped right away with the lift.

What is surgery like? I have never known anybody to quite adequately describe the grisliness of any of these operations so I now will *try!* My nose was shortened and straightened—we took out a bump—eighteen years ago, so I remember that procedure least well, but do recall the first day after surgery was a nightmare; your nose and eyes ache, your face is swollen to twice its size, you can't breathe. The day after *that* you begin to get more comfortable, progressively so every day, and in two weeks you can go out in public.

With dermabrasion, skin is deadened (in the doctor's office) a small patch at a time, with sprayed-on grain alcohol, then lightly abraded electrically with steel wool by a doctor (Dr. Orentreich for me) with a steady hand. The abrading doesn't hurt; skin deadening *does*. The procedure takes about an hour for the whole face and you come out looking like raw hamburger—a bloody, gooey *mess*, though oddly enough, you don't *hurt* too much after it's over because salve, which you keep applying when you get home, keeps you soothed down. In a few days you start bathing your face in milk; finally scabs form and drop away and you have baby skin. My dermabrasion was recommended because of long-ago acne scars, and I *think* it was worth it. . . . The skin came up fresher.

The most recent operation—removing circles from under the eyes, eradicating slightly drooping upper lids—is probably no more disagreeable than the others, but since it was recent it seems worse. I had "outpatient surgery" with Dr. Michael Hogan. You check into the hospital very early in the morning, are made drowsy but not knocked out with sedation, have the skin deadened with Novocain, get scissored away at and sutured for two hours—that's not *such* a tiny amount of time, is it, to be under the knife? And people always told me eyes were "just nothing"! Hah! A friend or loved one (my housekeeper, Anna) takes you home an hour after surgery with stitched-up eyes, looking like a cross between Raggedy Ann and Frankenstein. You keep fresh ice on your eyes *constantly* for twenty-four hours to keep swelling down and stave off black-and-blue. We blew that procedure in my house. David was just home from a long trip and I didn't feel like having *him* sit up and change ice packs every fifteen minutes all night. I meant to do it *myself* but kept dozing off from the Valium so I was a *jungle* of purple, blue and black, eyes swollen nearly shut for days. (David, on my arrival home from the hospital, took one look and swore— not so softly—"Jesus, the things you *do* to yourself—the self-*inflicted* pain!" True! If somebody other than a doctor beat you up like that you'd hope to have him *killed!*)

The swelling goes down gradually, the black-and-blue gets to be yellow-and-chartreuse, finally leaves. I nearly went *mad* with boredom the first few days because you can't read or *do* anything but listen to the radio. Once I "cheated" by sneaking to the typewriter, unable to *see*, but I could touch-type, and I wrote this account. One week after surgery I ventured out in dark glasses to hear Frank Sinatra at Carnegie Hall. You are *not* in shape that soon to go visit your idol backstage after a show, but Mr. S. seemed not to notice that his ardent longtime fan looked as though she'd slugged it out in a street brawl. Ten days after surgery I went back to the office, covered with makeup, hoping people would think I'd only been out for a D and C. It's tempting to babble about your operation, particularly if you like the way it came out, but I would advise, *don't*. Every time people look at you they think "face-lift." Just let them guess.

Now, we surely must be just about *finished* with our beauty discussion—I feel as though I'd been writing about fifteen *years* and *you* must be exhausted. I'll just say this to conclude: Regardless of what you were born with or born without, what you do to fix yourself up, some days you like you, some days you *don't*. One day you are crazy about your small breasts, curvy hips, intelligent little face, actually kind of all swelled up with pride, and then one measly *day* later you are so disgusted with this same group of parts you'd like to put yourself in a big manila envelope and mail yourself to *Bolivia!* You think you've *won*—that now, finally, you accept *your* Special Look—then it backs up on you! With the help of some sainted men you get convinced men *prefer* small breasts, small is young, adorable, then you watch some full-busted goddess felling all the males at a party, and it's hard to get back to believing your propaganda!

My own insecurity attacks come most frequently in travel away from *Cosmo* and New York—*my* special world where they reward *brains*. Plunked down among the haughty, snooty gorgeous ones of Venice or the French Riviera, one can get a virulent breakout of self-doubt about *looks*—not much *else* anymore, thank God. Well, I've found, after a little suffering you emerge, once more triumphant, on the *sunny* side. You don't look any *better*, you might not even look as *good* (lack of sleep, didn't put on the right lipstick), but it's just time to start feeling *good* about yourself again. Ready or not, world, here I come—quite *almost* beautiful, you know. Isn't it incredible? What beauty does for us and *to* us?

Now shall we discuss *clothes?*

Chapter Six

CLOTHES

We already said the *beauty* whirl was silly—having to try to be gorgeous when you *aren't* (though we also decided to go *along!*). Well, fashion is even *sillier!* How can anybody with any brains take seriously what we're supposed to *wear?* Every season we hear decreed hems up, hems down, waists pinched, waists free, shoulders skimpy, shoulders padded, lift that barge, tote that bale, hup two three, you there, you're out of step! . . . A girl could *croak* trying to get it right. Nothing true last year seems to be true *this* year. And how can you put your trust in designers, manufacturers, fashion magazines who have *totally* misplaced lilac, magenta, rose, ruby, lime, almost anything really colorful for daytime wear for about twenty years (although they did allow purple out of purgatory in the fall of 1980 and a small reprieve for turquoise in '82), while successfully foisting off on us gray, rust, slate, taupe, beige, mouse-brown as the only acceptable daytime colors? Why do we *do* it—take it all lying down?

Well, deep breath, here we go again. . . . We do it because we *like* it! Fashion is fun!

For all its craziness, fashion is a way of being new and fresh every year, of not boring yourself to death. Ex-*Vogue* editor Caterine Milinaire says, "Life would be totally dull if you didn't explore the possibility of expressing yourself through clothes." Diane von Furstenberg says, "Clothes help us project whatever image we want to project when we want to project it. Different moods, different outfits . . . that is the great joy of being a woman." Emilio Pucci says, "Fashion adds joy to your life."

I agree. Out of all the idiocy and slavery and rushing about trying to find a three-and-a-half-inch *raisin* suede belt or strappy sandals to go with *both* walking shorts and evening pajamas comes a kind of *joy*—creativity.

The Mouseburger and Clothes

Beautiful clothes are *not* an integral part of mouseburgering—i.e., having a great career and loving a man. What helps a girl with her *career* is her brain, willingness to work hard and getting along well with people over, under and around her. As long as you are clean, not even neat, but *clean*—though others don't agree with me on this—I believe your brain and drive are about all that matter and people don't give a *toot* what you wear except in the fashion business.

Clothes will not get you a man, that's for sure. Men respond to the sexiness of you, your sweetness, your rare sense of humor. Many a man has not even *noticed* that the girl he took to a party seems to have been dressed out of the rag bin, while we all know great dressers who haven't got a man to *take* them to a party. Clothes cannot *hurt* romance, of course. I think one of life's top ten (top *five?*) pleasures is shopping for the lingerie, party dress and swimsuit you're going to wear with *him*, but you're really shopping to shore up *your* confidence as much as for his delectation. As for work clothes, a closetful of Perry Ellis separates could not slow *down* a career (unless you went bust paying for them), but well-dressed girls *also* lose jobs, promotions. What clothes are is one of life's *pleasures*, bringing more joy to *us* than to our beholders, though we all love to look at well-dressed women. Clothes are one of the *rewards* of mouseburgering—work long and passionately and you can afford to buy lovely clothes. May I philosophize one more minute?

Loving Clothes "Too Much" Is Not a Sin

When people criticized Jackie Onassis for spending millions of dollars of Aristotle Onassis' money on jewelry and clothes the first year they were married, I always felt, if she could get her hands on the money to *spend,* how wonderful! Her spending wasn't going to bankrupt him; they gave plenty of money to charity, and he had, after all, got *his* hands on the most eligible woman in the world. Jackie obviously enjoys clothes (understatement) and I enjoy her *enjoying* them.

Clothes, it seems to me, are a reasonably innocent—if expensive—addiction. Some of us get hooked early in life. In Little Rock, Arkansas, where I grew up—during the *Depression* yet—clothes were *important*—your Sunday School dress, Easter dress, school outfits, *new* dress for a party, costumes for school plays, an *evening* dress when you were eleven. Somehow my mother, who sewed beautifully, managed these things for my sister and me. Of course you learn fairly early that what you put on your body isn't as important to the opposite sex as the shape of the body you put it *on* (and possibly having naturally curly hair), but *still* you care. I love my clothes and sometimes go into the closet just to visit them—all my Adolfo suits and my one Chanel, Ralph Lauren jackets, Cal Klein silk dresses, evening gowns I wear once a year, and those thirty-two blouses. . . . They are my *friends!* I have yet to learn the system of having only two terrific outfits you switch back and forth every day for six months, then you put together two *new* ones. Such spartanism wouldn't make me happy! We'll get to you in a *minute.*

You Can't Look the Way People that You *Envy* Look Without Spending the Money

There are no exceptions to this rule. Yes, well-dressed people sometimes pick up incredible bargains and, yes, that long evening cape you admire may have been in her wardrobe since Kappa Kappa Gamma days, but *usually* the fabulously dressed ones have indeed paid one hundred fifty dollars for the simple sleeveless tank top (which they have in six other colors) and their yearly clothes bill *does* exceed your rent. Last summer in Cannes I dropped into Rive Gauche, the Yves St. Laurent store, during a sale, with two friends, one in the Ten Best-Dressed List Hall of Fame, the other younger but getting there. They each left with a thousand dollars' worth of clothes. I left without even a T-shirt because I couldn't hack the prices. Those two will always be better dressed than I, not *only* because of their taste but because they're willing to *spend*. Of course I spend *plenty*.

Okay, you're not trying for the best-dressed list; neither am I, and you can make up for a lot with clever buying and taste; but I'm just saying nobody can be one of the drop-dead ones with *only* cleverness.

Pure Elegance

What about elegance? That is different from fashion flair, but elegant men and women *also* mostly don't manage without money; they buy rich and buy often. If you are practicing *up* for elegance, one of the secrets is that you practice when you're alone, not just for company; you are hosed down and exquisite at all times, plus you have roses on the dresser because *you* enjoy them, eat off Limoges and dry off with Porthault towels. Some of us "put-it-out-for-company" ones are *never* going to get the hang of it.

Acquiring Chic

Forgetting elegance and spending (and some spenders do look *godawful*, to be sure), aren't there certain fashionable women who do *not* spend that much? Certainly! We call them chic. They seem to *sense* when to tuck the blouse in or leave it out, stand up the collar, chop off the pants to make Bermudas, wear chokers instead of chains, eschew the satin skirt for satin knickers, pair them with a backless rather than frontless halter. So how do they *know*?

Well, many of them live in the fashion world. I rarely see a fabulously pulled-together *non*-rich woman who *doesn't* have something to do with the fashion business. But can *we* acquire chic? Unequivocally yes, says Carrie Donovan, fashion editor of *The New York Times Magazine* and previously fashion editor of both *Harper's Bazaar* and *Vogue.* "Ralph Lauren is from the Bronx, so is Calvin Klein. *I* came from a farm in Lake Placid and Bill Blass is

146

from Indiana. The first and *only* thing you need is desire. . . .
You have to *want* to have taste. Some people have inherently *bad*
taste. Their problem is really not the bad taste—that can be fixed—
but that they don't know they have it!''

Carrie says you start with *desire,* after which ''You study . . .
pore over fashion and decorating magazines, books, newspaper
clippings, absorb, osmose! This is your sinking-in period and may
take years. You experiment. . . . Try on and discard, try on and
discard, reject and endorse. You work at it until your eye gets better and finally you are . . . *there!* Try to examine beautiful clothes
even if you can't own them,'' says Carrie. ''Get the *feel* of what
those designers did. It *does* rub off. If you never *associate* with
anything but cheap, your taste cannot get better. No, all this association *shouldn't* create envy . . . it educates you.''

Cosmo's fashion editor, Nancy Benson, says fashion flair requires a
little *nerve* . . . feeling that *you,* by God, can bring it off. . . . Going
right out there proudly in your assembled concoctions.

Now, all this presupposes that you *want* to ''follow fashion,'' to
be chic. You don't *have* to. Plenty of normal, beloved women do
not, nor are any of us really ''helpless pawns of the industry.'' If
you decide to ''sit fashion out,'' you can always dress from what's
in your closet plus a few non-faddy *new* things. Stores in every city
carry basics. My opinion is that having the kind of chic and flair
Carrie is talking about is like sex after forty. You can decide to let
sex slip away, *not* participate, or you can get on the train, hang on
to your seat around the curves and have a great sex life. You can
sign *up* for fashion and enjoy it as a game and art form, rather than
just pass it by.

The Modest Plunge

Okay, let's say you're not going for the whole immersion course
but would like to follow fashion a *little.* How do you get the ''new
look'' each season, for example, soon enough to do some *good?*
As my friend Carol says, ''By the time I've gleaned that shoulder
bags have had it and we're into envelopes—which I buy—envelopes have had it *too!*''

There are three places to get help: the stores (they *do* stock new
stuff fast), fashion magazines (try to sort out what's going to
''take'' from all the blather), pulled-together friends (maybe the
best source—more later). Plus use your instinct. . . . What was

wide *last* year you figure will probably be skinny *this* year. A wardrobe can certainly be perked up. Examples: Putting the hem up or down a few inches isn't going to *kill* you. Pants-leg width changes; knife *in* the wide ones if skinny is back—unfortunately you can't do it the other way around. Lapel widths, too, can be whittled at. You can chop off the bottom of a silk dress and wear it as a tunic. I've made three expensive Ultrasuede dresses seven-eighths length and wear them now over pants and skirts as tunics. If you don't see square scarves on smart ladies, put yours away for a while and wear long-skinny. There isn't any question that fashiony people abandon the old a lot sooner than the rest of us.

Considering that you'll be buying a certain amount of clothes anyway, if you want to be in fashion you just start the cycle *sooner*. Buy and wear the new heel shape at the *height* of its vogue instead of finding the new shape after it peaks and wearing it to senility. Yes, to *start* the new cycle you will have to discard some things (with lots of good still in them!) sooner than you'd like, but anything *good*—pure silk, pure wool—you don't necessarily throw or give away; except for shoes, place it in "purgatory." My twenty-year-old pink mohair sweater came back in this year—furry was dead for *years*. Some well-dressed people give away clothes to friends or charity (for a tax deduction) quite casually and don't try to recycle. That act is hard for a mouseburger to get the hang of. We had so much trouble getting the money together to *buy* the purple wool princess coat, how can we be expected not to wear it to tatters? Nobody says we can't . . . it's just that fashiony women have the guts to lay aside, maybe give away, *sooner*.

The Image

Fashion mavens all say we need an *image,* but I don't think you necessarily start *out* thinking nymphet, earth mother, ice maiden, street urchin, Faye Dunaway (in *Network*) or Scarlett O'Hara. As you experiment the way Carrie Donovan was talking about, you just inexorably *gravitate* to a kind of look that pleases you—an image—and so you begin to choose frilly over tweeds, somber over gaudy—or the other way around. Looking around *Cosmo* I see all *kinds* of images . . . French schoolgirl, sassy-kid look, department-store proper—and I'm certain the owners just "osmosed" there. I hope you osmose to a *good* image. . . . A soccer shirt and dungarees seem so sexless to me—but whatever makes you happy!

Wear What's Right for Your Figure

You can actually wear almost *anything* unless you're fat, but some lines work better than others with your special bones. We haven't room to say what to team up with a large bosom (you fortunate person!), narrow shoulders, wide hips, short legs or whatever, but you probably already *know*. I think, rather than compensating for figure flaws, you pick the things that please you, and usually they *are* the ones that compensate for flaws. Once in a while a designer will create something that works for *all* of us—that great Diane von Furstenberg wrap dress, Emilio Pucci's little empire-waisted, no-fit-from-the-bosom-down skimp dresses in gorgeous colors (I've saved my favorite Pucci to be *buried* in!). You just automatically get to be expert by *looking* at yourself in your clothes.

Your Favorite Designer

Some designers seem to have our number, so *go* with them if you can afford to and stay loyal as long as they stay talented. Sometimes designers get bored with what they've been doing and go into a new craziness that doesn't suit you, or they just run out of steam. When they start getting silly, jump ship sooner rather than later . . . you don't have to stay faithful. I've had a dozen favorites so far and expect to have many others. Rudi Gernreich is in *my* Hall of Fame.

Status Names

For people who can't *afford* a Rolls-Royce or a Lalique chandelier I don't see anything wrong with having our *own* little status symbols—an Hermès scarf, the Gucci belt. The Rolls and the crystal *got* status-y only because of beauty and fine workmanship. So did the Hermès scarf and the Gucci belt for the same reason. Some S.S.'s may not be quite as status-y as they *were* because of so many of us buying them. You see about as many Gucci satchels on the subway as on the Concorde, but that's no reason not to buy them. With status *prices*, I doubt they will ever get *that* common and, besides, they're usually an investment. I've been carrying the same

Vuitton tote on airplanes—manuscripts, apple and cheese, newspapers, makeup, tickets, handbag, *everything* goes inside it—for fifteen years, and I think you'd have to take a *blowtorch* to it to do any damage. Louis, I'm *happy* to carry your initials! These are the names of some *other* status symbols (because of beauty and workmanship): Fendi, Elsa Peretti, Cartier, Charles Jourdan, Maud Frizon, Bottega Veneta—and, of course, Rolex is the watch of the moment. Designer jeans are probably kind of a "rip," not any better made or handsomer than non-status jeans, but if it makes you happy to have a famous name on your bottom, wear them by all means.

You Can Be Better Dressed
When You Own a Lot of Stuff

You see someone looking fantastic and you say, Ah yes, she knew *just* the sweater, belt, scarf to buy to put that look together. Probably not true! She very likely did it with stuff she already owns plus a *little* of it is new. People who always look sensational, as well as people with fabulous apartments, rarely buy "just enough"; they always "overdo" it. Yes, maybe one great bag will go with nearly every daytime outfit and you shouldn't try for complete *sets* of navy, brown, black, taupe and red accessories, but *more*—and I know this is different from what you usually hear—may be better. You can put together a great look more easily with enough *different* belts, bracelets, scarves to choose from. No, it can't be junk—the quality must be okay—and you can't buy copiously and collect marvels when you're poor, but A.M. (after mouseburgering), you may want to.

Wearing *Your* Colors

Cosmo recently ran some advice on color—an excerpt from a book. We should have been *arrested!* They (we) said, Don't wear white any brighter than your teeth (that would rule out everything but pale yellow), only wear beige the color of your skin (does Anne Klein know what color my skin *is?*), brown the color of your eyes (do you take the iris out and lay it beside the sweater?), etc., etc., etc. I think you can wear *any* color if you love it, and usually the colors you love are the ones that do something for you. If a color makes you miserable on *you* but you like it in *life*, have it in kitchen curtains. If it's not your *best* color but you love it, keep it away from your face. Black makes me look *exhumed* so I wear it in camisoles, and the black doesn't *start* until the bosom down, or in a black dress slashed to the waist, filled in with pearls and crystal. Cindy Adams, the columnist, is the only woman I've ever known who wears just one color—red, her trademark. It's wildly becoming, but I can't imagine giving up all those other nice colors for life. *You're* the color expert for *you*.

The Sale

Having never had any luck at sales, I've asked *Cosmo*'s fashion coordinator, Gretchen Parks—who looks *great* and buys about 30 percent of her clothes on sale and the rest at discount stores—*her* rules: Gretchen's rules:

1. Good things to buy on sale: lingerie, shoes and boots, coats. Nearly all coats go on sale in January. If you need one before that, just suffer and wait!

2. Shop expensive stores and departments during sales. This may be the only time you'll go near them, but here's a chance to study good merchandise and possibly acquire.

3. Ideally you try to fill up holes in your wardrobe, but you can go *crazy* trying to find the perfect navy blazer or wine slacks because those aren't what's on *sale*. Just try for great classic stuff that will "upgrade" your wardrobe . . . something good and terrific that will enhance what you already have. *Once* in a while you can abandon all reason and buy something insanely impractical but beautiful.

4. If you fall in love with a separate but it doesn't go with anything else you own, skip it. Or buy something else on sale to go with it so you'll at least have a whole outfit.

5. Stay away from what you already have seven of—pink blouses, gauzy peasant dresses. You automatically are drawn to your favorites, but if you don't really *need* any more, try to resist.

6. Try to go for all wool, silk, cotton—stay away from blends. (P.S. If anything blended in your wardrobe pills, use a razor or fine scissors to remove the balls.)

7. Don't buy anything too small in the hopes of losing weight.

8. If it's a rotten color, skip it.

9. After making your selections at a sale, hide them behind other clothes on the rack, then go sit in a phone booth for fifteen minutes and think it over to be *sure* you know what you're doing. If it's gone when you get back, the worst that's happened is you've saved eighty dollars.

The Mouseburger Clothes Plan

Now, what about a specific clothes plan for *you*, darling, deserving mouseburger? I asked two women with wonderful taste and not much money—*Cosmo* fashion editor Nancy Benson and free-lance fashion stylist Jill Cassidy—what advice *they* would give a girl on a budget. They worked separately but agree on so many things that I'm lumping their advice:

Put the bulk of your clothing allowance into *good* office clothes. You spend eight hours of every weekday on your job; you might as well look great.

Each season, buy either a skirt or two pairs of pants or a pair of pants and two skirts in basic dark or neutral colors. Have a couple of new blouses or shirts. A twin sweater set will deliver extra mileage. Buy one well-cut jacket each season.

Buy a good winter coat. This is what the public sees you in most, and you'll want to look your best by choosing a classic in a color that blends with other things in your wardrobe. Forget fur until you can afford it. You really *can* live without. Have a good raincoat. These exist at all price levels and are the perfect solution for between-seasons dressing as well as for rain/snow.

Don't buy more than two pairs of shoes per season and don't save them—*wear* them, as shoe silhouettes change drastically from season to season and you can't make shoes over. Purse styles don't change so rapidly. You're fairly safe in putting money into one good new handbag per season.

Don't be afraid to fall in love . . . with a luxurious angora or cashmere sweater, with a pair of satin pants to team with sweaters for evening, a pair of witchy shoes or boots, an extravagant item of real jewelry, anything really special and right for *you*.

Use accessories as personality accents, perhaps a lot of neck chains or bracelets to express the gypsy in your soul, perhaps brightly colored scarves to tie a special way to become your fashion signature, perhaps a wide belt with a big antique buckle to last for years and years. Once you fall in love with an accessory, never throw it out; set it aside for a while and come *back* to it.

Jill says, for evening, concentrate on silk separates. One top can be bare, one not so bare—again your great belt. You can also wear the silk shirts to the office with daytime bottoms. For an evening wrap in winter, Jill says a cape in a neutral color is dramatic, warm, not too expensive even in wool. Nancy suggests fake fur. Cape or fake can also work in the daytime.

In summer you can "fake it" with jeans, T-shirts, terrific sandals, again your great belt, and one of the good bags you've been acquiring. Don't put money into summer clothes. Jeans are okay in many offices. You'll know best about yours.

Suit yourself about owning a dress. You may want one good basic one to dress up or down for evening, for the office.

Buy whatever you can at discount stores. Watch for sales but buy only what you were looking for anyway. Keep your blinders on with other stuff. If you have decided one little black wool blazer will pull your wardrobe together, don't get seduced by a plum velvet skirt no matter *how* fabulous a bargain (these girls are tougher about sales than Gretchen). Postpone impulse buying until you have money. Investigate the possibilities of the five-and-ten for bras and panties, socks, hats, sweatshirts. Buy pantyhose at the supermarket or drugstore.

Never throw anything *good* away—real wool, pure silk. Put it away and wait for it to come back.

Your clothes must *fit*. Alter them so they will.

Clothes must be scrupulously clean—snaps on, spots off, crisp, bandwagon fresh. It *matters*, and fresh perkiness can make up for other things. (That goes for hair, makeup, fingernails, toenails.) Everything in great condition compensates for a small wardrobe.

One word about having something *very* expensive in your wardrobe. What good is *one* thousand-dollar Christian Dior suit—supposing you somehow scraped the money together—if everything else in your wardrobe is modest? Probably nobody will even *recognize* the "authentic Dior" surrounded by your "regulars." This doesn't mean stay away from the sinfully swank sweater or belt or shirt or whatever thrills you, *once* in a while. I admired some leather pants Nancy Benson—not rich, she supports herself and six cats—had on the other day.

"They're Fiorucci," she said. Fiorucci, ah yes . . . that's two hundred dollars' worth of pants, but she got them on sale, had them on with her red tennis shoes and thirteen-year-old cowboy belt, and she was *very* special. I just don't want you pining over Nancy Reagan's Galanos ballgown or saving for your basic Givenchy coat *yet*.

Bring In a Helper

Let's say you've developed *some* fashion flair but haven't the time or *drive* to haunt stores or study fashion like the stock market. . . . How can you get help?

Why not make use of people who *do* study fashion? I'm going to do another testimonial. Listen, I'm not some dopey female who thinks clothes and hair are the most important things in life, but I do get really thrilled about anything I can *fix*. Clothes and hair are frequently more fixable than *parents* or a man who drinks or your neighbor who plays his stereo all night. Testimonial: I am standing at the glasses counter at Saks one day next to this great-looking woman—black velvet knickers, black turtle sweater, black boots, newsboy's cap, blond streaky hair, silver-buckled Elsa Peretti belt, bracelets clear up her arm to the elbow and I say to this stranger as is sometimes my wont—usually nobody's going to *hit* you!—"You look terrific!" "Thank you," she said. "Fashion is what I do for a living . . . I'm a fashion coordinator." She said if she could ever help *me* in any way, she'd be glad to. I took her card and put it away—for three years! Then one day, closets jammed and nothing to wear, I said to myself, Listen, you get help in every *other* area of your life when you need it, why not a *fashion* helper (me, who's supposed to *know* about clothes and advise *Cosmo* readers!). I didn't know what to offer to pay her or even what she might *do*, but we made a date.

Well, darling, if anybody had told me some strange person was going to come over and straighten out my *closets* for six hours and I would *pay*, I would have said they were crazy. Closets you can do *yourself*, and what has that to do with chic? Well, you see, from being so *close* to your clothes and your closets, finally you can't see what you *see* and everything needs a fresh appraisal. We organized like maniacs, stacked and folded, put all the summer stuff out of sight in the *back* since it was now winter. I urged Jill to help me dump things I was keeping for sentimental reasons (the dress I met Queen Elizabeth in) and some of my Mistakes (that gray coat that makes me look like a small gray *elephant*), but she didn't throw out that much. Next visit we put together *outfits*—skirt, blouse, jacket, belt, shoes and bag—maybe a couple of dozen combinations. She didn't want me to write them down but to absorb what she was doing so I could do it *myself*, but in the beginning I wrote down. I just never would have *thought* of the old loden wool jacket with *gold* lamé camisole and the peach velvet skirt. I *loved* the shaking up. Jill now comes twice a year; we *still* organize the closets because I have perilously little space, then we put together little outfits, figure out where I have a hole so I can pick up the missing item. I will never be as fabulously dressed as she is, but I'm better than I *was*.

Regardless of who helps you or doesn't, you need to spend *time* in front of a mirror trying things together . . . doing Carrie's experimenting . . . it's the *only* way to find out. French girls do this without shame for *hours* . . . so must you if you want specialness.

Make Your Own Clothes

Home sewing is on the downswing. I don't know *why*. Nevertheless some people sew with great success. I've asked one who does, book editor Nancy Coffey, to give us her rules. Says Nancy, "I'd advise most young women to go out and learn to sew *tomorrow*. With prices so wild, how can you *not* sew!"

Beginners' mistakes to try to avoid: Choosing stiff fabric for a drapey dress and vice versa, picking too complicated a pattern, buying too complicated a machine. One that sews forward and backward is adequate even for an advanced sewer.

Stick to simple, uncomplicated designs with classic lines. Choose basic patterns and styles that look great on you and repeat them in all colors and fabrics, dressy and sporty, summer and winter, etc. You get to know exactly how each pattern will turn out, so after a while there are no more mistakes and you can whip up a skirt in a couple of hours.

For beginners, best bets are slightly A-line skirts, slacks and unstructured jackets (sans lapels, collars, etc.). One can always buy great-looking blouses, sweaters and tops to go with them and you save more money on major wardrobe pieces by sewing them.

Evening clothes are fun to make because you can experiment with outrageous fabrics, again sticking to simple patterns. *Vogue* patterns, though expensive, have the most clearly explicit directions.

Always buy the best fabric . . . cashmere, silk, pure linen, whatever. Clothes turn out better and last longer. It's more expensive but you're going to put a lot of time and energy into whatever you're sewing, and the results should look spectacular. Fabulous fabric is always noticed.

Press every seam, inside and out, right after it's sewn and before it is joined to another section of the garment. This rule is important. Seams then look razor-sharp and the entire garment hangs more fluidly. Re-press each seam again and again so by the time garment is finished, it's been pressed several times.

Last tip—don't be intimidated by the *idea* of sewing. There's no great mystique to it. Just proceed slowly and confidently, making sure you understand each step along the way before going on to the next. The secret is not to attempt anything too complicated— possibly *ever*—so each garment can be a success. Enjoy being creative.

Travel Clothes

I've always found there is no *way* to pack the perfect clothes for travel (sorry to be so negative!). It helps that you can't take along all your *junk*—you usually settle for what's new and fresh.

Still, four things screw you up: ONE—weather. It is not doing in London what *The New York Times* said it was when you left home. While you are in the *airplane* they start a warm spell the British Isles haven't experienced since 1904, and there you are in your woolies. Two—events. Things come up during the trip you didn't know you'd need clothes for. The cocktail party for which you brought the cocktail dress has suddenly been changed to a western barbecue in your honor, so, of course, you *die* in your black strapless chiffon, with fifteen pairs of jeans at home in the closet. THREE—while you're *here, "there"* is kind of remote and unreality sets in to zap your packing nerve. Even if you've *been* there, you can't quite *remember* what the place "feels like"—how people look in restaurants, offices, streets. How can you pack *only* diaphanous cottons for Puerto Rico while outside the window where you are six inches of snow have fallen? How can you stow thermal underwear (even though seven people told you you'd freeze your tail in Peking without it) when hot-blooded you sleeps between sheets in *January?* FOUR—natural Inferiority. No matter how meticulously you plan (this time, by God, you are going to get the clothes thing *right!*), sooner or later you will see a woman in the visited city so well put together you will want to throw you, her and all your terrible clothes right into the canal. There she is in her perfect slub-silk suit, Ferragamo sandals, handbag made in Italian heaven, twenty-four gold bracelets (you only brought your tank watch and grandmother's brooch), and out of her perfect Italian silk blouse is rising this perfect Italian silk face—Devastating! Well, even *without* the perfect Italian silk face and despite the four travel-packing curses, after a couple of days in the new city or country you will absorb the atmosphere enough to start looking *better* wearing what you brought combined with maybe a couple of new purchases. That's been my experience at least.

A word about packing.

1. Don't pack full. You will expand as you travel. *Everywhere* it is written you should only take one bag and fit everything in, but I don't see *why.* The airline allows you two bags; you have to wait in the luggage-claim area for *whatever* you bring, so you might as well take *two* pieces of luggage. This isn't so you can pack *more,* but just so everything won't be so jammed in and you won't go crazy trying to get the bag zipped up or the top down. If you're going to lots of *different* cities, then, yes, one bag is probably better.

2. You can't possibly take all the things you might need, so try to figure out how to double up a little on bags and shoes. Navy, after dark, looks *almost* black, and vice versa, so perhaps you can get away with navy *or* black accessories though you may take navy *and* black clothes. You might try for one perfect daytime bag that goes with a *lot* of things. My one and only (tan) woven Fendi seems to make it with brown, black and burgundy.

3. Take one thing warmer (a sweater?) and one thing less heavy (a silk dress?) than you think you'll need for this place at this time of year. It may be *the* thing you'll wear every day.

4. Take two or three eight-by-ten brown envelopes. Shopping receipts, newspaper articles clipped in travel, addresses of new friends need someplace to go rather than the pockets of your suitcase.

5. When you get home from a trip, replenish your makeup bag immediately. At that point, you'll remember what you're running

out of. By the next trip you'll have forgotten and will have to investigate the whole mess.

May I say *this* about clothes, whether you are traveling or staying home? One thing that separates chic girls from others is that the former wear enough *things*. Fearful girls *skimp*. . . . They'll do the Peter Pan collar but never use a brooch to clip it together. Or they've got the collar and brooch, so why would you also need *pearls?* They refuse to go the distance—jewelry, scarf, belt, handkerchief in pocket, knee socks, whatever! Bracelets may be the *most* missing item from "skimpy dressers." The first time I saw Diane von Furstenberg—*her* again!—I couldn't count the things the woman had on—though she never lets anything interfere with that incredible *shape*. I counted choker, necklaces, lapel pins, earrings, two belts, wristwatch, mid-calf boots. No, she wasn't kitsch but she was *complete*. Geraldine Stutz, elegant owner/president of Henri Bendel, is *always* complete. *Not* to go to a Fashion Group lunch but to the *office*, Gerry wears earrings, bracelets, rings, pins, maybe a cloche. If I'm making these women sound ridiculous and loaded down, *forget it!* They look divinely light and *un*burdened. I think more mouseburgers *don't* wear enough stuff, not because they don't *have* it—bracelets come from the *dime* store—but because doing the whole *thing* means you're taking yourself and fashion seriously, and what will people *say?* They'll say *bravo!*

All of this may be more than you want to know, not only about packing but about clothes generally. There's a catch to every fashion rule anyway—if you *only* put your money into things you wear most, you'd never have bought the art deco evening bag that's the love of your life and has been amortized over twelve years. And why *not* have "too many different colors in your wardrobe" if kaleidoscopic color thrills you? As for dressing to suit *your* figure, ruffles, pleats and flounces may *not* go with hips, but your phone never stops ringing, etc. Listen, the only rule in the world, as we've already said, is to have fun with fashion and let it bring you joy.

Now let's go right to sex and have fun with *that*.

Chapter Seven

SEX

The Sex Connection

Sometimes I think sex is like a big gray cat! When you *want* it to come sit on your lap, it's just as likely to stalk off and go look for a plate of Tender Vittles; then, later, when you're reading in bed or visiting with friends and couldn't care *less,* this arrogant, *miserable* feline will climb up on your stomach and start purring its head off! Murder! Well, sex can be as arbitrary and arriving-at-the-wrong-time as it *likes,* it is still the most sinus-clearing, mind-blowing, intoxicating, illuminating, exhilarating experience in the world, don't you agree? I believe one emerges from a night of making love closer to the human race—especially closer to all *men*—than you can ever be at any other time. Some barrier is removed . . . some intimacy born. I remember splendid years of slipping out of the Beverly Hills Hotel at dawn to pick up Appletrees, my fourteen-year-old Buick station wagon (parked on a side street because she really wasn't up to being seen at the Beverly Hills Hotel porte-cochere), feeling as alive as an eel from having been at it all night with a New York friend I had a long liaison with, and another time leaving a lover at the Plaza Athénée in Paris to taxi across town in rumpled red chiffon to *my* eight-dollar-a-night room at the

Normandie, loved senseless, and feeling enormous affection for every street cleaner, flower vendor, tram conductor, traffic cop, schoolboy. There is *no* feeling like that one. George Sand said, "Sex is the most respectable and holy thing in all creation, the most serious act in life." Agreed.

I am *still* preoccupied with sex—as a concomitant to love, yes, but also for its own sake. (There *is* sex without love and, no, hair doesn't grow out of your fingertips when it happens!) I have been a faithful married woman for many years now, but am grateful for an active sex life long *before* marriage, from the time I *gave* (not lost!) my virginity at age twenty. I have known all my life that sex was *good,* that it was somehow a compliment when a man wanted you "that way," and believe me, it took some *doing* to figure that out in Little Rock, Arkansas, in the thirties when I was a teenager. Young ladies were told *hourly* (is there such a thing as minute-ly?) by their mamas to keep little boys' hands *off* them until they got married, and should a girl feel something flutter *before* her wedding night (*on* her wedding night, the opening of the Aswan Dam was promised), it meant she was trash, her *family* was trash, and she was also probably mentally defective. Through all that garbage I *still* knew that sex was *good,* managed to repudiate my "training," and by some miracle, to keep sexual feelings intact, although God knows one felt guilty about feeling the *feelings!*

Then gradually, while keeping a good-girl profile and also managing to keep my virginity—you just removed hands from wherever they weren't supposed to be and you ran a lot!—a Little Rock girl in the thirties and forties would have run in front of a *train* in order not to go "all the way"—I began to discover, around age nineteen, that being wanted "that way" gave a girl a kind of power over men, that though most girls were *prettier* than I, they could not and *did not* necessarily get men more turned on. Perhaps my "rivals" kept themselves more in check. It was supposed to be ruination to show *any* signs of sexual response, and God *knows* nobody would marry you if you actually *had* sex before marriage or even went "too far," but I got pretty shrewd at figuring out how far too far *was* . . . when to stop in order to drive a man (if you could call a seventeen-year-old man a man) almost to suicide and yet remain chaste. I found this could all be accomplished with one's clothes *on,* so when I finally got around to taking them *off,* it was like a cook who has worked out thirty-two things to do with chicken and is then introduced to filet mignon and Camembert.

Anyway, straight through my first attempted assignation with my own *uncle* (he was thirteen, I was nine) in my grandmother's attic in Osage, Arkansas (only we couldn't manage *anything* because of anatomical differences—he was a very mature thirteen, me a scrawny nine), through all those nonobligatory passes in Little Rock Pulaski Heights Junior High School (nobody had to encourage *those* boys, they were randy twenty-five hours a day), through high school in Los Angeles (*more* boys, even randier), through my first affair (age twenty), through *other* affairs, and, finally, married at thirty-seven, I've managed to believe that it—sex—was/is *about* the best thing that ever happens to us. If I had to choose between sex and food, I would choose food, but I'd choose sex over *nearly* everything else.

So, what could there possibly be left to *write* about sex? . . . And why would one even *try* to add to the sexual lore we don't need any more of? Ego! Pure ego. I want you to know *my* thoughts on this most fascinating of all subjects. I'm not even going to offer hints from other men or women who might know something more than I, because I'm not sure you can *mix* sex advice. . . . Dr. Helen Singer Kaplan, lumped with Masters and Johnson plus a dab of Wardell Pomeroy. No, this sex-sagery is *mine*. So knowing that you don't need it, that the only sexual knowledge that means *anything* is your *own*, here are my thoughts on the subject.

What Are the Different Kinds of Sex?

There are five kinds:
1. MAGIC SEX, which happens when you are falling in love.
2. INTIMATE, COMFORTABLE SEX with somebody you know well and adore—your husband? Longtime lover?
3. FRIENDLY SEX. You know and like him but he's not that special in your life.
4. CASUAL SEX—anything from a one-night stand to three-weeks-without-a-future, but it *feels* okay.
5. SCRUFFY SEX with a new or old lover and you wish you hadn't.

I've had *all* of these. Have you? (I prefer one and two!) Let's explore.

Making it with someone you adore *is* magic. The crazy-loveliness of being with this *one* person, remembering between times what you did to each other the *last* time . . . well, it *is* possibly the best thing that ever goes on in our bodies and minds, don't you agree?

The trouble is, you can't experience that incredible magic indefinitely. When people live together, sleep together, work together over the years, sex can be loving and satisfying, but sexual tension vanishes. Can't you keep it alive? Well, if he travels a lot, so you're a bit like strangers when you do get together, or if you play games and torment each other, or he has other girls and one of you is unsure of the other, married love *may* stay somewhat more "intriguing," but those acts are expensive emotionally, and who wants to be worried sick about your *husband?* (He's supposed to be there to make you feel cherished and secure.)

No matter what you do, I devoutly believe it's hard to maintain *magic* sex with someone you've been married to or living with longer than three years. Just the *status* of not being married to each other is a sex plus, of course, and you may be able to maintain the sex-craziness for seven, eight or even more years if you are *not* married (and don't see each other constantly); married, I would give us only three!

That, obviously, is why many people change friends often if single, get a divorce and marry somebody else if married, or, in some cases, take a lover. Some married couples who are *not* unhappy with marriage or with each other and wouldn't consider divorce, do long for that incredible-falling-in-love *magic* sex again, so they start a new "friendship."

If married, that's for *you* to decide, my dear. I had twenty years of amour *before* marriage and got falling-in-love sex more or less out of my system! (We do sound smug, don't we? You should have seen me in one of my *suicidal* periods before marriage, or even *now* about other things!) If you marry at twenty and stay married, I don't know *when* you're going to work magic sex into your life more than once, but I won't worry about you. Maybe you'll totally disagree that magic sex can't continue indefinitely and you *will* continue. Cheers!

Intimate, comfortable sex and friendly sex seem self-explanatory; we don't need a blueprint. What about casual sex—sex *without* love? It can, indeed, feel good, moralists to the contrary notwithstanding! Don't you imagine that's what it's like with animals?—never mind who your partner is, just get in there and copulate! There's nothing wrong with that procedure except the animals are missing one of the sexiest accessories humans bring to sex—the brain! Though not *required* for the act of sex, "brainwork" (relating to your partner emotionally and intellectually) does make it more delicious. You could also say sex without love or deep friendship is like getting a massage . . . it feels good but is very impersonal. Masturbation is massagelike also. Listen, I hope you'll have a smorgasbord and enjoy most of the possibilities. I believe *any* kind of sex is better than doing without.

Nobody Is Attracted to Both Sexes "Equally"

If somebody is so-called bisexual, the sex he or she is fondest of is usually his *own;* almost never is it the other way around—that *he* sleeps with men *and* women but prefers women, or she sleeps with both sexes but prefers men. Dalliance with the "opposite" is frequently a step taken to try to prove, to himself/herself and others, that he or she is *not* gay. I don't know where this *gets* us; I'm merely pointing it *out.*

How Sexy Are You?

Sex drive means, I think, not how often you go to bed with a man because it's friendly, because there's nothing to watch on television, because you adore him and/or you want him never to leave you, but how often you feel like having an orgasm—in other words, how often your body needs a physical fix. It's kind of hard to separate the motivations for sex from the capacity or drive—some of the most sexually active people are driven more by *mental* demons (e.g., Don Juan) than by pure physical lust. But then there is the documented case of that barely literate dirt farmer in South Dakota who doesn't know from chasing girls but has had sex with his wife twice a day for the past thirty years—that's what one would have to call a *sex* drive. Why are some of us strong and some of us "weak" sexually? Let's see.

How Much Sex Do You Need?

Dr. Don M. Sloan, director of the Sex Therapy Clinic of New York Medical College, says we all started out in infancy sexually equal, but school and parental training, plus other influences, deadened *some* of us, while others were left sexually intact. Sexual needs *fluctuate*, of course, even after we're grown and our sex drive generally already determined. You've noticed surely that at times you can practically *think* yourself into orgasm, while other times you can have tried everything but starring in your own sex movie and *still* remain "unconsummated."

So what are your basic needs now? They could be *anything*. People lie a lot, but unquestionably some *do* require frequent (daily or oftener) sex; others *don't*. When I was young, my dear little friend Candy said she had orgasms if a man just breathed on her, and I figured the minute I stopped seeing the attractive but non-sexual athlete I was seeing and was breathed on a lot, like Candy, I *too* would be multiorgasmic. It never happened. There are undoubtedly women who require six orgasms per night (though I never met one!). If *your* body doesn't, why push? In an article in *MS*, Sara Mandelbaum quotes an interviewee: "The ideal sexual encounter is to take plenty of time and when you can't stand it another minute, make it!" That about says it, and you don't need to do that a hundred times a night, right? As we've said, sex drives differ, so whatever amount of sex is right for you, go!

Okay, is a nonstop orgasm-achiever sexier than someone not so "prolific"? You're not going to get *me* to admit a thing like *that!* There is so much *else* to do in bed than peak, and everything, in its way, is sexy. Bed is where you, a mouseburger, are possibly your *most* content—as well as your most accomplished. (I know you're just supposed to enjoy yourself in bed and not "achieve" so I'll defend "accomplished" in a moment.) Sexual activity is our *oxygen* . . . lifegiving, peacemaking—everything, from flirtation to being spread-eagled and ravished all night long and not getting any sleep whatever, is important, never mind that orgasm is *also* pleasurable. We are, I would say, passionate. Passion comes from your head as well as from your loins (isn't that a sweet word!). One doesn't *have* to have more than one or two orgasms per night—or none!—to enjoy sex. (If *you* have more, I forgive you!)

Help for the Non-Orgasmic

Let's talk a moment about not having *any* orgasms. That's rare these days with masturbation being so acceptable and vibrators creating orgasms practically in a *lamp*post, but let's say you're not climaxing with a *man* and would like to. As my friend Judith said recently, "People just don't realize an orgasm isn't that easy to *come* by!" Well, shrinks and other professionals are not always the *most* helpful in sorting out this problem. They will be sympathetic, but the only way you can get things *fixed* is in the *arena*—during the *sex act itself.* If you aren't having orgasms with a man, these are among the things you will want to do:

1. Learn to masturbate alone and get used to the feeling of having orgasms; then you may better be able to get the same result when lovemaking with a man. Don't rule out the idea of needing to do things *yourself* as you make love to a man to actually peak.

2. Change partners. . . . Sometimes it *is* his fault, or at least your lack of enthusiasm for this particular man keeps you from climaxing.

3. Have an orgasm with a man any way you *can*, not necessarily when he's *in* you—that's the *least* likely way! Bravely try to show him what you want him to do. I think the best talk is with *body* language rather than spoken words—taking his hand off *there* and putting it somewhere else, or possibly drawing back a bit if he's doing something you don't like so that he can't get *at* you as well. . . . Men *do* get "messages." I think "sensible" before-the-act or during-the-act conversation about what *you* like and what *he* likes is a passion killer. I wouldn't. Once in a while, a "Don't stop" may be in order, or you could *occasionally* murmur a "would you mind," then describe an activity you fancy. "Listen" at all times with eyes, ears, brain and body, since he's probably sending *you* messages, too.

It's not that easy to do all this, especially with a man you've been sleeping with for the past seven months or seven *years!* ("Why is she showing me this now? Does this mean the witch hasn't enjoyed herself in seven years?") Nevertheless, if you love the man, or he's going to be your sex connection for some time to come, you have to *try* to get beyond this shame phase and reach for what you need. There is almost no chance that you are technically frigid. You really can be orgasmic if you're determined.

About masturbation—whether to masturbate is academic by now. All the women I discuss these things with say they wouldn't have survived without it and *still* couldn't. *Where* to masturbate? Any place where you won't be disturbed. Feminist writer Betty Dodson recommends a complete ritual including music and incense. As for how often, that depends on how often you *feel* like it. In *The Sensuous Woman*, "J" advises that we rev up to twenty or more times in one session. I got to four once and was ready for a *respirator!* Don't *force* interest in your sexual self, but don't fail to acknowledge and respond to it either. I don't think I'd go *too* many days without masturbating if that were the only sexual activity available. After doing *lots* of masturbating, however, I think you occasionally have to abstain . . . you get *too* preoccupied. And if you masturbate *instead* of making love to a man when you *can,* you may just have gotten lazy and scared of men.

Final thought: If you have been having trouble reaching a climax with a particular man, consider "saving up" for a day or two—no masturbating—so that you're really hungry when you meet him and almost anything will carry you over the brink.

(P.S. Men usually don't like to *think* about your masturbating— like you should save everything for *them.* Don't tell!)

Let's just say masturbation is one of life's free, harmless, deserved pleasures.

Getting to Feel Desirous When You Aren't

If you would like to feel more sensuous and turned on more of the time when somebody is making love to you, I suggest something very simple: *exercise.* All that stretching, bending, rolling about seem to put one into touch with one's body—to get one's organs shifted around. I find, every morning of the world, after an hour of flapping about, I feel somewhat turned on, and this one special exercise is an almost infallible passion-arouser, for me at least. *Exercise:* Lie on your back on the floor, knees bent, and tuck your ankles under your buttocks. Now lift fanny off floor as high as you can (shoulders, neck and head are still on floor) and slowly bring knees together. Hold for a moment or two, then lower your back to the floor again, one vertebra at a time. Do this ten times. It *does* seem to unlock the viscera.

How You Feel About How You Look
Affects Orgasm

If you basically *like* your breasts, hips, hair, pelvis and tummy, the sap will probably flow and, no other hang-ups pressing, you'll have an orgasm. If you are *uneasy* about any of your body parts, a logjam (or sap-jam) can result. Of course, you are the same basic *you* all the time, but sometimes you look at yourself and feel lush, and other times you look and think, Who is this *gargoyle?* Your body proportions have nothing whatever to do with orgasm, of course—we *know* that. We also know you're supposed to love yourself even if you're a *toad.*

But if your mind turns *off* because of the way you perceive yourself on a particular day, then that does *indeed* affect whether or not you can climax.

So what are you supposed to do about all this? Well, one thing that makes *me* feel desirous and desirable is having a flat stomach. I can't even *have* an orgasm if I look down and see my stomach all pooched out. Full, bushy hair makes me feel sexy—skimpy hair (as in dirty) is a libido sapper. I think it helps to wear pretty clothes to a rendezvous. If you're living with a man or *married* to him, not being grease-streaked from cleaning the oven or dust-dappled from reorganizing the attic can also make sex pleasure more *likely. He* will be turned on no matter how dust-dappled or grease-streaked you are—can a television crew and three rolling cameras keep a hungry Afghan from his Alpo?!—but we're talking about making *you* feel sexier. Surely there will be times in your life . . . we hope *thousands* . . . when nothing can keep you from orgasm, but there will be other not-quite-so "automatic" times when thinking you look *great* (a cross between Empress Josephine and Cher) isn't going to *hurt!*

Don't Give in to Nerves

Orgasm doesn't happen easily, or even *happen,* if you're nervous—but, how, pray, are you supposed to relax when you are one big nerve ending because this man is so *important* to you, or this is possibly a secret assignation and you shouldn't even *be* here, or you're afraid you *look* scruffy? Also, as a successful career girl, you are sometimes going to arrive at your assignation tired and preoccupied. Well, you can be tense, tired and preoccupied as a fox at the hunt, but you don't have to show it. Jagged and jittery are the *death* of passion. . . . Force yourself to put aside the world you brought with you, to be languorous and slow, to *seem* to be at ease. Can you playact a little? Think sloe-eyed Turkish harem seductress until you actually *feel* calmer. When you get to play *itself,* slow and deliberate are always better than anybody marching in on football cleats to "strike up the band" and trying for a touchdown. The lovely things that are meant to happen *will* happen if you'll just try to relax. That's undoubtedly why some people have the good sense to take steamy and relaxing showers and baths together before anything *serious* begins.

To Fake or Not to Fake

I think faking is like using drugs—okay *sometimes,* but you don't want to *depend* on it/them. I can't imagine not faking *ever.* To say one must never fake is like advising somebody never to *lie.* How could *any*body get through life without an occasional (good) *lie*—"I had a lovely time at your party," "You definitely *don't* look fifty-three," etc. Believe me, men would fake it if they *could*—I feel sorry for them because they *can't*—at least not very effectively (more in a moment). Why is "making it" so important? Aside from the physical pleasure it provides, *not* to have an orgasm or ejaculate seems somehow to indicate to one's partner (though it shouldn't) that one isn't masculine or feminine enough to produce this ultimate proof of sexuality—a little *embarrassing.* Well, a woman can *pretend* the "display," then later, alone, really finish everything (masturbate); nobody has to know at the time you didn't "make good." Alas, a man can't so easily get away with that.

At any rate, after someone has made love to you with skill and

168

grace, an orgasm is a way of saying you enjoyed yourself, even as you compliment a host on a wonderful spinach quiche. A man is supposed to be able to *tell* when you are faking, but I don't think any man can *physically* tell—how could he? Some particularly sensitive and sophisticated men are able to *suspect* fakery and will question you; if you've got one of those, *don't* fake! I have just never been with a man who couldn't be "faked with" so that must mean that I'm either a better actress or my men are dumber, or both (dear me). May I say if you fervently want *not* to fake, then don't *start*—not one little fake! Faking can be like taking thyroid pills; once you take the artificial kind, your system stops producing its *own;* once having started the fakery with a particular man, you will have to keep *on*. If you're planning to get there naturally with him, you have to *admit* when it isn't happening and keep trying for the real thing.

How bad *is* fakery? Well, not reaching orgasm with a man some or even all of the time doesn't hurt you physically, and, were it *about* to, you could always masturbate later—but it can make you resentful. There he is, all spilled over and happy as a sand dab, ready for slumber, dinner or a Jets game on TV, while you, sensitive creature, are faking your head off and left with this unsatisfied, hollow feeling in your stomach . . . *not* happy, *not* complete. Eventually, both angry *and* guilty, you're apt to confess, and then we have *trouble!* It's hard on a man for you *not* to have orgasms after you've been "having" them, and a chill may settle on your friendship unless he's able to produce the real thing for you and *soon*. If you have more than *one* lover, possibly you'll have an orgasm with the one who turns you on but not with the others. That rare glory—sexual chemistry—usually *doesn't* exist with *every* man you sleep with. Anyhow, I don't think you should *always* fail to have an orgasm with *any* man and depend on fakery with him plus masturbation later or you will grow to resent him. Whoever he is, he should deliver this peak experience *some* of the time. Listen, now that Shere Hite has corroborated that most of us have orgasms *not* by penetration, but by clitoral stimulation, and if enough men *know* that, or we *tell* them, we can now have more orgasms *during* lovemaking and faking won't be so necessary. Happy ending!

Sex After Forty

When you get to forty or fifty (will you *ever* be that old?!) you may have to "go for the orgasm" at the start of each lovemaking session, and when you *do* decide, then be gutsy—*ask* for what you need (with body language) and do *yourself* what is needed. Get into the right position, *change* positions, stop one thing and start something else until you have it right! Help with your own hands if necessary; have him play with you *while* he is f——g you. This is a fairly dumb analogy, but I think declaring to yourself that you *will* have an orgasm is not unlike a politician declaring that he will run for office. You have a better chance of getting nominated and elected if you "declare"—very few politicians get *drafted*. You don't declare *verbally,* of course, only to yourself. This commitment to an orgasm probably won't be necessary when you're young—sex is quite automatic in your twenties and thirties—but it may be appropriate as you age. Incidentally, *you* will be sexy until the end of your life; you are a mouseburger! The way to do that is never to stop f——g. Find and keep someone *always* for that purpose.

You Turned On (Not Faking) Is the Most Aphrodisiacal Thing in the World for a Man

Somebody working away at you like beavers building their dam—slap, slap, pat, pat, paddle, paddle—is *friendly* (and gets E for effort) but if that somebody is squishy-mushy *himself,* is he nearly as satisfactory to you in bed as a man fully aroused? Of course not! Conversely, being hot yourself simply makes *you* better at what you're doing to *him.* One is not always hot, of course, and you can be *"good"*—make him happy—even though not turned on yourself (otherwise, prostitutes would not be so well paid). However, you in honest heat put an extra magic into lovemaking; the hotter *you* are, the hotter *he* will be. If, indeed, you are under full sail, you can *forget* all the rules about lovemaking, certainly including these, because a girl gripped by passion somehow *knows* what to do with her hands, mouth, toes, knees, etc.! You are *not* hot all the time, however, and at those times you must use your expertise if you want to complete the sex act satisfactorily. Now let me issue a warning: When you are *not* turned on yet but *expect* to be, it's tempting just to go on *doing* nice, arousing things for him because he *likes* them so much. Possibly you should let *up* on him a bit and wait to feel something *yourself* . . . he will then feel even *more*—when *you* are aroused—than if you just kept going and "finished him off."

Never Underestimate C—— Power

Not only will a man kill for you if yours (the most secret part of you) is the one (although few of us put him to the trouble), he will worship you, forsake *nearly* all others and act as silly as a Saint Bernard who has drunk his own brandy. A man sexually in love is one of life's marvels—so vulnerable, so dear and puppylike!

I've written a lot about how *rotten* men can be in the next chapter, and they *can* be, but that's only part of their sum. Another part (a very wonderful part) is their being almost *demented* because of what we do *to* and *with* them in bed, because of this special thing between our legs. I'm not talking about somebody a man merely f——s, but the one he *adores,* the one with c—— power (I promise not to use that word, or facsimile, too often, but it's really the only one that will do in this particular explanation!). He loves you, the *person,* yes, but just *thinking* of this special section of you gets him crazy and erect. Kings and lesser men have been *toppled* by this power of ours, but you and I don't want to *destroy* anybody—we just want to enjoy a man's being totally hooked on our . . . Oh, damn, I *promised!* Anyway, I'm *convinced* this particular power is the best of all kinds. Used properly, it hurts no one but simply glorifies and gladdens us all. Glory to the *power!*

Okay, perhaps you, a single girl, wonder why the man doesn't leave his wife and *marry* you since you have this terrific attribute. Because she has *another* kind, you see—wife and *mother* power! She's his *mate,* but more importantly, she's the mother of his little look-alikes; they grew in her and she *got* them here. Many men are *very* dynasty-conscious—I think *they* frequently want children more than *women* do. And don't forget that his wife, your rival, may have supported him emotionally through the bad times and he has some sense of loyalty though you don't want to hear about it! Based on his description of her, she's The Thing! But he's probably "keeping two sets of books," and powerful she *is.* Both kinds of power are rewarding—power always *is*—but of the two, I prefer *ours.* It doesn't always win out over wife/mother clout, but honestly, darling, some of the men you *think* you've got to marry, you really *don't!* They'd be *disaster,* you just can't see that *now!* Incidentally, be prepared to *lose* some of your c—— whoops!— power if you marry—*some* of it, not all (the man will begin to cherish you for other reasons and, my God, first thing you know you've got the *wife* power!). Enjoy the other kind full strength while you are single; married you can get *later.*

His Beautiful Penis

We know men worship our female equipment to the point of near craziness—isn't it odd how little is ever written or said by us about *their* beautiful equipment? I will say it now!

A delicately rosy, silky-satin, somehow innocent, always-vulnerable erect penis is *probably* the most fascinating object in the world. I mean, can the cockpit of the Concorde or a cymbidium orchid or a frog drinking water backwards even *compare* in fascination! Of course not! Size isn't supposed to matter, of course, any more than a woman's breast size matters. Well, you know perfectly well breast size *matters*—they just say that to cheer up us small-chested ones—and there is nothing like a *big* (anything over four inches erect), longing-to-be-appreciated, grateful for *anything* you do to it, show-offy, lovely male penis to bring tears to the eyes and joy to the psyche. I hear about girls who don't *like* this part of a man's anatomy—the late Helen Lawrenson wrote *vehemently* about it in her book *Whistling Girl.* Said Helen, "I was lying on my back with him kneeling over me when suddenly, with no warning, he thrust himself into my mouth. I thought he was going straight down my throat and I was in utter panic, as well as gagging. I lay there paralyzed, my eyes shut tight and I was, of course, unable to speak. Finally, I managed to wriggle out from under, scurry into the bathroom and throw up."

What an odd reaction! A penis may or may not send you into rhapsodies when it is *in* you, but it's *his;* he loves it and, in an aroused state, the penis is an absolutely sure sign he finds us attractive. Do we *want* one? Good God, *no!* The day Freud came up with penis envy, I think his brains *had* to have been out to lunch, but I *am* definitely grateful every *man* has one. Do you enjoy looking at pictures of men's penises in *Playgirl* and other magazines? I *don't.* I always thought I *would* until the pictures materialized a few years ago. Somehow this accessory and the man have to be in the room *with* one—and the man has to care about me and "mine."

So what do you do about all this perfection? *Admire* him, of course. Men are *so* insecure about their priceless possession. You think *you* worry about your thirty-two **A-cup** size and thirty-nine-inch hips! Well, with vaginas we at least have *auxiliary* sexual equipment, i.e., *breasts*. This one erogenous zone is *all* he has, so *you,* pussycat, must appreciate it. Just touch, pat, caress as you feel moved to do so, sort of like you cuddle and caress a puppy or kitty-cat. These are admiring things to *say* to a man: "This is the most beautiful one in the world. . . . This is the *biggest* one in the world. . . . This is the most *adorable* (sensitive, incredible, responsive) one in the world. . . . I absolutely *worship* this penis. . . . I can't go too long *without it.* . . . I'm kind of crazylady about this thing. . . . I am *wild* about your pr———, gorgeous!" etc., etc., etc. Listen, he will welcome and believe nearly *anything.*

Love His Entire Body

He has *other* valuable parts as well as a penis that you must make him happy about. Pick one or two and begin. You can endear yourself to a man so there's no ungluing him if he thinks *you* think his entire body and face are beautiful. Do you think plain man are *not* vain . . . that they couldn't feel *comfortable* with compliments about their tiny shoulders, bony knees, ordinary behinds? You are wrong. The homeliest man (or woman) cares *outrageously* for the various parts of himself, sometimes *more* than a beauty cares. The *less* gorgeous will work *torturously* to make whatever it is *better* and lavish attention on the not-so-beautiful part, like parents with a slow-learner child. I guarantee that if you *do* love this man's penis, knees, ankles, elbows, ears and toes as though they were those of a beauty, you will get to thinking they *are,* and he will get to thinking they are, too. What a fabulous gift for somebody you love.

"Good in Bed" Is *Still* Possible

As we've said, there is *endless* sex instruction now, so who *can't* be or, indeed, who *isn't* a splendidly functioning sex machine?! Just about everybody, that's who! Knowledge and "being allowed to" simply don't make you "good." You can *still* be "sexier" than other women if that appeals to you—and it always appealed to *me*. Enlightened as your rivals may be, do you suppose there's any comparison between *you* in bed with your need to please, your craving for affection, your passion, energy and well, *drive,* and other women in *their* narrow or fat little beds? Don't be ridiculous!

You know how talking to 60 percent of the people you talk to is *boring* even though they know plenty of words and can put sentences together. Well, for the men of the world, so is going to bed with at least 60 percent—possibly a higher percentage than *that*—of the *women* in the world boring. Those women don't talk like you or care like you or try like you; in a word, they don't make love like you. Yes, I know spontaneity and romance are the Big Two these days, that one is not supposed to prove anything in *bed,* for God's sake, just fall in with a dear person and satisfaction for all will ensue as surely as stars fall on Alabama. How shall we put it? . . . Well, the stars fall more wondrously—especially for *him*—with women who *try*. We don't want you not to enjoy *yourself,* obviously, but there are *several* reasons a mouseburger would want a man to be happy making love to her: she loves him, she wants him to stay *with* her, she wants a mink coat(!), etc., etc., and she's willing to make sure that he *is* happy. And then there's *pride*. Do you always want to be a guest at someone else's party, a passive little thing who waits for invitations, or do you want to be a fabulous hostess and make people happy in *your* home . . . responsible, exciting, grown-up. Well, that's somewhat like the choice between merely enjoying *yourself* in bed (to the point of reaching orgasm) and being "good in bed." Repeat: Being good means you are not only done unto, you take the initiative.

If they say you are Good in Bed, rejoice. It means *he* had fun, *you* had fun, and the sun is smiling down.

The Specialty

On the subject of "good in bed," may I add one suggestion, and now I'm going to be personal—I hope this doesn't embarrass us *both*. I have been so unhappily in love when I was young, a playback of some of the scenes could have us both weeping into our Beaujolais, also so inept *socially* you'd have longed to get me out of the room before I *destroyed* myself, but I do have, or *had*—I've been faithfully married a long time now—this thing which endeared me to many "friends"—the ability to bring a man without *fail*, to orgasm.

"Neither snow, nor rain, nor heat, nor gloom of night stays these couriers from the swift completion of their appointed rounds" . . . or something like that. I was, you might say, a sort of "never-fail" machine. I only remember *twice* somebody in my custody not making it. . . . What terrifying experiences. If hanging by my toes from the third floor of the Chateau Marmont could have done any good, I'd have tried, but *nothing* worked!

Well, anyway, it's not a bad little specialty to have—bringing a man inexorably to climax—and I'd like to encourage you to have it. Not all men, by any means, *need* to be helped, and certainly not when you're young and most of your men are also young and bursting with life. It's just that *no* man should ever leave you not happy with his performance. There isn't a great deal *to* this specialty. You need stamina, of course, but anybody who can get not-quite-thick-enough cream to whip or get a cat to let you clip his toenails can get the hang of it. Now, obviously, all your "successes" can't be achieved during intercourse—women are not the *only* ones who peak more easily when the man and woman are not *necessarily* bumper to bumper. *You* may not reach orgasm at *all*, or not until later. Why would a woman be propelled to such "selflessness"— always making sure *he* is orgasmic? Three reasons: One, usually you like or even *love* the man. Two, one is always proud of a specialty, whether it's growing African violets or making your own mustard, and you tend to want to improve that specialty. Three, this skill keeps a man *glued* to you.

So would you like to be his never-fail friend? These are the rules: Quietly assume when you begin to make love that you are not going to leave the bed (couch, floor or ceiling) until he has had an orgasm. You don't *communicate* this purposefulness. . .

175

Teeth-clenching would be particularly bad in certain phases of the evening; you are soft as marshmallow, playful as Lassie, sometimes even *passive*, but in your head you know you are going to succeed because you always *do!*

Okay, what will be your M.O.? Ah, that I can't tell you because it has to be based on what *he* likes; men *are* all different! The important thing is not to stop doing *something* until "it" happens. You could take a lesson from *you*. You know sometimes when you are close to orgasm and don't quite reach it but *could* if he would keep doing what he's doing *longer,* or do something else entirely, only you haven't the courage to tell him? Okay, he can *also* make it by your doing the "right" things and doing them long enough. He may not be able to tell you what they are, but some combination of routines—and just plain patience—will work. Don't give up.

If you keep right on enjoying your "work" and simply won't take no for an answer, you probably *will* bring him to orgasm. But what about the times when, no matter how relentlessly and lovingly you persevere, *it* doesn't happen, and then he really *would* like you to stop? How do you know when it's one of *those* times or the other kind, when you should keep going? You *don't* and nobody can tell you! What one wants to *avoid* is forcing some little cry from him like, "Susan, could you knock it off, I'm getting a cramp in my knee!" You're probably safe in continuing any one specific from three to five minutes—yes, that long—before you decide to stop doing that and start doing something else. Whatever you stop doing, don't stop suddenly—jerky and sudden are the *death* of sensuality. No amount of experience can ever tell you for *sure* when to stop or start but I have confidence in your *instincts.* P.S. I think I've explained that you don't approach *any* of this like a polar bear dipping into the frozen lake to spear a trout; you are languorous but *determined.*

The Coup de Grace

Okay, suppose he is practically turning *blue* and still nothing has happened. His penis may long since have come out of you and you are now "loving him" manually, but even *that* isn't getting results. Then gently take his hand and place it on his own penis and encourage him to masturbate. Keep your hand *near* him, possibly on his testicles; it isn't that you have *abandoned* him, but we all know masturbation is the *easiest* and most "comfortable" way to achieve a climax—there practically isn't *anyone* who can't reach orgasm by masturbating, though not necessarily with an audience, as is the case now. If you gently indicate you *want* him to do this for himself—that you are fascinated and not unpleased with what is happening—you may just get him to do it and the orgasm will come. One has to decide whether this "minor humiliation" for both of you (his achieving orgasm on his own) is worse than his leaving your bed frustrated—I think hardly *anything* is worse than his leaving your bed frustrated.

Suppose he is still orgasmless. Having him masturbate is not for *you* and you've tried everything but resting his elbows in ice water (said to be the late Aly Khan's technique for maintaining erection). Okay, stop making love and do non-*carnal* things for a while. Have some champagne (not too much) and start again later.

Very likely he *will* be able to finish when you resume—he wants to as much as you want him to. You can make the mistake of assuming that because the orgasm doesn't happen easily the man doesn't care for you or even care for sex (one idea is almost as repugnant as the other, don't you agree?) and send him home. Mistake. A man nearly always cares *madly*. . . . He's just having a little trouble.

Stay with him.

How to Go Down on a Man

Listen, just in *case* you don't know how to do this, let's go back to a big basic. I got these rules from a friend who claims to be "the best in the world." I always thought *I* was pretty good, but why should we not hear from the avowed champion?! (Probably nothing here you haven't already figured out for yourself.)

1. Take hold of the base of the penis or slightly higher up—don't grab too hard—with either your left or right hand, it doesn't matter which.

2. Now, using only your lips—keep your teeth *behind* your lips—open your mouth in a big O and put the head of the penis in your mouth.

3. Flick your tongue around this nice penis head and move on *down* the penis, putting more and more of it down your throat. If not entirely stiff, the penis may be lightly held with *both* hands but pretty soon you should be able to take one of your hands away.

4. Put more and more of the penis down your throat. Only a

177

very *large* penis will gag you, and you can always stop and come up for air if you're choking.

5. Now come back *up* again with the same semirelaxed mouth. And go down again.

6. Use your tongue as you go up and down, flicking your tongue about a bit, but don't use your tongue *all* the time.

7. With your left (or right) hand holding the base of his penis, you may use your *other* hand to keep him stiff, if that's needed.

8. Remember to keep your lips firmly down *over* your teeth but not tucked *around* them—you want your lips to be making contact with his penis, but your teeth not bared so they can *hurt* him. Your mouth will be *somewhat* taut throughout this operation; let some saliva run out.

9. Keep going—up and down, up and down, tongue flicking, stopping sometimes to kiss and lick the head of the penis.

10. Doing what you are doing, you should *reasonably* soon bring him to orgasm. In that case, swallow what comes out of him; it's a sign of affection. If he is *not* coming, you may want to stop fellatio (what this divine act is called) and start stroking his penis . . . that way you may be able to *"talk* him home" with dirty, loving language, something you can't do very well if he's in your mouth.

Some men like you to take their balls into your mouth and suck on *those.* Just try that and *see* if he likes this. Again, use your lips, not teeth. You don't have to choose one ball or the other—they just sort of all mush in *together.* You might do this *before* stroking or sucking his penis, or you can stop and do it in the middle. While you are sucking his balls, you may *also* be stroking his penis. Your head will be between his legs when you do this, of course, but you can still reach his penis with your hand. God, I'm getting dizzy!

If you are bringing him to orgasm by stroking, but want to swallow what comes out of him, you can lean down and take his penis in your mouth just as it is about to come. This isn't really necessary, of course, because men rather enjoy *seeing* what they produce—it *is* a kind of achievement. *Whatever* comes out, admire! He is very proud of himself. You may want to spread it all over your breasts, and if you are small-busted like *some* people I know, it goes a long way.

Well, I think that about covers *this* subject, don't you? Just practice and let your instincts and his responses move you along. P.S. Not likely with your man because you're too young, but if a man has had a prostate operation, there will be no ejaculation. Assure him that it doesn't matter, and if you like him it *won't*. You may not actually say reassuring *words* very often but your attitude tells him this is so. Believe me, he cannot be reassured *enough*.

P.P.S. Seems a little mild to mention this after the foregoing, but sucking on a man's *fingers* is sexy, too. Just get one or more of them in your mouth and act as though they're *ice cream*.

The More Sex You Have, the More You Can "Tolerate" and Will Want

Many women over thirty-five are inclined to slack off sexually because they don't *practice*. Slacking off may not be your problem *now*, but as you go through the years, it is vital that you keep active sexually if you want not to start getting brittle, prissy, gray and defeminized. *Whatever* you are good at and quit doing—tennis, trapshooting, speaking French—will tend to grow rusty—and so will sex. The less, the less. I hope you will never go without it for too long. If there is no man around, masturbate, of course, but sex with a man is what keeps you *womanly*. Find *someone* and keep on.

Are You Promiscuous?

Sleeping with more than one man on the same day or in the same week could be considered promiscuous, I suppose, yet I think you can do quite a lot of that and *not* be promiscuous. Maybe liking sex is comparable to the way James Beard feels about food; he cooks and eats a *lot*, but his attitude is never *casual*. People who have a lot of sex are not necessarily casual about it *either*. Now you can't have sex with *everyone* who asks you or attracts you . . . you'd just get too frazzled, and also, sex would lose its *meaning*. Nevertheless, I think you can be multifriended. When I was single (me again—I hope this isn't tacky), it never occurred to me not to have plenty of this pleasurable thing. If, in one week, two of one's dearest friends happened to be visiting (in my case, Los Angeles) from another city, why would one not fit them *both* in? There are, after all, twenty-one breakfasts, lunches, and dinners in one one-hundred-sixty-eight-hour week. It seems to me you can *certainly* accommodate more than one love if neither is classifiable as *the* man in your life.

179

When you are single, *timing* can be ridiculous, of course—too *much* sex available at one peak period, then no men at all for weeks. Also, if you're in love, you may prefer only *one* man (though my credo was always that total fidelity is only for the married!). Make your own rules about "promiscuity." I think enlightened *selfishness* is a good one!

Are You a Nymphomaniac?

Most psychiatrists say there is no such thing as a nymphomaniac, a woman who "can't get enough sex." Some females are so unsure of their appeal to men they only feel "safe" in the act of sex . . . receiving a man's "ultimate tribute." That's who is usually *referred* to as nymphomaniacal. As for needing to have orgasm after orgasm, as we've said, few women actually have that "blight" and those who *do* generally manage with some nice man they are married to or already sleeping with—not going out in the streets to *recruit*. You and I may be semi-nymphomaniacal in terms of feeling more content and *appreciated* in bed than anywhere else, but we aren't insatiable. I'm not anyway, are you? A nymphomaniac, then, is not to concern yourself with being or not being.

Being Kept Is Sexy, But Wearing

I was kept once for about six months. He was a rich New York banker—the quintessential WASP (talk about hating *Jews*—this man could have given Hitler pep talks), old (forty-seven!), and married. I was poor, young (twenty-four), gauche and determined. During my year with this wonderful "find" (I was his secretary), I planned to acquire enough capital to take care of my mother, sister and me for the rest of our lives—no more hives and colitis at the same time while trying to support myself and send money home on fifty dollars a week. Our association began when my "friend" winnowed me from about three dozen other secretarial-job applicants—I tried hard to give off just the right sexy-waif impression— and the "keeping" began a few days after my arrival when he sent me, with his car and chauffeur, to have a suit custom-made for my twenty-fifth birthday—baby-blue gabardine with a peplum! After that, he *picked* my clothes, and the liaison escalated with my moving to my own little apartment on South Curzon Street.

Alas, I was a *terrible* keptee! I kept pestering the man about *money*. I'd been promised a lot he owned above the Bel-Air Hotel on Mulholland Drive, across the street from Ginger Rogers' house. We drove up to look at it one Sunday morning and I said yes, it would do nicely! But then, three weeks later, and subsequently three months after *that*, when it hadn't been transferred to my name, I began to pout and whine a bit. . . . Not good keptee etiquette!

Our relationship did *not* flourish and escalate. The state of being kept—though I never enjoyed going to bed with him, and it didn't bring much money—*was* sexy. I think now almost *any* twenty-five-year-old girl is desirable enough to attract any forty-seven-year-old (rich) man for *this* purpose, if she behaves or misbehaves properly, but, at the time, being "picked" was a particular thrill for me—a breakthrough! All my life men had "respected my mind." Even as a frail young little thing in those days of raging male chauvinism, when men were not supposed to recognize the female's brain if it came up and laid *eggs* on them, people were always recognizing *mine*. Some of them recognized my *sexuality* too, true, but when all one longed for was to look like Ava Gardner and have men destroying themselves over you, parents, relatives, friends, neighbors were always saying things like "Dear little Helen . . . such a good *head* on her shoulders!"

Okay, here at least was somebody who might not have thought my *head* resembled Ava Gardner's, but one's body is right *underneath* one's head, so to speak, and *it* was being recognized for *itself* alone. . . . Somebody wanted me *only* for my physical self, oh joy! I had the *most* beautiful lingerie—ivory satin peignoirs with clouds of maribou, jeweled mules, empire-waisted black lace nighties, and I just loved whooshing around in them. I also had pretty daytime clothes to wear to the office, not bothering much about evening wear—who went *out?* My apartment was furnished; I was given a wood-paneled station wagon named Appletrees, already in his car fleet, but I never got *close* to solvent, let alone wealthy! The more I pestered him about the purchase of a few securities, the cooler he became.

I must have been *really* subtle, like a diesel truck! Finally my keeper went to Europe for the summer with his wife, leaving me with *very* little splash-around money, and I had to get another secretarial job. It's a good thing my little arrangement *didn't* work and that I was so lousy at being kept (one afternoon when he'd lost a million dollars in a bad real-estate deal—a million *meant* something then—I literally went to sleep while he was telling me about it!), because otherwise the rest of my life wouldn't have happened to me. I wouldn't have married David; he wouldn't have helped me write a book; you and I wouldn't be together now. Be kept if you like, but I sort of hope *you're* as bad at it as I was.

The *Almost* Stranger-In-The-Night

One-night stands have a bad name. They shouldn't. I once jotted down some notes in the afterflush of a one-night (I am not going to say *stand*) friendship in the Holiday Inn in Memphis, Tennessee, when I was doing swimwear promotion at a department store. It was a freezing January morning and my new—by then rather *old*—friend, an American Airlines pilot I'd met in flight the night before, had gone off to instruct some young pilots, while I got ready to advance on Gold Brothers. I wrote, "It's like having won a beauty contest, the Grand Prix, the decathlon . . . we made love so hard my teeth nearly fell out and I was somebody *else* for a few hours, wilder than the usual me. I think in one way this kind of instant liaison is *better* than gradual seduction because, once you decide you are going to bed with him if he asks you, you don't have to be coy or giggly or shy or hold anything back when it happens. Once you get to bed, you can pour in your whole self like maple syrup on waffles because you probably are never going to see him again. . . . You feel sort of dramatic and wanton and . . . different! Maybe sex can only happen that intensely when you don't know somebody well so you don't have to be your usual snake-charming, thoughtful, considerate, man-pleasing self and can just please *you* (hmmmmm . . . this may be revealing more than one *should* of one's usual sexual self, but you already know about me by now). Anyway, in this rubber-stamped Holiday Inn in downtown Memphis I have been somebody else and sex has been *total!*"

Pity a girl can't feel like that every day, hmmm? Well, if you're in love with a man, especially if you love him a bit more than he loves you, you are frequently a little apprehensive. Will you marry? Does he have other girls? Is he really committed? Sex is the plasma of a serious affair, but sex in a motel without commitments, without having to prove how lovely, intelligent, thoughtful, caring and *devoted* you are, can be more carefree. There can be aftermath blues, of course, if he's somebody you *want* to hear from again and he never calls, but if you don't have "casual sex" too often and are able *occasionally* to appreciate sex just for itself, heartaches will be minimal.

I never saw that man again or talked to him on the phone, and casual sex was not usually for me, but I hope the captain is still flying one way or another, and that you have your *own* American Airlines pilot once (twice? thrice? oftener?) in a lifetime.

Tristesse in Coitus

Do you have a tendency to get wretchedly hung up over a man just because you are going to bed with him—to let him really get *to* you? Sex *is* so intimate, orgasm so cataclysmic, it's easy to understand why the man in your bed seems so important, but are you being daffy about a *nothingburger?* We've all done it. To quote my friend Giselle, "I nearly worried myself insane over two sinfully mediocre men. One, a near-moron, also *drank* a little, but he was *so* good in bed it never occurred to me during the entire year together that he was almost *criminally* dumb. I cared for him like a Nobel Prize-winner . . . worried, fretted, agonized to the point that my friends nearly gave *up* on me (Giselle, don't you think he's a *tiny* bit limited? they would understatedly inquire). So ridiculous! Now I resent every insecure minute I squandered on such a nit."

A lover of *mine*, rather a passive man, was due at my house for brunch one Sunday with nine other people and called half an hour before the party to say he had a touch of flu, could *not* come over, not to worry about him, blah blah blah. Not to *worry?!* Partly because I needed a host for the party, but mostly from insecurity about a "love relationship," I became *crazy*. He *must* come to brunch, I pleaded, and reluctantly he did, but for the rest of the week I used up eight thousand calories a day charming, sexing and pleasing him. I mean he was a *squirrel* who deserved *no* anxiety, *no* special treatment, but the act of sex sometimes makes us quite idiotic (it happens to men, *too*).

Let me say all this another way: Don't assume just because you're having sex with a man that you have to (1) fall in love with him; (2) get into a big emotional dither; (3) marry him!

183

The Man Some Other Woman Owns
Won't See You

He is a big huggy-bear, and handsome. . . . When you dance with him, however, you might as well be waltzing with a stuffed giraffe. You don't exist for him as a female because he's *hers*. How does a woman keep a man so indifferent to other females? She pumps herself into him, that's how. Let me tell you about a huggy-bear-waltzing-giraffe *I* know. His now-wife got him away from his *then*-wife five years ago. . . . It took her ten years to do *that,* so now she surrounds him like Saran Wrap, as though he were a big asparagus stalk! Nobody can get under there *with* them—she embraces him as lover, husband, father, son, comrade, playmate, and throw in Congressman from your district. She also embraces his son and daughter because *they* belong to him (she's not one of those silly women who repudiates a man's *children*). Before his dying mother died, she also embraced *her*. This girl won't even open a *present* unless he's there to share the opening.

So here's my point: Whereas he possibly *could* get it on for someone else, why should he *bother?* He'd have to get the *stake* out of his heart! So shall we simply plan to live *without* any playback from these men? *I* can, though I mostly think it's better for men to make women feel like *women* even when they belong to others. If two people can *only* respond to each other and make the rest of the world feel like encroachers, I think those people are a little *funny*. No, married people do not have to stray to prove their sexuality, but the most sexual and sensual people *I* know give off warmth and sunshine to *everybody*. My pussycat husband does that, and though I know he is sometimes tempted, tempted and giving in are two different things (thank God!).

How about loving only one man all your life? It happens, of course; you find him when you're a baby-person and that's *it*, though that seems to me like living on soyburgers when there is also beef Wellington, goose stuffed with cherries and pine nuts, little French lamb chops and puréed chestnuts. Anyway, I think the kind of woman I was just *describing*, who burrows into a man to the point of somehow blocking out all other women—as though he had had a frontal lobotomy—is a terrified woman indeed. She pours all her love and energy into *one* man not *so* much because he is magic, but because he is her *haven;* it would just be too scary to have to think about finding and wooing *another.*

A man should like women *more* because of you, though, hopefully, his "more" is kept under control.

You Can't *Have* Everyone You Fancy, Even for Sex, and Even If He Has No Other "Steady Girl"

"Packaging" (how you look and what you offer) is important. Your package can attract many men, but not *all.* A novelist I know was in Hollywood recently and looking forward to meeting two of the most important and attractive male movie stars of our time— both bachelors. One of them, on arriving at the restaurant meeting place, checked with the maitre d' before going to the table, found the woman he was to meet was around forty-five, *not* pretty, and simply left the restaurant. (I love his type, don't you?)

The other man kept the date but spent the evening taunting and chiding the lady; he was not nice. "What did she expect?" asked the woman who had arranged the "date" and was, indeed, fond of her writer friend. "Maggie fantasized that she'd knock either one or both these men right off their space shoes and they'd go back to the Beverly Wilshire for a night of love. Ridiculous! She's witty and articulate and attractive but those movie stars—both much younger than she—can have anybody, from sixteen-year-old princesses to twenty-*three*-year-old novelists, and they're not going to be turned on by a lady who's *not* ravishing and in her forties."

Yes, you can *usually* move out of your league for a brief sexual fling—committing to a woman for one night or a week is not a heavy investment for most men. Still, the most desirable men can have the world's most desirable women—you *know* that—and you must not make yourself unhappy with somebody whose "package" is a lot different from yours.

Everybody *hates* this package idea, many "romanticists" refuse to acknowledge "packaging," but everybody *does* come with one. This might be yours: You're young, charming, energetic, healthy, full of sex appeal, poor, somewhat gauche, not a full-fledged beauty, and you work as a biochemist at a hospital. A mouseburger! Him? He has money, power, fame, charm, sexual drive and possibly also a wife and family. And you're mad about him! The list of "attributes" (never mind the liabilities) that you bring to each other can cause a real *sexual* conflagration, but he may simply be too far "over your head" to spend much *time* with you, much less want to marry you (divorces *cost*). You just may not, indeed, finally make it with this man . . . you may *lose* him. Yes, certain nubile flight attendants (*and* biochemists) *do* marry powerful, famous, rich men (ex-stewardess Shirlee Adams married Henry Fonda) but not often.

The way you can cope with this inequity, which even your sexual dazzle can't alter, is to get important at your *own* work. The man you are now hurting over—too rich and too all those other things—may not be around when you are in your prime, but there will be plenty of others and that is what this book is about. You eventually get into or closer to *their* league, and being in that league is very good for sexual enjoyment. You can have whom you want and nobody will leave you because your *package* isn't satisfactory.

To be personal, I've now "passed up" all the men I was ever miserable about who were too heady a package for *me*, and I became more successful (and sought after!) than *they* ever were. Hah! I worked *hard* to do that and it took years—years—but it makes me happy, literally *happy*, to know that not one of those men who were once "over my head" could now begin to equal *my* dear little package. I know I sound like Medea wrapping Jason in his poisoned flammable coat, but I'm no Medea . . . men are for loving. It's just that living well *is* the best revenge when someone hasn't loved you back! You, little mouseburger, can beat the present sexual tristesse by quietly moving on and up in your life and someday passing him by. You can have your *pick* of good men and you will, as your package improves. Of course, when you're fifty—will that time ever *come?*—promise me you won't lust after a twenty-two-year-old rock star.

186

When *Your* Man Doesn't Want You in Bed

When you're twenty-two, *most* men you're involved with will desire you most of the time—you are at your tender, wantable best. Someday, however, you will be with a man on a date who likes or loves you but, incredibly, is not trying to get you out of your shirt and jeans, though you would like to get him out of *his!* Possible explanations: he's "overcommitted"—he may be "servicing" (oh dear, how equine!) a wife *and* you, and last night was *their* night to make love. Perhaps there's another girl or two in his life and you are his new woman; he may actually have been in bed with one of them just *before* seeing you, and isn't now what you could call *needy!* Perhaps he is a bit older and *tireder* than nubile you, involved with business, a lawsuit, a difficult client, difficult children, and they've sapped his strength. Alas, men *do* have to ration sex at times in their lives. Be tolerant! You're a big girl now—an equal—and you must give a man the same privilege that *you* occasionally "enjoy"— that of being not quite in the mood or physically up to the act of making love.

Your Sexual Past

What about confession? Don't! Reviewing your previous sex life with a new man is the worst idea you ever had! Remember when *you* have been confided in by a *man* about his sex life with another *woman?* Didn't you feel as though you'd just swallowed a live five-foot python? He may *encourage* you—"Tell me about your other lovers." Don't be tempted. He doesn't mean it. I can't stress this point strongly enough. There *are* no exceptions.

A Man Wants You for Something Other than Your Body . . .

When you are very successful in your job, you may discover, to your horror, that many an attractive man doesn't think of you as a woman now but as a repository of knowledge and influence. Having been used to being a sex object first, a valued worker second, you will either love this switch or hate it. . . . I have always *hated* it! I don't mean that a man should be trying to tear your dress off at the same time he is making his sales pitch, but it *is* a little depressing to be regarded with all the warmth a man might accord your Steuben ashtray. I forgive, however. Since a man's work is frequently as important as the woman in his life (and that's how I feel about *my* work, it's very important!), one probably shouldn't be vexed if some men *only* want us as business friends, literally for what we can contribute to their professional lives. . . .

My sisters in the Women's Lib movement would say that's what we've been *after* all these years. We'll just hope—because no other possibility is tolerable—that some man loves you for your sexy core as *well* as your brain!

You Can Love Somebody Without Wanting Him to Get into You

Heaven in *this* life is desiring someone so much that you must *claw* your way off to the nearest bed, but sometimes you are *not* that hot for a man you're having an affair with. Yes, you may be in love with him, mad for him, and never want another man, but there are other things about him just as important as sensuality to have caused your desire: his charm, looks, glamour, brain, background make him "desirable," and sex sort of builds out of *that*. You never hate the idea of going to bed with him; on the other hand, you are not half-crazed with longing (after you *get* to bed you get aroused). You can have the most sexual, sensual nights of your life with this kind of man, for he is the one who gives you romance. Before you marry, love him but don't *necessarily* do without sex with somebody other than him. Does that sound reasonable? I hope you find *both* blessings, *all* blessings in one person, but, if necessary, while you are still single you might have to find them in *two*. (More?)

Sometimes the *Scene* Makes Up for the Man

Has a friend whisked you to Nassau not *just* to splash in the surf but he isn't the friend you happen to love (*that* friend you said goodbye to three months ago and are still torching for as though they poured gasoline on you every morning and struck a match!)? Have you laughed and chattered the night away with a dear, older man in a Paris *boîte* but, alas, he doesn't make you tingle even down to your *knees,* let alone to your *toes?*

Listen, torching girls sometimes need to put their torches down and ultradiscriminating girls to forget tingling clear to their toes and have a nice sexual experience just because the scene is *magical* and the man *acceptable.* Let me tell you the experience a young Chicago friend recently recounted to me: "I was in Los Angeles on business and though nearly everyone drives out there, my tycoon picked me up in his chauffeured Bentley and whisked me off to lunch at his house in the Truesdale Estates. It was the iciest California day I can ever remember and fires were burning in three fireplaces. A Japanese houseman served Dom Perignon, filet de boeuf, Caesar salad, brie, chocolate mousse, coffee, brandy, and off we went to make love. In *my* dressing room was a voluptuous pure silk kimono laid out on the chair—no, I didn't get to take it home, alas! Mr. Tycoon and I met in a bedroom darkened against the California sun (I *like* darkened rooms). Cio-cio-San sang her heart out on the stereo—and sang and sang and sang! Could this man make love? Yes, in terms of doing *enough* things to make one feel rosy and desirable. Was one ever deeply moved? No, but I really wanted *him* to enjoy the afternoon and be happy with himself. I knew I probably would not be back with him again because I really didn't like him in bed, but I liked *it* . . . the incredible lovely way he had done everything, his being made happy and *my* collecting an experience."

Is that selling out to go to bed with someone you're not attracted to? Not to my friend it wasn't, nor to me it wouldn't be. It's just the kind of thing that doesn't happen to girls who are too prissy and careful and selective and busy torch-bearing.

Greeting Somebody Frontally Is Highly Effective

You know, of course, how to hug properly—tummies touching lightly—but hugging *improperly* with bosom and pelvis crushed against him, actually ground *into* him for a moment, is dynamite! The impact is sexiest with somebody you don't know well, or shouldn't be hugging that way. An office friend? A man who was never your lover but should have been? Somebody you haven't seen in years? The frontal crush is highly gratifying for a man when delivered by a girl not known for her sexual generosity, someone a little prudish. Start from a few feet back with open arms; walk into the man and throw your arms around him. Do save this embrace for special occasions or you'll get a reputation for being a human Cuisinart.

Places to Make Love

You *can* just make love in a bed, but since the *brain* contributes to sexual pleasure for humans, an offbeat place can add a little sparkle. These are possibilities: Your office, his office, tourist section of an uncrowded airplane en route to Europe late at night with lights off, also the john of a 747. Cars are marvelous. If the car is *moving*, you'll have to confine your activity to fellatio—one of the *best* places for that provided you're not stuck in traffic next to a truck. The resourceful girls at *Cosmo* also came up with *these* places to make love; each contributor swears she really *did* it there.

—**Standing up in the Tower of Pisa**
—**On the chairlift at Vail**
—**In the New York Jets locker room**
—**Inside a sleeping bag while waiting in line for the Kentucky Derby**
—**In the wine cellar of Château Lafite-Rothschild**
—**On the Cyclone roller coaster at Coney Island**
—**In Edgar Allan Poe's bed at the University of Virginia**
—**In a hammock suspended between two palm trees**
—**On the observation deck of the World Trade Center**
—**Every Saturday in a sauna**
—**In the pilot's compartment of the Goodyear Blimp**

—In a sailboat
—On a pool table
—On a bed of pine needles in a pine forest
—In a hansom cab riding through Central Park
—In the sand trap of the fifteenth hole of a golf course
—On the second floor of a skeleton of a house under construction
—In the back seat of a Volkswagen
—On the *Michaelangelo*'s top deck
—In a coed john at the Citibank in Paris
—In a canoe
—In a marble bathtub—*without* water
—In a marble bathtub—*with* water
—On the conference-room floor of a very large ad agency (during working hours)

For fellatio only, *these* are possible locations: in his Eames or other chair, at his desk while he phones (especially his mother), on the couch while he watches television, at the dinner table during diet time when he hasn't had dessert for days (of *course* I'm serious!). Speaking of tables, there hardly is a man who doesn't like to be under-the-table *groped* (in restaurants and at dinner parties) after you're already lovers. Before that, proceed with caution. In their courting days, it's said that a beautiful Italian courtesan used to tell one of America's most powerful businessmen at parties, after a certain amount of under-the-table grope, she couldn't wait another minute to satisfy all her hunger, and they would rush off to the bedroom. He was apparently *crazy* about her hunger, for he divorced his wife of twenty-four years and married her. (Alas, *they're* divorced now.)

Just don't fail to use your imagination about love places and what you do in them. (Variety may eventually pall and you'll sink gratefully back into bed again, but there, reminiscing can be fun.)

Alcohol and Sex *Do* Mix

One bottle of cold champagne for two warm people is an aphrodisiac, especially if you drink it on an empty stomach and especially if it's Tuesday morning, Friday noon or some other not-quite-"standard" time to make love. *Any* kind of alcohol—gin on the rocks, a bottle of chilled Mersault, a Piña Colada—can get you *out* of yourself if you are a constricted little creature and tend toward nerves. Heavy drinkers should drink *less* when loving, of course, but small-to-medium quantities of booze for *not*-heavy drinkers can help with your responses. My favorite drink is a French Seventy-five. An authentic one contains sugar and lemon juice. I just pour a shot of brandy into a glass of cold champagne and make do nicely. A peeled perfect *peach* at the bottom of a glass of champagne is heaven . . . and romantic.

Try Different Positions Only
If It Pleases One or Both of You

If the missionary position is the one you truly enjoy, no need to keep working your way back and forth through the *Kama Sutra*. Perhaps you should work your way through *once,* however, just to be *sure* you aren't missing anything. *The Joy of Sex* by Alex Comfort is a *modern Kama Sutra* with descriptions and illustrations of *nearly* anything sexual that feels good. The positions you two figure out together are best of all, of course.

Sometimes Forget Being the Bright,
Successful You—Simply Be a Body

After you're successful, there will be times (thousands, we hope!) when what you are more than a glossy career woman is *horny.* On some of those occasions, you simply "forget" to impress a man in other ways. Don't talk too much or show off your brain too much or be too newsy or charming or full of language. Just feel *whorish* for a change; don't try for anything else. It will make you vulnerable to give up the other "assets" that you usually impress him with, but the vulnerability won't destroy you, and the contrast is good for you both.

Because a Man Is Not Erect Does Not Mean He Isn't *Interested* in Sex

A tumescent state for him is probably comparable to *our* being *quite* aroused. Well, you may not be *that* aroused, but still like going to bed with him, yes? (We've listed reasons before.) Yes, seeing him lying there soft as a melting popsicle with taut and eager you at his side *is* a little discouraging, but if he *wants* you to rouse him by playing with him, why *not?* Men do that for *us* all the time. An orgasm reached by your having instigated sex is no less "authentic."

Helping Out

Some men like a pillow under your bottom so they can get at you better; this is particularly true for a small-penised man, but can be true for *anybody.* If you know he *likes* that, then why not skivvy up on your own little pillow or hand him the pillow to put under you.

More Helping Out

Contract your vagina around his penis when he is inside you; that feels nifty to him. Practice when you *aren't* with him. . . . Contract your vagina . . . pull it toward your tummy and hold for a count of five or ten. Let go. Do it again. You can also practice by stopping the flow of urine as it comes out of you: Stop. Start. Stop. Etc., etc. Sometimes it's hard to *remember* to contract and let go when a man is *in* you—you're concentrating on other things—but it is *very* nice for him and you should do it. Good for muscle tone, too.

When He Wants to Make Love and You Don't

Do it anyway. No, it *isn't* bad for your health or, I think, even bad for your psyche. Loving when you aren't sexy isn't, to me, any different from listening to a man talk when you'd really rather be reading your new *National Geographic*, or going to a dinner party when you'd rather stay home and have a chicken sandwich. You don't have to rev up and have an orgasm. . . . Indeed, perhaps you *can't*, but as you go along, you'll probably get in the mood *enough* so that you won't "suffer." As accomplished as you are at making love, it seems to me *not* to when the man you love *wants* to would be like not singing, not acting, not cooking, if *those* are your specialties. This is your *thing*, so of course you do it! If he isn't your *special* man, that's something else. In that case, just do what your body says.

Doing What You *Don't* Like During Sex

Should you ever compromise and do something to *him*, or let him do something to *you* that makes you feel, well, yukky? No, of *course* you shouldn't. And neither should you ever get menstrual cramps, dark circles under your eyes, hives, sunburned or bitten by mosquitoes. Every sexual encounter should be soul-lifting and exquisite, yes, but sex, like life, my dear, is *not* perfect, and *you*, Miss Faintheart, may not always be able to squirm out of a sexual situation just because it's making you feel a little *queasy!* Perhaps a man you adore as a friend, or someone you owe a lot to, is simply terrible in bed . . . that doesn't mean you *shouldn't* sleep with him. Perhaps a man with marvelous "credentials"—he's glamorous, famous, exciting, takes you fabulous places—is also an indifferent bedmate. Well, maybe Jackie Onassis could say goodnight at the door, but not *you*. . . . Sex is part of your *package*. Maybe you like the man sexually, but don't care for certain *things* he likes to do (you don't want your nipples kissed *ever* and he insists on kissing them constantly!). If you *mostly* enjoy yourself in bed, not being turned on some of the time or even turned *off* isn't going to hurt you. It hasn't killed *me* yet, anyway. Sex is still the *best* thing you do and the thing you *enjoy* doing best, a few scruffy moments notwithstanding.

P.S. We're not talking about whips and chains or anything really ugly, just "normal" sex.

Don't Forget to Remember—Sex Is Naughty!

It's almost a shame sex is so acceptable, clean and friendly now, like eating Granola with skimmed milk—not that it doesn't still *feel* very nice. Whatever you can do to keep sex naughty in your life, I hope you are doing . . . reading pornography (I love erotic Indian and Chinese art), seeing naughty movies, having fantasies, either in your head or talked out with him. Years ago, when I was in analysis, I confessed to my well-meaning therapist how much I loved fantasy and depended upon it to feel my sexiest self. This "enlightened" soul, in the *vanguard* of people who believed sex was okay for everybody (singles, marrieds, hermits, water buffalo, gerbils, you name it), was so distraught that anybody should think sex "dirty" he set about to "right" the misconception by yammering away by the *hour* that sex was *clean*. "Obliterate all those dirty thoughts from your mind," he would say. "Think good, clean natural!" Dear Max . . . he just about sex-is-cleaned me into total frigidity! Giving up my fantasies and thinking about tubfuls of soapy water, or trying to think of nothing at all, can be very *unsexing*. Fortunately I only followed his doctrine for a couple of months before I went back, sensibly, to thinking sex was naughty.

Fantasies are one of life's sex-chargers. Some women won't even *tell* their favorite fantasy for fear of dissipating its "power." There are two kinds: those you play in your head but don't discuss, and those you "conduct" together as you make love (you are the saucy maid, he the Edwardian employer; he is the satyr, you the wood nymph). Both kinds can be marvelous and *any* head-fantasy is acceptable—you know that. *Whatever* gets you off is practically *sacred!*

Oh, I guess we'd better mention threesomes, foursomes, orgies and the like. I can't tell you about them because I never had the experience. Sex with one man was always (well *usually!*) so agreeable that adding other cast members seemed to me (a) kinky; (b) unnecessary. As usual, you're on your own.

How to Be a Delight the Morning After,
When He Stays Over

This advice may sound as old-fashioned as *Godey's Lady's Book* but you *ought* to pay some attention.

1. Somehow get the old makeup off—maybe skip out of bed after he is asleep—so he won't see you in it in the morning.

2. When you get up and start moving about, put on something pretty—a peignoir, perhaps. Try not to look like a dead octopus.

3. If he wakes first and shakes or touches you, not necessarily to make love, but because he has to leave, try to show a *touch* of sprightliness. Don't groan, moan, look as though you'd seen the specter of death at having to get your eyes open. Smile and *seem* to be awake. Every man has experienced—and detested—the girl who wakes up groaning that she has a terrible hangover. A torpid body when *he's* moving about is also not attractive.

4. The minute he's awake and sensible, you must convey that he was wonderful. The language is up to *you*. "You were fabulous and that's all I'm going to say." "You moved me very deeply last night." "I loved having you kiss me . . . and everything else you did." "It was wonderful to go to sleep in your arms." You've got to take the posture that it was *marvelous* without making a big deal out of it.

5. Never, *never* convey that you're sorry. Only the gauchest dummy would announce, "God, I don't know what happened . . . I don't *do* things like that," or, "Jesus, it must have been the joints we smoked last night!"

No matter how awful—or good—it was, *do* not *make him feel guilty!* There are other ways to convince him you aren't a sleep-around girl. Never indicate the happening was anything but fabulous and you aren't 2,000 percent glad it happened.

6. If he *wants* to continue the sexiness of the night before, okay, but there's every chance his heart won't really be in it unless you're away on a fabulous romantic vacation. In the city, you should try to be a bit *different* in the morning—now you are intelligent, listening, pleasant, but not pulsating—a *friend*.

7. It's best to move the scene away from the bedroom rather soon so he can *see* you in a different way. Take him to the kitchen or, if you're only going to chat, to the living room.

8. Yes, you *must* offer him breakfast. It can be the simplest thing in the world, but do it nicely. Have a pretty dish, a china cup

and saucer—go out and buy one *now* if your cupboard only features peanut-butter jars and cracked china. No, he isn't expecting prewar Plaza Hotel service, but stop figuring that sex, youth and charm are all he's going to get, or ought to expect from *you*—a man is affected by your *trappings*. Give him *real* coffee instead of instant; bring it to him with a cloth napkin. If coffee or breakfast goes to him on a tray, use a fresh doily with a real flower, if possible.

9. Do not extract from him a commitment as to when he'll see you again. He *ought* to commit himself right then, but if he doesn't, don't push. Do not seem clingy and insecure; you *may* even want to make it possible for him to leave your apartment *early* in the morning. Say something like, "Listen, if you have a heavy morning, I *do* understand." Or "If you need to get to your office, not to worry. I promise not to feel abandoned!" He'll then feel freer to *stay*, but if, indeed, he *leaves*, you will have "given permission" and that's face-saving for *you*.

10. Some *few* men may like making love to a bowl of tapioca, but the affair—if it's to be that—will probably go better if you *don't* seem to have the rest of your life to spend with him in that apartment (unless he's the delivery boy and you're Barbra Streisand—then your availability could be flattering!). You should seem to have some plans of your own for the day.

11. Before he leaves, you might want to consider giving him a present . . . not something that seems to come from your handy-present file, stocked for just such occasions (even if it *is!*), but a *spontaneous* gift you want him to have because you're so happy and feeling such friendship for him. Suggestions: one of your own silk handkerchiefs ("I think this would look *super* in that coat pocket"), a special book (Rupert Brooke in a sweet, mock-leather edition or Elizabeth Barrett Browning's sonnets), some small *objet d'art* from your apartment—a small brass lion (because *he's* a lion), a papier-mâché knight on horseback because the knight reminds you of him.

12. *Smile* when he leaves.

If you're spending the night in *his* apartment, get the hell out the next morning—not abruptly, but don't have him panicked over what he's going to *do* with you. On the other hand, don't make such a quick exit he's insulted. Just be a gracious lady with things to do. If you leave *then*, perhaps he'll ask you to lunch.

Listen, your problem could just as easily be getting *away* from him or getting him out of your flat. I know you'll do either tactfully and with charm.

197

Never Expect Anybody—Except Possibly Your Analyst—To Be as Thrilled About Your Sex Life as *You* Are

You think you and your dear one may possibly have established a new Guinness record . . . why shouldn't *everybody* be happy for you? My dear, we *are,* except possibly we thought *we* were the only couple with pure sex magic going for us and here *you* are with *your* achievements. And God help us if there *isn't* any sex magic in our life at the moment—do we need you on our hands totally blissed out? Near-jealousy may not be the *only* reaction as you recount the thirty-two positions you and Mr. Wonderful got into in that beach house with only a hammock, prayer rug and some wet sand to work with. You may be *boring* us! I sat next to a man at lunch the other day who had "found sex"—moved away from home, moved in with his beloved, and gotten blissed. "It's the most incredible thing," he kept burbling. "In eighteen years of marriage, I never knew there was sex like this, and we're in bed *all* the time." Bully for him, but did I *need* a radiant lunch companion? I'm never altogether keen to hear a man rave about *any* other woman, are you, even if it's just about her sensational blintzes? In recalling sexual bliss, I think you mostly preen to *yourself,* like Scarlett waking up in her big downy bed after being ravished by Rhett the night before. My feeling is that you mostly keep love and sex happiness just for you and him. It is *not* all that attractive to outsiders.

Say No with a Little Class

And what of the men who woo you whom you can't *stand?* We've said very little about *them* so far. Well, as I've mentioned, I've always thought a pass more of a compliment than a put-down, no matter *who* is making it. Also, since we're sexually wooing *men* some of the time now, what is there to be so sanctimonious about? Still, there is involuntary revulsion when somebody comes at you for the squeeze, the grab, the kiss, who ought *not* to. What to do? There is no better way than just to be cool. Don't squirm. Don't thrash about. That's what I wrote in *Sex and the Single Girl* twenty years ago, and defensive tactics haven't changed. A wildcat will turn him *on;* a cool, unresponsive girl will calm him down. Though some may have the appeal of wet thermal underwear, one can only pity them for being gauche, silly, dumb and undiscerning, but not *censure* them.

The few times I have pursued a man and he hasn't pursued back, I have been devastated—who *needs* it? Well, if we had to take all the rebuffs a *man* takes to his sexy ideas and to his hands, mouth, penis, we might never leave the *house* in the morning. I really do admire their *courage.* Say No thank you in the nicest way. Lie, if you will (I have the flu, I have rabies, my husband carries a revolver, I'm frigid, I'm gay), but be ever so gentle and kind, even to the creeps. I hope you are affectionate by *nature* and like *most* men you know to hold your hand, kiss you on the cheek and touch you, even if the activity isn't sexual. I just think life is *better* that way. There almost isn't *anybody,* man or woman, whom I know well I *don't* like to touch. Oh, well—maybe that's extreme or insecure or something. *You* decide for you.

And now let's talk about romantic love, a really incredible thing when it happens.

Chapter Eight

LOVE

Love . . . What *Is* this Thing?

Love. What original, profound thing can *anybody* say about love? Shakespeare, Tolstoy, Homer, Flaubert, Colette have all had a go at it. . . . "We are never so defenseless against suffering as when we love," "Love is, of all the passions, the strongest, for it attacks the head, the heart and senses simultaneously," "Love is a human emotion that wisdom will never conquer," "Love is blind, and cannot see the pretty follies that themselves commit," blah, blah, blah.

The *rules,* if there are any, are inconsistent: One set says, Give all, hold nothing back, devote yourself utterly to the beloved and you'll "win"; another school (my school) says, Do all that and you could be a candidate for the Bellevue psychiatric ward—at least if you do it too *soon* or don't check the effect it's having on the beloved. Nevertheless, for some of us, loving casually is about as possible as trying to assemble a main-frame IBM computer from a box of component parts. Yet, if getting love counsel from a sufferer (me) is like getting investment advice from the Franklin National Bank or consulting Dracula about your anemia, how can you even think of discussing love with a *non*-sufferer? A woman who has never had a moment's insecurity with a man . . . what does *she* know? May I tell you then what I absolutely *think* I know about love, one mouseburger to another?

1. Once begun, a love affair is like a train headed through a tunnel. . . . It is absolutely going to go through because it's been *programmed* to do that back at the station. There is no use whatever trying to control it.

2. Mostly, men are rottener to women in love than women are to men.

3. It is not unusual for a man to disappear *totally* after having had with you what you thought was the best night of his life—that's what he *told* you—and certainly of *yours*. He never calls again or not until months later anyway.

4. The *only* reason a man doesn't call is that he doesn't want to. He has *not* been taken to the emergency ward of Mount Sinai, thrown in the slammer or spirited away by the Reverend Sun Myung Moon's Unification Church. Only not wanting to has prevented him from lifting the receiver.

5. Men and women *can* love equally. Just because men are frequently irresponsible and behave detestably does not mean they cannot love deeply. *However*—big however—the man who loves as deeply as that may not be the one *you're* in love with . . . he's just got it in him for *some* woman *some*time.

6. When men are having a bad time in love, they *can* suffer worse than we do, and these may be outstanding men, not losers.

7. There is no pain like the pain of having a bad time with a lover. . . . It's *got* to be in the top three pains (hard to think of what the other two could be!).

8. Love changes. A man who is giving you fits can actually get to love you more than you him; *you* can detest somebody you adored, though right now you could sooner conceive of scalloped kneecaps or green blood than not caring for *this* one the way you do.

9. When you fall in love again (and you will), you can hurt just as much over the new person. (P.S. This knowledge never helped anybody feel any better while suffering her present pain.)

10. One person always loves a little *more* than the other.

11. Being romantically in love is *sick*—you're subtly deranged—though you can be normal in every other way while it's happening.

12. Deranged or not, love is the biggest joy and excitement-producer we have.

13. There is no better way to get to know someone than to have an affair . . . it can save years of lunches.

Now for a few details of love. May I?

People Who Are Ready for Love and Who Need It, *Get* It

Love doesn't just drop on you unexpectedly; you have to give off signals, sort of like an amateur radio operator . . . "Calling C.Q. C.Q. C.Q. Whiskey Two India Ocean Yankee calling. Hello, Whiskey Two India Ocean? This is kilowatt six Delta X-ray King. Do you read me? Blah, blah, blah."

Any man lured away from his wife was *lurable—he* was giving off signals. Somebody with a really closed-down shop *ignores* the signals when encountered and doesn't give off any of his own. Even though love sometimes *eludes* you (dry spell), if you keep your shop open, your signals clear (I like men, I approve of men), love will happen. Any woman can have a man, we *know* that—if not a great man, then at least an *okay* one. After forty, you must look (work!) harder to find one; after fifty, you must look (work!) really *hard* for male companionship. Between ages twenty and forty you don't have to do very much unless you want a special and *outstanding* man (kind, successful, attractive, faithful, solvent, amusing, etc.)—then you have to "work" as hard as the forty- or fifty-year-old woman has to to get *anybody*. The crux of what I'm saying is this: You treat finding a man like finding a job—you look—and give off signals. You can't force or be desperate or make man-finding your sole occupation. Do that and it *doesn't* happen. "You can't get a man with a gun," sings Annie Oakley in Irving Berlin's *Annie Get Your Gun,* but you also can't stay indoors reading gothic novels and expect him to find you.

Maybe we only encounter someone to really fall in love with every few years. Maybe, eager to plunge into a sexy *la dolce vita* afternoon or night of love, nobody's there even for *that.* Doesn't matter. Your general mood is that of "ready," pores open, accepting and tolerant of men, not "after them" only for marriage (more later) but "after them" because they complete your life. You *will* connect.

Where to Meet Men

Let's discuss for a moment how you might *meet* a man to have a romance with. The two *best* ways are: (a) having friends introduce you (David arrived that way)—they give him your name and he calls you or you call him or they arrange a get-together with both of you there; or (b) through your work.

Those are the big two. At parties and social events I always found the prettiest girls carried off the spoils (i.e.—men)—I never did well there. Aside from personal introductions and sinking in through your work, we'll list some places where men at least *are*. Compiling the list is easy . . . *Cosmo*'s young editors helped me. What may *not* be so easy is getting acquainted with a man just because he's *there*—i.e., getting yourself to talk to someone who may not be paying any attention to you at all. Gretchen, dear Gretchen, says when you've picked one out, just say *anything* to him, it doesn't matter what . . . "Can you tell me the fastest way to get to the library (airport, post office)? Could you help me with this tray? Are we in the south or north wing? What time is it?"

The most banal beginning will do. If the talked-to person doesn't talk back, it probably isn't personal—he's just not friendly; try with another. Even if you get your first words out and he responds, the conversation may close right down if you don't keep it going; that's the *next* challenge. Some girls can start a conversation with a stranger and move it right along; some can't. If you look friendly, are accepting of men, really *like* men, somebody attractive may get the message and start a conversation with you. We'll hope. No matter where you go to find men, you ought to be there to have fun or to be enlightened or for some purpose other than acquisition. So here is the list of places where men congregate, and some of them allow for a "sink-in" period *longer* than just a few minutes or an hour, so you'll have a better chance.

Spectator-sports events—Men turn out in droves for football, baseball, basketball games, tennis tournaments, boat races. Go with a girlfriend; talk to all around you.

Active sports—*You* play tennis, handball, golf, ski, swim.

Health clubs—Executives often go before work but may not be in the mood to chat. After work there are little health bars where you can get acquainted.

Library—Law, medical, university. Have something to look up, a reason to be there, but ask questions of male researchers—"Am I in the medieval history room?" "Where are the card catalogs?"

Art galleries—Men do go there; prowl, then stand next to a prospect studying a Jasper Johns or a Utrillo.

Tiffany's at Christmas—Filled with men shoppers.

Brooks Brothers or any other establishment-type men's store. (Bloomingdale's or other chic emporiums may attract more homosexual men than you need.)

Big busy wine store

Roller disco—Fading but still good

In line at the movie

In line at the cash machines at bank

Supermarket on Saturday or late at night—Look in his basket and ask where he found the dill mayonnaise. (If his basket reveals too much cat food or sanitary napkins, forget it—he has other interests.) If you always talk to the help in your market, nobody will think it odd if you also bring the man next to you at the checkout stand into the conversation.

Country bar or small-town bar (not so much else going on in town to entertain people)

Video game store or any video store

Mercedes-Benz showroom

The park on weekends—Divorced men will be there with their kids.

Theater, opera—Stroll at intermission, talk to "strangers."

Book stores, especially the photo department.

Take classes men attend—Power boating, stock-market analysis, business courses; stay clear of "Understanding Your Psyche" or other female-oriented subjects.

University clubs—You don't have to belong to the club to attend some of its events.

Church, church choir

Hospital volunteer—You'll have to work but will meet male visitors, patients (they recover!), doctors and hospital staff.

Place a classified ad—Some *Cosmo* girls have reported interesting results.

Ski trips for singles—Planned singles get-togethers are not always rewarding but ski trips can be the exception.

Singles bars—Don't dismiss them entirely. Lisa reports better luck at brunch—go with girlfriends—than being raked over by the nighttime bar lineup.

Alcoholics Anonymous—Excellent! Go as a visitor.

Political campaign—You'll have to telephone, address mail, *contribute,* but these people *need* you and friendship may continue after the candidate is (or *isn't*) elected.

Flying lessons—Expensive but you cannot *miss.*

Walk a dog—Still the *Numero uno best!*

Okay, that's where they *are.* Let's say, one way or another, you've now *connected* with a man. How does *love* happen?

Love Happens When Two People Shoot Each Other with Magic-Poison— Or One Person Shoots the Other

Why does it have to be *him* . . . *that* one? Because those thousands of other men just as good, possibly better than he, haven't been injected with your poison. Everybody has a supply and we inject each other. A man who is gaga about a woman has given *her* a big injection. When a man looks like Pinocchio but to you he's Placido Domingo, *he's* had an injection.

What I'm saying is that *Cupid* doesn't do it with bows and arrows, you do it with this sweet, efficient "poison." In the best of worlds, we're mutually poisoned, but we can't shoot ourselves . . . *your* supply of magic-poison is only to shoot other people. Some shoot many times (you can get refills). Others use up only their original supply, if that, and die with most of their magic-poison still in its little vial. The cost for refills gets a bit *high,* especially for men who *marry* each poisoned lady and have to pay off the *old* one in cash or other hard goods, but for women, too, shooting frequently is costly because falling in and subsequently out of love is quite an emotional drain. Most of us, especially when young, get shot once or twice by *somebody.* Rich, famous, powerful men get shot *continuously* until they die, and some (Mickey Rooney, Rex Harrison, Richard Burton, Alan Jay Lerner) do continuous shooting of their own all their lives. Some women only shoot men "over their head"—a movie star, a rock musician or a man (possibly homosexual) who never shoots *back.* It's called "hiding out" . . . picking a totally ungettable type so you can't actually become involved, but the shooting is all involuntary, can't be consciously planned.

If you pick a victim because you think he might be *good* for you (suitable) but for whom you feel no attraction, the magic won't "take." Many of us keep shooting the same "type" of man over

205

and over, however. My friend Diane shoots only "baby boys." . . . "They are so cute," she said in *Interview* magazine. My southern-belle friend Linda Rae likes only Oriental men, etc., etc., etc.,—falconer's *choice*. God knows you don't always shoot the most suitable victim . . . later you find he has a soft white cruddy underbelly but, while full of your poison, he is Superman. We can't see what other people see in *their* victims, of course, because we haven't *shot* them with anything and friends haven't used any of their magic on *our* beloved, so they wonder seriously about our choice. One of the blessings of shooting many *different* men is that each enhances your life in his own way, moves you into *his* world. I can't imagine poisoning only *one* man in a lifetime or receiving only one injection yourself. People who are too careful—who subconsciously hunt and hunt and hunt and hunt for one *perfect* "prospect"—surely miss a lot of living. What they tell you is *true*: the only regrets you have later on are for what you *didn't* do. Shoot away!

The Machinations of Love

You will have dozens of encounters with men—dates we call them—and little romances and affairs. No big deal; but once in a while . . . *once* in a while *love* comes. I want to write about *that*.

First, a few ideas about how to enhance yourself to him. But let's stop right there! Don't *you* deserve pleasing, *too*? Definitely, but a statistic or two, if I may. The latest U.S. Census reveals that, between the ages of thirty-five and thirty-nine, there are 13,000,000 women for every 10,000,000 men. Between the ages of twenty-five and forty-nine, women outnumber men by 1,250,000. These figures don't reflect drug addicts, alcoholics, men locked up in jail, the homosexual population (four million acknowledged but 15 percent of total male population show "tendencies"), none of whom do us much good as love partners, so the reality is even worse than the statistics. Bottom line: There are too many of us, too few of them, and of the possibles, only a few will really interest you.

Being a mouseburger, you're always going to attract whoever is out there, God knows—like lint to navy-blue serge—and when you're young—teens, early twenties—these statistics will not yet mean much to you and you'll love, *be* loved, without much effort. Maybe the man in your life is so crazy about you, the *last* thing you need to think about is how to please *him* but, even at *your* age, I think men can be like apartments. When you go out to rent or buy an apartment or house, you know what you like *always* exceeds what you expected to pay, no matter *what* you've budgeted. Well, the quality of man you need, regardless of your age, sometimes escalates to *just* exceed your ability to "pay"; the more credentials *you* have (brains, looks, success), the more *he* has to have to please you.

P.S. I have no guilt whatever about saying some men are better than others. We are all born equal in God's eyes, yes, but not in each other's. So if he's *good* (a lovely, sexually attractive man, also attractive to other women), *you* have to be *better*.

Sure Ways to Please a Man

Be on time. Women rarely are.

Compliment him a *lot*. You almost *can't* overdo it . . . his clothes, his taste, his dog, his feet, his cooking, his charm, his family (!), his rock collection . . . they are all the greatest.

Rave about his brain. "What a brilliant idea!" "That's a *perfect* solution." "How did you think of that?" "Well, I'm sure *that* got the meeting moving again!" etc., etc.

Pay attention to what he drinks and learn to mix it flawlessly . . . the perfect martini (with Bombay gin?), a Manhattan (sweet or dry?), gin or scotch on the rocks (with a twist?). If he drinks beer, carry *his* brand. Get Russian or Polish vodka. For a non-drinker, carry his special favorites.

Learn how to light his cigar—like Gigi. It's a precise little routine and takes practice. A man, not necessarily this one, will show you.

Research any project he's interested in. Helping him in his work is a nearly foolproof way to ingratiate yourself.

More Things to Do in the Early Stages

Listen. Don't talk too much. No matter how often he says "Tell me about *you,*" don't go overboard. Who you are will gradually come out. It is somehow wrong for a woman ever to do a complete history at one sitting, deliver a monologue—and *never* announce chirpily one afternoon (presumably having soul-searched for years), "I think I'm getting to like myself better!"

Research *his* life totally . . . from what he says, by talking to his friends, family, coworkers. Read anything written about him. Men love to talk about their past even if they aren't that old, about college days, favorite relatives, summer vacations. If a man has been in *any* war—World War Two, Korean, Vietnam—you usually can't go wrong in asking him about it. (A few will demur, most like to talk.) That experience is a Big Deal. Tell him the period fascinates you . . . what was it like?

Whatever he tells you one day, remember to ask him about it the next. Make written notes after you see him if you need them to remember—people in his life, organizations belonged to, products made by his company. Your reintroducing these specific things later will be so flattering he will *faint*. Most people don't even remember you told them you were having your gallbladder removed.

Summation: Listening is the best weapon ever forged for a woman to get through to a man. It just about takes the place of a gorgeous face or body or having to be too smart *yourself.* Mouseburgers are terrific listeners. May I say there is *nothing* like intelligent you looking out of your intelligent eyes, understanding every word he says, saying intelligent things in return to intelligent him. . . . It is the sexiest. May I also say there probably has to be some bullshit in every love affair . . . I mean you *deliver* some if you care.

Now I'm going to try to defend *that* idea.

Acceptable (Necessary!) Bullshit

I distinctly remember telling David Brown I didn't care if he went out with other women. . . . *Nothing* could have been more untrue but I didn't want to terrify him. Women have said—guiltlessly!—"But I *love* bald heads," or "Don't be silly, what girl *wouldn't* pass up the ballet for a chance to see the Rangers play the Philadelphia Flyers," or "I think it's adorable that Chester (three-hundred-pound sheep dog) sleeps on the bed."

All this stuff is *okay* to say—it's for a good cause. You are *accommodating* during courtship, and the gesture does not have to be totally *sincere*—I mean you don't have to have a primordial, throat-clutching *desire* to help his little sister sell her raffle tickets or "Let's wash your Porsche this Saturday" for you to say it and do it! You Xerox the article about him from the trade paper and send it to friends . . . be sure he *knows* you did. The cassette of his speech . . . could you listen to it one more time and play it for your father? That terrific letter he wrote to Consolidated Freightways about their new forklifts . . . could you have a copy? Snapshots of him at tennis, squash, salmon fishing, in bathrobe and in tails are Scotch Taped to your mirror to the point you can hardly get your mascara on. You wear the T-shirt he gave you eight straight days on vacation.

You don't like my calling this stuff bullshit, right? Okay, call it anything you like (and of course you're doing it because you *love* him), but just *do* it!

Still More Things to Do

If you are in love with a man, you have to be careful not to bore him (it wouldn't hurt not to bore *anybody*). You're in the car and he's deep into a monologue about the Salt II Treaty (possibly he could be boring *you!*). You pass an apartment house where you used to live or a school attended as a teenager. I see no reason to stop the Salt II talkathon to point out the house or school unless he's an *architect*. Point them out another time when he's not so caught up with his subject. Truth: A man will always interrupt *you*. Why the old double standard? Because of that thirteen-million-of-us, ten-million-of-*them* situation, of course, but also because men have never got the hang of when to let us talk and not interrupt. Your *friends* are for confidences and tears and your dissertations and pointing out old houses and schools attended. A *lover* is for loving and charming and going to bed with and having a passionate, unforgettable moment in history with—not for total bilateral friendship. That will come if you stay together long enough. To continue:

Don't put down his ex-wife or present wife or even the girls he admires, except in the most teasing way. Strong people say good things about weaklings, and if you say good things about his wife or ex-wife, you have more of a chance of "weakening" her than if you attack; criticism only shows insecurity. Of course, if somebody is a real bitch you can say, "My word—that woman is really *something,*" but you do it like Madame de Staël commenting on a servant girl or the ingenue observing some pitiful virago of an older woman. . . . You are sweetly compassionate, operating from *strength!* You don't necessarily defend her when *he* attacks. You sympathize but don't pitch *in.*

Never telephone just to chat. If you're completing weekend plans or he has *asked* you to call, okay, but random telephoning just because you're lonesome, or, God forbid, suspicious ("I was just thinking about you, darling, and rang up to see how you are" or "I haven't heard from you since Wednesday . . . what have you been up to?") is going to do you so much harm I can't warn you away from it *enough.* We've come a long way with equality . . . you have the tickets, you ask him, you have the dungeness crab, you invite him, but random telephoning is still better left to *him* if you're crazy about the man. Boy *pals* are something else; them you can call.

Don't get into arguments. You cannot, must not. If you keep those two things *alone* under control—telephoning and arguing—you're way ahead. Argue with your cat.

Be selective about what you tell him. You want to be intimate, of course, not to have big flubby secrets, but utter candor is questionable . . . for now. You may mention—*once*—your ulcerated colon or needing three grams of thyroid a day to keep from fainting, but do not bring the subject up *often.* I would spare him the details of your visit to the proctologist—or even your sister's husband's disappointing job hunt. Only dumb people equate intimacy with openness on *every* (un)-fascinating subject.

Now, all this stuff I've been telling you to do, I suppose, could depress a free-spirited girl. Certainly it doesn't sound like *1982.*

Manipulative! Obviously advice for nit-brains and women who do not truly *love*. Integrity-rich, equal-to-any-man-who-ever-lived *you* does not need cheap tricks! Oh, come off it! Your honor is not going to be compromised and these are not cheap tricks; they are endearing and they *work*. And we are only talking about using them on the man who is a very Big Deal in your life. Sometimes when I read advice in women's magazines, certainly *Cosmo* ("leave your scented hanky under his pillow, offer to walk his dog when he's out of town, take his mother to lunch"), I, too, am inclined to think that is cute, foxy stuff meant for other people . . . sweet but not for *me*. Yet when a friend offers the same ideas, one *accepts*. They seem sane and valid. Please, then, consider that I'm a *friend* and we're chatting. This is *not* girlish nonsense.

Sinking In

Be wonderful to his friends. They are *sacred* to him. Try not to see the ones you hate too much, but even them you have to be nice to.

Never criticize him in front of others. *Never.*

His children are going to be part of his life forever! Get along with them as best you can. They won't love you immediately—don't even *try* to win them quickly or come on too strong—but they can *like* you if you're attentive, non-gooey and fun. Let's hope their daddy keeps them from being little *brats* around you.

Enjoy, if you can, the things he introduces you to and wants you to enjoy, leaving out drugs, group sex, gambling parlors cops raid, cockfighting and a few other aggravation-makers. I'm thinking about *innocent* pleasures like restaurants, museums, books, movies, records, canoe trips that thrilled *him* and now he hopes will thrill *you*. Does that include sports events? Ah, yes, the old carbolic-acid test! Well, even if sports do not move you right down to your metatarsals and you can barely get a volleyball over the net, you can enjoy the *drama* of the event and just being with *him;* a tiny touch of enthusiasm does not constitute selling out. A young friend of mine tightened her vaginal muscles throughout two entire football and three basketball seasons. "It was the only muscle tone I *had* during that period," said Millie, "but all that contracting got me through the games and I think it helps you have orgasm; it *certainly* keeps your insides from getting flabby.''

If your interest in sports should wane a bit later on (after you're married? It did for Millie), didn't you once adore pistachio ice cream, three-inch heels and Bruce Springsteen and find your adoration channeled elsewhere *later?* Well *okay!*

More Sinking In

Do whatever he suggests immediately if you can. Check out the dress he saw in Saks' window he thinks you'd look good in, get the tires rotated on your Toyota, buy two shares of the stock he's bullish on, read the Ken Follett thriller he loved. *Do* it. *Respond!*

What about his dating other women? Let us not concern ourselves—I mean let us not let him *know* we are *concerned*—about them just yet. Too soon. Eventually they'll all have to go—we *hope*—but don't insist on that yet.

The Affair Is Blossoming

Let's think of some ways to make your hours together memorable. Ask if you can borrow him for four hours on Saturday; plan the four hours based on what's available in your city—photography exhibit, street strolling in a special part of town, sidewalk art show, any kind of show (flower, boat, cat, antiques), French, Italian or vintage American movie (movies in the morning or afternoon are special), a little shopping, probably two or three things incorporated, then brunch/lunch, before or after, at an al fresco restaurant in summer, cozy bistro in winter. The four hours may or may not include a slip into bed. What's wanted is to make these four hours *fun*. *You* take the initiative.

Lightly Does It

Do not scare him. You can be attentive, flattering, ador-able. . . . Do all the things just suggested but not be sexually heavy. It's okay to steal him for four hours for your Saturday-afternoon adventure—maybe he won't even see you for dinner that night—but early on it is *not* okay to say that friends have lent you a beach house for the weekend and can he come out. He may not yet be ready to see you wall to wall for forty-eight hours straight. Too much. Too heavy. Men are still fragile about sexual pursuit. . . . Do not move *in* on him. And if you tell him early on you're looking for commitment, I'll *kill* you!

The Affair Is Spinning Along

After one of your assignations, send him a flower—maybe a big African daisy (a rose is too federal) with a note—"Last night was wonderful—love, Eloise."

When he's away, write sexy notes to reach the hotel when he does or tuck them in his luggage. Sexy notes are not federal sex pursuit like pinning him down for a weekend. Take him to or pick him up at the airport. Distances are horrendous, yes, and it seems a shame for both of you to travel traffic-clogged freeways but seeing off and greeting a man you love are sweet, sexy things to do. For his homecoming, put gas-filled balloons in his apartment—or yours—with a big gag card; chill the champagne.

Taxi and Auto Etiquette

When you get out of a cab or his car and head for a building, turn and wave at the loved one left in the cab or car. If *he* gets out, keep watching as he heads for the building or skims down the street—he may turn around and wave at *you*. It's ghastly to wave to somebody either from street or car because you miss them already but *they* never turn around to wave at *you*. Be a waver.

Things You Cannot Sooner or Later
Go Wrong *Saying* to a Man

"You've had such a profound influence on my life."
"You've changed my life."
"You've taught me so much."
Elaborate.

Giving Gifts

Now, as soon as the friendship ripens, you must begin to give him presents. Start this early in your young life, not late, if you please, even though you're poor . . . a medal, a poster, a book, a paperweight, a box—something antique, something funny, something carefully picked out just for *him*. Many women think the fact he is f———g you is your ultimate gift and one doesn't have to do another thing.

Wrong. Your *love* for him may be the ultimate gift but f———d he can always get. The idea that you are doing him a favor to go to bed (unless you *are* doing him a favor) so no other gifts are required must be banished from your brain *forever*. Even if he is half-crazy wild about you in bed, if you enjoy yourself there with *him*, it's present time. Presents say, I value you, I dote on you, I love your body, face, hair, heart, soul! I spent money to pick out this lovely bauble just for you.

It's quite simple really: Just about everything you ever thought a man should do for *you*, you should reverse and do for *him*. Now a man may not give back quite as much in the beginning, and if there is no reciprocity ever, stop. But if he is just *slightly* unable to catch up with your generosity, that is okay. Generous is better than stingy. Girls always on the take never operate from a position of strength and when they get to be forty, run into trouble. You can't *buy* a man with presents, and I know few women who would even try, but if you go a *little* overboard, pay too much for gifts for him, it isn't the worst insanity. Frankly, you'll have very little trouble with *any* man about accepting a present. They love it—especially flowers. And they also don't mind being taken to dinner.

Finding perfect presents is a challenge. They have to be utterly "custom-tailored." You know, having to do with *his* psyche, *his* hobbies. . . . Yes, hobbies! Fishing, driving, hunting (ugh!), music, literature, wine. If he has a car stereo, get him cassettes. Tickets to the show or game *he* wants to see are always good. I remember a Don Juan to whom I gave a picture of myself for his birthday. Talk about your ugly mistakes! A scrapbook of the entire Ford Model Agency would have been more suitable. Another friend—somebody wealthy—I gave Mickey Mouse little doodads for his den . . . one gets the shudders just *remembering*. Well, you learn. If he travels, consider the electrical plug that converts DC 220 to AC 120 in foreign countries, traveling Water-Pik, a super passport case, a little alarm clock. Anything monogrammed is perfect—Sterling bookmark, staple remover, key ring, bottle opener, handkerchiefs. . . . It doesn't have to be expensive, but should obviously be bought for him alone. Each man has a style or image, just as we do—Western, continental, Saville Row, tweedy-rustic, Fred Astaire. Whatever you buy for him to wear has to be compatible with that style. *Presentation* can be interesting. How about cuff links in the bottom of his grapefruit? A tie tack perched at the center of a spider chrysanthemum? Remember that present-giving is not the act of a desperate girl trying to buy love but of a generous and thoughtful one expressing pleasure in her man. No strings attached.

While we're into presents, could we talk about *class*? Class is *paying* for the food processor he gets you wholesale, not accepting it as a gift. Class is writing a check for the charity he believes in—the check can be small. I'll never forget a friend sailing to her feet to make a personal financial pledge the night her lover was honored at one of those charity dinners. . . . She gave fifty dollars while wealthy folk around her were pledging thousands, but her man loved it. Class is putting a bouquet of fresh spring blossoms (that does cost) in his apartment for no reason, filling the tank after you borrow his Pinto, *meticulously* returning what you borrow—handkerchiefs, sweater, money; not running up a bill to call your folks in Toledo from his office though he said you could. Non-class is *never* taking him to dinner or buying a gift because him rich, you poor. Class is unrequired, uninvited, *voluntary* generosity. It could *one* day be giving back his mother's onyx brooch if you break up.

Still *More* Sinking In

It is sexy and loving to *baby* a man, care about his health. I learned this *late* in life. One of my early beaux had ulcers—he used to devour *me* devouring *food*. . . . My eating all the things he *couldn't* was apparently orgiastic for him. Well, during our time together I *never* asked how he felt, though I cared for him. *I* was healthy and the idea of anybody being *sickly* was, well—unacceptable, even unimaginable. Years later at a Foote, Cone and Belding office party at the Town House Hotel in Los Angeles, a wildly attractive account supervisor—my date for the evening—went through a swinging door just as a waiter came through the other side and hit poor Nelson's forehead so hard you could see the door imprint on it. We got the hotel doctor and nurse, and since he was my date for the night, I stayed *with* him. Well, he was so grateful, I finally kind of got the hang of it. Jesus, I was already thirty years old, and this was my first taste of gentleness and caring and Nightingaling. Men are to baby! It gives you power but it's *enjoyable* to be so emotionally supportive and soothing and adorable. Ask. Care. If he's gone for a medical checkup, inquire. How did he make out at the dentist's? This is not the same as being responsible for a *sick* person—we're not asking you to do *that*—but concern for his health is *de rigueur*.

His Other Life

When one is a callow girl (early twenties), it's hard to *know* what men are needing, especially if he's older than you and possibly more successful. You're so wrapped up in your love affair and how he's treating you, you can't even think of him as needy. When you get a little older, you realize—surprise!—men are quite *human*, like *you*—and have a few problems! I mentioned the man who lost a million dollars in a real-estate deal, and that, the afternoon of the sale, I dozed off during our rendezvous. Later he said he just didn't see how I could *sleep* on the day of his great loss. Well, I was *reasonably* young—twenty-five—and didn't really understand what was going *on* in his life. . . . I was too callow, too dumb. I hope you'll learn to empathize, be smart and care a little *sooner* about things having nothing to do with you. I'm afraid you just *aren't* all there *is* in his world.

The Disappearing Act

Should you disappear sometimes—play hard to get? It's confusing. Every "adviser" in the world says lean *back* occasionally, make him lean forward, come looking for you. Yes, but he has to *want* to look. Presumably, *every* man wants to look for Victoria Principal—or whoever is the reigning ten as you read this—plus all the runners-up who are nines . . . fantastically pretty and lush. Would you mind if I just directed these words toward *us*—the mouseburgers? Yes, we *too* sometimes have to lean back and be scarce, yes yes yes, but we have to be in *position* to do that.

Two different women have told me this week that their now-husbands pursued them in their single days like madmen—the more the girls ran away, the harder the men pursued. Great. One woman is a famous actress; the man who chased—and got—her is a troglodyte, if you don't mind my saying so. The other woman is a twenty-nine-year-old dancer with the loveliest little body one has ever seen, her pursuer a sixty-year-old druggist. These women were in a *position* to be chased—their "package" was better than that of the pursuers.

We, with an "equal" or a man "better" than us, can go into hiding, and who's looking? You wait there in your little box, *suffocating,* and nobody comes to open the lid and get you *out*. Obviously, you must keep dignity and self-respect in an affair, not roll over like a Lhasa Apso just because its master has said roll over. You know when to move plans around because he's called suggesting something wonderful but you were already booked, and when to stand pat with previous plans. I'm just saying enthusiasm, availability, delight with his asking are certainly *part* of a mouseburger's arsenal; let Princess *Caroline* say she is booked for the next ten Saturday nights.

All the Trimmings

Now that you're deep into romance, may I hope also you're deep into some of its lovely trappings . . . champagne brunches, sangría lunches, crêpes at midnight, trips *à deux,* getting dressed gorgeously for *him,* being tipsy on margaritas in Puerto Vallarta, staying up all night in San Francisco, clinging dancing—and you aren't wearing any underwear under your pajamas—toasting in the sun, falling down in the snow, making love *everywhere.*

Sound like a 1930s movie? Good. You ought to *be* a movie heroine a few times in your life.

Some people's love affairs consist of movies, pizza and one more rerun of great moments in basketball. That's okay, love is love, but sometime in your beautiful young life I hope you have it with all the trimmings. There's *Christmas,* the *most* magical time if you don't screw up (*why* is Christmas so fraught with split-possibilities?). There's tree trimming, partying with him, hot buttered rum, buying his gift, glitter in your hair, satin on your body, fur. It's *magic.* Listen, Christmas can be the *pits* . . . no beaux, no parties, no *nothing.* . . . I've spent some like that, so, when love *is* there, I think we must *gobble.* I hope *many* lovely sparklers contribute to the intensity of at least *one* of your romances.

What besides Christmas and travel contributes to intensity? The kind of *man* you're with contributes. This is a favorite theme of mine, but I think the sexiest love in the world is between you and a somewhat "over your head" person—sought after, good-looking, respected—who could love battalions of women other than you but who thinks, by some miracle, *you* are the young Grace Kelly crossed with Lola Montez; who cherishes you as his lover but also as much as he cherishes his mother, daughter, friends, profession, model airplane/lithograph collection, you name it. When a man like that (you are equals but he is somehow *more* equal) loves you, possibly even a bit *more* than you love him, that is the most romantic setup in the world. *Other* intensity-makers: the darling *younger* man; the just utterly sensuous *snake,* never *mind* whether anybody respects him; the married man (ah, yes!); the widower who needs your adorableness to put his life back together. . . . Oh, God, the variety . . . how can you love only *once?*

Role playing contributes to sensuousness. Nearly all love relationships have some, not deliberately assumed but just there because of age and personality differences. Just as marriages have secret contracts (see Chapter Nine) in which husband/wife agree unspokenly to behave in certain ways, lovers have their "roles." I think the father/daughter relationship one of the sexiest, present in nearly every love affair in which he's at least fifteen years older than you. Then there is somewhat worldly, wicked, woman-of-the-world *you* indoctrinating slightly inhibited man into pleasures of the flesh—sensational! Utterly alike in age, interests, ideals . . . like Donny and Marie Osmond, only not brother and sister . . . *that* has its charms! Listen, if I'm sounding like a food critic comparing the homey delights of cheese fondue to the sophisticated allure of ragoût à l'ancienne, why not! Have fun with your roles before the fondue hardens into *problems*. Speaking of problems, maybe we'd better get to . . .

The Married Man

I don't see how a single girl can survive *without* an occasional married man—to fill in the gaps, stave off hunger during lean days. Many people (especially married *women!*) feel married men are off limits *totally,* for moral reasons (you ought not to confiscate somebody else's property) and practical ones (he can never see you Saturday night, goes home, even on Tuesday, right after dinner—or *before*).

True, true, true, but, to me, avoiding married men totally when you're single would be like passing up first aid in a Tijuana hospital when you're bleeding to death because you prefer an immaculate American hospital some unreachable distance across the border. This is my reasoning about married men: (a) When you're single, it's important to have heterosexual male companionship. You must *connect* with men. (b) All the connecting doesn't have to be with someone you could marry. (c) You should not go without *sex* too long. (d) Married men *need* you and are some of the horniest, appreciatingest, lovingest, most accomplished of our men sexually, and are *there* during a drought. (e) You can "use" them selectively, to sleep with if you're needy or just to have dinner with if you're lonely. Some take you to marvelous places, especially those on expense accounts away from home.

Now, one can't say *enough* about how unsatisfactory they are to fall in love with. They *don't* get divorces. We don't have statistics

219

about how many men leave wives to marry girlfriends, but 9 percent seems about right to me, and, since the ones who marry are the ones you *hear* about and frequently we *don't* hear about affairs that never went public, 9 percent may even be *high*. Further, when a man divorces, he frequently marries a *new* girl he hasn't *met* yet, not his loyal present friend. Married men are also not available to take you to your sister's wedding, to the company dance, to dinner on your birthday, at Christmas, or, as we said, possibly *any* Saturday night.

They also continue to sleep with their wives. This shocks some single girls practically into unconsciousness, and the girls never *do* admit that is happening. Even *divorcing* men will sleep with a wife right up to the signing of the papers and *after*.

To continue enumerating M.M. flaws—he does not always level with you about his needs nor cooperate on behalf of your *own*. Realizing that he is *not* the divorcing kind, you may have nonetheless decided to have a sexually rewarding friendship with the man. Possibly he is looking for a happy sojourn with a lovely girl while Pamela and the kids are in the country (just what you had in mind), *or*, for ego reasons, he may be looking for a heavy love affair and commitment, *sans* marriage, of course, *ever* to you. The reason he didn't *tell* you he's going to demand that you fall deeply in love is that if he did, you wouldn't go *along*. Later he lies and lies and lies . . . "We're going to be together, Madeleine, I *know* it" (listen closely and you'll find he never says *when*), but, as long as you are hearing from somebody those words you need so much to hear—I love you, I love you, I love you—you stay pinned.

Having painted such a gloomy picture, why am I recommending a married man to you at *all?* Well, for the reasons given (drought, expense-account dinners, etc.) but also because dating married men is not automatically tantamount to falling in love with one. And *should* you fall in love with one for a little while, *that* is not tantamount to breaking your heart, to hoping and waiting and waiting and hoping for *years* that he will divorce—you're probably not that silly. *Don't* be that silly! But I think you can *go* to the laden buffet table at a sumptuous Jewish wedding feast or a lush resort hotel and sample a few of the desserts, the sturgeon, the pasta primavera, without keeling over at the foot of the table because you have O.D.'d. You *can* enjoy the fling as *he* does, get the good out of it and move on.

What about *her?* I never worried about her. She's got a problem but you aren't *it. He* is it. A cheating husband will cheat with *somebody*—you are not that special. People always ask if *this* is my attitude—what would I think if *David* were cheating? Well, I would be *devastated*, but live by the sword, etc., etc. If someone can lure him from me, she's a good woman and I'll just have to deal with it. . . . I'm trying not to have that happen.

Trouble in River City

Let's say you are *not* with a married man, but are in love and have been wonderful, knocked yourself *senseless*. If you were any more adoring and divine, they'd have to cast you in bronze as a love goddess, give you a Pulitzer, write Broadway musicals about you. And what *else* are you? You are totally, absolutely not *sure* of him! Anxiety has set in. . . . It just *does* sometimes. Never mind whether it's another woman—he definitely doesn't spend enough *time* with you. His work (children, social life, sports, cronies—fill in your own enemy list) takes too much of his time. Forget *marriage*, he won't commit, *period* . . . maybe won't even say I love you. Sometimes he's remote, unreachable, and then there was the Disappearance when he didn't call for two and a half *weeks! Merde!* Oh, sometimes there isn't any question he adores you and you're delirious, but one measly *day* later the chill in your bones is so deep eight blankets and a quart of Napoleon brandy couldn't warm you up.

Well, darling, everybody from Proust and Shakespeare to Andy Warhol have written about love's ghoulishness—how the torture is frequently *not* made up for by the ecstacy. Shakespeare's Richard the Third says, "I have snakes in my heart . . . my heart has turned to stone . . . I strike it and it hurts my hand." Another sage: "We are never so defenseless against suffering as when we love . . . loving is a painful thrill." A third: "Love is a state of mind that begins when you think life can't be any better . . . and ends when you think life can't be any worse." Napoleon declared, "The only victory over love is flight," and Los Angeles sex therapist Irene Kassorla, author of *Nice Girls Do*, says, "The minute he or she falls in love with a mortal, they're in trouble."

Part of your unease is that you don't feel *equal* to him. You think you love *more* than he, yes, but not only *that*—and this, to me, is

221

the real meaning of the "inequality" you feel—you figure he can *cheat* more than you if he wanted to because (a) he is not so *hooked* on you as you on him and (b) he's got more *stuff* with which to be unfaithful if he desires.

Aside from men *always* being in demand because of the disparity in numbers, you believe that gene for gene, line for line, he is a more beautiful man than you are a woman, plus he's just got more charisma, more push and *charm*. Whenever he sets foot outside the door, you're certain he's in danger of being loved to pieces by a woman who merely *sees* him and keels over. And if she doesn't go toes up immediately, all he need do is *use* some of that considerable charm and charisma to tip her over. . . . You feel he almost can't *help* himself, he's so sexy! And you? Well, you got him in the first place because you're good in bed and you're sweet, and you hang on to him by being adorable and loving and caring and grateful and flattering and thoughtful and protective and supportive and generous and cooking and present-ing and succoring, but if you ever *stopped* any of that, he would obviously drop you like a scalding, wet bath towel. You keep him, unworthy as you are, by dint of *great* energy expended, great cleverness, even great chicanery, and great myopia on his part. Besides, he's *comfortable* with you . . . you're there. God knows you're available. It's no trouble at all for him to get a date with *you* on Saturday night or any other night with *no* notice, but it's always an anxiety-fraught game you play. . . . One could never say you're winning, just that you're hanging *in*. You decide only the merest whim of fate has kept him from having another woman already, but who is going to want *you* besides that strange little person in the mailroom who brings you little ethnic candies, and possibly your second cousin Ralph who has had the hots for you since you were ten?

My dear, you paint a very strong canvas of *his* assets, *your* liabilities. The only thing is you are full of shit. Ah, yes, there is the utterly glamorous, famous person who picks you up for the briefest moment and drops you again—him you haven't as much clout as— but celebrities are not what we're *talking* about. As for the non-celebrity, he is *not* that much more attractive than you, even if he is *physically* more attractive. Yes, you may be unequal in some ways. He may be richer than you; you can't compete with that. He may be further along in his career; he's a hundred-thousand-dollar-a-year man, you're at twenty or thirty thousand—for the moment. He may be socially more at ease, but on a human level, the level at which you operate with him and with all other men, you are perfectly as okay as he even if you're feeling *wildly* outclassed. You did *not* get him by some fluke or manage to keep him by sheer energy, willpower and guile. You manage to keep him because you're *okay*. Your *brain* is okay; your looks are okay. You have a warm and pretty body—pretty *enough* anyway—and if the time comes when you need to get another man, my darling, you can and *will*. All it takes is the need and wish, and then, finally, the act.

The thing that is keeping you from doing that *now* is not your lack of ability or talent or beauty—it's your lack of *wish*. And should you, at some time in your life, ever decide to go for numbers instead of one man at a time you can, yes, have *numbers*. We can't absolutely guarantee the *quality* of all the men you'll attract, but are all *his* admirers so chock full of quality? Supply depends on need—and energy!

So much for the pep talk; let's discuss present realities.

Fact: After the first fine days of passion and romance, so quickly over, there probably *is* not equality for lovers. One of you is simply *more* in love than the other, or less *sure* of the other. One is leaning forward, one is leaning back. At the very least your *timing* is different; your aching desire to see him may not coincide with his to see you. *Cosmo* once asked Elizabeth Taylor, then married to Richard Burton, "In your marriage, Elizabeth, whom would you say has more 'power'?" "I never heard such a dumb question in my life," said Elizabeth. "Tell *Cosmo* that is *sick*. When two people love each other, there is no such thing as power."

Wrong, Elizabeth. At that very moment *he* had the power, though at other times, when they were making *Cleopatra* together and she was the "new girl in town," glamorous, bewitching, married to another man, not yet his, *she* had it. Ah, yes, womanizers always have the power until they lose it, but back to vulnerable, anxious *you* going out of your mind! Further truths:

1. As things stand at the moment, I believe woman usually give 55 percent in the love relationship, men 45. What with the man shortage, women working harder than men at nearly *everything* we do, and possibly us being more shrewd and knowing a good thing when we have it, is that percentage so bad? I can live with it, can you?

2. Crazy ladies make love better than uncrazy ones. Your virulent anxiety about him somehow produces the purest kind of sexuality. . . . You're on edge, hungry, a Bengal tiger (the *best* kind!) when you get to bed. I'm not sure you can have that kind of sexy love *without* a touch of (though maybe you've got a touch too

223

much of) anxiety. When you're unsure of him, the affair just gets riper, juicier, headier, *more* addictive. . . . You're into pure passion. Of course mouseburgers tend to be passionate about *everything,* appropriate or not—it's part of our package. And everybody seems to feel great attraction to something that is unencumbered and free . . . a child, a playful puppy. We want to scoop up a *man* who is ignoring us and hug him to pieces.

3. Don't fret too much that you can't play it cool. As we said earlier, there is something about the act of f———g that does remove a certain starchiness from the most starched of us . . . not being affected would be like spinning around three or four hundred times like a top and not getting *dizzy.* Even with somebody you don't care that much about, the starchiness goes. In the act with somebody you *love,* even intelligent, liberated, "equal" and successful *you* can get into the crazies.

4. Whatever your passion and anxiety, your wokr is not going to suffer . . . at least you'll have *that.* Give or take a bad morning or two when you'll want to gulp down the pink liquid soap in the ladies' room and get your pained life *over* with, being an emotional extremist (Truman Capote's phrase) does not interfere with your being good at your job. The passion you put into the affair is the kind a mouseburger also puts into her work—which makes you *good* at it. You don't stop doing that.

5. Don't place too much emphasis on one bad night. Eight rotten evenings in a row might justify cyanide but one or two duddy nights go with the territory. . . . You can make a comeback.

Incidentally, when he is "free" and you are "trapped," does that mean you love him more? Yes, if you define love as *need* . . . you *need* him more, but if we are talking about pure *love* . . . affection, adoration—he *possibly* could love *you* more, might even be more sacrificing than you if one had to give up one's life as with Sydney Carton in *Tale of Two Cities* or something like that. Do you think his love is nothing just because it isn't anxiety-ridden? I'm just saying it's *possible* he's as hooked on you but behaves differently. Finally, if he's given you too much trouble and you have given him too much unrequited love, you can grow to *hate* him (the tables turn . . . revenge!) but we are not at the table-turning stage yet, we are merely suffering. What to do?

224

The Confrontation—How To Avoid It

Let's say you are really *quite* uneasy and want to *tell* him of your pain. . . . Would he please put his big woolly arms around you and reassure you? My dear, despite everybody pushing you to have "open and honest relationships," and despite your own mouse-burger inclination to *be* direct, I think forever blabbing what's on your mind is only for securely married people who can't/don't leave each other easily. In the flame of a big, splashy love, all that honesty, that confessing of how *unsure* you are can cause him to freeze over like a mud puddle at sixteen below. Most men—may I generalize?—provided they're not professional torturers who need "testimonials," seem to prefer a "stable," together girl. You must *try* not to splatter like an egg on concrete if you can help it. Contain! Even though you're a little sickened by some development and long to say, *No,* you may not go to that party with another woman, may *not* spend Christmas in a ski lodge with your brother, you said you were shopping but Alice saw you having cocktails with your secretary . . . pressure on the man is intolerable. Pressing will only get you spit at. . . . You must operate from strength. Strength comes from quietly hanging in.

Example: A young friend of mine has been left in the city for the weekend while her boyfriend whom she dotes on and wants to marry is off in Connecticut with a couple of old schoolmates and their wives . . . nobody *sexy,* still it's midsummer—a girl could *kill* over such a development, and Andrea longed to tell him he couldn't *do* this to her. But he's a "catch," he's also basically sound and good. It's *okay* for people to need other friends than you in their lives, so Andrea dimmed down her pique, went about dredging up anybody still left in the city she could get her hands on to have dinner, lunch or museum with that Friday, Saturday and Sunday. She doesn't have him *yet* but I think she's on her way.

Sometimes you have to *act* stable when you don't feel it, and if you *act* stable, the scene you were working yourself up to may not take place. Could you postpone a bit? Tell yourself you will wait at least until the following day . . . or maybe a week before you go to pieces—buy a little time!

The Christmas David and I were courting, I gave him gold cuff links from Cartier. Expensive. He gave me a skimpy pearl necklace from Saks while gifting the maitre d' at Romanoff's with a check twice the size of the cost of my pearls (I checked!). I was so sputtering and squirmy leaving Saks after the checkup, you'd have thought I'd swallowed a can of lighted Sterno. It wasn't the skimpy pearls, honestly—David had no money then—but the thought he could value a restaurant employee more than me . . . really! Well, at the time I was in therapy, had *never* made an emergency call to the therapist, but instinct told me this was the time. "Cool it," said the doctor. "Doesn't mean you can never discuss the Christmas present with David, but this is a man you love. He obviously doesn't know much about Christmas presents but he's been 'good' most of the time; don't pile on."

I reeled in, never mentioned my rage until we'd been married three years. (He thought it was funny.) By then I was on my way to bigger pearls and tipping maitre d's myself. I was thirty-six at the time of the pearl-episode, had made a hundred thousand mistakes with men but now had the benefit of therapy and a loving, nonexploitive *Possible* in my life. A girl does learn . . . and get lucky.

Containing

Maybe things are just not happy generally between you; you're miserable and feel a soul-search coming on. Of course, the last soul-search was a disaster. . . . He *loathes* soul-searches. Knowing you can't control yourself forever—it isn't you—can you maybe control yourself for what—ten days? *Sounds* like forever but ten days might be long enough to buy yourself some thinking time to figure out carefully what to say when you *have* the talk so you won't be into twitching, out-of-control, glassy-eyed madness. Your despair can be because you hope to *marry* the man and he's balking, or he's remote, or he's *impossible*. . . . *Whatever* the problem, you need to gain a little confidence and tranquility.

Once I was *so* depressed over a man, I consulted my friend Charlotte. Knowing I was going to Mexico in two weeks, C. said, Couldn't you hang on for those two weeks, not have a big scene? You're going to be okay in Mexico no matter what, because *he* won't be there. So I hung on, got through our meetings before departure by all but Scotch Taping my tongue to my teeth and swallowing alum to avoid telling him how miserable I was, got myself to make love without big sighs or even one sob (it wasn't easy—I felt sobby), got myself *onto* the plane and south of the border.

Okay, the trip really *was* fun. . . . When I got home my sadness had dissipated some, the keen edge worn down; I was fresh from Acapulco with a tan and a together feeling. Nothing had changed exactly . . . I just somehow *saw* him differently.

Gretchen reports a similar experience. "One summer when I was in *pain* over a man, I went to St-Jean-Cap-Ferrat and lay low for two weeks. I put the burner way down . . . it was still *on* but like the kind of heat you use to make yogurt with. For once I didn't scrounge around the shops looking for his perfect present or write him perfect postcards. I didn't even fantasize or think much about him, just sat this one *out,* and when I came through the airport shops at Orly on the way home, *still* resisted the urge to buy him an Hermès scarf or ashtray, which he would have loved. Well, when I saw him again, he hadn't died for lack of me, but for once I hadn't died for lack of him *either.* I was calmer than usual, still eager to see him but *calmer.* It had been good discipline and I've done that a few times since."

Gretchen continues: "I've come to believe, having *usually* done it the other way, that instead of blowing up a love affair with the dynamite one always has stored up for these occasions, i.e., fracturing your heart with the big-deal enormously painful (to *me* anyway but rarely to *him*) scenes, it can be better to let the affair wear down 'naturally' if it's going to or at least to end it quietly."

Interesting. If you finally *do* discuss—at a time *deliberately* picked by you—your anxieties or specific problems, I'd suggest you try to be flattering, contained, charming, nonaccusing and dear . . . *quel* assignment! Bringing a present along to the confrontation sets a good tone—a present not out of desperation, but because you think he's adorable—only you've got this *thing* on your mind. You know not to weep all over him *ever* if you can help it, especially if *he's* unemotional. Weeping is out of control and, in some ways, as bad as a temper fit which is *also* out of control. Think about the people who cry around *you.* . . . Don't you feel really rather, well, *detached* as you watch them sob away?

P.S. Never say to a man, "Oh, I could love you so much . . . could make you so happy if you'd *let* me!" What you mean is you'd make *you* so happy if he'd let you love him, that *you'd* enjoy getting your hands on his time and soul—but it's pretentious to think he wouldn't already have handed them over if he thought *he'd* get anything out of it. Face the reality that he hasn't any hidden happiness to be mined by you if he doesn't think you're the one to mine it.

Another Her

We have been talking about just run-of-the-mill anxiety with your man. . . . It *could* have been about another woman, but I have saved that little torment for a special section because other-woman jealousy is so much more *hideous* than other problems.

Let's declare right now that what's going on is probably *not* all in your mind. Observing suffering friends—and myself through the years—I've found one usually has *reasons* for that feeling you've been kicked in the stomach. When some dear person declares sweetly she is *never* jealous I know she's (a) lying; (b) hasn't been involved with somebody who's acting like a shit; (c) she's feeling it all right, but refusing to call what she feels jealousy.

There is no *way* anybody seriously, sexually in love cannot be wounded if her man gets into bed or anywhere close to bed with another woman, and that's *final*. True, us less "secure" mouse-burgers feel more jealousy perhaps than others, feel mortally threatened if a man gives his secretary a *book* for her birthday or a ride home in a blizzard, and, ideally, we'd have him write his lunch order on a pad and send it up the aisle to the flight attendant rather than *talk* to her. We know a lot of terror all right, but still we're *pretty* much okay unless he commits what seems to us an atrocity.

Right here we ought to define the man. If he's a Don Juan—a human sausage machine who must continuously be fed new girl-sausages—the problem is a little different than with a man who has just committed random naughtiness. A real *womanizer*—from girl to girl to girl like a bee into blossoms—might as well wear a black hood with slits for eyes and carry a cleaver like the executioner of Marie Antoinette, for that's what he *is*—our executioner! Dealing with him is different from dealing with a random transgressor. You and he will eventually part so it doesn't matter *how* badly you carry on; good behavior isn't going to save you or get you anywhere—sorry to be so negative!

Of course, you may *exacerbate* the suffering with your suspicion and snooping . . . all for very sound reasons, of course. During my long involvement with a Don Juan I went through wastebas-kets, coat pockets, desks, beds, briefcases and garbage *looking* for evidence, never failing to find it. With a certified D.J., his cheating practically becomes your *raison d'être*. Hope Cooke says in

228

her autobiography, *Time Change,* about her husband, the Chogul, "Although I feel powerless to effect any change, I am obsessed with his infidelities. Worse, in worrying so much about his flirtations, I've begun to identify with him, act like a silent pimp, picking out in my mind the girl I fear he will go after next. One day as I'm jeeping along a rutted road through the jungle in North Sikkim to join my husband, who's preceded me by a few days, I see a very pretty girl through a fringe of trees, walking down the valley from the spot where his camp is. She is carrying a spray of white orchids and wears one in her hair. I know he's given them to her, or if he hasn't already, he will."

P.S. Don't expect a womanizer to stop chasing women just because he gets married. Unless he also gets sick or impotent, he will always kill again. Are you then a neurotic crazylady to be involved with such a person? Of course not! *Any* sane woman is capable of having a D.J. in her life, and it does not mean you have low self-esteem or *hate* yourself unless you pick D.J.'s over and over again. Liv Ullmann, Angie Dickinson, Julie Christie, Diane Keaton, Jackie Onassis, Audrey Hepburn—to name a few famous "nice" women—have all suffered the blight. You just don't want to go through it *twice.* If you're with one *now,* however, I think you just get the "good" out of him (he *is* divine in bed, is he not? and life is heady and romantic) and prepare to suffer.

You, Him and Her

Okay, your man, possibly not a Don Juan, has shown interest in another woman, and, though he may not yet have gone to bed with her, you're in agony. May one suggest you are probably not so much jealous of another person (especially when you *see* her—she isn't Bianca Jagger) as you are scared absolutely witless by your own inadequacies . . . threatened not so much by a winning *her* as by a failing *you?*

Don't try to find out much about her—I *mean* it! I'm for doing anything, God knows, that would *help (Non tricarus est excessus inferus*—no trick is too low) but investigating her will *not* be helpful because very likely *she* is not the problem. . . . His *needing* her *is.* If a man doesn't *want* another girl, Natasha Kinski in her undies won't move him, but if he *wants* another girl, there are so many for *any* man to pick from we really don't have to worry much about her as a person. Yes, you can go squirreling about trying to

229

find out where she works and who her friends are, but if what you want is to get over your *jealousy*, it would be better to leave *her* rather amorphous. As beautiful black model Beverly Johnson said when she just missed qualifying for the 1968 Olympics in the one-hundred-yard free style, "Don't worry about what the others are doing. If you look around to see where everyone else is going, you lose the race. The trick is to keep swimming." Keep swimming!

Living with Love Angst

Let's say it *hasn't* blown over with the other lady—he's seeing you *and* her—or he has stopped seeing her but *other* things are wrong and you're dying. . . . Your affair right now bears *no* resemblance to the courtship of Lady Diana by the Prince of Wales and you're in pain. He sees you less often. Your need to have him telephone at this exact moment is equal to your need for oxygen—and in direct proportion to his need to do no such *thing!* Lover's equation: Naked need in one breeds dispassion in the other. You do the old staying-home-*by*-the-telephone routine, knowing what an utter fool you are, interspersed with taking the dog for a walk, hoping to invoke magic by not being there. . . . Zilch, says the answering service. (You *know* you can't call somebody you haven't heard from to tell them you don't want to *hear* from them anymore but are tempted!) At the office you've alerted twelve people to get you out of the john, out of the elevator, out of *hell* if he telephones.

Then one morning when you are nearly dead of pain and waiting, he does. Lunch? Fantastic! Only this lunch, which ought to be a frisky, happiness-producing *extra*, turns out to be the *only* thing he has in mind for the week—dinner isn't mentioned. Oh those treacherous little lovers' lunches of roily stomachs, frozen tears and barely touched escargots. The *night* you've planned for three weeks and plowed *everything* into—the apartment, the food, the wine, *you*, perfumed, coiffed, dressed like Scheherazade—and *pffffffT!*

I recall maybe the *ugliest* night of a long affair. Around five in the morning W. tells me we will *not* be going to Europe. . . . Santa Anita has been a disaster this season (how a girl can pick somebody who likes women *and* horses is incomprehensible!). I go toes up! It isn't *just* that he has been unfaithful but *everything* is rocky, and I had counted on our being together for two weeks (Eiffel Tower, Schmeifel Tower, it didn't *matter!*) to glue us back together. I slide out of bed like a little greased seal, leave him smug and sleepy, drive barefoot and bathrobed in my Restoration Chevy, Catherine Howard, straight to the Santa Monica pier (twenty-five miles away) racked with pain, sorrow and sobs. It didn't help!

So what do you *do?*

Hanging On

Until you decide to break up, may one suggest your work ought to be your solace at this time and, rather than *ignoring* it because you're so gone and crazy and worried about *him,* you ought to invest. During my years with "bad men," I always found everything that went into my job I got *back*—with interest. Putting everything in a man—that particular man anyway—one might not get back one's original *investment,* not that you don't continue to invest *anyway.* So, even though, at the height of the trauma with him, you feel like a crab scrabbling up on the rocks even to get out of bed in the morning, let alone do anything about your *job,* do it! Show up on time. Line up a certain number of projects you're going to do every day and *do* them. Make phone calls you've been avoiding which could *further* a work project. Attend meetings, write the report, turn in ideas. Discipline! I do not say your heavy little heart will be *in* it, but the work is there to solace and reward, help you get and keep your balance.

Aside from work, picnic-lunch in the park with an office friend—you bring the lunch; make an appointment with somebody you've wanted to spend time with . . . go to that person's office or flat for tea if he/she is too busy to spare you a lunch date; God *knows* you'll want to check into a health club . . . pure oxygen for ladies suffocating in a love-fit. Stay in touch with a shrink or close friend. There are times when one's life needs an *editor* . . . the raw manuscript needs straightening out. Do not leave everything to your own confused thinking but let your "editor" help and advise. Trust. For now. Later on, your life manuscript may need virtually nothing at all and you'll be advising (editing) others.

The Spite Fling

What about having a new romance to make him jealous? Well, I'm a firm (almost hardened into concrete!) believer that you stay friendly with many men all your life.

Lunch, cocktails, phone calls. *Never* wrap up in a love cocoon so that you can hardly *see* anything beyond the silken strands.

It's also okay morally to have more than one *sexual* partner at a time if you want, but having them at the same time you are madly in love is like trying to get in your car and drive to Philadelphia while you are still on the airplane in a holding pattern over the airport; you can't get *into* a new romance when you're wild about a man. As for faking interest in somebody new just to stir things up a bit, well, for mouseburgers, action is always better than passive suffering, but for some reason you can't really do it to him while he is doing it to *you*—whoever does it first is obviously the one who *needs* an outside person, the one who causes the real impact and commotion—you're only playing defensively.

An actress I know tried to make her husband jealous when *he* strayed by having a little showoff spite fling of her own. It was easy—Molly's beautiful and charming. Her husband pretty soon stopped his cheating and Molly stopped, too, thinking she and he would quickly fall back into each other's arms. Not so! Husband simply started a *new* affair. Whatever was wrong with their relationship couldn't be fixed by jealousy and they were subsequently divorced. "It was like I was going for the jugular," Molly said, "and I merely wound up biting him on the leg."

But now, regarding seeing other men, I have something to suggest which is new and different, so pay attention. I think in case a man is torturing you with somebody new, not on purpose necessarily but just because he really wants to see other women, you, too, should see somebody else but not tell him . . . *not* do it to make him jealous but to cheer *you* up. It works differently when you do it for *you* but don't tell. You just quietly conduct the new affair or heavy friendship with another person for your *own* sake, to gain some equilibrium, to get away from his stranglehold for a moment and not take him *quite* so seriously.

I have done that. Yes, life gets a little confusing, keeping dates and times straight, but I don't think for a moment it is unsavory or promiscuous. How could going to bed with somebody nice and sweet and lovely that you like as a friend be *promiscuous?* And this is the point: You wouldn't be conducting this second affair if it weren't that your beloved were giving you a very hard time. I believe you can do your jealousy some good by proving to *yourself*, never mind Mr. Wonderful, that you can charm and bewitch another man.

Pick a *good* man—there is really no reason not to. You don't care if he loves you passionately or is yours forever or if you share *him* with another woman—you need him only as a loving, if temporary, companion, so might as well try for a prince. Funny how easy it is to *attract* new men when you're "safely" in love with somebody else. But never tell your true love. This is for *you*.

Jumping Ship

When do you leave? There's a very simple way to know: When the pain outweighs the pleasure, you go. When you cannot take one more hour of this suffering, you cut your losses. The end may come "unexpectedly"—you didn't know this specific night was going to be the one although things had been rocky of late and you also didn't know this would be the *final* goodbye after so many previous "trial" ones. I remember a final-final in my single years. Baby Julie, his new love, was out there pounding on the door of his apartment at four in the morning with me inside *with* him, and B.J. is wailing, "Let me *in*, Joe darling, I didn't *mean* it . . . I *love* you . . . Let me *in* . . . blah blah blah." Well, darlings, something finally snapped. This is *ridiculous*, I said to myself, two of us grappling like Japanese fighter fish over one silly man, and I got dressed and flew out of there *forever*. . . . So much for quiet discussions—I'd *had* all *those*. No one can imagine—unless she's been there—how much silliness, and for how long, one puts up with *before* flight.

Sometimes you will be leaving a man who is *not* a rat but who, nevertheless, simply must be left (he's *killing* you). In Nandi, Fiji, David and I are boarding our plane after a few days' holiday en route to Australia. Nandi was then a South Pacific fueling and crew-change stop. The pilot is the most attractive man I've ever seen—a blond *Viking*—you could kidnap him. His lady is the assistant manager of the hotel we have stayed in. I hear from one of the flight attendants that the pilot is married and has children. I watch this girl, obviously far, far gone on her man, she so young and busty and attractive, weeping as he kisses her goodbye on the steps of the hotel, and I feel I am witnessing a classic case of girl who must bail out before her heart is utterly broken. *She* doesn't know it yet but *I* know she must leave him, and, in his case, the replacement will probably not be easy. . . . How many men like him does she see for more than a day or two tucked away in Nandi? But I wanted to tell her, though I barely knew her, It's going to be okay. . . . There *will* be another man for you . . . there *always* is.

When an affair has been going on a *long* time, leaving is toughest. (Poor Jean Harris—fourteen years with Dr. Tarnower. She should have left at least by their seventh year when he took a mistress, not waited until she really couldn't handle the jealousy and rage.) It is a bold but life-preserving, eventually life-*enhancing*, investment to leave. My husband told me recently, "I changed my life when I stopped needing lovers who were not friends . . . when I decided life *was* too short to get hurt and wounded again and again by difficult women when another kind of woman could be just as sexy and actually *love* you." (He's talking about *me*!) That happened to *me* too . . . with men, with *him*. Somebody who is *good* and who really *loves* you can be just as sexy. I adore this man with whom I have now been twenty-three years more than any of the others.

The Goodbye Girl

You've left him. Or he you. Leaving is not the superior position it sounds. The reason you leave is that you're getting your *head* beaten in! When a man leaves *you*—or doesn't return after the fight—he may also not be the "fortunate one"; you may have been giving *him* a bad time. Whichever is worse, leaving or being left, it's *over*. You've gone through all those partings and makings up and this one you pretty much know is going to take.

These were my survival rules.

Rule 1. You do not lock yourself in your room with his photograph, his platinum record, a bunch of joints, a fifth of Scotch, the Nembutal, and play and drink and smoke yourself—literally—to death like the daughter of a famous entertainer did a few years ago when her man walked out. A little self-pity, yes. A *lot* of grief, yes, but you are not going down the old tube in self-hate, paralysis and masochism. I would suggest you *not* browse through mementos, sleep in his cashmere sweater, go anywhere *near* the hi-fi to play Your Song. Nevertheless . . .

Rule 2. In the first hours and days after a breakup you don't *fight* the pain. It may not even *come* immediately. The fight, the drama of it, may have left you somewhat numb, or even exhilarated. . . . *Later* comes the pain: Stunning and pure as a forty-carat diamond, pain like nobody has ever felt before, except you the *last* time this happened, only this is *worse!* Well, you have to let the pain *occupy* you, like an invading army (or like the barium swallowed for the G-I X-ray series that spreads all around your intestines, the G-I series being the *only* thing I can think of that is *almost* as miserable as a busted love affair).

Rule 3. You cry. Tears are part of Nature's Recovery Plan. You don't gouge your Poor Tortured soul to feel *good* ("Shape up there, soul!") right away but rather let your P.T. soul lead and tug where it will. The fight may have been so dramatic you're anesthetized for the moment and won't cry but pretty soon will feel so awful you'll say to your P.T. soul, "What *is* this shit? I cannot stand it another minute!" and *then* the tears will start, slippy-sliding a few at a time, later gaining momentum until you're splashing and sobbing like a Greek tragedienne and, if you happen to feel your forehead at that time, it feels like *rocks* were in there, all knotted up into something that must look horrible. . . . Don't *look!* As the sobs and wracks and splashes continue, your brain softens to the point you're sure you should never have left him! You feel ghastly and wonder how you'll ever get back to feeling even as good as you did before you started *crying!* Not to worry. Fifteen minutes later, when you finally run down, you'll feel *cleansed* . . . cauterized and, dare I say it? better. At least you can go on with whatever you'd planned that day and, yes, you were *right* to leave him, birdbrain! (Second, third or even fourth subsequent cryings are not unusual for recoverers.)

Rule 4. Sleepless you will probably be. At night on Bonnie Brae Street in Los Angeles when I couldn't sleep after a bad breakup, I used to get out of bed, take all the pillows, collect Spam, my first Siamese cat, go to living room, spread pillows out on couch, lie on top of pillows, put Spam on stomach and talk out loud . . . sort of like a lawyer, giving a deposition—this is what *he* did, this is what *I* did, this is how we got to this stage, this is how *I* feel, this is how *he* feels. . . . After an hour I would say, "Okay, cat, and okay, pain—I'm going back to bed now. You can both come *with* me if you like. When did I ever deny either of you access to my body? . . . The welcome mat is *out*. If you decide against now, I'll be around later (when pain knows it *can* visit you, it occasionally lets *up!*), then I would go back to bed, maybe with a glass of milk or hot chocolate, and fall asleep, *that* night done for. I never tried to cheer myself up before it was *time*. Trying to force cheer is like trying to get a green banana to ripen by putting it in the *oven*.

Rule 5. Sooner or later—probably sooner (you may have called her immediately after the breakup), you will want to enlist a friend, somebody to tell everything to. This particular friend will listen not only attentively but *endlessly* . . . let you talk yourself to pieces. Maybe this friend can now level with you a little more than previously, gingerly mention problems of his that have obviously *got* you to this stage, but if she is a *good* friend, she will never say you were a fool to have loved him or that he didn't love you *back*. You may be tempted, now you've parted, to remember only *adorable* him; she may gently remind you of the *other* him.

If you have no close friend to confide in, we'll have to *get* you one (Chapter Ten), but for now you can make do with an office mate or an acquaintance. One afternoon a young *Cosmo* editor we'd just hired came to me almost destroyed with man trouble. Frankly, I had a lot of things to get done that afternoon and could have done without my young friend's trauma. Nevertheless, I listened for about an hour and a half—a long time for me—and then I counseled. I'm just saying if selfish, first-things-first (like *Cosmo* business) *me* can pause to render first aid, I'm sure you'll find someone.

Rule 6. Get professional help. There is *nothing* like somebody smarter than you about emotional matters. My friend Charlotte is a better shrink than most shrinks, yet I want Charlotte *plus* somebody less involved with me . . . a professional. Even when I was the poorest girl alive, I somehow squeezed out the money for a couple of sessions in crisis time. Your decision to get help is simple if you've already been in analysis and can just check back in with the same therapist, more complicated if you haven't. One of your friends or your doctor will surely know somebody. I can't recommend shrinkage *enough*. Just one or two sessions can help ease the pain.

As the days post-breakup slip by, you will want to surround

yourself with as much love as possible. I have always found office friends *invaluable*. Even if they don't know what is the matter with you (let's hope you haven't told *every* little star about your love problems as they unfolded), they can still be supportive. I used to stay near these people like a family just letting their friendship osmose *in*. You can do that. A real family, depending on the kind you've got, can also lighten the load.

The Long (or Maybe Not So Long) Road Back

The first *week* after the breakup you won't be worth much to yourself or your company but at least show *up*. I always found work—though on a lower level of energy than usual—kind of *soothing*, practically the *only* way to get the time to pass. Don't head off on a trip the first few days or weeks of your grief. You'll just be taking the blues *with* you and won't have anything but a so-so time or, if you manage to smile while *there,* you'll get soggy again once home. I can't stress enough that you've got to have a proper period of grief, although you don't let it paralyze you at work. Just keep on the back burner the knowledge that this *will* get better—you don't have to do anything ambitious right now. As the days and weeks go by, try some of *these*—nothing new here but all useful: night school (will you finally learn Italian, cost accounting?); classes in cooking, painting, ballet, modern dance; gym or health club; outdoor exercise—tennis, golf, archery, swimming, horseback riding, squash, jogging (some you can do alone); lunch, dinner with friends (invite them to your house sometimes; don't freeload); visits to elderly relatives, people in hospitals (during one "recovery," I danced with the mentally retarded patients at Sawtelle Veterans Hospital in Los Angeles . . . I hated every minute but it took my mind off *me*); career (*Numero uno* priority. You've got all that time and energy to pour into your work now and it will repay you. Success—living well through success—*is,* as we've already stated, the best revenge). During a recovery (me again) I entered a *Glamour* magazine contest—Ten Girls with Taste—won a trip to New York, Joseph Magnin wardrobe and two weeks in Hawaii. From that contest came my moving from secretarial work to writing advertising copy to writing *Sex and the Single Girl* to you and me being together now.

237

The New Person

Let's mention *him* one more time. Is he hurting like this? Not likely. He may be uncomfortable enough to call you several times ("Linda, can't we even get together to talk about this?") but he is probably not in pieces. His lesser pain is not your problem. *He* is not your problem anymore. Your problem now is to get *over* him and on with your life, and that means, sooner or later, finding a new man.

Your challenges are three: One, you are about as capable of emotional involvement now as though you'd been hacked to death with a machete. Two, if you should *want* to care about somebody else, there's nobody like *him* . . . perceived by you *still* as a cross between Christopher Reeve and Dan Rather, with a touch of Johnny Carson thrown in. *You* you perceive as having little to offer. Three, he, right this minute, can date two dozen women. *You,* right this minute, would be lucky to get it on with the bottled-water delivery man. Listen, hasn't the time finally come for you to *forget* how many women he can rack up? And you have your memories . . . the most wonderful memories they can never take away from you. Memories! . . . who could possibly care about *them* when your heart is broken, but one day you will pour them over you like Chanel No. 5. Memories of love affairs contribute to the total you, your *image* of you, which in turn creates the *world's* image of you—a woman who has loved men, who has been loved by them, somebody, well—if you can get your mouseburger self to come out of that brown paper bag and *admit* it—fascinating . . . not like those sane, careful creatures who only love once.

Now we come to the present. Pay attention. There is *no* mouseburger so unprepossessing that she cannot turn up another man or several. What appealed to the first one will appeal to others. I don't know a woman, I mean not *one,* who has ever failed to turn on another man, frequently better than the one she is currently deranged over.

Example: One of the most gifted female writers of our time (critics rhapsodize), definitely a mouseburger—shy, diffident, not pretty—I remember *before* her fame and success as *suicidal* over a married man. K., now married herself—not to him—is the object of attention of one of the biggest *movie* stars of our time (my dear, I *only* tell you true stories). He is interested in her *brain,* of course—

such a lovely brain—and her talent, but whatever appeals to a man *counts*. They are not having an affair but she is being lovingly pursued.

You don't have to be a famous novelist with a movie-star admirer to constitute a testimonial to this fact: You were *not* invented to please only one man, to have only one man catch your special beauty, the essence and charm and lure of you. There are, oh, my God, so many others!

Dating Again

Oh, my, what a scruffy bunch, those early arrivals! Have Frank and Terry lost their minds to think you'd want to go *out* with, let alone form an *attachment* with, this thing they must have dredged up from the bottom of Lake Erie? Some recoverers won't even accept blind dates—life is too short and all that.

Okay, *stay* choosy and exclusive, but *I* always thought it better to date all the men one could muster, hustle or be fixed up with quite *soon* after the fall. You're not really going to be *over* "him" for possibly a year or longer, and I don't see how you can wait that long to begin your new life. These new people take your mind off your dumb broken heart. Even if they are second-rate, you have to pay attention when they talk, make an effort. I just always liked having men—a man—*around* and thought of the sad, lovely Cole Porter ballad from *Can-Can*—"It's the wrong time and the wrong place, tho' your face is charming, it's the wrong face; it's not his face but such a charming face that it's all right with me . . ."*
—even if he was decidedly *not* Burt Reynolds. One didn't have to *sleep* with him but one could get *something* from the encounter, even if just a better fix on his field . . . politics, law, architecture.

So you ask your friends who Know People to fix you up . . . you *do* accept blind dates. You do *not* require that every evening with a stranger—or friend—be meaningful. You ask men to a movie, lecture, exhibit, concert . . . you *cook* for them, but don't pick on people too far over your head or you'll get your feelings hurt by their rejection. You bless every late-afternoon coed business meeting that lasts through dinner.

Just being *with* men is important, but remember, you are not desperate. Desperate women do not find anybody. You are open,

---

*Copyright 1953 by Cole Porter.

friendly, tolerant and reasonably *patient*. One day you get back in the swim sexually. A divorcee I know, sexually and emotionally dormant for two years after her divorce, recently went to bed with a man and said it was *not* good. "He's dull *out* of bed so why would he shine *there*, but he's 'turned me out.' "—Las Vegas expression for a man who sleeps with a girl, gets her hooked on him, then "turns her out" to sleep with other men, possibly as a prostitute. My friend has now been "turned out," not like the Las Vegas girl, but freed to sleep with and get sexually *interested* in men again. The bland man did that for her. God forbid it should take you a smidgeon that much time.

Well, finally, one day you are *over* him. They bring out the old pulp tester to see if there's any life left in the tooth (your late love affair) and there *isn't*. . . . Eventually you will be a bit aghast, maybe even ashamed, that you ever took him so seriously. . . . *Him?* Why couldn't you just have enjoyed the sex and headiness of it all without being so federal-case out of your *brain* about him? You couldn't. You never *can*, and you must never apologize to yourself for the man you've given all that passion to. He was the one at the time, and if you cared, you cared. God bless.

Chapter Nine

MARRIAGE

Why Marry?

Man as a meal ticket is as quaint an idea to a mouseburger as keeping a dinosaur as a pet; when (if) you marry, you'll go on working, earning and achieving. Marry for sex? Don't be silly! That's better *outside* marriage. Companionship in old age? You two may *not* make it together to old age—one marriage in every two is rocksbound. Also, women outlive men by an average of fourteen years . . . the dear thing may have perished. Acquiring somebody to daddy children might motivate a woman to wed, but millions of divorced and widowed women are bringing up children *without* a live-in daddy so you don't *have* to have one for that purpose either. So why *do* so many of us marry when we don't have to? Because we think we can't live without a particular person, usually. . . . We come down with that "we've got to be together forever" feeling no matter *how* debatable that idea may seem three years later. The prospect of being alone any longer may be too hateful for a single woman to bear, and here is this Possible Person in her life; or we want public and legal recognition that we've *captured* somebody—*plus* all those reasons just said weren't the reasons to marry but still *are (plus ça change, plus c'est la même chose).* What *has* changed is that we don't get married just because we're (a) pregnant or (b) think he may be our very last chance.

How do you have a *good* marriage?

Trying to describe a good marriage is like trying to describe your adrenal glands. You know they're in there functioning but you don't really understand how they work. Mutual support is probably the biggest ingredient of a good marriage. "They" (the outsiders) are wrong, you are right, no matter *what* the evidence to the contrary (or what either of you is really thinking!). Author Judith Krantz *(Scruples, Princess Daisy)* says, "When you consider family and friends, however dear and close, you come to realize there really is no other 'best friend' than your husband. This does not mean unhealthy interdependence—a large measure of independence is necessary in order to admit that you *do* depend on someone else—but life is a thousand percent better with a husband behind you." Meredith Brokaw, NBC anchorman Tom Brokaw's beautiful wife (they married in college), says, "In marriage you get all interwoven . . . you get so *close.*" Betsy Cronkite, Walter's wife, says, "When I think of how sorry I feel for widows, I guess you'd have to say *companionship* is the biggest ingredient." Casey Ribicoff, married to the ex-Senator from Connecticut after a long, romantic love affair, says, "I trust him completely . . . only one other person in the world do I trust that much, and you can be totally *yourself* . . . there is nothing to hide, no truth he can't accept." "I really would rather do things with Jerry than anybody else in the world," says actress-comedian Anne Meara of husband Jerry Stiller, "and he's *there* . . . I don't have to get a date with him!" I like this definition of a good marriage. "It's having someone to telephone wherever you are and somebody who takes your work as seriously as you do" . . . the new acid test.

Is marriage a compromise? Compromise doesn't quite say it for me . . . compromise sounds like sitting down at the negotiating table and talking out your terms. Well, husbands and wives really don't *discuss* terms that much (I will water the lawn if you will feed the Airedales)—you just *do* it. Balancing is more what a marriage is . . . balancing *your* needs against his and trying to see that both sides get taken care of. Many marriages get *better* as they go along. "Our marriage didn't really take until nine years in," an advertising man told me recently.

I think part of the reason women say they *don't* want to get married is that, yes, they really *do* like the single life—all that freedom!—but—here we go again!—there also aren't that many men to marry! One of my good friends, a widow aged thirty-nine, has been saying that she really *enjoys* being with other women because you don't have to carry on like a fox terrier on visitors' day at the pound trying to get adopted the way you do with men, or turn into a glazed doughnut *listening* to them. It is so much more comfortable and real being with women, she was saying, when whammo, her second year into widowhood, she met somebody, and now being with women isn't all that fantastic—she wants to be with *him*.

Part of many a single woman's defense of singlehood, then, is wanting to deal with the *possible*, not set herself up for discontent by insisting on a husband when none is available. However, when as with my friend, a Possible hoves into view, you begin to think of marriage. If one can choose the timing, I think it's *probably* better to be single in your twenties and thirties when a lot of people have the hots for you and you can have as many affairs as you care to fit in, and married when you're older and not so *many* people want you; but just because that's the way I did it doesn't mean it's the best or only way. When you're older and snugly married, the marriage may disintegrate anyway, so you're never *permanently* "safe." Whatever your age, a man can always leave you for another woman or *die* (of the two, I think dying is preferable). Listen, marriage is an *adventure* I would wish for you *sometime* during your mouseburger life, if not *all* the time.

How to Get Married

We all know women who manage to marry when there are *no* men. This is what you do:

1. Determine that you really *want* to be married, that you are not kidding all of us and yourself by saying that's what you want— and not really wanting it.

2. Be ready to compromise in your marriage choice. He will not only have minor flaws but probably a couple of major ones that appear on your *least*-wanted qualities list (Stingy? Slobby? To the right of Jesse Helms?).

3. Do not think the man you are desperately in love with *has* to be the one you marry or that you must be deeply in love to marry. Out of your skull in love and getting married should probably be *less* frequent handmaidens than they are for marriage to last because passion blinds you to the real *him* . . . the one you'll be

spending your life with. Writer Irma Kurtz says, "Wise people go to bed in love but get married friendly." Be happy, grateful, if you've turned up a *friend*.

4. If you marry *just* to marry, that isn't the worst idea! Should you live all your life without marrying *once?* I'd vote *No*. Take a chance! And if you pick a decent nonloser and dedicate yourself to him and the marriage, it has a very good chance of succeeding.

5. Try not to be discouraged because there are "no men." It's *true* "the pickings are lean" but it only takes one, just one measly man out of all those millions and millions. I believe you can *have* your one (perfectly good) man. Most women who marry didn't have fifteen chances—they had one. You can have a happy marriage with your "one chance" if that's what it comes down to.

Okay, you've sighted the man you want to marry, whether he feels the same way or not. How do you "get" him? Two more basics: First, he has to be a *possible*. You may meet and fancy, date, sleep with, live with a man who is just not a *marryer*. There is no more marrying him than turning Hugh Hefner into a Bible salesman (Phyllis Schlafly into a feminist?). Have "fun" but forget that man to marry. The marry rules don't work with him. Second, *timing* has a lot to do with marriage. Sometimes a man is just "ready," even if he doesn't know he is. You may not be among the women he has loved most of his life, but you are the one who is there when he is ready to be fertilized. Fine, but if his time is *not* now, you have to ascertain whether his time will be *ever*, or ever with *you*, and if not, you may have to forget him. An attractive man I know who has never married and fells girls like sparrows though he is faithful to each until The End says, "When they get the old lower-lip wobble and say, 'I want to have your baby,' I know it's time to move on." Touching.

Okay, if he *is* Possible—and try to face the truth about this—you do all the things mentioned on pages 207 through 216 when you are merely in love. They are as sound as the rules that govern weight loss. If you want to lose weight, take in less food. If you want to entrance a man (and maybe marry him), you are *good* to him, easy with him, a joy to be around. Some men marry neurotic women who give them a bad time, but usually they *don't* (though the woman may be enjoyed in bed). Usually the disturbed, neurotic, difficult creature *loses* men. You are cheerful. A brief synopsis only, please, of your year with runaway colitis, mere mentions of people you loathe at the office, your neighbors who play punk rock—*loud*—all night. You don't actually have to *be* happy to seem happy with *him*. Trust me. You will not "get" a man if you are a walking mound of sadness or venom. Think about the divorced men you know who kvetch so about ex-wives and present alimony—how you'd just as soon escape while they're in the *men's* room and never look back. You are adorable to be with, got it? You really *like* men. If you secretly *dislike* men, you need psychiatric help, just as you need it if you dislike *you*. There could be no better investment.

And now into the stretch. Do not push. Do not nag. Do not bring the subject *up* unless he asks what you think about marriage, and then be cagy. Pretend not to be *certain* what you think. Marriage *sometime* maybe . . . you just aren't sure. Do not *lunge* (the Baskerville hound presented with a bleeding human heart!). You know whether he is a real Possible and you must handle him as carefully as pastry dough. Do not, however, let the moment pass—by moment I mean the year or possibly longer when he is *keen* for you, hopefully getting keener. You must firmly, quietly move things ahead. Close.

I knew I had a live one with David, knew I wanted to marry him the night we met. (I knew a lot about him before that night; he was wildly eligible and, on meeting, thank God the chemistry "took.") Now, as the whole world must know by now because I talk about it so much on television, he did *not* want to marry me, he had been married twice already—"Why can't we go on like this?" he would moan.

It took me a year and three months. Sometimes a longer investment is necessary. A young friend of mine has finally married her man of choice after *three* years, but she was getting stronger all that time, not weaker. I *generally* think a year is a pretty fair time to invest if you're in a marrying mood. Wait too long and his ardor may have peaked, cooled and started down the other side. Finally, if necessary, you walk away. "I adore you, I love you, I want to spend my life with you but I think we should be married. If you don't want that, okay, but then let's not see each other any more"—and you leave. Mean it. Know that you are *not* coming back if he doesn't acquiesce.

Many many girls get married that way. I did. If he won't marry you, there's this to consider: he may recognize certain facts you *re-fuse* to—for example that you'd be *miserable* married to each other, or he'd be miserable married to *anybody*—it *couldn't* have worked. You think if you could just get him to the altar, he'd be so happy. You are possibly *wrong!* Don't force further—you *can't*. You've given it your best shot. Fall back, recoup your strength and look elsewhere.

What About Living Together?

If you're single, I think you should be *single*—live by yourself and lead the romantic life you never can lead again once married, no matter how divine your *amore*. If you live together, you might as well *be* married and have the fringe benefits—yes, there *are* some.

Living together is *grubby* a lot of the time. The *housework* is grubby. Your looking not exquisite 87 percent of the time may not be grubby but it's love-*dampening*. Being with each other every night, every day, every weekend with just a little time out for errands and jobs is surely going to take the soaringness out of *sex*. More gloom: Women living with men get stuck with *more* of the domestic stuff, no matter how unfair (more later), and if you'd like to "share equally" his financial acquisitions at breakup time, one resists, but not *quite*, mentioning Michele Triola Marvin: for all her suing Lee Marvin for palimony, based on their cohabiting for six years, she has so far collected nothing—a judge reversed her $106,000 award.

Living together as the way to get married? Don't count on it! Says my friend Bernice, "With you as dependable as Lassie and as available as a box of Grape Nuts, why would he *marry* you?" True, some men get so *used* to and dependent on the person they live with they haven't the strength or gumption to "break in" someone new and *do* marry their roommates, but it happens just as often the other way. If marriage is on your mind, I'd recommend you stay close to him and subtly keep the pressure on, but don't move *in*. Oh, well, you're not going to listen to me, *are* you? That's what I thought! Hundreds of thousands of single men and women *do* live together and the numbers *grow*.

Whom Do You Marry?

You're going to marry (as well as live with) whom you're cuckoo about no matter *what* I or anybody else tells you, so why am I wasting my *breath?* Well, in one way, it doesn't matter *whom* you marry because 30 to 50 percent of a good marriage is luck anyway, and it can take years to figure out if your luck was good—i.e., if you got the right person. For a long time you think you did and you "go along," and then one day, when it is *very* late indeed, you realize this man and his life style (raising chinchillas to sell to the furrier? nurturing four stepchildren *all* of whom dislike you and need braces?) aren't what you really wanted at *all!* "Life style" is the last thing usually considered, of course, when signing up with a man; as long as you love each other, figuring out his limitations, who your friends will be, how much money you'll *eventually*—not necessarily now—have to work with is unromantic and tacky, right?

Well it may be unromantic but it isn't *tacky*. As my friend Ursula says, we spend more time checking out a *refrigerator's* possible durability than we do a prospective husband's, yet it's *probably* he who's going to determine whether we live in a city penthouse or on a dirt farm, have gambling debts instead of vacations in France, mingle with dullards or enlightened peers—things like that. You will be marrying not just a *man* you see but his potential way of *life*. Now that's not always discernible when you marry *young!* He has yet to do his growing, or not growing, but few women think much about what they want their lives to be like later when the opium of sex will be less potent, when it's so potent *now*. I *did* think about that when *I* got married. . . .

Oh, God, I am so sensible, but it's *easier* when you marry late. Growing up in the Depression in Little Rock, and later while helping support my mother and sister, I always knew I didn't want a husband to be a box boy at the A and P; I wanted him to be *dynamic*—and that's the kind of man I fell in love with and married. Of course, when David left jobs a few times after our marriage, I thought God was punishing me for my sensibleness. And the summer when *Sex and the Single Girl* was so successful and I was whooshing around the country promoting, and David (unemployed) met me at the airport one night and said "I've got this great idea, we're going to start Helen Gurley Brown Enterprises," I nearly threw myself under the car—*me* the little person our finances were going to revolve around? Never! Of course *Cosmo* is indeed a spinoff from *Sex and the Single Girl*—but David returned to Twentieth Century-Fox shortly after that conversation and our business lives have never since spun around *me*, thank God! Enough about my "sensibleness." The good news is that, regardless of whom you marry, the marriage-luck can be good just as often as bad, and here comes another not very profound "profundity": If the luck didn't take hold in one marriage it can in the *next!*

So are there *any* guidelines for picking a husband? These are mine. Marry a *nice* man. Since *life* is out there handing you so many horrors, how can you cope if the biggest horror of them all is *him?* You can't be attracted to a man *just* because he's nice, but if you're lucky, the sexual chemistry will develop between you and a *sweetheart.* Two, marry someone who loves you at least as *much* as you love him—more would be better! Admit it or not, there is a lover and a beloved in every relationship. Stendhal delineated these roles as the victim and the darling, and, though you *may* switch back and forth, one generally *keeps* his role. The lover (the "victim") is the more exciting part. Loving "more" keeps you up on your tippy-toes and it's frantically wonderful, but all that frantic wonderfulness can get quite wearying, especially as you age; so I think it's preferable to be the "darling" yourself if possible. Three, even if you love *more,* hope to marry someone who will cherish you. Not to be cherished is possibly the worst problem of any for a wife, maybe an insurmountable one. A beautiful lady I know is divorcing a *Time*-cover mogul, not only brilliant but a total *charmer*—with everyone but *her.* For years he has said nothing nourishing or lovely to her, and she feels bereft. Did she bring on this condition? We don't know, but at any rate, her life is intolerable without love and she is getting a divorce. If a man *does* cherish you, that is the best thing that ever happens to a woman, and you can put up with a lot of faults and foibles for that special gift.

What else should a husband have or do? Whether he's a good father to your children or a fantastic lover, *I* don't really care, though those requirements may be on *your* list. If he should be successful in his work, that I would consider a *terrific* advantage, because I think work—and it doesn't matter *what* work—is him. I can no more imagine marrying a man who just barely tolerates the work in his life than I would think of signing on with a convicted criminal— but that's *me,* and you may not care a bit how he spends his days. I can think of six or more marriages in which a man brings in hardly *any* money nor even holds a job at *all,* and those couples seem happy. These women may be mothers who need a baby-man to succor or need his successlessness to make *them* feel Very Important, but so what? Also, a baby- or marginally successful man is apt to stay with his succoring wife. . . . Where will he get another like her? Anyhow, any marriage that *works* is okay by me.

Don't Tailgate or Envy

You think *their* marriage is sexier, more civilized, less boring and certainly more *normal* (does Claudia's husband sleep with Mallomars under his pillow?) than yours and you'd like one like that. Forget it! That marriage probably isn't *any* of those things, and different couples can't have the same marriage *anyway*.

Are you allowed just a *tiny* twinge of envy for Beautiful People unions with their beautiful houses, parties, boats, tennis tournaments, children, travel and all that beautiful *money?* Well, not from *me* will you ever hear the consoling idea that possessions don't bring satisfaction. They *do,* but "beautiful" doesn't make a *marriage* happy. . . . Those people divorce oftener than *anybody*. Beautiful People *conversations* are frequently drearier than anything you could imagine under sedation with a migraine and even the Beautiful People *themselves* frequently long to be home with their cat and a cup of cocoa instead of at a Beautiful People charity affair. As for possessions, you can *have* them if you mouseburger now, you *know* that, so don't get racked up by envy.

The only thing that matters is that your marriage *suit* you. If you're both gregarious, then surround yourself with people, give parties. If you're quiet and reclusive, stay to yourselves and *don't* give parties. If you love houses, buy and fix them. *Nobody's* M.O.P. (marriage operating procedure) has anything to do with yours. If another wife, beautiful or otherwise, seems to get *treated* better than you, that is something else, but you mostly do get back what you put in. I understand envy and am very good at it, but not about anybody else's *marriage!*

Forget Orthodox

While we approve all kinds of arrangements for single friends and their lovers, once married, we expect people's lives to be only one way—traditional! . . . Partners faithful to each other to the death, husbands and wives sharing each other's interests *totally,* he the principal provider, she the helpmate, the couple rarely apart except for war and hysterectomy. My dear, a *few* marriages may be cut from that cookie cutter, but most are *not* and they can still be good marriages. A man I know pours it *all* into his *wife's* career.

Yes, he is "living off her," but she couldn't make that seven-figure income without him. A woman I know uncomplainingly supports her husband who doesn't do *anything* except look great in evening clothes and bake nine kinds of quiche. God *knows* there's nothing wrong with a man *cooking*. Actor Roy Scheider does *all* the cooking; his film-editor wife, Cynthia, takes care of household repairs. (I wish we had one of each of those at *our* house!) Whoever does what in your marriage, it's *okay*.

There Is a (Serious!) Catch to Every Man

Whether they admit it or not—and many women *don't* ("George is the finest human being God ever created!")—there is not only a tiny catch to every husband but something so big, so disagreeable you could star it in a sequel to *Poltergeist* or send it in to negotiate a union contract during a transit strike. This doesn't mean your husband isn't *wonderful*, only that he is human—i.e., *flawed*. Could I mention a couple of flaws I observe at rather close range? What about a man who bellows at you from a room on an entirely different floor from the floor you are on . . . "Helen? *Helen!*" and, whether you answer or not, starts talking to you so you are forced to go downstairs to see what this person is saying or let him sit there talking to himself, which seems unfriendly. What about a man who cannot glean, after you have told him two thousand times and even after a Broadway play was so titled, that nobody can hear anybody when the water is running. (I have been talked to while water ran from faucets in bathrooms and kitchens all over the world.) How about a man who looks as though he has pinecones sticking out of his pockets, operating on the theory that he might *need* his Philippines Airlines timetable, the treasured letter from a friend who has passed on, three bankbooks, *all* of his keys including those to houses in Southampton he won't see for several months, plus a roster of the Century Club and *most* of his credit cards? ("God, no! purses are for sissies!") Have you tried to say "Bless you" to a man whose sneeze rattles dishes, causes paint to come loose from ceilings, cats to run under tables, coat hangers to come down from their racks? (You know you *ought* to say "Bless you" but your nerves are too frazzled to get the words out.) These are only the minor catches of one's dearly (dearest) beloved; suffice to say, murder is possibly too mild a term to describe what you feel you ought to do about the major ones; extreme irritation doesn't even come close to defining your reaction. When my friend Lola's mother points out to Lola that "Every man has *faults*," and Lola says, "Yes, I know, but I'd give five million dollars for the chance to put up with somebody's besides *Charlie's!*" we all know what she means. So why, then, is this the one person in the world, faults and all, you could not possibly live without, hope you will die sooner than and would literally *kill* for? Don't ask *me!* I'm just saying it's silly to pound your little forehead because of a man's faults; he's not pounding his forehead—or *you* (we hope!)—because of yours.

Every Marriage Has a Secret Contract

According to psychologist Kenneth R. Mitchell, formerly of the Menninger Foundation and now with the Dubuque Theological Seminary, every marriage has *three* contracts: the legal one represented by the marriage license, the informal *verbal* one (you talk over where you want to live, how much money you'll try to save, how often the in-laws can visit, etc.), and the *secret* contract, which deals with what you will expect the other to do to make you "happy." Get ready! One's gut emotional needs are usually not anything you like to admit even to *yourself,* let alone another person, and so, though binding, the contract is not discussed.

Example: He will drink a lot. You will harangue him about the drinking but put up with it. By your constant haranguing, *he* expiates guilt, and this allows him to go on drinking. *You* get to think of yourself as a moral, *superior* person, putting up with this inferior one, plus you've got a fellow who isn't going to leave, because he needs the "punishment" you mete out, etc., etc., etc.

Another secret contract: He will accept your flagrantly promiscuous behavior before marriage providing you don't expect *him* ever to amount to much in his job *after* marriage.

A third contract: You will be emotional, hysterical, unstable to the point of nearly burning down the house and he will be supportive and never complain, because your "craziness" makes him feel important and powerful; you also add fire and drama to his life, which he, constricted creature, is unable to produce for himself.

Do you see how this all works? Actually, divorces or serious disenchantment can result when a person changes the *terms* (his tacitly agreed-on behavior) of the contract *during* marriage—the drinker stops drinking, the wife declares her husband *does* have to achieve in his job, the crazy lady goes sane and stable. . . . You can't *do* that to the other person because that isn't the contract you "signed" when you got married. It's interesting to figure out your *own* secret contract, though, of course, you won't discuss it with him, or possibly with *anybody*.

All Marriages Have a Money Personality

Frequently one partner is oral (generous), the other anal (stingy); that's okay because you balance each other. "Money escapes from Willie like marbles rolling off a glass table," says my friend Bianca. "I have often collected wadded-up bills from his night table, smoothed them out, added them up to maybe a hundred dollars and thought how easy it would be to steal a couple of tens or a twenty . . . he would never *know* . . . it would just be money that 'got away from him.' On the other hand, if he were as cheap as *I* am—I take bread home from restaurants—we wouldn't have any friends!" David (*my* beloved) enjoys giving money to people it will make happy. I like to give people money it will make happy if I *know* them; handing twenty dollars to a hotel maid I'll never see again doesn't create a single joy unit in my breast, it creates *anxiety!* David thinks I am the cheapest and I think he's the most extravagant!

Sometimes a *wife* is the oral one. "Betty will have nothing to do with 'wholesale' even if it's a brand-name television set I could get for two hundred dollars off," says an anal spouse. "She wants us to march right into Macy's and 'pay the two hundred *dollars,* for God sakes!' " From another fiscal conservative: "Ellen never worries about friends who let *me* pick up the restaurant tab four times in a row, nor will she *not* send Dom Perignon to people who wouldn't know Dom Perignon from the dome of the Illinois State Capitol building!"

Oral David says to me, "You have a pinched little face whenever we're hit with any unexpected expenses." He's talking about the night we found out the plumber had put the dishwasher in backwards (it was full of dishes at the time) and the whole thing had to come out and be put in *frontwards!* David rues my devoting "precious, irreplaceable time" trying to find a cab going "our direction" instead of climbing into anything lit up, even if we then have to go around eight extra blocks to start heading *home*. I hate his prying my luggage loose from me to turn over to a porter when all I'm carrying is a Vuitton tote and my purse. Listen, you frequently *complement* each other. If David were as careful as I, he would never have "recklessly" left Warner Communications with a year and a half left on his contract to go into independent movie production with Richard Zanuck: No *Sting, Jaws 1* or *Jaws 2* money! On the other hand, *I'm* the one who arrived in our marriage with eight thousand dollars (from hoarding and scrimping all my life!) to pay his son's private-school tuition, the rent and a few other trifles (David was broke and *owed* money when we married).

I think I've been a good influence about conserving; he has helped me enjoy spending (listen, it's not too hard to get the *hang* of!), though you keep getting new jolts. I recently had a letter from his beloved shiatsu practitioner, Yukiko Irwin, which said, "Your husband is the least stingy patient/client I have ever had. Who *else* [who indeed?!] would think of raising a fee voluntarily—he is the only one who has."

Recycling a sandwich Baggie for my brown-bag lunch the next day, I couldn't resist asking myself why he didn't just mind his own business and leave Yuki's fees up to *her,* but then I recalled the rest of the letter: "He is a real gentleman inside and outside and that is a dying species." How could you want to change a man who evokes such a nice response in women, especially one for whom he totally *disrobes* twice a week?

Every marriage has a different money structure. In some, all income is pooled; in others, his salary goes for food, house, car payments—the basics—yours goes for vacations, *your* clothes and extras, and you keep separate bank accounts. I like the pooling system since my husband makes more than I and I have access to the *more!* (At one one point *I* made more, however, when *Sex and the Single Girl* sold to the movies, and we also pooled.) As a working wife, you have money *clout* because you contribute, and whichever one of you has the most money-*sense* would be the one to handle the books, I would think.

Even with this insane inflation, you *can* manage if at least *one* of you is shrewd. As a starving secretary helping support a family, I ate and dressed okay, never *owed* money, and had a sweet little life. Being thrifty wasn't any easier then than *now* . . . passing up cashmere and even croissants one couldn't afford—but that *is* how it's done . . . a mouseburger is just *careful.* Never having *been* an idiot about money, it's hard for me to see how married people get in so much trouble. If neither of you is thrifty or careful, perhaps

253

you need an adviser. The tax man who has brilliantly advised David and me all these years and kept us out of trouble was my wedding present to David—I found him when I was single. You may need somebody like that in your life to get you both to behave.

Postpone a little pleasure—the Peugeot, the armoire, the lynx coat, the Betamax. They'll still be there when you can afford them and sweeter for the waiting—but who needs preachy *me* to tell you *that!?*

The Advantage of Being Married that Nobody Talks About

When Scarlett O'Hara was widowed in *Gone with the Wind* at age seventeen, she had to wear black and mourn for a year. *Unwidowed* wives didn't have it much better. They couldn't dance with or talk with men at parties, only chatter with other wives on the sidelines. Some women, with terrific help from their husbands, *still* act like circa-Civil War wives . . . hanging out only with their own sex at parties, finished with gaiety and relating to men, *de*sexed, you might say. Well, I don't know about *you,* but it seems to me feeling and acting totally sexless with anybody but your husband is a good way to get really depressed! Nobody wants you to flirt wantonly and "frighten the horses" or be a *sleep-* around wife—ugh!—but I think you can enjoy the company of men more because you *are* married! You're stable. You have a wonderful husband to whom your first loyalty goes, and everybody knows it, but from *within* your safe snug haven you can dance, flirt (decorously . . . never in a way not appropriate to a woman in love with her mate), befriend men and have fun. What *is* flirting? Simply making a man aware that he is a man and you are a woman—what is so criminal about *that?*

But why "operate" at all? Why *need* the awareness of other men? Because you are a female and want to *stay* female and *alive* as long as you live, *n'est-ce pas?* Wouldn't the man you're flirting with be nervous about attentions from a married woman? *Au contraire! Single* women are the ones it is not particularly safe for him to enjoy without complications. Single women so frequently are looking to get him committed or get him married or get him *something,* not the *least* of their needs being to keep the man to *themselves.* A securely married woman has no possessiveness about her . . . she has her permanent man to adore, her darling, and wants only to add life to her life by having friendships with men not her husband. The chosen man/men can be married *or* single, and they may be heavily involved with a wife or girlfriend but *you* are "safe" to dance with, pay compliments to, *enjoy* because you don't want *anything* but their temporary attention.

People who have affairs in a marriage are scathingly said to be trying to prove they are still attractive to the opposite sex. Damn right! What, pray, is so loathsome or hard to understand about *that?* I just don't think you have to carry anything to the affair stage to enjoy still being womanly.

Matchmaking is an agreeable activity for married females . . . it's satisfying to put people you're fond of together. A businesswoman can help other women's husbands or beaux with her influence and advice, with introductions to people they'd like to meet; a married mouseburger *enjoys* dispensing favors. If there's a man *you'd* like to meet, not to have a romance with but because he seems interesting and asking him to lunch would be too bold, you can ask him *and* his wife to dinner. . . . Marriage does provide a power base. Marriage is being with a man you love and trust and would be utterly lost without, but it is *not* for forsaking the world or the men in it.

Passionate Love and Marriage Do Not Necessarily Go Together

Psychologist C. A. Tripp says, "Familiarity breeds fatigue." He also says, "There is a spark between strangers. If you get close, you risk the whole enterprise." Ah, yes. A man I know who loves his wife returned to the city the other day without her. "Laura stayed in the country to put the silver and china away, she'll be in tomorrow," he said. My dear, that's what marriage *is*—or part of what it is: somebody staying in the country after a party to put the silver back in its little bags while the other person gets on with *his* chores. Not very romantic, but then marriage *isn't*. How can marriage remain exquisitely romantic when romantic love thrives on suspense, uncertainty, newness—on *not* getting together—while marriage thrives on trust, comfort and *getting* together?

But marriage has compensations—as if you didn't know. No longer must you worry yourself into a heap of corn flakes about *does* he love you, *will* he get rid of his other women (or wife), *are* you the craziest in bed he ever met and all that tension-producing stuff! Marriage isn't the *end* of sex, of course, even of good sex. Though you no longer feel as though you're coming down with scarlet fever just because he's in the room, you do still *adore* him and have fun in bed.

Now, if cliff-hanging sex only lasts about three years or less with people in close proximity (Dr. Tripp—he's really *into* this subject—says, "Friendship and compatibility eventually *kill* zestful sex"), then possibly a woman who doesn't want to settle for "nonzestful sex" shouldn't *get* married.

Author Irma Kurtz says, "Few divorced women in the world were not once madly in love with the strangers they made the mistake of marrying." Listen, people are playing it both ways. A beautiful television actress I know subscribed to the philosophy "Married you can always get" and didn't, even for the first time, until she was forty. Another friend says, "F——d you can always get—marry, but for more *important* reasons!" and she, now married, has affairs. We'll talk about those in a moment. At any rate, marriage cannot *have* the same quality sex that an affair—at least in its early stages—has, so let us all not pretend that it can.

You Can't Take Too Seriously a Man You Are Married To

There is no *way* your husband can be the same hero, to be worshiped at the feet of, that he was before you married him unless you decide to live in a Tupperware dish and never come out of the refrigerator. In social situations, it will be much easier to see his silliness and shortcomings than his virtues and blessings, no matter how impressive he "once was." You don't lose your *respect* for him, just your awe—especially in company. That he is still smart and other people *acknowledge* that he is and listen to him attentively doesn't help—you just wish he would be smart a different way sometimes—you've heard him be smart all his *present* ways a million times before!

Flying to New York from Los Angeles one day, David and I sat behind an entertainer whose wife was giving him hell. "So get involved," she is hissing at him. "Get *outside* yourself. . . . You're so *self*-involved." This to a man who takes two million dollars out of Las Vegas every year and is thought to be a comic genius. Some other female—not his wife—would undoubtedly have cooed, purred and sympathized because *she* wouldn't have been so *used* to him. Wives *do* get to feeling, well, *safe,* and safe to criticize. Safe is okay; criticizing is not. The man does not have to be perceived as the god he was before we married him but he does have to be *listened* to. Never, never tune *out.* That is the most dangerous and divorce-producing activity in any marriage. And, unlike the lady on the plane, you must try not to put him down in public *ever*—that is the worst! My point is, don't be surprised or mad at yourself for sometimes thinking this dear person is a little silly. . . . He's your *husband!*

The Next Generation

Though I never wanted children, from my observations children can both strengthen and destroy a marriage.

Let me jot a few thoughts from mothers who say that kiddies are the sun, moon and a double anchovy pizza. These are all women I know personally who do indeed have *terrific* kids—and the mamas work.

Diane: "My first child was murderously difficult and things didn't go too well. Then, when she was four, Michael came along, and, from the beginning, he was an angel. I fell in love. It is just incredible to love somebody that much . . . it's a love you never feel for anybody else. Then when Karen was nearly grown, *she* started being okay. I look in their eyes sometimes and joy simply overwhelms me."

Agnes: "It doesn't make any sense what you have to give up for kids . . . you have to look after their bodies, their minds, their teeth, their bowels, their stomachs (they're always eating), their lessons, their clothes, their tuition . . . you do *nothing* but give up and spend, but then you're polishing this perfect little jewel or jewels so who's *counting?*"

Yvonne: "They're my support system. Maybe all children aren't so wonderful but mine have been there in every difficult hour of my life. We're a troop . . . marching on the enemy!"

Magritte: "If you think how you laugh at a puppy or kitten doing something absurd, multiply that by two hundred and twenty thousand and you've got kids. They're *wonderful.*"

Roberta: "Some of the wonder of motherhood is that it makes you a better person, concerned with something *outside* yourself. To be so emotionally involved with another human being is always a good thing even if it sometimes hurts."

Mallen: "When they are little, you are the center of their universe, and it is simply indescribable joy—your attachment to that other person."

There, isn't that a hard sell if you ever *heard* one? As for how children affect marriage, the news is possibly *not* so terrific. Says Roberta: "Children are possibly the one thing you and your husband can enjoy *equally*. They bring pleasure to each of you individually but they don't make you happier *together* . . . you couldn't say children *cement* a marriage." Jessica: "Sometimes childless marriages are happier because husband and wife devote themselves utterly to each other, no 'outside' competition from kids." Mallen: "Children can make a marriage *worse!* Nature provides that a woman will become interested in her baby almost to the exclusion of everything else, including him, and, except in rare instances, a husband is no longer king of the roost after the baby arrives. Some men can't handle that and you have *trouble*."

Well, my dear, to have or not to have children *may* be the most important decision of your life and certainly restructures a marriage. The children will be there, of course, after he *isn't* (in case of divorce or death), and that can either cheer you or chill you. Thank God it's now okay to go either way.

Try to Make It Work with His Family

Occasionally you fall into a lovely set of in-laws who dote on you and treat you like a daughter; just as often they're apt to be a little grabby, tacky and suspicious (especially his mother and sister!). At best, they are *different* from you. Well, just because he picked you or you picked him doesn't mean you would have picked *them!* If he's close to his folks, but you don't get on all that well, why not let him visit them oftener than *you* do. Even if you *do* get on well, why must visits always be from the *two* of you? I see my sister in Oklahoma much more often than David does; he sees his stepmother in New York more often than I do (and I *do* forgive her for sniffily asking David, early in our marriage when I was beavering away on some manuscripts out under her banyan trees, "Doesn't your wife have any *hobbies?*"—she who has practiced her violin four hours a day every day of her adult life and is now ninety).

If they are mean and unfair to you, and he always sides with them against you, I can't see how the marriage can last; you've *got* to come first. Once that's established, you must be respectful of his family, and try never to allow a real rift between *him* and these people who raised him or between *you* and him and them just because they're a little *funny*.

Your Man's Work Is Him . . . Encourage Him

How can you be jealous of a man's *job,* for God's sake? Work defines a man, gives structure to his life and also to your marriage. All workers, whatever their occupation, enjoy the camaraderie of work friends and the joy of a job well done, give or take a few carburetors falling out *after* you leave the garage or your bedroom walls coming out puffy instead of satiny after the paint job. A woman whose husband *doesn't* enjoy his work is the one with the problem.

When a man repudiates work or decides to make it only a small part of his life, he's apt to look to you and his hobbies to supply the joy in life, and that's a very big order for *both* of you! Anyone who has ever had a mother with little in her life except her children knows the burden of trying to supply daily joy-units to someone with few other interests. . . . You are *much* too closely scrutinized. Underemployed people *want* their version of perfection in *you*—it's a burden.

Yet so many wives are unrealistic about a man's work life. I can't count the women I've heard whimper and pout because the man doesn't get home at five o'clock every evening to play with them and the kids, at the same time they love (do they *ever!*) the perks and life style his labor brings. Even if you could live with a simpler life style than this man's job supplies, is it *fair* to ask him not to do what you know perfectly well he was going to do when you married him—devote himself to his work and put the hours in? Actually, work is a better mistress than a *mistress*, if you'll just think for a moment.

Whiners also frequently think the tycoon who is putting children through Harvard and Wellesley and them into mink coats ought to clean out basements, brick in the patio and go on weekly visits to the wife's family. Do they suppose his energy is *endless*, that chores come automatically with husbands like ferns come with forests? If you want him to be happy and *you* to be happy, I suggest you dole out house chores (if you're in charge of them) carefully and do everything possible to encourage him in his work, nurture his ambitions, smile on his business friends, and smile when he spends *time* with it and them. If he is spending large amounts of time away from you for his golf buddies, alumni pals, fund raising for charity, his boat, ham radio, health club, children from a previous marriage, possibly *wife* from a previous marriage, *plus* work and work buddies, then you've got something to complain about and should do so—*loudly!* P.S. Obviously he should let you have all the time you need for *your* work, and maybe somebody will write *him* a book about that. If he doesn't give you *this*, you've got serious trouble.

A Husband Comes First

No matter what else is in your life, a husband gets priority—when he wants to see you, talk to you (in person or on the phone), go to bed with you or whatever he has in mind. That really shouldn't be much of a problem if you've got a *liberated* man who understands your need to work and achieve. I can't imagine having any other kind of husband, of course, but I know many women who have had to try to turn a chauvinist into a man. *What to Do with a Liberated Woman* by Shelley Roberts and Fred Hilliard (Smuggler's Cove Publishing) is a rather charming book on the subject. Just consider this: Out of every twenty-four hours, you can sleep eight and *still* have sixteen in which to put a husband "first" as *well* as fit in an important job, friends, lover, parties, politics, whatever is important to *you*. Commitment to children I must leave to another adviser, as we said, but I would *think* your husband comes before them, too. *My* husband gets the grade A, number one treatment *always;* his breakfast and dinner (if we're home) get cooked by me; I run the house and am available for every single business or other kind of engagement he wants me for. One is a little *busy*, to be sure—but I get my hair done, get *Cosmo* to the printer, *and* for years I've been writing this book. Organized—and maybe a little dizzy!—is what I think you call it, but one's husband doesn't suffer.

Humor Him (for God's Sake!)

Some of a husband's requests will be totally ridiculous. If complying doesn't take *too* much out of you, why not comply? Says an indulgent friend, "My husband thinks that if paper is left within five feet of the stove, the apartment is going to catch fire. 'Carol, I'm telling you, you're going to burn the place *up* someday!' Well, the stove and counter tops are fireproof; let's suppose a paper towel *did* happen to waft over to the stove all by itself and somehow connect with the pilot light; it would burn up, a few ashes would float about and that would be the *end* of it. I have pointed this out to my beloved until I feel like a burned-up paper towel myself and have finally decided, to hell with it; I now move the tiniest scrap of paper virtually out of the *house* when he's home! It doesn't hurt me." A husband said to me at a party the other night, "If Alex would just do something—anything—because I *want* her to—never mind whether it's logical!" Shouldn't Alex? Shouldn't *you?*

Be as Nice to Him as You Are
to Other People

You probably don't have the *nerve* to be really rotten to an aggravating *taxi driver*, or turn away and start rearranging a cabinet while a friend is in your kitchen boring you, but your *husband*— aha!—he *belongs* to you, and him you snap at or ignore while he is talking to you all the time. Well, engrave on your forehead, please—and I promise to engrave on mine—politeness begins with *husbands*. Does the man who loves you, married you, puts up with you—and who, in eight states, cannot leave you without turning over half the community property—deserve *less* politeness than a stranger who probably wouldn't even try to keep you from being *mugged?!* No!

The Best Thing You Can Do for a Husband Is
Listen to Him

Before you married him, you listened like a telephone-answering service to every message; now, as a wife, you're just too *busy* to do that. What you really are, of course, is *bored!* Wouldn't any *sensible* person rather read her *New Yorker,* organize her closets or hide out under a cucumber mask in the bathtub than have a discussion about the shutout Dodger game or the oil-depletion allowances? Unless you're a heavy baseball fan or investment banker *yourself,* the answer to that is *Yes!* Of course, there are *fun* husband-discussions . . . when you gossip about friends, plan your white-water trip on the Snake River, talk politics or whatever interests you *both,* but I'm talking about the *dull* stuff. Well, if your husband wants to talk, you probably ought to stop whatever you are doing, look in his eyes and *listen*—really listen—every single day, to the dull stuff along with the good stuff. It will keep you out of divorce court, and divorce lawyers from getting all your money.

Don't Use Your Husband for *Everything*—
Have a Support System

Although your husband is your *best* friend, it is one boring little wife who has *only* her husband to share with and confide in and he only her, don't you agree? Selfish, narrow, smug, *not* loving or trusting outsiders—I *hate* those people! To have a really rich life, I think every woman needs four to six "main people" in her life apart from her husband, plus about ten to twenty *peripherals.* One might think of each of us as a planet with a satellite system around us; you're a body in other people's satellite systems, too. Us satellite folks give variety and *juice* to each other's marriages. Dumping all your problems on one man is too much of a burden on him anyway. So what do you dump on the satellites and spare *him?* Endless health concerns, for one thing. When I was scheduled for a D and C, I told David the night before I went to the hospital—did he *need* three weeks to fret and worry?

Certainly it's better to defuse your anger and disappointment about *him* with somebody else, especially if your complaints are things he can't really do much about. The best friend doesn't have to be a girl. Rona Barrett's *two* best friends are men: Shelly Davis, financial packager of entertainment projects, and Bob Marcucci, film producer and personal manager. Ralph Davidson, chairman of the board of Time, Inc., is the best friend of Pat Collins, CBS "Morning News" 's pretty (married) movie reviewer. My support system consists of three close women friends, a shrink, an old beau in California, some *Cosmo* editors I work closely with, a fashion helper, a housekeeper, two hairdressers and perhaps six other people life would be infinitely thinner without. . . . Who are *yours?*

Total Togetherness Is Usually Too *Total*

You do *not* have to be inseparable—in each other's pockets, as Elizabeth Taylor described her marriage to Richard Burton. Apartness works, too. Actress Connie Towers, who appeared three years on Broadway and on the road in *The King and I* while her husband John Gavin managed the kids and ranch in Los Angeles, said a new kind of bond was forged between them. Charlotte Curtis, Op Ed editor of *The New York Times,* and her Cleveland brain-surgeon husband see each other on weekends. They're devoted. For years ad tycoon Mary Wells Lawrence ran her agency, Wells, Rich and Green, in New York, commuted to Dallas to be with (then) Braniff head husband Harding Lawrence. For two years after they were married Marlo Thomas kept a flat in New York—husband Phil Donahue's residence was in Chicago, where his show is produced. My husband has spent half his time in California putting movies together or on location filming them for years! I not only don't get lonely, I don't even get *bored* (but then I am a workaholic). Vacations I'm not sure you take apart—you might *miss* something—and vacations are, indeed, a time for sex and marriage renewal. Still, maybe to me they seem important to share because David and I are apart so often.

I do know you need friends of your own and activities away from him if you're to stay vital to each *other.* You don't want to smother each other.

Compliment Him. There Is No Such Thing as Too Much Flattery

Maybe there is nobody much in the world to tell him he is wonderful *except* you. It really doesn't *matter* if the flattery you heap on him is close to baloney—heap away! It has yet to be decreed that only people who utter the truth are going to inherit Beverly Hills real estate—truth is a *killer!* Scout *around* for the good stuff . . . there's got to be some.

Friends like to hear you "brag on him," too—possibly because husbands and wives more frequently *attack*. At dinner the other night, a hostess raised her champagne glass and said, "I want to toast my husband. If it hadn't been for Bobby, I wouldn't be here tonight with all you beautiful people!" Well, she knew most of us *before* she married Bobby, but everybody thought her toast was great. At another dinner, somebody started the "What person in history would you most like to spend the afternoon with?" game. I couldn't think of *anybody* decent and said Julius Caesar; another woman contributed Carl Jung; the third piped up with "My husband!" Well we *honest* ladies just sat there in stunned (jealous?) silence. Her husband on *good* days is about as scintillating as a bowl of watercress, but you have to give her *credit*. Nobody, *especially* husbands, doesn't need flattery.

Do this for me. Even if this very morning the word "orangutan" crossed your mind as he ate three bananas before lunch, come up with something wonderful to say about him next time other people are around; it won't hurt to repeat it when you're alone.

Oh, my God, I sound like Marabel Morgan, but she advises women who have *only* a husband in their lives; you've got a lot else, but he's a beautiful, valued *asset*.

The Glue that Binds Marriages Together
Is a Sense of Humor

Novelist and screenwriter Garson Kanin said on television recently that humor has kept his long marriage to actress Ruth Gordon a happy one. "The day doesn't go by that Ruth doesn't make me laugh," he said. Jack Howard, charming chief of the Scripps-Howard Newspaper Howards, says, "I look forward to the drive in from Center Island to the city so I can hear Eleanor *talk* . . . she breaks me up!" Nice, isn't it, that those women are so amusing and so beloved by their mates. The challenge for *some* of us is that we are not particularly *funny* . . . we earnest little things, out there expecting life's mine fields to explode under us. I would *kill* to be able to make the reply my friend Carrie did when her husband suggested that if Carrie would only learn to cook, they could fire the cook and cut down expenses. "Leonard," she said, "if you'd learn how to f——, we could fire the chauffeur!"

Well, I've decided if some of us can't be actually funny, we can at least train ourselves to be *amused* by life. Example: When one's husband loses his door key, cuff links, collar stays, glasses case regularly each day and takes the house apart looking for them, one can just think of the scene as a television sitcom instead of getting exasperated. When the snow is sifting in underneath the window you've just weatherproofed, you could *try* to smile. Serious, heavy-handed little mouseburgers have to *practice* thinking funny. I'm *practicing*. Are you?

Splitting the Housework Usually
Works only in Theory

Ladies' Home Journal editor Sondra Enos says, "Clive certainly does some things around the house, but he gets to pick which *ones*. . . . You couldn't say we share equally." Another young friend on the subject: "Mark is fond of telling people he *helps* me with the housework. . . . It's still designated as *mine,* you see. . . . He just pitches in occasionally like a good soldier."

Never mind that Women's Lib was *supposed* to have delivered up to us equal shares of the grubby stuff—even *young* brides with supposedly enlightened mates tell me their share is heavier. As for women my age, there isn't any *question* that the house, at least the *menial* stuff, is our domain—even if we also run a corporation! My husband's sole housekeeping responsibility is giving the back elevator man a dollar when he comes up for the trash on Saturdays and Sundays. Yes, he puts his used dishes in the sink, but he *doesn't* run hot water on them! In discussing this inequity with Sondra the other day, we asked ourselves why we *tolerate* it and decided maybe our being so well organized (she has young children, besides) and strong makes us feel a bit *superior*. That I can fall out of bed, exercise one *hour* every morning, cook David's breakfast, do mine in the blender, get my makeup, hair and clothes together, leave typed instructions for the housekeeper and *still* get to my office sooner than David (virtually choreless) gets to his, *almost* amuses me.

To be fair, David can cook his own Cream of Wheat in dire *emergency;* he handles our finances (complicated), our Southampton property and deals with painters, plumbers, electricians at the apartment, but how often do we paint or plumb?

Hopefully the present generation of mothers is training its male offspring to *love* cornering sheets and sorting laundry, but for now you may have to be content that your husband handles some stuff you don't care much for—car servicing, yard work, household repairs. Dole out extra assignments when you must, but let *him* pick when to do them. It doesn't have to be this very night or this very Saturday. If he won't *ever* do chores, you may be picking the wrong ones, or have picked the wrong husband. Use shortcuts for the house and insist—since you *contribute*—that some of the family income go for household help.

Give Presents

Nobody doesn't like presents, and your husband ought to get them frequently, not just on his birthday and at Christmas. Husbands are good present-*prospects*. With a husband, even if you get carried away and spend too *much*, it isn't too *much* if you know what I mean. Husbands give nice presents *back,* though reciprocity isn't what motivates you. *What* to give isn't hard to figure out because husbands drop a thousand hints a year even when they don't *know* they're dropping them. "I can't find the goddamn screwdriver!" Get him *two* for Saint Valentine's Day. "Did you notice these onyx cuff links Frank had on?" Ask Frank where he got them and buy the same ones. He likes medieval history, cymbidium orchids, the paintings of O'Keeffe, the wines of France—then *cater* to those interests, at least with *books*. The best present I ever gave David was a handmade birthday card with glossy photos and personal messages from each of twelve women he once told me he thought sexiest in the world. The messages took some doing because several of the women didn't *know* David, but I started early sending photos and asking for personal messages from Jackie Bisset, Geneviève Bujold, Lee Radziwill, Barbara Walters, Marisa Berenson and seven others; all came through.

One woman I know had her husband's raincoat lined with her not-that-old mink coat (yes she got a new one for Christmas but she didn't *know* she was going to). Another invited her husband's entire college graduation class to a surprise birthday party; she corresponded and telephoned for a *year*. (If *I* did that, my husband would dump me in the river but you know what *your* man likes.)

I used to be so *skimpy* with presents but have improved and have more *fun* with them now. All presents can't be perfection, but if you give enough, *some* will be. What about a music box playing his favorite song (Rita Ford Inc., 19 East 65th Street, New York, will supply), two dozen fudge brownies, tickets to a ballgame for him and a buddy (not you), Henri Bendel's Agraria, the best-smelling stuff in the *world* to keep on his desk and sniff (ten dollars to thirty dollars), almost *anything* antique—silver goblet, scissors, magnifying glass—with initials engraved I.H.T.H.F.Y. (I have the hots for you), a bottle of Sandeman port—can these *hurt* your marriage?

Wear and Appreciate the Presents He Gives You

Some of us are careless about wearing and carrying husband presents or we exchange them for something we like better. You ought to keep exchanging to a minimum. "For years I took back everything Ralph gave me," says my friend Ellen. "Why pay fifty dollars for an ounce of Arpège at Saks, I figured, when I could bring it home from Paris for twenty-five dollars (those were the good old days!). Well, he finally stopped giving me *anything!* He's started again, thank goodness, and I wear and use *everything!*"

A few men believe they ought not to have to "pay," that they should be loved for themselves alone. These men must be taken

Firmly by the Hand. Of *course* you love him for himself alone, of *course* he doesn't have to pay, but presents are a talisman of love. Men *always* give presents to women they love. . . . Such a sexy and pleasurable act you don't want him to miss the fun of. Make a big to-do about anything he gives you—wear it to *bed* unless it's a toaster. Keep educating, encouraging.

If It's Precious to Him, Stay Away from It!

Sharing doesn't have to include his thirty-year-old Kentucky bourbon, his secret cache of shelled pecans, Godiva chocolate or sunflower seeds. If these are *his* little treats that he likes to dip into, show restraint! Not sharing could also apply to his Sulka robe and Panama hat. Do you want *him* borrowing your Gucci luggage, Bal à Versailles bath oil? I'd like to report that your mouseburger guide (me) didn't have one *grain* of the pound of Beluga caviar she gave her husband for Christmas even though it's *perishable*. He offered halfheartedly *once;* I refused and he relievedly gobbled it for breakfast, lunch, dinner and snacks . . . talk about *brownie* points! Keeping your hands off this stuff is different from the things he *wants* you to wear (his old letter-man's sweater) and drink (the Napoleon Brandy that makes you horny); a girl can tell what is and isn't off limits. Incidentally, some *big* things seem to belong to only one of you, though you bought them together and technically have joint ownership. I think of David's and my apartment as *his*—he selected it and dotes on it; my jewelry is *mine*, though he *paid;* the den is his; the bedroom is *mine*. Our cat somehow belongs to *me;* the house in Southampton is *his*. I really think it's better that way. . . . Everything shared would be Communism, and that wouldn't be any fun. Now for public behavior.

Be on Time

There's nothing to explain here. Are you so disorganized, such a nit you can't get anyplace when you're due there? No, you're just *careless* (selfish!), fitting too much in on the theory that *they* can wait a few minutes . . . always them, never *you!* Well, waiting for a late arriver is *aggravating*, as you well know, and the one waiting should not be your *husband*. Lateness is one of the top seven things I hear husbands complain about: She can't get dressed on time, arrive on time, do *anything* on time. In my family, we have finally reached detente; no longer do we surprise the hostess in her curlers and wrapper, but having decided on a reasonable arrival time—fifteen minutes to half an hour after the invitation suggests—I now get into my clothes and my face made up without any lollygagging. Our contract has been in effect a couple years now and I know David appreciates my promptness (though he still can't really believe a hostess doesn't want you there a few minutes early—to show your enthusiasm—and *I* think, with thirty other guests, what difference could it make if I'm the last one in the door?). Do your own negotiating.

He's Your Date for Life

This is a matter of honor—that you *not* be one of those couples everybody can tell is married because you look endlessly around the room or stare straight ahead and never talk to each other. Ask him questions. Gossip. . . . This is your *date!*

Behave Yourself with His Secretary

A good secretary is part of his support system; God bless, and aren't you lucky he has her? With this paragon, if she *is* one, you are friendly, generous, unstuffy and appreciative, but don't forget she belongs to him . . . you mustn't try to take her away. You're *friends,* of course. If it weren't for David's secretary, Pamela Hedley, in Los Angeles, I doubt he and I would ever have got married. So *many* women were in David's life at the time, and Pamela sort of helped him sort through . . . "Keep this one . . . Don't see much *here* . . . Might try one more date" . . . she could have disqualifed me at any time. (How there could have been any choice between sensible, employed *me,* who had just paid cash for a Mercedes-Benz 190SL and that heap of seventeen-year-old "starlets" who could barely get their Hamburger Hamlet lunch money together every day I can't imagine, but you know how it goes.) David's New York amanuensis for eighteen years, Grace O'Reilly, is also a dear friend, and if I were compiling a list of people I would want to be in a foxhole with, Pamela and Grace would both be on it. Still, they are *his*. Grace and David have a Scotch at the end of the day (so I can delude myself he doesn't drink, since he *doesn't* when he gets home); *Pamela* and David are as devoted as J. R. Ewing and Miss Ellie, though Pamela is a young woman *also* devoted to a husband and two sons. I'm glad my husband is flanked by such darling women.

Entertaining Together Is One of the Best Parts of Marriage

People rarely mention this—they keep talking about the Serious Things in marriage, by which I presume they mean having somebody to shovel snow, pay for the children's orthodontia, and hobble with you to the old folks' home—but giving parties with a husband *is* more fun than giving them alone. . . . Deciding what guests will work with whom, what you are going to feed them, will you do it indoors or out? Enjoy!

Your Loved One Is Not Coming Off as Badly as You Think

Sometimes at parties he embarrasses you to the point of near suicide . . . if he tells that story about him, President Ford and the tennis sneakers one more time, you think you will crawl under the couch. Ah, my dear, not only can they *tolerate* what you consider his idiocies, they may not even *recognize* them as such, indeed, may find him charming and interesting. They haven't been exposed to the tennis-sneaker story as *often* as you, you see, and your problem *may* be simply a tiny touch of the old if-he-belongs-to-me-how-can-he-be-any-*good* malaise. Wives are often *super*sensitive. Husbands do it to wives, too. David is always trying to keep me from asking "How much did you pay for that Chinese export plate?" or "Have you thought of seeing a dermatologist?"—things I know they are *dying* to tell me! I would like *him* not to brag so much. Even if your husband *is* awkward and people *do* notice, you don't have to think of yourself as joined to him at the hip. You are *not* his mother; he is not your little boy. As a shrink I knew once said, "You are not responsible for the behavior *of any other human being.* . . . The only person you are responsible for is *you!*"

The Time for You to Be His Mother
Is When He Is Sick

Is there a wife so mean she won't remove a glass sliver from her husband's foot, kiss away his hangover or make him hot lemonade with honey and bourbon when he has the flu? I can't *imagine* such a person. You are younger than I, possibly living with a Women's Lib-trained man, and, presumably, your husband also does these things for *you*. At my house there isn't much wife coddling during illness, but then nobody female is ever *ill* at our house so the unilateral sick-care plan works okay. David is such a serious hypochondriac, he's really rather sweet (provided he snaps out of it before *I* snap totally in *two!*). The other day when I told him his temperature was eighty-seven (I was reading the thermometer wrong), he said, "Oh God, that's just how Brownie (one of our cats) died . . . his little life fluids just ebbed away and he was gone. Do you think I have that?" Dear David. Anyway, caring for a man when he's sick makes you—or makes *me*—feel very feminine and important . . . it's really rather *pleasurable*. If he's sick longer than two days, of course, keep the cyanide out of reach because you're going to be tempted to give it to *one* of you. But if he's *trying* to get well, this *is* the time to be Mommy.

Always Have a Little Money You Can
Lend or Give Him

It's so classy *never* to have the shorts—to be able to reach in your purse for the money for tips, magazines, taxis, even though you aren't *expected* to. It's good to be able to say, "No, thanks, I don't need any" when he offers *you* money for taxis and tips. Being able to buy somebody a present is satisfying, as we've already mentioned. An Englishwoman I know who started a successful cosmetics firm with her husband's help gave him a Rolls-Royce for Christmas—just had it out in the driveway Christmas morning, isn't that *heaven?* (a heavy mouseburger that one). Another friend got a bank loan to buy *her* husband a Model-T car vinted the year of his birth. Being given money or presents by a man is sexy, we know that, but you can't *always* be the receiver, the paid-for one. Be a financial grownup and carry cash.

When He Won't Talk

Some men *cannot* say the words—they want you to love them *without* their being required to "pay." If they have to give compliments, encouragement, I love you's, then they think your love is "bought" (like men who can't give *presents*). A woman married for many years to a silent man told me he finally got a compliment up to the surface the other day. "Loretta," he said, as they were driving to the country, "I guess you're really a part of me." "What part?" she asked quickly. Long pause. "A kidney?" "You have *two* of those," she said. "If you lost one, you could still get by." "My heart?" he said, nearly choking on the words. "Better!" she said, very *very* grateful. Listen, if he loves you and is good to you, then you can probably survive his frozenness. I *told* you there was a catch to every man.

To Get a Man to Do What You Want, Try an End Run

We know you can't change a man, not the basic him, but you can *influence* him and sometimes change his *actions*. Women have got their husbands to be less stingy, attend the ballet, take up squash, try God, etc., etc. A newly slim Frank Sinatra told a friend soon after his marriage to Barbara Marx, "We have something new around the house . . . it's called half-portions." Neil Simon says his second wife, Marsha Mason, "taught me about living today instead of trying to stay loyal to a marriage that had ended in death." My husband's business partner and closest friend, Richard Zanuck, has been coaxed by his third wife, darling Lili, to be more social and go to parties whereas before he would have preferred going to the *dentist* (his stay limit is still *limited*).

We've all seen people who got a *little* nicer, a *bit* improved with marriage, possibly because they began living with a True Believer—some women have enormous faith in a man. Partners can also have a *non*-benign influence on each other. Sometimes at *Cosmo* we deal with a writer who is so suspicious, so almost *paranoid*, you'd think we were trying to *destroy* the poor little thing instead of get her manuscript published. When you poke around a bit, you frequently find a *husband* has been coaching her—"Now, Jane, I

want you to go down there and tell those bastards blah blah blah!''
You can almost *see* them sitting around, reinforcing each other's
darkest suspicions about the human race, setting each other *up* for
squabbles, scenes, contention. There but for the friend who introduced me to David go I, I sometimes think . . . silly, frightened
little person who thought people had to be watched pretty closely
or they would do you in (my mother frequently thought that).
David is so trusting . . . whether it's his laundress, his buddy, his
President, he always figures they're *trying,* and he's kind of convinced *me* not to be so sniffy and critical. If more people were living with David, I sometimes muse, perhaps *they* could be saved
from grievance-collecting, hating their employers, making such
horses' asses of themselves. Anyway, a benign influence is what
you want to exert on your husband.

So how *do* you get somebody to change, maybe not his whole
character (impossible) but just do something a little differently?
Well, first you have to be sure that "right is on your side"—that
the change is going to be good for him or bring better treatment for
you, that you're not just trying to change his act with which nothing is wrong except it's different from *your* act (he likes city
clothes, you want him in jeans; he comes alive at night, you're a
lark). If you devoutly believe the change is justified, here are some
rules:

One: Show by example. If you are a Good Person, tolerant and
kind, and *doing* the thing (dieting, exercising, nice to his mother,
etc.) you want *him* to do, you have a chance.

Two: Don't criticize. Criticism only makes us defensive, *rein-
forces* rotten behavior. If you want somebody to change anything
forget the "you're lousy" approach.

Three: Manipulate—yes, manipulate! I can hear you screaming,
Manipulation is bad and you're never going to do *that!* Calm
down. Manipulation—*handling*—is *not* necessarily evil; it simply
means using tact and diplomacy to get people to do what you need
them to do and the "what" may even be lifesaving for them.
Whole nations have been saved from war by the use of tact and diplomacy . . . who are *we* not to use them with a husband?

But you'd prefer reasoning and logic . . . just honestly present-
ing the facts so he can see the rightness of your cause? My dear,
hasn't logic been tried by you *before* "for the cause" and didn't the
man tune you right out?

So, how do you manipulate a husband?—still sounds crummy to
you, doesn't it!—for a good cause? You repeat a theme, with a sug-

gestion, over and over—lovingly—until you get through. "Joey, you have the best legs in the world and the cutest tush . . . now if we could just get thirty pounds off the *rest* of you!" Or "My mother adores you . . . she tells me how lucky I am you married me until I could *hit* her. You don't need to see her very often—maybe just every six months—but if you could see your way clear to get home from Denver Thursday night instead of Friday morning, we could take her to dinner on her birthday and *two* women would die and go to heaven."

Now isn't that more effective than saying "You *owe* this to my mother, you really do; why are you so everlastingly selfish and never think of anybody but *yourself?*" or to the plump one, "You're piggy. You don't have *any* willpower." Manipulation.

Suppose you don't want the man to do anything except not be so *bloody difficult* all the time . . . to be more fun, more gentle. Maybe a touch of humor will help. Him: "Goddammit, Adelaide, somebody's taken the last tube of toothpaste in the house and I can't brush my teeth! I left it right here on the counter!" You: "Poor baby, did somebody swipe its toothpaste and now it's going to have to get around all day with furry *teeth* . . . dreadful!" The *Los Angeles Times* arrives without the news-analysis section . . . he's in a *state!* "But that's terrible . . . they left out the most important section of the whole paper and now you won't be able to talk to anybody all day because you'll be a *dummy!*" He's grouchy. "Joe, you are so sour . . . you really depress me!" is going to get him even sourer. "Dear darling Atlas . . . you've got the whole world on your shoulders. Well, just for one hour while we have dinner, I want you to set the world down on this table . . ." etc. etc. etc.

When a man comes home grumpy from a trying day, you must ungrump him, of course, before he takes it out on *you.* Meet him at the door with the offer of a drink, a foot massage, a rubdown with icy alcohol . . . offer to wash his hair. How can he be mad at you when you are such an angel? You're not really such an angel . . . you're just trying to protect yourself from abuse, and it *works.*

As I make these suggestions I feel you may be saying, "For God's sake, *why,* why would I be doing all these things at *this* stage of man/woman development?" Because some things don't change. Men are still difficult, and if you want to live with one, *any* one, he simply requires handling, as we've said, even as *we* do, but this is a handbook for us with *them;* somebody else will have to do one for them with *us.* I *don't* think you ought to do double rollovers to please a man who is critical or complaining about *you*. The harder you try to please that man, the more you may reinforce his being grouchy the *next* time.

Can you ever change a just plain miserable human being into a prince? Well, maybe with insane amounts of love and encouragement, a few drinkers *have* quit drinking, belters have stopped belting, philanderers have stayed home, but that kind of changing is rough to bring off. It's so much easier *not* to have to reform one of those, *or* a man who doesn't understand your need to achieve through your work or who hangs out only with his male cronies, not you, or who isn't basically kind and generous. I've already suggested you marry *only* somebody decent . . . the kind you can maybe fix up a *little* but whom you can live with fairly well *unfixed*. May one suggest that when you have determined your problems together, or when serious faults of his cannot *be* fixed, you simply LOWER YOUR EXPECTATIONS. You may have to admit that for some problems there are no solutions. There is such a thing as incompatibility, of course. Nobody's rotten, or necessarily right or wrong—you are just very different from each other and want different things. What a pity we can't glean this *before* we marry—who and what we really want. You can always try with another. Second and third marriages *do* frequently turn out better.

Don't Surrender Your Soul

We have been talking about the use of manners, politeness, diplomacy to get what you want *for* him, not *from* him, but your needs must also be met. Even if he hates what you are saying, on your own behalf you have to keep plugging away . . . probably in many different conversations. Is it a neighborhood you've got to get away from? More (less?) time together? Freedom from football? Do you want to have a child? *Not* have a child? Go into business for yourself? If whatever you want is reasonable, then *have* it. Stand up to him. You *must*. All the placate-a-husband advice in this chapter has only to do with trying to have a happy marriage, a peaceful existence with a man . . . it has *not* to do with surrendering your soul.

Speak Up *Firmly* When It's Time

To assume that someone—even someone as close as a husband—*knows* what's bothering you from subtle hints, pained looks or no words at all, is idiotic—unless he's just announced his sister and her family are coming to spend six weeks and then he can sort of *glean* what you're thinking. To put it another way, passive resistance, the silent treatment, are maddening and *not* effective.

Pick a good time to talk, when he isn't depressed or distracted. "I have something to tell you, can we talk for a moment?" One night in London at Claridge's I sat David down to discuss two things I'd mentioned a thousand times before but which had never sunk in; manipulation had *not* done the trick. He later told me I looked so grim he thought I might be announcing that I was sending in my attorney but I simply told him first, his weight *bothered* me—never mind *health* is supposed to be the only reason a woman would nag a man to get skinny, I *respected* him less for being chubby, and second, it was absurd to pay five hundred dollars for custom-made Dunhill suits, to shower twice a day, change *shirts* twice a day, only to have dandruff on his lapels. Something about the time, the place and my seriousness got through to the man *this* time, and the pounds and the dandruff were eliminated, though he'd already been presoftened for the diet by a friend.

Demanding doesn't work any better than icy solitude or passivity, of course. You must be assertive—speak up quietly but nicely when it's time. *You'll* know when to contain, to pass it by, and when to confront. The problem may not be so much getting a man to pay attention but to sort out between the things that *can* be settled by a talk and those that *can't* be, and not to keep haranguing and be assy over the latter. Getting aggravated and having big discussions about stuff a man can't change is *wrong*.

The Fight

Is it good to fight in marriage? Some people seem to think so and whole books have been written on how to do it properly. A friend of mine, recently married, says she's going crazy because her new husband *won't* fight. . . . "He just sits there tight-lipped and purple but never lets *go!*" Different indeed from her *first* husband—I remember the night I met him he was trying to push Clair out of the car while it was moving. *I* go along with the group who think fighting is *bad*—that, as the Emperor Constantine said, *"Every* war is a tragedy."

Husband-and-wife fights really accomplish *nothing* (did you ever *win* one?). Usually nobody is right, nobody wrong, you just have a difference of opinion. But then, doesn't fighting clear the air? If it *does*, it also splatters the ego, rends the heart and raises the blood pressure. . . . Who *needs* it! If fighting were really such a good idea, wouldn't we do more of it with friends or even strangers? Aha, with *them* we wouldn't dare because fighting makes us ugly and unattractive. . . . They wouldn't put *up* with us; no matter how blotchy and disagreeable we get, a husband *must* put *up.* Like Clair's husband, some women don't have the *problem* of not fighting with husbands. Their men, more placid by nature, or at least more controlled, somehow are easier to be around, and fights just don't seem to happen. Well, I didn't marry one of the placid ones and perhaps you didn't either. My husband *believes* himself to be benign and ever polite while me he accuses of being a *cobra,* but as they say of certain people, "He doesn't have ulcers, he *gives* them." Well, my husband doesn't have fights, he *gives* them, at least that's my opinion. David can be so irritating, so unreasonable at times, that first thing you know *you* have said something nasty to this "pacifist" and whammo, you're fighting! Is that perhaps how it is with *your* beloved?

Okay, if you believe, as I do, that fighting is bad, destructive, debilitating, how do you *not* fight? I think the most important rule is: Watch out for stress times. The worst fights happen when people are tired and pressured. It's not each *other* you're mad at initially, but when the airline gives your seats away on the last flight home from San Juan or the confirmed hotel room isn't *there* when you arrive at 4 A.M., you start picking on each *other.* My two killer fights of the past year were both pressure-based.

Close to Christmas we had been going out every night and I was in bad shape. Christmas is always a rough time for me because I have to get so many presents bought and dispatched to people who help David and me all year—secretaries, nurses, receptionists, building employees, tradespeople, plus the *Cosmo* staff and Hearst executives, plus family, friends (and you can't give them all the same *things*), that from December third on my office looks like Macy's shipping department, plus there's *always* too much social stuff *plus Cosmo* comes out every twenty-two working days regardless of what holiday it is, plus plus plus. Well, one night, having been out four evenings in a row, we were seated at a charity dinner to which David had suggested I ask some Hearst executives and I realized it was going to be a long, *long* night with only little *children* . . . not Tony Bennett, *not* Eydie Gorme, but little moppets entertaining.

"What are we *doing* here?" I whispered to my mate. "Shush," he said. Ten minutes later I repeated the question, now really curious. "Shush," he said again. The reason he was shushing me, and the reason we were *there*, it turned out, was that an ABC executive sitting at the next table was not only in charge of the evening but in charge of negotiations for the purchase of David and Richard Zanuck's *Jaws I, Jaws II* and *The Sting*. I swear David hadn't told me ahead of time about this man and our special need to attend his charity evening; he said he *had*. Anyway, I didn't know or remember at the time why we were there and just got restlesser and restlesser and madder and madder. If *we* had to be there, which, at that moment, I didn't understand, why in God's name had we asked my Hearst executive friends, who were *also* worn out from Christmas and definitely didn't need a business banquet in the middle of the week but *had* to accept because we'd asked them?

Finally, crazed with fatigue and pique, I began the Bent Teaspoon Trick. Procedure: Take a hotel or restaurant teaspoon (you don't want to destroy your own this way) and, with all your strength, bend the handle down to the spoon part—in other words, bend the two ends together. This takes about eight minutes if you are tiny, as I am; then you place the crushed spoon in the hand of the person you're mad at. I did three teaspoons in a row and, by the third one, David was getting quietly apoplectic since he felt the ABC man at the next table could *see* me bending teaspoons (I'm sure he couldn't) and I was also destroying hotel property.

When we got home, the fight lasted about eight hours. *Nobody*

278

slept. We dredged up everything ugly we could lay hand on—devastating!

One more blockbuster? We have finished dinner with friends at Le Grand Vefour in Paris and decide to walk home through the Tuileries gardens. Summer night, cloudless sky. We get *into* the gardens okay but, after covering half a mile or so, can't get *out* because the gates have now been closed and locked. Well, our enterprising little group decides to shimmy up the gate—about twelve feet high (there are foothold places)—then let ourselves partway down the other side, again with footholds, jumping the rest of the way. Everybody but David jumps with stomach facing gate, fanny in the air, lands clean. David gets over the top of the gate okay but lets himself down the other side *rump to gate,* catches his never-before-worn Dunhill blazer on a gate spike as he jumps, and rips jacket neatly in two. I cannot *believe* a thinking human being can come over the top of a gate that way, as though he were stepping into a taxi, and am *enraged!* It doesn't help that the gendarmes then took us into custody and my fractured-French-speaking husband has to plead our case in *tatters.* Finally back at the hotel (we promised the Gs not to do that *again!*), we got into such a fight that Warren Beatty in the next room (he later tells us) crawled out on the balcony that surrounds the hotel to peer in our room and see if we were *killing* each other. Not this time, Warren. Reason for fight: I was attacking something my husband couldn't help—lack of terrific physical coordination—thus flouting a mouseburger rule for husbands I just got through handing down!

So, okay, the point is, *whatever* makes it happen, I am *against* fighting, have taken the vows of abstinence (am doing *pretty* well so far this year) and would ask you this: Are you possibly *also* a summer soldier and sunshine patriot . . . sweet and jolly when *life* is sweet and jolly but let Zeus drop a hot bolt on your job, friendship, cherished plan, and the summer smiles turn to snarls, not necessarily directed at Zeus but at *him,* your husband, the handy substitute? Then you must watch it when you and he have been standing in a snowdrift for twenty minutes, unable to get a cab *or* a bus and are slowly freezing to death, or when people you didn't want to ask to dinner anyway are now forty-five minutes late, or *whenever* either or both of you are good and pissed, okay?

Go Underground When He's in a Fighting Mood

Let's go a little further with avoid-the-fight guidelines. He comes home frustrated from his job or wakes *up* feeling black and blue. . . . Pressure and tension are all around you like mustard gas. As actress Margo Channing says in *All About Eve* as she commences one of her famous rages, "Fasten your seat belts, it's going to be a bumpy night!" Bumpy it *may* be, unless you can pilot the plane through without a rollover . . . a real little test of character! Says my beautiful friend Ursula, "When Woody is black and angry (not at me but at *something*), I find him so disagreeable I want to strike out, to say *Stop* it, I can't *stand* it!—but knowing he'll strike back and then we'll *both* be miserable, that he will have sucked me in, I say to myself, No siree, I'm sitting this one *out*, and I try literally to stay away from him that night." At *my* house I have learned to sit it out, too—to express sympathy to a discouraged mate, tiptoe around him a little, hide out in another part of the house, only going to check on him occasionally until he gets defused or goes to bed. Would something like that work for you?

Stay Out of Mined Areas *Generally*

A year or two of marriage will flush out the topics to avoid. In my family, I just never mention that I don't really *like* to be read out loud to, that I'm not crazy to hear stock-market quotations even when they're "good for the Jews," that I hate watching television when there are so many more *interesting* things to do (like rearrange my scarf drawer or finally finish *Breasted's History of Egypt*).

David *knows* all these dislikes and if he still wants to read to me, quote stock prices, insist I sit down to watch the eleven o'clock news, then we have to figure his *need* is stronger than my aversion and I will go along—at least *some* of the time. The other Saturday morning, right after breakfast, he decided I should read *The New York Times* stock quotations to *him* while he checked them off against our own portfolio. Jesus! These were fresh and frisky Saturday morning hours I had *specifically* put aside to work on this book and my heart sank right out of sight (like a kid on his way to play baseball and his mother calls him back to clean up his room).

You may *think* I could have said something like, "Look, darling, could we do this later?" but to my husband that would have been a hostile remark—it just *would* have—and probably have started a fight. I spend so *much* of the weekend hidden away in my bedroom writing or editing that staying fifteen minutes longer in the kitchen seemed no extraordinary request to David, nor *was* it, I suppose.

I quietly swallowed (just like a dutiful child . . . at *my* age and *my* station in life!) my pique, gave up fifteen minutes of Golden Time, lost a *little* of my momentum on the book and did the stock quotations. It was over soon enough and I escaped. You know *your* mined areas.

Disappear for a Bit When
You're the Ticking Time Bomb

A fight hasn't started but you're mad and *peaking*. Well, my darling, just remember the pleasure when you peak will be like wolfing down a pound of almond rocca . . . delicious going down but you will have to *pay later*. I've *never* been in a fight in which I didn't have to "pay" (i.e., go apologize, mop up the mess). You get it all off your chest, all right, but then guilt, remorse, anxiety about whether-they-now-despise-you will send you straight back to apologize . . . there is *never* an exception. Try not to *do* that damage to yourself. Get out of your husband's presence. Go to another room or leave the apartment. Don't *stamp* out but explain you're going out to cool off. See how you feel an hour later.

"Distancing" works for me *all* the time at *Cosmo* because I know I can't *afford* to get mad at employees . . . too many temper tantrums establish you as a bona fide horse's ass. I'm cooling it all the way down with my husband these days, too . . . better not to say the *first* rotten word . . . like you don't take the *first* drink or cigarette if you're on the wagon. Oh, God, all that self-denial! When you are *about* to be critical with your husband, just shut *up*. What you have to be is Very Disciplined. Breathe deeply . . . literally . . . and try to get your mind to glance off to other subjects. Think of England—think of your new Perry Ellis sweater. Keep doing that until the rage passes.

Start Laughing

Let's say hostilities *have* broken out, and you're both saying *ridiculous* things (You: I don't even want to *go* to Guadalajara if you're going to wear that horrible sweater. Him: The last time we had any peace in this house was when you had a strep throat and couldn't *talk!* etc., etc., etc.). Hard to say *which* of you is being sillier. If you can start *laughing* at the things you're saying, at the way you're both acting, the fight may evaporate. A friend told me that during a grisly fight, he said to his wife, "Get your coat and leave this apartment!" She went to the closet to do just that and he locked her in. They both started laughing—end of fight. (P.S. Some of us who have *no* sense of humor at fight times can't get this plan going!)

Once the argument is raging, I have no advice except to watch your language. Try to avoid terms like "You're wrong . . . you're *lying!*" Say, instead, "I don't agree with you. That isn't how I see it." Whatever language you're using, once started, a fight usually must run its course—like Hurricane Frederick. Some people say you should try to keep it from *escalating* but I think you might as well try to get a scrambled egg to unscramble. Bombs away!

Apologize When It's Over

Go to him and say you are sorry, you were *convinced* you were right but you must not have been or he wouldn't be so angry. (You may *still* think you were right but don't say *that*.) Apologize sincerely even if, as is the case with me sometimes, your "quiet" husband who never loses his temper or starts an argument *himself* has said or done the assy things that cause *you* to do so (which makes him just as guilty as having the temper fling *himself*, don't you agree?). After the fight, discuss how it might be avoided next time. *This* time you've had "a breakdown of communications" and hope to stay in touch with each other better in the future.

I'll tell you what helps *me* apologize quite *sincerely*. I say to myself—and I mean every word of it—You are lucky, *very* lucky your husband married you, my dear, that you now *have* a husband. Should your marriage end, there is no big storehouse of possible *new* husbands for you to get yourself one from; at your age that bin is practically empty. The bin that he gets a new *wife* from is *not* empty. . . . That bin is always full. Your husband is rich, attractive and *nice,* I say to myself; he can get somebody younger, prettier and better-tempered than you *any* time! That kind of thinking might drag you off your nagging, screeching, criticizing kamikaze course; it frequently sobers *me.*

Some arguments are settled in bed, of course. It's an okay place to settle them. Don't feel you got seduced or copped out—anything that diffuses anger is okay.

Now to problems other than fights.

When Your Husband Is Left Out of the "Fun"

The deepest sads a woman may ever experience are wanting somebody near her to be loved and popular and instead, he is being dumped on! I'm not talking about the little stuff—his best friend cancels a golf date, the restaurant gives his table away—I'm talking about *major*—somebody else got the promotion, they're leaving him out of meetings these days, people he is telephoning are not returning his calls (ah, that memorable day eighteen years ago when my beloved said, "Jesus, I can't even get my *agent* on the phone!"). Well, when he's wounded, *you're* wounded. You hurt *for* him, of course, but may I suggest another possibility? You also hurt for *you!* There is something a little narcissistic in wanting a loved one to be popular. If people dote on *him,* they must admire *you* for being his dear one; if he's a pariah, you think his bad luck brings *you* down! Don't feel too guilty—if *you* got wounded in *your* work, he'd feel the same way: brought down. I'm just pointing out that part of our hurt is love, part *vanity,* but never mind, the hurt is *genuine.* How do you cope?

You are sympathetic in the extreme. Even when you begin to feel a bit more irritated than *grieved* by his wound (he is so surly, so pouting, so disagreeable, like a little boy!), you are in total sympathy. He is right, they are wrong, that's all there is to it. Never mind that you may possibly be wondering what he did to bring *on* this trouble, out loud you say anything that might lessen his hurt— how unimportant the lost prize, that you're sure people are *not* avoiding him the way it seems, that he is one of the most respected people you know, that he has great honor and integrity—whatever good qualities he really *has* that you can call forth. Then can we get a little objectivity going here? Think how you treat your dearest friend when she (he) is down. You love her, you are supportive, but you do not *grieve* with her. In troubled times, you can actually be more effective with a friend than with a family member because that person does not *belong* to you. Well, actually, neither is a *husband* your possession or appendage. One must keep *remembering* that.

If you've got one who can't stand on his own, okay—that's the kind of person you married; you can either divorce him or live with him as he *is*—something of a bleater. You must *not* suffer yourself into a bleeding colon, however, because of *his* sadness and pain. See a shrink if it's *that* bad.

He's Depressed

Now let's go to a different blight—depression. A man depressed about *something*—job, children, finances—can be a terrible burden, but a man depressed about *nothing,* or nothing you can pin down, is a soggy, boggy *mess.* He mopes, he withdraws, he's a walking *rain* cloud you wish would burst and get it *over* with! Okay, what he is possibly suffering is endogenous depression; the problem may be physiological (programmed into his genes), not psychological (caused by a bad current event). Two gifted men, the late composer Richard Rodgers and writer-director Josh Logan, both plagued with endogenous depression, said they were helped with drug therapy (lithium). If your man is viciously depressed, without cause or *with* it, you must try to get him help, probably psychiatric.

More likely his gloom isn't serious or long-lasting enough to be treated by a doctor. A friend tells me her husband goes into a fog around Christmas every year . . . something about his childhood not having contained any happy Christmases makes him simply *lugubrious.* Nora says after her initial sympathetic reaction what she'd really like to do is *drown* him for being so morose, but of course that isn't practical, so the family leaves him to be morose and operates *around* him. My experience is that a depressed husband is really not to be jollied *out* of it . . . you just ride out the gloom as you would a cold; treated or untreated, a cold takes up to fourteen days to disappear; *mild* depression usually goes away sooner. My darling is occasionally depressed and seems to be *dying* of it. Well, I have mercifully discovered husbands *don't* die of their worries. Love them. Wait it out. Get out of the house . . . it will pass. If it *doesn't*, get help.

He's in Trouble with His Job

Possibly the trouble he's in with his job is *him*. So, seeing what he's doing wrong, can you not set him straight and send him back to the office to do it *right?* Not likely. First of all, hearing only his side of the story, you'll have trouble figuring out what *is* his fault; listening to him, they are all *idiots*, he totally in the right. Being loyal, you'll want to *believe* that—easier to blame them than face the idea that the man you're *married* to is a dum-dum. Second, even if you somehow glean that he's in the wrong and ought to go in there and *say* so, you're in trouble because you don't want to seem to side with *them* . . . from you he has to get total approval and support no matter *who* is right or wrong. Three, as I've often pointed out, even though you are supportive in the extreme, you are not his mother. He must handle his *own* life, including bungling this job if necessary. You can't "do it *for* him" anyway; though you can coach a *little* from the sidelines, he's the one who has got to go down there and *do* it every day.

Tact and diplomacy—you've heard about them *before!*—are required. In times of job trouble, you have to act nicer than you have been known to act in your life. "My God, Ralph—you've screwed up again!" is not dialogue for the day! This person must be handled like fine Dresden china or, again, as you would a *friend*. Hoping to help him save the situation, you are now a double agent, keeping two sets of books. Yes indeed, somebody in his company is a *jerk* and, yes indeed, *that* person is the one who has screwed up, but now comes the double-agenting: "They are bastards all right but somehow we've got to deal with them. Why don't you think about giving up those two people in your department they want you to get rid of and *see* how you get along?" or "Why not check your stuff with this new man for a while? He'll probably be very dumb and won't last very long." Get him to do whatever you feel he *has* to do to keep his job at the same time that you are his ally.

Now suppose, and this is more *likely*, they really *are* jerks in that company and he is *not* wrong. Same advice—back him. Encourage, plot and plan with him, say he can quit if he wants to, but, again, don't go down the drain suffering.

He's Being Forced Out

When David was being forced out of Twentieth Century-Fox thirteen years ago, along with his friend and now partner, Richard Zanuck, it was like gradually getting your *foot* amputated; the forcing out took a *year*, so we all had plenty of time to writhe in agony. Dick's father, Darryl Zanuck, was chairman of the board of Twentieth, Dick, president and head of production, David, executive vice president. David's position at Twentieth and his friendship with the two Zanucks, also Darryl's wife, Virginia, then separated from her husband, had always been a source of pleasure and pride for me. David was so close to father *and* son, the three men were a kind of triumvirate. Dick lived in California, Darryl in New York and, since David and I were also in New York, we saw a great deal of Darryl and his friend Genevieve, a young French girl. I don't know what security is for *you* but for me, in those days, it was having Darryl telephone every Sunday morning faithfully to say, "See you at nine at Trader Vic's."

Then one autumn it was all over. David and Dick fell out with Darryl over the issue of placing Genevieve in a movie. The stockholders were restless over some recent flops, and Dick and David thought it was bad timing to risk casting an inexperienced girl in an expensive film. Darryl was furious. He thought Dick and David were plotting to wrest control of the company from him and that David, in particular, was the Svengali, as he put it. That was the beginning of the forcing out of my husband and—since he would not abandon "Svengali"—of Dick Zanuck.

It was grisly. Along with getting the sudden freeze from Darryl, whom I adored and by whom I'd previously felt so loved, his young friend Genevieve left me like the skin of a molting snake. Ugly! Dick was probably hurt the worst. He adored his father. Also, having grown *up* on the backlot of Twentieth Century-Fox, he had never known another professional home but David, a highly regarded executive at Twentieth for eighteen years, was also in shock. To make things even blacker, one of those who did not lift a hand to keep David and Dick from being turned out was someone they had only recently hired to help them shape things *up* at the studio; his first shape-up act was to go along with the directors who voted to request Dick and David's resignation. Loyalty!

Okay, during a time like this you want desperately to *help*. All wives of being-forced-out executives become strongly protective if not downright aggressive! Judith Schlosser said, when her husband was asked to step down as president of NBC (he's now executive vice president of the parent company, RCA), "The pain was devastating." I decided *my* best move was to go to Genevieve, from whom I was now totally estranged, and say, "Listen, G., you've got to use your influence to persuade Darryl to tell the board of directors not to fire Dick and David. A *terrible* mistake is being made!" Some innate sanity made me tell David what I had in mind the very afternoon I was planning to dart over to see her, and I thought David was going to (1) strangle me and (2) have a coronary. He got all blotchy and red and said I was *not* going to see this woman and I was going to stay *out*—OUT!—of this affair, did I understand?

Foiled in that endeavor, which even *I* realized couldn't have helped, I decided *without* consulting David to go to see William R. Hearst, Jr., senior family member of the Hearst Corporation, which owns and publishes *Cosmo* and who happened to be on the board of directors of Twentieth Century-Fox. Wearing my prettiest Pucci, coiffed and perfumed like a Crazy Horse girl, I called on Bill at his office to suggest with all the charm I could muster that *he* intercede with the Twentieth board to keep David and Dick from getting fired. I pointed out that there was something a little *inconsistent* in Bill's being involved in a move to force David out of his job when this same man had *everything* to do with Hearst's most profitable product, *Cosmopolitan.* I reminded him that David had created the format for *Cosmo,* had written cover blurbs and decided on articles from the beginning, and was as intimately involved with *Cosmo* as *I* was. Having planned *not* to, and fighting valiantly to keep the vow, I wept . . . sob, sob, sob . . . all over my hoped-for deliverer, but, sympathetic and kind friend that he was, he confirmed that the die was already cast, there was nothing one director could do. He *did* stay away from the board meeting at which the firing was done and therefore withheld his vote.

In retrospect I can see the two situations—David's life at Twentieth and his contributions to *Cosmo*—had nothing to do with each other, but wives are desperate people. So the weeks during which the ax was descending crawled by, and I ached and hurt and died. David had given me the precious gift of a big career (editing *Cosmo*) and I decided if his own career was in permanent decline, *I* would be the breadwinner. I always had unmitigated faith, as you can see, which David is fond of pointing out!

Well, I could have saved myself the sobs and rationalizing. A few weeks after the firing, David and Dick set up their own production company, Zanuck/Brown, produced *Jaws I*, one of the biggest movie box-office hits in history, as well as *The Sting*, *Jaws II* and many other important movies. They even returned to Twentieth with the most incredible deal ever given a producing team and were welcomed back by the very man who did not stand up for them at the fateful board meeting. "Welcome back Dick and David" read the big sign at the entrance of the Twentieth lot.

Funny! But this is *now*, that was *then*, and the firing, accompanied by pain and trauma, nearly broke my heart. Let's talk for a moment about fired husbands.

He's Fired

Living with a fired husband has *got* to be one of the woolliest things that ever happens to a wife. If he doesn't find another job reasonably soon, the strain on the marriage can be *enormous*. The two most famous husband firings of recent history must be those of Richard Nixon and the Shah of Iran—think what *their* wives went through—but *any* firing is the pits. It's not just the loss of income—his severance pay may tide you over—but the ego blow and loss of status can be *horrendous*. His feeling about himself as well as the way people start treating him begin to be very *"funny."*

What do you do?

I have no business giving advice, as I was devastated and worried all during all David's job vicissitudes. A friend of mine's *mother* brought a shopping bag filled with twenty-five thousand dollars in cash over to the Regency Hotel when her son got the ax from an important network job ("so you shouldn't have to take a new job in too much of a hurry"), but nobody brought a shopping bag over to *our* house. But the truth is, a firing *isn't* the end of the world—surprise—it just seems that way.

Good people get fired every day, every *minute*, and survive. Maybe getting ousted will even be the precursor of a wonderful new professional *life*, as it was for my husband. At any rate, a good man frequently gets a better job or eventually works into one. I have known fired men who were in limbo for a year, even *two* years, and then a sensational job just *dropped* on them. Your own job will *help* during this period. It guarantees nobody is going to starve but, more importantly, it will take you out of the house away from the gloom and occupy you for eight or nine hours a day . . . you can't spend *all* your time worrying about *him*. When you're in the house *with* him, put on the act of your life. You *must*. You are *not* worried.

Now that's easy to do *some* of the time, but you have to keep *doing* it. Everybody visits a person in the hospital right after surgery, right? But then "business drops off." You have to not *let* business drop off during his entire unemployed time. Think of it as an illness; if you were ill, would you not expect him to be utterly supportive and to stay cheerful until you got well? Of course you would. Worry over him with *friends* as much as you like, but not with *him*. This is a gut test. I didn't pass with great marks but you *will*.

Now that we've been on very stormy seas for a while, shall we get back to sunnier territory? May I tell you my thoughts about connubial *sex?*

The Way to Keep Your Marriage Sexy Is to Keep Having Sex—and Put Some Dash in It

Dr. C. A. Tripp's warning about familiarity breeding fatigue notwithstanding, *everything*—simmering cioppino, Swedish ivy, Pomeranian puppies, children—responds to care and attention. Why should your married sex life be any different? You keep it alive by doing all those things people are always telling you to do. Treat him as a sex object. Dress up. Smell pretty. Be ready for love. Do you know what ready for love *means?* It means you are juiced up ready to go, or *almost* ready to go, with your *husband* most of the time, the way you were when you were single . . . it doesn't take an act of rape to get you to bed. Can you *remember* how you acted with a lover? Husbands respond to that stuff *too*, you know. At a party I attended last year in London, a young couple arrived forty minutes late, breathless but not very apologetic. The wife later told me that she and her husband had stopped on the way to make love in the Land Rover. "We always do it spontaneously," she said, "anywhere, any time . . . Tom likes the craziness of it . . . the danger, if there *is* any . . . and we are still genuinely aroused by each other's bodies after seven years!" Bravo!

Another couple I know made love on the eighteenth hole of the Siwanoy Country Club while other members and guests dined on the veranda. People tell us to change the scene . . . check into a motel. No *wonder* we're admonished to do that—it *works*, you see. A husband I know says he and his wife of twelve years "make love like minks in Paris . . . there is something so pervasively sexy about Paris we have to remember we came here to *eat.*"

Paris is expensive; the back of the Land Rover is *not*. Doing sexy married things is really less a matter of money than having the energy and desire to create them . . . it's so easy to be lazy and get utterly, if comfortably, routinized.

Ali MacGraw once said, "The trap about long-term relationships is that everyone stops trying. . . . It's a shame."

Half the problem of continued sexual activity in marriage is keeping *him* interested. We now get to the other half—keeping *you* that way. . . . Men aren't the *only* sex who may start ho-humming about sleeping with their mates after a while. Okay, the sex will usually survive if you keep the *marriage* dynamic. How do you do *that?* You have to fight boredom . . . boredom is marriage's worst enemy. You have to keep moving and growing, being interested in things outside your home and yourself. I don't have to tell *you* to "get out of the kitchen"—in terms of what you *talk* with him about, you're *out*—but you must also get out of the *office* (laboratory, store, television station). Resist the urge to tell him first thing when you get home about the cretinous temp who bungles phone messages, the auditor with skin rash. . . . That news will keep an hour or two or maybe *forever*. Resist the urge to tell him *every* detail of life.

Change in a woman is good, not bad. To be the same innocent he married means you haven't *grown* . . . you should be *smarter* every year, and lovelier and more chic . . . and funnier. The maintenance of *you* must go on every day of your life and is expensive (time *and* money)—the good haircut, manicure, exercise class, massage, but then, you have the money because you're a mouseburger. Spend it on maintenance . . . and on beautiful clothes. They may not notice what you wear very much when madly in love but that was then and this is *now*. Pretty clothes cannot hurt your marriage, especially if the man didn't go into Chapter Eleven paying for them. If you take inventory, you'll *know* whether you're a sexy, dynamic wife or whether you've grown sluggish and dull, whether you complain too much these days and aren't any fun, whether you need to Shape Up. A dull, complaining (not about him but about life) wife is a sexual *turn-off*.

Now for the *good* news about married sex: M.S. has it over casual sex because you can *always* have an orgasm—no performance anxiety! He knows exactly what to do to turn you on, whether to talk or shut up, stroke or pat, where and how long . . . and you know what to do too. Married sex is really very satisfactory and *doesn't* go away if you don't want it to. Toward having it *not* go away, may I make one vital suggestion? Here goes. . . .

Never Refuse to Make Love, Even If You Don't Feel Like It

Exhaustion, preoccupation with a problem, menstrual cramps—nothing is a good excuse for not making love unless you happen to be so angry with the man in your bed your eyes are darting around their sockets and your teeth are grinding. He won't ask you then anyway because you look ghastly and he's probably mad at you, too! Refusing to make love is a rejection of one's very *being*. . . . Who *needs* it? If anybody ever told *you*—and maybe somebody *has*—"Sorry, I've got a headache," you know it's demoralizing. Making love when you aren't revved up doesn't hurt you. Even if you can't crank out an orgasm—that would be asking too much—you can be sweet and friendly and *almost* enjoy yourself. What one *never* wants is for him to stop asking. You already know *I* think having a man want your body is about the highest compliment he can pay you. Your body is the most *intimate* you. If he starts rejecting *that,* he's abandoning your *core!* Oh, dear, I'm sounding like Marabel again—he master, you slave . . . treat big chief heap good or he go off reservation! Well, Marabel probably doesn't do her ladies any harm, but, as I said before, I'm not Marabel and you aren't *them.* As a mouseburger, you have almost every good thing in your life or the potential *therefor.* A husband is only part of your fulfillment, but a lovely part, and *you* want to be the one with whom he grooves sexually.

Expect Impotence at Some Point
in Your Marriage

According to respected shrinks, 80 percent of all men go through not tiny but *prolonged* periods of impotence. Women don't *have* this problem, of course, because even if we're feeling as turned on as a plate of cold lasagna we can still perform. What to do when he becomes afflicted? Do *not* get defensive; it isn't your *fault*. Do not put any *pressure* on him; orgasm is beyond willful control. You can flex muscles, blink eyes, move ankles around in their sockets —yes, all are voluntary motions; orgasm is more like snoring, digestion or heartbeat . . . *involuntary*.

During his "difficult time" surround him with love and show no anxiety whatever. None! Should you discuss the problem with him? Yes, if he wants to, but don't overdo it—discussion doesn't cure sex problems; patience and "laboratory work" *do*. Never discuss his poor performance in bed *in* bed. . . . That's the *last* place! Since impotence is frequently stress-related, you can talk about his *other* problems if you like; when *they* are cured, so may the impotence be.

Don't try too hard to be extra sexy yourself while his pilot light is off or let *him* strain too much. The harder he tries, the more elusive becomes the erection. Some night or day when he is not really trying, he will feel sexy again and you'll resume. If the problem goes on too long, see a sex therapist. There *are* such people and they do not exist just for "crazies." If you care, you can fix *nearly* anything.

The Affair—Yours

Whether he's impotent or a stud, mad for you or cool for you, whether your marriage is strong or weak, some married women *do* have sex with people other than their husbands. We don't have copious statistics about infidelity. *The Hite Report on Male Sexuality* reported that 72 percent of the men who had been married more than two years engaged in extramarital affairs.

In *Cosmopolitan*'s 1979 Sex Survey, responded to by 105,000 women, 54 percent said they had had an affair during marriage. In the European upper class, affairs are virtually *de rigueur*. . . .

Marry someone suitable with whom you have lovely, suitable children and spend the rest of your life with him, but also have a mistress or lover. Many American women's magazines, which supposedly reflect American mores, don't even *acknowledge* female adultery, but if we all know plenty of people who *don't* cheat, we also know plenty who *do*.

Example: A friend of mine was staying at the Beverly Hills Hotel and missing *most* of his sleep because of the fairly heavy nocturnal activity next door—both rooms' beds shared a mutual wall, and there were moans and love-type yowls from the *people* plus creaks and groans from the *furniture*. Sleepless the third day, my friend called a pal in the hotel hierarchy to see who was *in* the room next door, found it was one of America's leading advice-givers-to-the-troubled—a married woman with children, doting husband and *impeccable* reputation. When the creaks and groans started the fourth night, my friend telephoned the room next door and said, "Judy [not her name], this is God speaking . . . you are being a *very* naughty girl!"

He doesn't know whether the lovers moved the bed across the room, went someplace else or stopped the affair cold, but the noise died down. I cite this incident to suggest that if *this* lady (you'd faint at the name—though the arrangement may have been temporary) can, so could anybody. And so *do* a lot of anybodies.

So why don't *more* of us have affairs? Well, I think most people take their marriage vows seriously. Few of us get married with the idea that we will have little flings later on. Only when monotony, boredom, frustration actually set in do people usually stray. Even when those conditions exist, cheating feels funny and scummy to most participants. Other reasons for constancy: Most of us prefer *not* to risk hurting a loved one and/or to face all the recriminations. An affair is *time*-consuming . . . the *amànte* frequently wants not only your body and heart but large amounts of your *time*. Trysting is *expensive* . . . taking cabs, splurging on lingerie, renting trysting places (sometimes the woman's responsibility), buying presents—loved ones you aren't married to frequently require more presents than people you *are* . . . especially true for married men with single women. And then it tires the brain telling all the *lies* you have to tell: remembering where you said you were instead of where you *really* were, figuring out a plausible reason to leave the house Saturday afternoon when your husband *knows* Saturday afternoon is when you always stay home to wash your hair, etc., etc., etc. Hiding out is also restrictive . . . never being in a favorite bar or restaurant with this person because friends might see you. As for emotions, well, you do run the risk of falling in love with your lover and breaking up your marriage or falling in love with him and not breaking it up, both equally traumatic. And maybe the *most* important reason not to "sin": most people's *sex* drive isn't so high they *need* more activity . . . they may have just barely enough libido for *one* partner. To sum up: Secret carrying on takes so much energy and *chutzpah*, most of us are too plain lazy or too plain scared to get involved. . . . We think a giant avenging eagle will probably swoop down and peck us to death!

Okay, that's why people *don't* cheat, and that's a lot of reasons. You may think all people who *do* are seriously maladjusted. That isn't *true* despite the heavy propaganda from nearly every "authority"—church, psychiatrists, and those famous specialists, women's magazines! A strayed congenital cheater once told me he had a mistress because he thought it was "civilized." This man has a beautiful wife, beautiful children, several beautiful homes in beautiful cities, a beautiful seat on the New York Stock Exchange. . . . A mistress just completes his beautiful world.

More often the reason people cheat is the one summed up by my friend Pat Schoenfield: Says Pat, "Some people need romance after marriage, some don't. Those who need it go outside marriage and find a person who feels the same way they do. The rest of us stay home and stay faithful." Don't you think it's about as simple as that? *I* abstain because I got all the play out of my system by marrying *late* (age thirty-seven) and because of how I'd feel if David were cheating.

Well, in *case* you're one of the ones who doesn't want to stay home and stay faithful—and you *know* I want for you whatever you feel will complete your life—here are ground rules gleaned from some women I know who also don't stay home and stay faithful and have strayed more or less "successfully" for years. These women feel that breaking up a marriage, especially one involving children, to marry somebody you've taken a sexual fancy to would be lunacy . . . about as dumb as *denying* oneself sexual rejuvenation with a new partner. Marriage, they say, is *not* for sex after a while, but a bulwark against the storm, an institution based on loving friendship and respect, to be carefully preserved, yet exciting sex is too good to miss so why *should* you, blah blah blah. Oh, dear, let's don't start that again, arguing should you or shouldn't you. . . .

Let's just get on with the rules:

1. The most equitable affairs for the married occur between *two* married partners. Both have the same amount to lose and can understand each other's needs and restrictions. Affairs between married men and single women are still harder on *her* . . . she is alone on birthdays, holidays, always urging him to spend more time with her, to leave his wife, to come be her *permanent* love, etc., etc. *Married* women who have affairs with married men say it's a very different bowl of porridge from being the oh-so-vulnerable single girl who represents only *half* a man's paradise . . . you, *too,* have somebody waiting at home!

2. Having an affair to spite your husband because *he's* having one is disaster. Understandably, you may want to prove you are still attractive to men when the one nearest you has defected, so an affair is begun, but you don't necessarily tell *him,* the defector. Trying to make a man jealous can backfire—he'll take up even *more* determinedly with the person he's cheating with or even someone new—but *possibly* to prove to *yourself* you're still desirable or as a distraction while *he* strays, okay, go! (Gad, the trouble I'm going to get into with *this* advice, but I devoutly believe in it.)

3. Be *insanely* careful not to have your husband find *out.* That means not taking phone calls from your lover at home, not cuddling in public even if nobody you know is around (somebody is *always* around, you just don't see them), not being seen together in public very much *altogether,* not arriving at or leaving hotels, motels or apartments together *ever,* not putting *anything* in writing—no love notes, no signed birthday cards—not repeating things said by your lover to your husband, who will wonder where all those smart, well-informed ideas came from, not meeting your paramour if the date interferes with husband-plans, protecting your lover, too, if *he* is married because aside from that being a "gentlemanly" way to act, if *his* mate finds out, she can tell *yours.* No calling your friend at home or leaving lipstick on his shirt or perfume on his body. Most affairs of any duration get found out eventually no matter how careful two people are but you can postpone the discovery a long time if you are really careful. Most apprehended lovers are greedy for too much time together or are dumb and careless.

4. Tell virtually *no* one—for two reasons: First, you owe it to your husband's honor to have few people know you're cheating; second, every person who knows is a potential blabbermouth.

5. Your husband must come first at all times. If you want him

not to find out about your affair, your marriage to endure and your conscience not to be so heavy it sinks you, your husband's plans and needs get top priority. You were seeing your lover Sunday but "Daddy" decides Friday the whole family is going away to ski this weekend—go ski!—and you may not even be able to get word to your lover. If you thought you'd include Mr. Wonderful and his wife at a dinner party but at this "innocent" suggestion your husband says this party has to be strictly for his business pals, take *your* pal and his wife off the list. It's enough of a plus that you *have* a lover; your husband must continue to be number one in your life or you are a *fool*. P.S. If your lover resents your devotion to your husband, aren't you lucky?—so long as he doesn't do anything silly like phone you at home or *demand* too much time. The less available you are, the more he will probably cherish you . . . it was ever thus! Actually, you can be very good to your husband *and* your lover . . . you just have to be well organized and have lots of energy (and a cheating heart!).

6. Don't escalate. Because you're madly in love with the affair-ee doesn't mean you should leave your husband and marry him. Getting married is possibly the *least* good way to keep the sex and romance you now enjoy with your paramour alive, and seeing too much of him in your *present* arrangement is the *next* "worst way" to keep it alive.

George Jean Nathan, when asked why he had not yet married his longtime friend Julie Hayden (they finally married), said, "Just because you like beer doesn't mean you up and move to the *brewery."* A titled Englishman, urged to marry his mistress after the death of his wife, said, "But where would I spend my *evenings?"* A glamorous Latin American friend of mine has kept an affair going for ten years with what she calls her A.F.C. plan: "absence . . . Geraldo and I both travel a lot but not together; frustration . . . we can't show our affection in public and must always be secretive and careful; containment . . . we have never increased the *amount* of time we spend together." Smart woman.

7. Don't expect the affair to solve the *problems* of your marriage. People have said an affair can *improve* marriage because the straying one is now more content and so sexually revved up that sex with his or her *mate* may escalate. I've never seen that happen. The people I see involved in affairs are often so besotted with their lovers they tend to think of old Ralph or dear Josie as *ridiculous*. At any rate, if it *were* true, few mistresses would be content for long only to improve a man's marriage nor would a woman's lover rel-

ish that role. An affair may possibly add mischief and excitement to your life but can only occupy your mind and body *some* of the time. Whatever is wrong with the marriage has to be worked on with your *husband*. P.S. After an affair turns sour, *then* you might appreciate your husband more.

8. Don't confess. Some cheaters long to tell their mates in order to be forgiven or perhaps even to gain approval of their continuing to cheat. Wouldn't that be heaven . . . no more sneaking around! Well you might get the former but you will *never* get the latter, and, if you get it, you're signing the marriage's death warrant. As writer-director Marshal Brickman says, "Open marriage is nature's way of telling you you need a divorce." The minute he starts talking about his *girl* or you say you're dashing off to meet Larry, the marriage hasn't a chance. If you should be asked about the affair, deny everything and keep denying. If caught, you can at least make the absolute minimum of what's going on. The affair is nothing. You don't know what possessed you to begin it. Ever since your Yorkie died you've been behaving irrationally . . . this affair business is just one more manifestation of your craziness. The other person is *nothing* . . . absolutely not in your husband's league, they don't live under the same sun, breathe the same air, etc., etc. And if you continue the affair, be twice, thrice as careful as you were before.

9. Be prepared eventually to be found out no matter how careful you are. Some husbands are less suspicious than others. Some are busier with their *own* lives and don't have time or the desire to trail you about and keep up with your hourly activities, but some day, some time, no matter how trusting your mate, something will give you away; there are virtually no exceptions to this rule if the affair is of long standing. Carefulness means you'll be discovered *later*. At that time you decide what to do. An affair doesn't necessarily break up a man's marriage . . . it probably won't yours either. Most affairs finally lose their sparkle anyway. As they say in France, *Elle trouvait dans l'adultère toutes les platitudes de mariage* ("She found that adultery was just as boring as marriage").

A few may last as long as twelve, twenty, thirty years, but that's rare. Your *marriage* is what can be forever if you like. Whether you start another affair when the old one dies down will be decided by the same reasoning or instinct that guided you to start the *first* one.

Now, shall we move to another possibility: *his* affair—a very different kettle of bouillabaisse!

The Affair—His

We seem to have a *new* double standard. Of the 54 percent of women revealed in the *Cosmopolitan* Sex Survey to be having affairs, 80 percent said they didn't want their *husbands* to cheat. Seems reasonable, but suppose he *does*. A women's magazine once asked me to write an article on what I would do if David were cheating, and I tackled the assignment enthusiastically, writing that I would kill him—probably an andiron-bludgeoning, since we have no guns in the house—and that David would probably help me do it because he's so sweet about things ("Here, let me get that . . . that's too heavy for you"). That I would have no remorse whatever inasmuch as I think cheating is the worst thing a man can do to a woman. In my article I figured to spend no more than six months in the slammer because times are right for a cuckolded wife to get off light—cuckolded *men* have traditionally gone almost unpunished for having shot dead a faithless wife or her lover. I next said I wouldn't harm David's paramour or even be very curious about her . . . five cents a dozen paramours are. When a man gets ready to *cheat,* almost any reasonably okay female will do, and David's lady probably wouldn't be that evil or interesting. I figured she would be the "victim," not the "perpetrator." Oh, *occasionally* a man is lured to cheat by a woman who got the idea before *he* did, and *her* you might have a twinge of curiosity about (or be cross with), but usually a man is subliminally ready for infidelity; any "decent" girl who happened along at the "right" moment could be his detonator.

I've been a detonator, as you probably have, and at the time you think you're pretty hot stuff, but you're *not!* You're just *there.* I have sympathy for single girls with their married men, as you know. What *else* should a single girl do who is between lovers and there are no bachelors around that particular week or month or year but try to keep warm and cheered up with somebody's husband? As a single girl, with one exception when I fell in love, I always considered husbands like foraging in the refrigerator after you forgot to order in groceries . . . there might be only a few lettuce leaves, some mayonnaise and half an English muffin, but, though it wouldn't be a very *satisfying* meal, you wouldn't *starve.* No, I never considered husband-borrowing immoral because I didn't pick the husbands, they picked *me,* and if it weren't me, they'd pick somebody else. Nevertheless, about eight pages into my article I came off the "I'd ignore her, I'd kill him" routine and confessed the one I'd be *most* likely to kill would be *me*, that being cheated on by a man is something I just about couldn't stand. I couldn't take it when I was single and somebody strayed, and I would be less able to stand it *now*—married. I said it wouldn't help me to rationalize that a "head relationship," in which two people do not actually go to bed but are emotionally close, is just as intimate as going to bed—the old "so what's sex, just a *technicality*" rationale. David has had numerous head relationships since our marriage but thinking "what's sex . . . merely a technicality" wouldn't help me accept his having now got technical. Sex, by me, *is* the friendliest thing two people can do; sexual fidelity from a man is a total need of mine and sexual infidelity a *horrible* idea.

Okay, what would you *do* if he were cheating?

Should you have a "spite affair"? We've talked about that before. Maybe. Everybody says don't, but I can't see *what* is so foolish or unefficacious about trying to relate to another man or men inasmuch as the one you related to *most* has gone off and undone you. As I said, I wouldn't tell *him* about it because jealousy doesn't necessarily ensue for *deliberate* cheaters; only mindless, unmotivated defection seems to give anybody anxiety. If I had an affair I would hope to be a *little* attracted to my sexual and emotional "therapist"—maybe an old lover!—and not have to *bludgeon* myself to get to the rendezvous. Is this too equivocal a stand? I just don't think I would eliminate *anything* that might help me feel better and get me going with my comeback.

How else should one act after the initial shock and early discussions? Everything I've ever read on the subject suggests you forgive, trust and shut *up* once he says he's giving her up or you glean it really wasn't much to begin with. That sounds sensible and I would do that *some* of the time, but I would likely fluctuate between total sensibleness, even *adorableness*, according every word out of his mouth the respect usually reserved for a Woody Allen screenplay, and total relapses with one more round of weeps, screams and recrims ("What do you *mean* she's not your kind of girl . . . she was your kind of girl enough to take her to Bermuda for a week," etc., etc.)—perfectly fine one moment, then all catatonic and crazy the next. I'm afraid I'd ask *much* too often where is he going, whom is he having lunch with, when will he be home, etc., etc., feeling most of the time *utterly* insecure, vulnerable and

299

underloved. At this point there couldn't *be* enough love to fill me up.

And so my husband will either give up the girl because sex has waned (that takes a bit of a wait), because I've made such a horrible fuss and he doesn't care much for fusses (what he *really* doesn't care much for is splitting the community property), *or* he's not that keen about the girl or the trouble required to keep an affair afloat and was looking for a reason to bail out anyway—deep breath—or he *doesn't* give her up . . . and the affair just goes on and on—*then* what do you do?

I wouldn't divorce quickly. I don't believe much in divorce if you have a *pretty* good marriage—just this nasty *affair* business is wrong—*and* you're over forty (which we've already decided *you* will never *be!*). I have seen men so deeply smitten with a new love they *ask* for a divorce, really *want* the divorce at that moment but the wife doesn't *give* it to them, and, as sex wanes between husband and beloved—and even the most potent, gut-renewing kind *does* wane—there isn't the big *reason* for him to divorce and he comes back home. No wonder girlfriends (me in my time) nearly tear their squeaky-clean hair right out by its solidly planted roots patiently waiting for a still *more* Patiently Waiting Wife to give him up. Could *you*, as a wife, wait it out or, never mind this one dabble in infidelity, put up with a *perpetually* cheating mate? I don't know whether I could or not. Infidelity is a way of life for many men and some women—*more* women nowadays, as we've said.

Hardly anything (*especially* husbands) always turns out the way you planned it. Having a man cheat on you may be one of those ratty, rotten things programmed for *your* particular existence, like having a man die in your arms is programmed for somebody *else*. Infidelity is down the list somewhere on the causes for divorce—incompatibility is much higher. Being constituted as I am to try to *do* something about problems—the mouseburger way—I could probably cope with the *first* defection, strengthen my ties to him, try to change whatever he said he didn't like about me, try, finally, to shut *up* about his infidelity and see what the future held. There isn't really anything else *to* do, is there? I'd be lucky to have my job. A job has always sustained me in times of heartbreak and I assume would now. I would survive but I doubt I could take more than one or two infidelities without leaving him. Could *you?*

Time for Divorce

Millions of words have been written about divorce, and not having had one, I won't try to add to the observations. I'll just quote my friend Geraldine Stutz, president of Henri Bendel and not long ago divorced, who says, "The best life is one you share happily with another person but living peacefully alone is better than living wretchedly with a partner." So if your days are full of pain and your nights full of rain—or vice versa—you probably *are* better off alone. The same thing is true with a man you *aren't* married to, of course; when the pain outweighs the pleasure, you should *leave*. You may put up with the pain *longer* if you are married, but finally you figure life has *got* to have more to offer than this misery, and you split.

I don't believe in leaving without giving marriage a huge College Try; what's wrong with the marriage may simply be your expecting silly things from it like *bliss!* All men (and all *women*), as we've pointed out, are so flawed you might think you were selecting from the bottom bin at an eight-weeks-old close-out sale, so you might as well tough it out with *this* one as to go dashing off looking for a *new* Perfect Person (who isn't going to be perfect at all). And it *is* cold out there—particularly for mouseburgers not still young.

Judith Krantz says, "Single parenthood alone is so horrible to contemplate it makes for a hell of a lot of compromise in marriage, and compromise is what it's all about, dull as that sounds. When I look at friends who have divorced, I see that with their second or third husbands they finally made the compromise which would have kept them married to their *first* husbands if they had figured it out *then*." Divorces obviously "work," however. My husband and most of our friends have had *several!*

You'll know, after much (painful) soul-probing, whether it's time for divorce and, as always, in any serious life situation, I think talking with a professional can be invaluable. *Pay* the very high fee for a few sessions to get an objective opinion and to cut down the trauma.

Finally, I want to say this about marriage and men. When you marry, you will have a man at your mercy in a way—any wife does; she has tremendous power somehow not accorded single women. *Young* men get tired, too are vulnerable, are dependent on you. You can frequently act just about any way you please and nobody is going to toss you out, divorce you or even not love you, but I hope you will give him a break—let him up off the mat. Maybe he has done nothing special to deserve your smiles and approval but dole them out *anyway*, just because you don't want to become one of those harridans, one of those awful women who extract the maximum from a man while taking the joy from his life.

Now shall we get away from the oh-so-serious man-woman stuff for a bit—I'm wrung out, aren't you?—and talk about just plain *friends?*

Chapter Ten

FRIENDS

How to Be Beloved of Your Friends

A mouseburger's friends are, in some respects, like her lungs or liver—she can't get through life *without* them. Friends are almost a bigger deal than lover or husband. Those you *can* get through life without, at least for long periods, but *friends*—they are a staple of every *functioning* mouseburger. Once in a while you meet somebody who doesn't have *many*, who tells you he/she doesn't have the knack for *making* friends. That, to me, is like not having the knack for breathing. Friend-making works on principles as reliable as *geometry*—and a lot easier to get the hang of. You have things in common, then you are *good* to that other person and you've got a friend.

Attracting a lover is more difficult. You have to have the sexual *lure* for some other person, and romantic love produces all those emotional spills we're always getting maimed from and picking ourselves up and starting over from, but friends—well, they are the best life has to offer. As we've said, friends can actually be more helpful than family members in life's grisly moments. Partly it's because they don't *belong* to you, aren't joined to you by blood or contract. When you fail, they don't have to feel ashamed, because nobody *connects* them with you. Nobody says pityingly, "Oh, that's Daphne's friend—you know Daphne, the one who put the suede coat on her expense account and got fired." No, you can sneak away from cheering up Daphne and nobody even knows you've seen each other—but a husband, a family member or even a lover is immediately brought *down* by your trouble. . . .

People *associate* you with him. They don't hold your troubles *against* him but there *is* that connection. Also, the loved one may be so affected by your pain he can't give sound advice—all he can do is *hurt*.

Enough cannot possibly be said about the wisdom and efficacy of friend-counsel when you're coming apart. You can also come closer to telling your friends *everything* than you would a husband or lover. I mean, who else are you going to talk to about your husband or your lover? And aren't men *funny?!* They lay on you a heavy load . . . husband depressed and howling in pain, lover married to another woman and he's *killing* you, but no matter *what* they're putting you through, they will say searchingly, "Hey, you don't talk to Bonnie about *me*, do you?" Listen, do they prefer your talking to Bonnie (and getting defused) or getting themselves pushed off the roof?—a man has that *choice*. *Whatever* has fallen on you, friends make you feel whole again . . . not so stupid, not so klutzy . . . and not alone.

The Selection

How do we pick friends? Phyllis Greenacre says in the *Journal of the American Psychoanalytic Association*, "If two people are repeatedly alone together, some sort of emotional bond will develop between them." That may explain some of our choices, but I think a mouseburger just experiments through life with friendships. Many develop because of whom you work with—my closest friends have come that way. Sometimes you *live* near somebody who becomes important to you, or a woman belongs to a man who's a good friend of *your* man, so you take up with each other. Whatever, a mouseburger usually has a *network* of intimates who mean different things to her. In your life I think you need: husband or lover (your best *male* friend), close girlfriends, a shrink, a doctor, platonic men friends, office beloveds, a financial adviser and "helper" friends—hairdresser, dressmaker, masseuse, decorator—and you add on as you go along. You, of course, have your *own* list.

We've spent pages piloting you through the love affair—which probably won't survive the year—and we're only going to spend a paragraph or two on girlfriends who may last your lifetime. Why? Because girlfriends don't need explaining or piloting; they don't usually bring problems or traumas; they bring solutions and peace. The sweet, sunny, effortless, comforting world of women—steeped in each other, in love but not romantically . . . God forbid there should not *be* romantic love in your life, but even worse might be the world without the archangels who are "only" your friends.

I once wrote these words about my friend Charlotte Kelly: "A chat with Charlotte when you're blue is like coming in from a raw winter night and getting into bed with your heating pad . . . or sitting down to your first professional manicure after months of doing your own nails. Charlotte is Bonamine taking effect when you're on a rocky boat . . . weeping when it's time to weep . . . the big burp, cramps easing up . . . the room *not* spinning when you've had vertigo . . . Mentholatum . . . the blasting TV turned off in the next apartment . . . getting *both* nostrils free during a cold. The *worse* your trouble, the better you feel talking to her and the better she feels helping you." (Charlotte must have just pulled me back from the brink one more time when I wrote that. My friend Ann Siegel performs the same magic.)

Thank God, friends now tell each other how much we mean to one another. Women never *were* much for the old John Wayne macho hanging-out-together, but you never said how much you loved each other. Now, since Lib, we tell each other *often*. Some women have great men friends, close as girlfriends, and the same praise would be heaped on *them*. My best pals, aside from lovers, have always been girls.

Could we now talk about how you treat friends?

Some Friends Are for the Good News, Some for the Bad

I am at the airport breaking the news to a "bad news" friend (magnificent in trouble) about a trip David and I are about to embark on. "Doris? Listen, I called and missed you three times yesterday . . . just wanted to tell you I won't be in town for a week. Oh . . . Tokyo, Hong Kong, Bangkok (but before she can kill herself)—Doris, I don't see *how* David and I are going to do it . . .

we've only got seven days for the whole trip and you *know* we're going to be getting on and off airplanes like the cleanup squad . . . I'm pooped *already.*'' (Slight relief on the other end of the phone.) Doris: "But, Helen, you obviously have to *do* this if it's what David wants (gaining momentum); I know *you'd* rather just flake out somewhere and rest."

I've *convinced* her! By the "right"—or "wrong"—emphasis, and making this utterly wonderful trip sound disagreeable, I have given Doris a chance to do what she does *best* in life—cheer people *up.* Good news can only make her uneasy because (a) she can't help—helping makes her feel strong, competent, successful; (b) her own life is not that glamorous, so fantastic goings-on in *yours* can only produce envy.

That's just how this particular friendship works, and I'll bet *you* have friends like that. Other friends—possibly those a little more secure than you—can be happy for your *good* news, actually don't care much to chat if your life *isn't* moving right along. Depression bores them. Well, you just don't necessarily tell everybody *everything* unless you have the judgment of a gerbil.

Reciprocal Trade

Aside from what we *tell* each other—the good news and the bad—and how we comfort one another, what else are friends for? Charlotte once described it this way: You *do* for each other. You trade off. "Use" might even be the operative word here. "Use" means to take advantage of something somebody can tell, give or do for you. Like you *use* your Minox, your typewriter, your Cuisinart and don't think you are "mistreating" them, you use your *friends.* With your few *best* ones you extend unlimited credit—and you don't keep track. Reciprocity is the key. For your few closest friends you move your ass.

There Is No Free Lunch

Everything costs *something*. And so you may be a friend who gives selflessly, endlessly—money and gifts as well as counsel and cheer, without wanting a thing in return—but hold on a minute— you *should* want something in return. You hold that person's marker. Maybe you don't want to be paid back in *kind* or paid back this minute but you should be paid back eventually *some* way. Masochists and sacrificers aren't your role model. Friendship has to be *mutual*. Do we not all have friends for whom we extend credit indefinitely and then, *enough* already. If *you* should ever get dropped, you might ask yourself if you have not been "on the take" . . . trying for a free lunch. I've already written that you don't have to keep the *same* friends all your life. Feel no guilt if you move on or away provided they aren't carrying your marker— but if they are, repay before you go.

As Marilyn Monroe Said,
They Want *Pieces* of You

How far do you go for *non*-friends, just acquaintances, who make demands? You go as far as you can without splattering. The little stuff you do because it's no trouble and helping people is basic mouseburger. When the requests get federal, you stop. Sometimes you can't tell what they're *up* to. At the Private World of Leslie Blanchard where I get my hair colored every six weeks (we have no idea what color my hair is, nobody has seen it for years), my darling shampoo girl said to me one day, "You look so tired, Ms. Brown; I want to tell you about my church." She then described the Seventh-Day Adventists, with whom she said I could "lay down some of your burdens and find peace and renewal." Sweet. I said, Thank you, Celia, but probably not. Six weeks later . . . "Ms. Brown, you have so many responsibilities, so many people asking you to do things, my church would be a sanctuary for you." I am *quite* touched but no again. The next visit Celia tells me what religion means to *her,* again what it would mean to me, says the church is having a special seven-day program to which visitors are invited . . . would I not like to stop by for an hour? One little hour, how can I refuse? But I am *very* busy and a *genius* refuser. "Celia," I said, "if I should ever feel the need for your religion, I will tell you and we will visit your church together, but not just now, I think." Aha! Comes now the *truth!* "Ms. Brown, if you were to come to my church and be converted and tell everyone, it would mean so much, whereas if I, a simple shampoo girl, tell people the miracle of the church, it doesn't mean a thing."

Had! Me too!, she carpenter! The pitch was never for my salvation but for the church's vitality. I tell her then that I am an atheist, which is true, only let's not go into *that.* You have to say no to people who take pieces or there is nothing left (and forget thinking that church might have done me some *good!*). There is so much you can do that is appropriate, that takes guts and energy on your part without getting shnockered (my friend Lester Linsk's useful word).

Use some sense. A friend recently asked to move a camera crew into *Cosmo*'s lobby to get a shot for a movie—*Cosmo* wouldn't be mentioned. I said no. It would have tied up the office all day with the staff falling over cameras.

Another friend, highly successful in advertising, wants to meet my agent friend Sue Mengers, feels Sue might be interested in her women's group. Knowing Sue, I think not, but tell advertising friend to write me a letter describing the group, her wish to meet Sue, and I will send the letter along. Advertising friend irked that I will not simply call Sue and get the appointment. Well, Sue sees almost nobody outside her own world. If I did much requesting, she would stop taking my phone calls. On the other hand, Sue has never said the first encouraging word to one of her clients about letting *Cosmo* do a profile (movie stars are hard to get and we need help). "If they didn't like what you wrote, I'd be dead," she says. I *understand.* When you can, you *do,* when you can't, you *don't.*

Show a Little Class

What is class? Class is non-cheapness . . . non-cuntiness . . . doing the difficult but *appropriate* thing. It may be only a "gesture" but a *classy* gesture is sometimes *expensive. Cosmo* flies Raquel Welch to New York for Francesco Scavullo to photograph her for a cover; Raquel doesn't like the pictures, asks that we not use them. She's wrong, they're gorgeous, but we comply. In the next mail is Raquel's check for her plane ticket and the St. Regis hotel bill. Class. A girl I know gets disengaged from the scion of a wealthy San Francisco family. She gives back his grandmother's emerald ring though she's poor and he said she didn't need to. Class. The doorman lends me seventy-five cents for bus fare because I'm out of change that day and you can't get on the bus with folding money. When I try to pay back, he says, "Ms. Brown, you nice lady . . . let me treat you to the bus one day." Class.

Class is performed with humor, a touch of self-mockery perhaps, never with stuffiness or anger. It's calling somebody you usually want something from and this time not wanting something. It's not bringing up the money a friend owes you for two years (you just don't lend any *more*). Class is not taking things from hotel rooms, even ashtrays, not wearing the scarf and *then* returning it to the store. These are other class rules and, believe me, I'm still *working* on them.

1. Keep your word. If you say you will, do it . . . and soon.

2. Don't be cheap. Going dutch with the girls, do you throw your money on the table and somehow always manage *not* to include tip or sales tax?

3. Keep in touch when they're down and keep on keeping in touch. (When somebody's jobless or ill longer than a week, you know how most people care at first but can't go the distance.)

4. Remember who was good to you *when*. Don't get lost when you move on and they stay still.

5. Though you love gossip, friends shouldn't get bum-rapped when they aren't there. At least state your positive feelings about them even if you don't defend them to the death.

6. Never freeload indefinitely no matter how poor. There are ways to pay back.

7. Don't be so *stuffy*. Laugh a little when the joke's on you.

Respond When They Put Out for You

You can't *get* other people to have manners. It took a lot of pull to get a table at the Russian Tea Room the other night for seven out-of-town friends for cocktails at six-thirty, because that is the beginning of their dinner hour and the Russian needs all its tables for the dinner crowd. Okay, I *got* the table, and one of the guests is ordering the maitre d' (my friend) around like a lackey. I am about to die. No manners! Sometimes people don't *respond* the way they ought to. I recently gave a dinner party for which I knocked myself *senseless* . . . Donald Bruce White (New York's great caterer) food, bowers of flowers, *old* Dom Perignon . . . on behalf of what I thought were crème de la crème guests, and do you know I have yet to get a phone call or a note, let alone a basket of flowers, from *any* of those six couples? Sometimes you can't believe your not-ringing phone, your empty mailbox, the *silence* when people ought to be applauding because you've performed.

My darling, you won't *not* succeed in life without manners but manners (being kind, not causing pain) are *natural* to a mouse-burger, and I think *responding* is the next highest social virtue after listening. (More later.) *Do* it. People are waiting to *hear* . . . waiting for you to return phone calls, answer their letter, thank them for a present, a party, say whether they got the job, that you can't have lunch. I know . . . they crowd you so. Must life *be* a "meaning-less round" of have-to's, get-back-to's? Can't people know you *mean* well but you just haven't got *time* for all that responding? Of *course* you can ignore the "have-to" world but I sometimes think the ultimate hostility is not to let people hear from you who are ex-pecting to. If you get the response over with quickly, it doesn't have to be wonderful. You, my dear, are *not* a disappearing act or you can't be a mouseburger.

Doing It Is More Important than How You Feel About It

Never mind your motivation for doing good deeds—just *do* them! The most selfless love of all—mother love—isn't all that selfless, you know. A mother gives "all" because the baby is *hers* . . . an extension of her own body and psyche. To do something nice for somebody who *isn't* your child may actually be more unselfish. The point is, you don't have to *feel* the altruism to en-gage in it. Writing your check to the charity, showing up for a rally, visiting the hospital . . . *doing* the dreaded chore, whether your heart's in it or not . . . is a lot better than merely "caring," moaning and sympathizing and then doing *zilch*.

Forgive . . . Close the Books on *That* One

Comedian Buddy Hackett once said, "I never carry a grudge. You know why? While you're carrying a grudge, they're out dancing!" And I love this saying: "Acid corrodes the vessel." Isn't that wonderful? It helps me forgive to have David around. David doesn't *have* any hate bones so when I get even close to working up a good permanent snit against *anybody,* he simply wears me down by persuasion and example.

If somebody has done something rotten to you, he will repeat it with another "victim" and another, and finally victimize himself. I have rarely seen it fail. . . . *Life* takes care of villains. Of course life does in the rest of us at the same time—nobody escapes catastrophes—but I'm just saying you don't personally have to do the work of the gods.

Don't Worry About What They Say Behind Your Back

If we all heard every conversation in which we were mentioned unfavorably, we'd *mainline* on Valium. Don't *you* sometimes say rotten things to close friends about people you love? Could you trust anybody who *doesn't* ever complain about near and dear ones, even a husband (*especially* him!). That would mean they're too stuffy to admit *their* darling has warts. Not to worry what they say when we aren't there! When they gossip about you, it probably means you're important—or enviable. The *good* news is that we also say *good* things about each other *in absentia* and would probably defend each other with our lives if required.

Your Money Is Not Their Money—And Vice Versa

Does your would-be borrower work as hard for his money as *you* do for yours? If he is in a field that doesn't produce much money—painting, acting—that is his choice, but why should *you* support his "artistry" while you are nine-to-five (or nine-to-nining) in a job that enervates as well as pleases? Some people always seem to have the "shorts." Okay, loan a little—to the trustworthy—but this was always (still is) my theory: If *you* (I) can get by without borrowing, even when poor, why not *they*? Nobody had more financial problems than I when young and fragile (yes, fragile!). I only borrowed once—four hundred dollars from Alice Belding in *case* I needed it for my first trip to Europe. I didn't and gave it all back. When you have *made* money, I still think there are better things to do than subsidize the "needy." (I'm not talking about giving to charity.) Truth: A man will not *love* you for subsidizing him. He may not love you if you don't, but you'll still have your nest egg. Pay for him and you'll probably eventually lose money *and* man. The same thing is true with platonic friends—you lose them *after* you cut off the funds, or when they can't pay back, *they* drop *you*.

Pursue!

New friends add zest to life . . . just pick a potential or two and let go . . . you'll know pretty soon whether to keep *on* with your phone calls, invitations—they're responding—or they hate it and you should stop! Two new people got *me* this year. Being a workaholic and a *bit* reclusive, I can't even see the friends I *have*, but these two pursued and won. I'm glad. I pursued a couple of times, *too*, and lost—went after two businessmen with beautiful brains. We lunched—I asked *them*—but they haven't asked back. I may have been a *tiny* bit over my head. A *lady* who attracts me I also courted. She doesn't *mind* me, thinks I'm smart and non-treacherous (unlike others who court her for her husband's power) but she doesn't want me to close in . . . you can tell . . . so I stopped. Cool cats, these, who absolutely will *not* succumb to your charm! Okay, you can't get every man to love you or every woman or man to be your friend, but reaching out your arms is as natural for you as an elm tree growing leaves—*reach!*

When Really Lonely, Pick On "Possibles"

Other people's lonesome times will not necessarily correspond to *yours*. A famous designer used to call me for lunch, dinner, weekends at her country place . . . whatever I could manage. She pursued, I retreated . . . I was *frantic* at the time. Well, if I called her this *minute* for coffee and a bran muffin, I *know* she couldn't fit me in. Her life is different now. Pussycat, there is always somebody who needs you . . . who is having, if not a *lonesome* time, at least a *quiet* one and will be happy to rendezvous. Don't get your feelings hurt "picking on" people *not* in their lonesome phase and who, for the moment, are *booked*.

Now for a little etiquette.

Don't Be the Bearer of Bad News

As Richard Berlin, retired president of the Hearst Corporation, used to say, "The bearer of bad news is frequently the cause of it!" (They used to put the messenger to *death* in medieval times when he brought unpleasant tidings to the king.) Just shut up unless you've *got* to speak. I regret having told Elaine of Elaine's Restaurant the other night that the john in the ladies' room was broken. She was perfectly happy until *I* stopped by her table. Why did *I* self-elect to ruin her evening? Don't rationalize you've got to pass on rotten things being said about a friend "so it shouldn't come from a stranger." A stranger will do just fine! Don't send ugliness in the mail. I recently read this scurrilous article comparing *Cosmo* to *Playgirl*—*neither* of us came off well—saying we were dull, my personal column banal, our success predicated on copying *Good Housekeeping* (*Good Housekeeping?!*). You name it, if it was a knock, that article contained it. Where did this little number appear? In an obscure trade magazine. How did it get to *me?* Sent by a friend to my home address who "figured you'd be interested since it's about your magazine." Wrong! People who work for me are requested *never* to show me anything unfriendly so don't bother to send it! Why not try to be the one who sees the bad news *doesn't* get to your friend?

Get Rid of Them *Subtly*

I once telephoned a pal in West Los Angeles when I worked on the Max Factor account at Kenyon and Eckhardt to ask for a ride to work. Well, I woke her *up* and was greeted with, "Oh, my God, it's eight-thirty—I'm supposed to be in the office in ten minutes!" Me: "Well, listen, Sheila, could I be on the corner and . . ." Sheila: "For God's sake, get off the *phone*, I'm late!" Bang. That was twenty-three years ago and I still think about it . . . I mean if I hadn't telephoned that girl, she might *still* be asleep and those were

313

the thanks I got. When people are about to drive you insane (which obviously I was about to do to Sheila), you *can't* scream "Get off the phone, get out of here, I'm *busy!*" because that is fish-wifey. If you want people not to think of you concomitantly with the word *jerk*—or worse, hysteric—you must *quietly*, if steadfastly, get yourself extricated. It's called keeping control while coming apart (Stephen Sondheim lyric from *A Little Night Music*). In control, except in bed, is a pretty good mouseburger thing to *be*.

The Rude Ones

I can't imagine us being rude—not often anyway. We're too *smart*. Yes, I know some important and famous people can be rude, but if they *knew* how much people despise them for it, you'd surely have to put their continuing rudeness down to *dumbness*. Rude people who have terrible jobs—taxi drivers, bus drivers, waiters—may very well snarl because they're tired and have to deal with creeps, but I'll bet you and I in those jobs would handle it differently—I *know* we would. Rude isn't for us . . . we just *aren't*.

P.S. I feel polite/kind is something a mouseburger can easily *be* most of the time to enhance her life and other people's—one of the easy "possibles," so why not *be* it?

"Sorry, I Made a Mistake"

These are not *quite* the five most beautiful words in the English language but *close*. A dressmaker nips in a camisole so close under the arms I'm no longer breathing. She won't say she took too much out of the seams . . . insisted *I* did something to the seams trying it on. She *said* that. The dry cleaner shrinks my dress to a size two; it's the *fabric*, he says. The fabric is 100 percent Forstmann wool . . . I think they boiled it—but no way could the *cleaner* have erred. The restaurant kitchen chars your meat when you asked for rare; nothing but glowers when you point out *their* mistake. The taxi fails to make the turn on Sixty-fifth and you go two dollars out of your way. He's angry at *you!* These are the people you *don't* know well. In your office—*especially* in your office, where many are scared *publicly* to admit a mistake, it gets you *points* to quietly, not sullenly, come right out and say "I goofed." It's bad enough the mistake was made but to further aggravate the person inconvenienced by it by refusing to admit you were involved (unless you really weren't) makes him *twice* as aggravated. In your office, in your house, in your bed, you find friends not able to plain old say they made a mistake, sorry! Couldn't you be the one who can? "I'm sorry . . . I made a mistake . . . I'm really sorry . . . it's my fault." It's so refreshing!

Call Them What Makes You Happy

I call *everybody*—limo drivers, salesgirls, maitre d's, cleaning women, doormen—sweetie, honey, pussycat, without a twinge of contrition. Should you *be* so personal with non-beloveds? Well, it isn't lost on me that endearing terms so casually bestowed cannot have much meaning for the bestowed upon but I do it for *me*. I really do *like* our doorman, *Cosmo*'s new receptionist, the girls who help me buy lingerie on the phone at Fernando Sanchez, and so refuse to reserve my "sweeties," etc., etc., for dear ones only. (I try to call only David "darling" but sometimes slip even *there*.) What you call people is as personal as fingerprints and you shouldn't pay any attention to what I or anybody else calls them; do what makes you happy. P.S. You will probably address people differently as you get older and friendlier. In your twenties you can be more conservative.

Cry Carefully . . . or Alone

Crying is comfortable, loosens up everything inside, but makes you look terrible and people hate your doing it . . . even loved ones. Nobody ever joins in . . . you really *do* cry alone. I used to cry a lot—a *big* sobber—but don't any more. I can't remember my last big cry except when my mother, Cleo Bryan, died last year. The slacking off I attribute to good nutrition (getting sugar and starch out of my life), exercising, good shrinkage and mouseburgering, so as not to have much to cry *about* anymore. If *you're* a big crier, you might want to try some or all of the above.

The Divorce Go-Round

Do not come down hard on either side when a marriage is in trouble. Listen. Support. Sympathize . . . that's it. If the couple gets back together and you have badmouthed (with reason) one of them, they will never forget and you will eventually lose not one friend, but two. Later, if they split permanently, you can choose sides and be a little bit more outspoken, but it's still better to let the friend you've stuck by do most of the complaining—you just tsk-tsk a lot.

Don't Patronize Anybody Else's Heroes or Feel Funny About *Yours*

During my poor little girlhood in Little Rock, I was marvelous at pleasing rich mommies and daddies. "Bring home that little Gurley girl!" they would always tell baby Ann or baby Karolyn. Fraternizing with the rich I found was a way to eat good food, visit great houses, try on beautiful clothes in other mommies' wardrobes, and did I ever know how to be a good guest?! Maybe I hoped they'd *adopt* me though I dearly loved my own mommy and sister . . . maybe I hoped they would adopt *all* of us! Anyway, some of the posh rubbed off, even if it didn't stick, and I've had a crush on rich people ever since!

Is such a crush a bit inappropriate *now?* You bet, but I'm still *at* it! Rich, powerful men who run empires are my idols—just let me sit at their feet and hear how they cornered soybeans. Somebody once described a mogul I was carrying on about as having "an interesting combination of traits—mean and stupid!" I don't want to hear about it! The people in trouble, in my opinion, are the ones who *don't* have crushes and that isn't *us.*

Be Nice to Your "Betters"

Globbing onto a better-off one and driving him *crazy* with your attention, even if it's "selfless" (like offering to run errands or sit with his plants), is psychophantic . . . not rewarding . . . and you're actually "using" him to get yourself into his magic orbit. There is such a thing as *etiquette* with the rich, famous and "better" ones, however, and they do *notice*. One night we *didn't* go backstage to see a famous actor after his agent got us tickets to the show; he was hurt. Today I *did* go to a big-name funeral. At first I'd thought it presumptuous—I didn't *know* the deceased—but she was the mama of one of my employers and David *made* me. He was right. There may have been a certain "fawning" quality among all us employees at the funeral but the family *did* expect us there and appreciated our attending. Whoever you know who's a big deal will appreciate hearing from you (probably by letter) when he has performed well and been written up in the paper. "Betters" can always use praise, but don't go on too long; keep letters to about one paragraph and preferably typed. He or she *might* enjoy your detailed review of his performance or book if the entire thing is favorable, but even then it's usually egomaniacal to think your interminable thoughts are going to be devoured hungrily—brief is better. Just don't ignore a big-deal friend *because* he's big deal; a valentine is a valentine.

We've been talking about how to behave with people we like. Now for some *difficult* ones.

The Losers

Losers are people with a big problem or problems that make *your* problems look like the insole of your sandal came loose, nothing worse, and—important point—their problems *never* get solved. They *love* to get their waxy arms around *you* and squeeze until you are nearly squashed to death; the more you help, the more you *need* to help and pretty soon that's about all you're doing . . . helping . . . your time and your life utterly submerged in the loser's problems. (Feed the alligators and you get *bigger* alligators.)

Do you need these people? Well, surrounding yourself with losers and helping until you're exhausted certainly takes the guilt away from being a *winner* . . . you are obviously a Very Good Person to devote yourself to all this hopelessness. It also makes you feel *important*. There they are . . . mired down again so they send for Miss Wonderful to come counsel and console, listen and sympathize and . . . not get on with her *life!* God knows there is pain in the world, and we must all give money and support to charities, but in their daily life, most mouseburgers ought to associate with and help people who are helpable . . . people like you who have problems they try sincerely to *do* something about. My beloved shrink explained it to me this way: There is horror all around you. You can identify with, be obsessed with, the sad, tearing-each-other-to-pieces creatures, and worry yourself into the eternal ''sads'' about them, or you can get on with your life. It is quite moral to take care of *yourself;* every person's primary goal in life *has* to be his own physical and psychological health. This is the *sine qua non* of satisfactory living and hard to *do,* with pressures so great, if we are constantly associating mostly with gloom and negatives. So help only where you can.

People Who "Cost Too Much"

Not everybody who saps your strength is a loser. Certain bosses, lovers, husbands, secretaries, office managers, housekeepers (*especially* housekeepers), mothers, tradespeople and friends you *also* tiptoe around, scared to death you'll make them unhappy, at the same time wondering how they get away with making you *do* that when there are so many people you like *better* whom you don't have to tiptoe around. Well, at the moment, you may be stuck with the tiptoe person for whatever reason so you continue, anxiously, trying to please. Be encouraged. One day, especially if you've had shrink help, you're done with the emotional blackmailer. You either get them out of your life or their fangs get pulled. You don't care if you ever see them again; you don't want a *Christmas* card from them. God, I love to think . . . but only for the briefest moment . . . about some of the people who can no longer do that to me. Listen, you can't dump them all instantly . . . some may be *family* . . . but at least you can recognize what they are doing and *gradually* ease away.

Bitches Live!

You don't see bitchy women *often* these days but there *are* still some. And bitchy men . . . occasionally homosexual . . . funny and full of lure because they're so bright and amusing and know so much gossip, but then they lash out and hurt you. Director Billy Friedkin said of one of them, a writer, "It's like dealing with the tar baby. After you get hurt, you try to get back by hitting him in the chest (figuratively) but you only come away with hot tar up to your elbow!" For a long time you think it's inept, cloddish *you* who must have caused their disdain (mouseburgers *are* inclined to take all the blame) but later even *you* have to admit it's *them!* They just can't not hurt and maim—finally, almost without fail, doing it to *themselves.* I sat with a bitch at dinner the other night. She kept stopping the party cold, with the arrival of each new course, to point out what I *wasn't* eating. (I've talked about this before.) "I suppose you aren't going to *touch* the tortellini," she announced to me and seven other people. Again, "I guess you're going to pass up the mousse." Finally she came out with "Personally I like people who *eat!*" And I like people who mind their own goddamn business about *your* body, but it's not a mouseburger's way to strike back. If you have to spend a whole evening with a bitch, I think sweetness is the one thing she can't *stand* and it's our mouseburger *nature!* I even kissed this one goodnight!

The Hostile Ones

Hostility is heavier than bitchiness and you can run into it with people you never saw before in your life. Celebrities get it a lot. The marketing director of a liquor company sat next to *me* at lunch recently and said, when *Cosmo*'s publisher introduced me as one of the twenty-five most influential women in America according to *World Almanac,* "Were you number twenty-four or twenty-five?" and he wasn't smiling. This, after being forty-five minutes late to lunch, with eighteen people waiting, and announcing on arrival, "I gotta be out of here in forty-five minutes."

It comes sailing out at you like a flying wedge—their hostility. A man next to me on the airplane is incensed that I will try to work on my book—*this* book!—instead of talking to fabulous *him,* who has brought *nothing* on board to amuse himself with but his big mouth. "So you're going to work all the way to California, are you, little lady . . . my, my, my!" he interrupts again and again, unable to *believe* somebody would prefer her work to *him*. Men do it on dates. "Do you *like* living in this neighborhood?" to a girl who barely has rent for a ghetto *closet*. "Do you always keep your nails so short?" (to one who can't grow anything past the half-moon). "You have a perfect little barrel chest," a man once said to me (God took this one away with a massive coronary two years later—one *does* get avenged).

Well, you have *not* been singled out. The hostility is quite impersonal. And you'll learn some hostility is buried deep below layers and layers of what *seems* to be friendship except how come you come away from each meeting with this friend feeling so *terrible?!* It might be time to face reality: That person is *hostile* . . . nearly eaten alive with jealousy. No matter how they wound, it's better to be *us*. I don't think we're ever *hostile*, are we? Sad, disappointed, occasionally envious (and willing to say so up front!), but never trying to wound another to somehow make *ourselves* feel better. How unimaginable! How gruesome!

Drinkers Are Different from Us

Rich-poor, conservative-liberal, gay-straight . . . lots of categories to divide the world into, but I think one of the most life-affecting is drinkers and nons. It seems to me I've spent half my life having the drinkers drive me quite literally mad! As a young woman, I didn't know what the problem was when I'd been promised dinner and at twelve midnight we're only into pretzels . . . I thought they were just *cheap*. Gradually I began to realize that with drinkers "funny" things happen—fights get gotten into between them and others—not necessarily with you—and you can't really *talk* to a drinker . . . you and he are in different worlds. Drinkers are *slow* . . . they never want to get to the theater, movie, bed, food or check. . . . They just want to "set a spell" and have another drink!

I was with three the other night—one of the most divine women I've ever known—when she isn't nipping—and dear, limited Larry (What does she *see* in Limited Larry? I always ask myself and *know* the answer: Sarah likes weak men), and a doctor they hauled up from Washington, brilliant early in the evening, ossified at the end. When I decided at eleven-thirty that they planned to spend the rest of their natural lives in that restaurant, I departed. Limited Larry put me in the cab, mumbling the wrong address to the driver, so driver and I are soon barreling down toward the Battery instead of up toward Central Park where I live. This is what I have finally decided about drinkers: They should stay with each other and not hang out with the rest of us. (*You* probably figured that out already!)

P.S. Some famous, talented people drink and are they ever patronizing about us *nons?!* This is *their* problem—their silly little defense against the sure knowledge they will one day wind up with cirrhosis of the liver.

Care of Celebrities

Celebrities, though not necessarily difficult, are also *different* from you and me (I'm only a *small* celebrity so we're not talking about *me*). These are my rules for the famous:

1. Talk quietly. Don't burble. Say how honored you are when introduced but don't get all sweaty, agitated and babbly.

2. The more *facts* you have, the better. Familiarity with their *obscure* movie (book, play, concert tour, speech to the U.N.) will endear you. If there's an opportunity, *introduce* this knowledge into the conversation. If there isn't (other people are hogging your celebrity and you can't get on), don't have a conniption fit (as we used to say in Little Rock) or get pushy. Maybe you'll get a shot *later*.

3. Don't talk too much about yourself—important rule—even if encouraged. Just dole out tiny portions of your life or the celebrity's eyes will roll around in his head. There are very few "homey" famous people. They may *seem* homey (you are misled by their moldy tennis shoes and Midwestern twang), but never fear, they are fully aware of who *they* are (somebody) and who *you* are (nobody) and have reason to feel you are not as interesting as they. Even if you are genuinely funny (some mouseburgers actually *are*), I would keep a low profile because you're on celebrity turf and if *you* hold the floor, nobody—especially the celebrity—will be very comfortable. A celebrity has *earned* being center of attention . . . you have *not*.

4. Take the celebrity's *helpers* seriously. You may think, Oh, that's just his Cro-Magnon hairdresser or his masseur . . . nobody

. . . and feel free to ignore them, but these people, even though perhaps monosyllabic conversationalists, spend a lot of *time* with the celebrity and usually he gets *fond* of them. If you are ever in a position to help a helper, it wouldn't be a bad way to get closer to his/her *boss*.

5. Once friends with a celebrity, do *not* ask him to entertain at your company dance (they won't) or let you bring fifteen *other* friends to meet him (they *mostly* won't and who can blame them? . . . that's being "used," and you wouldn't like it either). You will learn they do not give presents. They also do not give any notice when they want to see *you*. They *send* for you ("Meet me at Romeo Salta in twenty minutes!") or show up at your flat unannounced and you are to drop everything, including your undies. They get *fond* of civilian girls but rarely marry them unless the girls are beautiful or rich. Celebrities are really more satisfactory at a distance—on the stage or on television or possibly at a party where you can just gaze at them—than they are in your life, but you'll need to go through one or two to find this out for yourself.

Now let's go on to a *problem* mouseburgers sometimes have.

We're Shy

I agree with Cleveland Amory, who says shyness is just selfishness . . . self-centeredness. You are so occupied with *you*, you get all restricted, even *paralyzed*. Well, knowing what it is doesn't keep it from *happening*. As a chronic sufferer, at least at parties, this is my appraisal: Shyness never goes *away* but you can fix it pretty well so that people can't *tell*. That, my dear, only takes the old one-two—self-discipline. I *make* myself talk to strangers. I try never to wait for an elevator or a bus more than a few minutes without talking to whoever else is there. Same for people next to you in the theater seat or the restaurant banquette . . . just a word or two. I unconditionally pet the dogs of strangers though there is a chance I will get my hand chopped off by the dog or my head by the owner, but I *try*. This talking to strangers may sound a little gauche or corny but it's *good* for little "inward" people like us. I have a role model: Liz Smith, the gossip columnist. Lizzie would talk to a fossil and it would talk *back;* she just doesn't know any strangers. I *frequently* think, How would Lizzie be handling this? You don't have to keep *up* the conversation, once started, but it's good to get yourself to open up for those few minutes . . . drag yourself *out* of yourself. The other day at Bergdorf Goodman a beautiful twenty-year-old blonde was surrounded by at least twenty-eight pairs of shoes, her mother and a salesman anxiously waiting for her to make up her mind. On the way out of the department, I stopped by them for a moment to say, "God, I hope she *buys* something after all you've gone through for her!" Three people—mommy, daughter, salesman—looked at me as though I were *crazed*, but that was my push-by-a-shy-person of the day.

You Are Not *Making* It with this Group

What about something that's *worse* than shyness . . . feeling "out of it"—alien—not like alien in a foreign country with the "natives," but right here at home with people more or less like *you?* It's a feeling some of us get at times, throughout our lives, and when it happens . . . the loneliness, the not fitting in, you see yourself a total failure. It goes deep and depresses the life out of you.

Okay, let's have it out. You are not a creep. Feeling that you don't belong sometimes seems to be part of our specialness. *Everybody* doesn't belong in *some* situations (the sixty-year-old business tycoon visiting his secretary's bridal shower because the girls good-humoredly invited him, the teenage daughter sitting around with her daddy's golf buddies at Saturday lunch, not to mention just standard social encounters in which people don't have that much in common)—but the difference between most people and us is *they* don't *take* it so hard. I have seen David with a group of fashion mavens from Seventh Avenue. David is about as interested in fashion as he is in handling a human brain, and I *know* he can't be comfortable or even know what they're talking about, yet when he gets home, he says he had a good time; like *most* reasonably "well-adjusted" people finding themselves in a "foreign" scene, he just tries to mesh in and not let himself take it very big.

I, on the other hand, am to this day nearly *destroyed* if I'm totally out of sync. These are just a *few* of the groups I (still) find myself out of sync with: Professional Wives . . . not working themselves, they make a profession of being devoted to the *man* in their lives. Professional Mothers. Again, not having a profession they get paid for, they have plowed it all into the children and, *having* none, there isn't much *I* can contribute to a conversation about

323

getting the kid into Buckley (New York's plush private school) or Cora Mae's teething problems. Movie Stars and Famous Entertainers. There is nothing like the glitterers—or the "twinkies," as Sue Mengers calls them—to make you see yourself as a nothingburger. New York's top models. So glorious, so long-limbed and perfect, how are you going to *feel* around them . . . exquisite? (And they are not necessarily great talkers!) Add the Men and Women in New York's WASP Society in their forever-pleated Mary McFaddens, chatting it up at their charity dinners or *après*-concert suppers (though I tend to get on better with the men because we can discuss *business*). And maybe the *worst* (for me) . . . the International Jet Set, who may *include* some of the others just mentioned. I remember a party at Ivo Pitanguy's (Brazil's eminent plastic surgeon) a few years ago in Rio at which I felt really *peculiar*. Ivo, the consummate host—although Brazilian hosts of his stature may not show up at their own dinner parties until after midnight—couldn't have been more charming, but I was *out* of it. They all seemed to be getting through to each *other* . . . smiles, hugs, laughter . . . but you are only getting through to you. It's lonesome! Eleanor Roosevelt said nobody can make you feel inferior if you don't *let* them, but on occasions like this, well, I tend to *let* them.

Here are some notes I wrote a year or so ago after having dinner with a blue-blooded Italian. "It wasn't that M. was hateful, it's just that I *bored* her . . . I don't quite know *how* because I never opened my mouth except to ask questions but she ate nothing at Pearl's . . . how could you eat nothing at Pearl's?! . . . *asked* nothing . . . not one question about my work, my husband . . . *nothing* . . . not a word about our recent visit in Milan . . . it was shuddery."

Listen, you can tell yourself until you're dizzy that *they've* got the problem and of course they *do*. So keep reminding yourself: Whenever people are acting really *funny* (and making you not like yourself), usually they do it with everybody . . . it's their *thing*. A famous movie star, now Broadway actress, is so snooty every time we're introduced (she never remembers the last time), it's like nude bathing in the snow, but she's snooty with *everyone*.

Whether you're comfortable sometimes depends, of course, on *other* people's skill and grace. You can be in the most "intimidating" situations with somebody marvelous at putting others at ease and feel loved like a kitty. Into my rose leaves again—Richard Zanuck, his then wife Linda, David and I spent an evening in the back room of Jilly's with Frank Sinatra and I wasn't even anxious

324

. . . my idol was relaxed and charming. David and I also spent the day with the late Jean Paul Getty at Sutton Place, his estate outside London, just the three of us and his attack dogs. When I didn't know what to do with the high tea spread out for us, he said, "You're the lady, Helen—you'll want to do this," and, seeing I couldn't quite hack it, helped me with it. Darling. Another time in the heart of the jungle in Brazilia with the U.S. ambassador and his wife and several Brazilian government people, I couldn't have been happier because they were so *adroit* at making you feel at home, but it sure isn't always like that, and it isn't always the rich or famous who make you feel funny . . . it can be *anybody*.

Maybe some of us sufferers haven't yet recovered from the trauma of girlhood "unpopularity" on a given (brrrr!) night or two. You stand there *now*, in your carefully pulled together little costume that looked great when you left home but you'd like to rip it to ribbons because nobody at the whole frigging party is talking to you and grisly girlhood memories surface. I have a blind date with an Aggie at Texas A and M at College Station during my one semester at Texas Women's University. Good loyal person, he danced every dance with me as other Aggies cut in right and left on other girls. It stands in memory as possibly the most humiliating night of my life though there have been several excellent runners-up!

I once went back to Little Rock and called up a boy I had worshipped in junior high school—one who had "rushed" me for a few weeks—an early Don Juan—dropped me and gone to my friend Elizabeth. For *years* I really didn't recover . . . it broke my heart. So I am in Little Rock one time before I became "famous" and I called him. He didn't remember me but came to the Marian Hotel to have a drink with me. Children, he was nothing . . . NOTHING . . . fat, sappy. I was almost sorry I'd gone back to lay the ghost—if you'll pardon the expression . . . so romantic and tragic remembering him as he had *been*.

Well, as we said, men are not necessarily a problem for shy girls. Feeling alone in a crowd *is*. Okay, this is what I think we have to remember, us sensitive ones.

1. When you feel you don't belong, it is selfishness, yes, and self-centeredness, yes, but it's also sensitivity. As I said in the opening chapter of this book, we *are* sensitive . . . like dandelions in the wind! We are also *empathetic*, so that if they think we're bland and boring, we *know* they're thinking that . . . our radar is infallible. Such sensitivity is both our strength and our weakness.

If we feel things deeper, take ourselves and our "social failures" too seriously, we also, because of knowing how others are feeling, are able to be great *friends,* lovers . . . to "connect."

2. Just because all of us have arms, legs and bottoms doesn't mean we can all be bosom buddies. You're going to go through life feeling alien sometimes—it hurts but it doesn't kill you.

3. Some of the best "belongers" don't do much else in life *but* belong. Put them with the Women's Temperance Christian Union steering committee *or* at a Malibu coke party and they fit right in, but nobody writes them up in the *Yale Law Review* or even the *Hollywood Reporter.* Shy mouseburgers have successes in *other* areas. The older we get, the more we tend to "specialize" with people who "appreciate" us.

4. Since one to one is still how you get jobs and get love, you don't ever have to *be* popular in crowds. Once, only once in my life, can I remember being a "star" . . . at a party in the British Transport Hotel in Glasgow, Scotland, with a bunch of book distributors and retailers when I was promoting *Sex and the Single Girl.* They don't have too much going *on* in Glasgow, you see, and tend to make a big fuss over whoever is in town, but, for whatever reason, I was a *lioness* that night, saying funny, coquettish things like Dolly Parton or Auntie Mame or somebody who wasn't me at all, and all the men were raising toasts and I was toasting right back—heaven! Maybe I was drunk. It never happened before and it's never happened again!

5. Mouseburgers may not be able to tell jokes at *all.* David Susskind told me a really funny, almost *foolproof* one recently, so, in mouseburger fashion (how am I going to get *you* to meet challenges unless *I* do?), I decided I would tell the joke to somebody (you guessed, I can't *tell* jokes!). Well, I practiced like a maniac, got my courage up to boiling point and told it to Bob Bernstein, chairman of Random House, one day at lunch. Did I pick the wrong tellee? What with being nervous about my debut, I left out part of the middle, which screwed up the end. Bernstein just *looked* at me and shook his head. . . . F—— it, I said to myself, let Susskind and Henny Youngman tell jokes, I will just be the world's greatest listener (more soon).

6. When somebody comes on *too* impressive, he may be in trouble himself, showing *you* up to make *him* feel adequate. A young man I knew slightly gave me a ride into Manhattan from the airport and began to come on . . . not to me but *for* me. He was chief counsel for a large corporation, divided his time between

New York, Los Angeles, London—okay so far, but then he quickly got to his large *staff* . . . "I've turned all eight attorneys loose on *that* one," after which I got the girl-in-San-Francisco, girl-in-Los Angeles, "double your pleasure, double your fun" recall, plus his ownership of *two* flats at the Sherry-Netherland . . . I was *exhausted!* Of course, if you listen as raptly as I'm going to suggest you do, to men and everybody else, you're going to get a lot of coming-on at, but think of it this way: Their bragging really puts *you* in charge, gives *you* the power, not the other way around. Repeat: Anybody who makes you feel like the stuff that comes up in the dustbag of the carpet sweeper is probably more insecure than *you* are—he's just coping differently.

7. Some of the time when you are feeling so uncomfortable and put down, what you really are is *bored,* only you don't recognize it as boredom . . . you just think you're *inept.* As you get older, you get a little better at appraising boredom and acknowledging that you *can* be bored with the famous singer, with people whose picture you see in the paper daily, with just about *anybody.* Boredom with dumb people—never with life itself—is *part* of life like fillings falling out and nights you don't sleep well. Accept.

8. Sometimes the people you "don't fit in with" are *tradespeople*—inappropriate to suffer so much. The men behind the counter at the Stage Delicatessen on Seventh Avenue can turn me into a *schoolgirl* (they really are rather unfriendly) when all I'm trying to do is take out some leek-and-potato soup. You go into a small shop to buy panty hose and three salesgirls, chatting it up with each other, act as though you're *bothering* them, are snippy, cross and suspicious. Them you *don't* fit in with, right, and you have to stop trying to please *everybody* (a hang-up of mine and many mouseburgers). Just get what you came for and leave.

9. Everybody who intimidates you is himself intimidated by *somebody,* or at least vulnerable. You *know* that, of course, and it doesn't help, but just thought I'd mention it. The aging millionaire is gaga about young girls, whom he *revolts,* so he lavishes presents, is utterly fixated on them and quasi-miserable (I know a couple like that, do you?). The successful businessman thinks anything breathing, even if bungling, in the nation's capital is a Very Big Deal and slathers over them (I think these worshippers are really *nuts.* Have you spent much *time* with politicians?!). Knowledge of *their* hero worship may not help *us*—somebody told me when I was young to think about a scary person as sitting there in red wool underwear with big holes in it. Big deal . . . so he's in his

red holey underwear and you're *still* scared, but I'm just saying the vulnerable—and impressed—among us can be in any echelon.

10. If you are *nowhere* with the information you need to keep pace with a particular group, you can keep *still*. You'd prefer to chime in, of course, but if the conversation is completely over your head, silence is better. Eventually somebody will remember they haven't heard from you for two days and bring you into the chatter. Meanwhile, try to turn up the corners of your mouth slightly (I think Mona Lisa at these times), get your jaws to relax . . . not easy, since they feel like Elmer's Glue hardened around pieces of beef gristle . . . and don't tune *out*. Keep looking at the talkers as though you *cared*. I've watched young people handle this assignment rather well when their folks are entertaining big shots. Nobody faults your not talking if you don't look miserable and seem to be enjoying *them*. God knows the talkers need somebody to listen to them.

11. Some of your *most* belonging times . . . now I'm going to get in a plug . . . will probably have to do with work, if you get where I expect you to get. *My* most belonging times have. The year Maxine Daley and I went to Fort Morgan, Colorado, and Prescott, Arizona, to photograph ad campaigns for Stauffer reducing equipment and played poker all night with the boys . . . marvelous! The many trips to Paris, Milan, London, Hamburg, Tokyo to launch new editions of *Cosmo* . . . joy! If this grown-up fun, which I think so much better than partying, is "being one of the boys," that's fine with me as long as I get *in* on it.

12. *Read Time* or *Newsweek* cover to cover every week, also a newspaper. I started doing this really *late*, after getting *caught*. I was in a limousine not *that* many years ago, riding through heavy winter traffic from my office at Fifty-seventh and Broadway to Brownie's health food restaurant on East Sixteenth Street with my friend Danny Kaye, *his* friends Schuyler Chapin, then general manager of the Metropolitan Opera, and James Levine, its thirty-year-old prodigy conductor. Kaye is with the driver in the front seat, I'm in back with the others. What to talk about? What I know about classical music is only slightly more fleshed out than what I know about sports *(nyet)* and what I know about opera *specifically* is just enough to get me into trouble. I've seen *La Traviata* twice and know that Puccini wrote *Madame Butterfly* and *La Bohème* (or is it *Bohemian Girl?*). The Metropolitan season is on, I know that because friends went last week, but damned if I can remember what they *saw*. The only conductors' names I recall are Toscanini and Stokowski, both dead, and Leonard Bernstein, who I think was

Levine's predecessor, so we probably don't bring *him* up—besides, what would I *say* about him? Joan Sutherland, Renata Tebaldi, Maria Callas (also dead), Beverly Sills are or were *stars,* I know, but do they sing at the Met? Levine is overweight—*that* I know, too, which tells me we're not going to be talking health or nutrition or anything I'm familiar with. Well, even to ask questions you need a *base,* and I am grappling around for my base like a drowning prairie dog. . . . You can't just dive in with "So tell me about life in the opera company!" It's possible this little crisis has not got you heavy-breathing, but we're in so let's finish! I bailed out with the most *minuscule* equipment. A thousand years ago I had interviewed Alfred Wallenstein, then conductor of the Los Angeles Philharmonic (one of my sixteen secretarial jobs was in the publicity department of radio station KHJ, for whom he sometimes conducted), and the one fact I'd retained through the years was that most opera companies operate at a deficit. I also remembered *seeing,* but not reading, an article about Chapin in *The New York Times Magazine.* With just this scant ammunition, I asked Chapin, "Did you *like* the article in *The New York Times Magazine?"* and "Does the New York Metropolitan Opera operate at a very large deficit?"—whew! As he answered, I picked up enough information to ask more questions. Levine I never managed anything with; he wasn't keen on dummies or maybe *he* was shy. . . . We know he's a *genius.* Well, you must learn what's going *on* out there much, much sooner than your guru—me. I now read at least the front section and the Op Ed page of *The New York Times* every day even if I'm in a stupor.

Change of subject. A few words about getting along—platonically—with men.

Never Underestimate the Ease with Which You Can Take a Man to Lunch or Dinner

Where are people *finding* these men said to be embarrassed when you pick up the check or who won't even *let* you? I haven't run into any . . . not *ever.* When I was a baby-tadpole worker at Foote, Cone and Belding, I rode home from a funeral with a client (me secretary, him head of travel association) and he suggested lunch. At its end, I said, "Listen, you're a client and I don't think you're supposed to pay for lunch." "Yeah, I guess that's right," he said, "but then, I asked *you.*" "Well," I said, "why don't I just pay for lunch anyway . . . I'm sure I can get the money back when I get back to the office." (I was in way over my head . . . I didn't have the authority to buy anybody a cup of *coffee*.) So I did pick up the check and I did get the money back, but I found out those *thirty* years ago that most men are just waiting to be asked . . . who doesn't like free? You're advised to tell the restaurant people ahead of time to "sign the bill," add tips and mail it to you or you'll drop by later in the day to pay so the dear man never sees you grappling with money or even your American Express card. I've found such precautions totally unnecessary. I usually pay *cash*—I hate the bills coming in later—counting out my tens, fives and ones right under his nose and he just studies the restaurant decor or chats with the blonde next door. Do I sound cross? I'm going to stop this second! The reason we can take somebody to lunch is now *we've* got an expense account and it comes with success. You can't have the E.A. and the success and still be paid for like a little girl, so I, for one, am not *cross*. You'll *have* an expense account if you mouseburger and will find the expense-account lunch a *heavenly* invention that lets you eat well, show off, and even turn business friends into lovers if you want.

You *Are* Flirting, Aren't You?

"Listen, I can drop everything," says my hard-hat friend, a quizzical, attentive look on his fine Sicilian face. I am bus-bound, skippety-hopping along Sixty-fifth Street in my new silk Calvin shirtdress, ten pounds of pearls, masses of hair (my own and Kenneth's), no bra, no stockings, nothing between me and the ground but panties and sandals. *"Later,"* I tell him, flashing him a dizzying, I hope, smile. On to the bus.

A few mornings previously I have been bus-bound but *not* so skippety-hopping in my sensible beige coat and he has said, friendly-like, "Hiya, doll." "Hi," I say back, but I know he doesn't really think much of my outfit; neither do I. He can also tell I'm not feeling like flirting this morning and he's matching my mood. To the bus again.

Some mornings *this*, some mornings *that*. That man under his hard hat—he usually wears it though some mornings his head is bare and his fine Sicilian curls are on view—well, I am almost as fond of him by now as I am of my cat, and no, I don't know his name, and no, we've never said more than six words to each other—we just flirt. When I was twenty, thirty or even forty, I didn't know how to get the good out of somebody like that. I would blush, duck, squirm, try to escape. When you get older you get friendlier—and your working on shyness helps. You realize people mostly are *not* planning to rape, rob, mug or abuse you. So, this is to suggest flirting as a good healthy pastime . . . with your man of choice. Possibly there used to be *more* flirting because nice girls "didn't" (go all the way) so you could flirt insanely and be "safe." Now that nice girls "do," flirting *can* be misconstrued. In a perfectly "safe" setting, like an office or at a party where you'll be going home with your *date,* not your flirt-object, however, flirting is innocent, "safe," and recommended. Director Jean Claude Tremont told the Duchess of Windsor at a party in Paris a few years ago that since he'd quit smoking he simply didn't know what to do with his hands. She searched his face, then body, and said, "You don't look to *me* like somebody who wouldn't know what to do with his hands." *Go,* Duchess!

Flirting takes a little gall and a partner. Older men are super objects. They like it, need it and appreciate it. And no, they don't attack you.

Flirting rules:

1. Pick somebody not "over your head" . . . too brassy to flirt with the famous author or chairman of your company or anybody you seem to like better than he likes *you.* Flirting is only comfortable if *you* are comfortable and feel "equal."

2. Flatter outrageously. No lengths are too far to go.

3. Convince him (if not yourself!) his remarks are the most amusing you ever heard.

4. Tease. "I can't *believe* anybody with such a flat stomach is only going to have one tablespoon of chocolate mousse." "If I thought I'd meet anyone as interesting as *you* at a Cordon Bleu cooking class, I'd register *tomorrow!*" "How do you get your sideburns to *do* that?"

5. Gaze at him. Never look away, no matter *what* they're doing across the room.

6. Do not say anything naughty or risqué. That would spoil everything.

7. Think of yourself as a totally assured, mischievous, slightly naughty but not-taking-the-whole-thing-too-seriously participator. If the flirting isn't working, stop. There's always another "victim." You are just trying to keep the *good* difference—the sexual polarity between men and women—alive.

Your Girlfriend's Man Comes On to You

Nothing is quite so easy as being attractive to the man who is giving your girlfriend a bad time. It isn't your charm, it's your *freedom*. *You* represent fun, adventure, playing the field . . . *she* represents drama, commitment, and every so often a scene or two he doesn't much like ("Where *were* you Thursday afternoon?"). We are not talking about a man who is in *love* with your girlfriend, only one who isn't . . . or not very much. She cannot possibly be as attractive to him as frisky, untethered *you,* because she is *hooked* on him—that immediately removes half her clout. Don't get dramatic. Just quietly turn him off and never *never* tell *her* he came on to you. P.S. If your man is acting spicy with one of *your* girlfriends, don't be too jealous. She *isn't* lovelier than you . . . just not in his pocket. If *she* were his girl, *you'd* be catnipping him.

Now, how about catnipping *everybody?*

Charm Is the Next Best Asset After Looks and Brains—And Can *Almost* Make Up for Looks

The great trial attorney Louis Nizer says, "Charm is affection that has become natural through practice." He apparently thinks you can learn it. Cary Grant says charm is a lethal *weapon* . . . I agree. This is my assessment: Charm is presenting yourself in a friendly, modest way to the world, thinking how it is for *them,* the person you're talking to, what they need to hear so you can give it to them, and nobody ever coming away from you feeling *worse*. It helps to *like* the one you're trying to charm, though that is not absolutely necessary. And you need a sense of humor—the hostile person can never be charming. A West Coast-dwelling, best-selling author is the most brilliant, articulate, entertaining man I have ever met and I could listen to him for *days* but, being a basic hater, he could never be described as *charming*. Then there's the British writer, not nearly so famous, who came to see me recently. Dropping by my office, C. says she's in New York to work with *Time* magazine research people (not bad) but could not *survive* without dropping by to pay her respects (nice). Then she says she read *Sex and the Single Girl* as a teenager, has probably *reread* it fourteen times (her copy *tattered* from rereading she says), and it changed her life (not bad at *all!*). A conversation proceeds in which she is all the things just mentioned (modest, quiet, friendly, drawing *me* out), until, utterly in *thrall*, I go get her a *Cosmo* canvas tote bag with Lovey the Cat on its front. Did she *need* a Lovey tote bag? Hardly. She is on her way to lunch at "21," where Lovey will be a little corny, but her eyes light up, she says "Oh, I love it," and instantly transfers all her belongings to the tote. Am I making her sound awful? She wasn't. And she managed to wedge in *her* achievements, never fear—two best-selling books in Britain, *beaucoup de* love affairs, two nice kids, but *I* couldn't open my mouth without her looking approving and *radiant!* A charmer.

Empathy is a big part of charm. Let's say a filling falls out on Friday afternoon in August and you call the dentist. He's left for the country, says the nurse . . . what New York dentist stays in town on summer weekends? Well, *you*, buried under a monstermound of paper, have not left for *anywhere* and think it rotten the dental profession supposes fillings only drop out Monday through Friday. You say to the nurse, "Jesus, I guess I'm the only one working this afternoon. . . ." Question: What is *she*, chopped liver? People other people love (the charmers) would say, "Jesus, I guess *you* and *I* are the only ones working this afternoon."

Can you learn empathy, charm? I'm not sure. I think maybe empathy is instinctual. Mouseburgers *have* good instincts, however, so charm is not far behind—we just need to move up in our jobs, in our lives, so we have all kinds of people to practice with. I'll bet you're already charming. Now I want to get on to an asset/accomplishment you *can* learn for sure, and one I think important.

Whether It's Love, Getting Ahead in Business or Just Being Liked, Listening Is Your Most Important Asset

That's a pretty big statement, but I believe it to be totally true: You absolutely cannot go wrong being a good listener. The beauty of this particular asset is that so few people *have* it; you'll be hugged and praised for something that requires no natural talent, no brains, no looks, no particular skills . . . all you have to do is *begin*. Some of us *are* almost criminally good listeners *already*. Like a boa constrictor (us) with a rabbit (them) the poor fluffy rabbit doesn't have a chance. I've almost felt sorry at times for the person trying to escape from him talking, me listening; he is going to be listened to if I have to strangle him to get him to talk. Listen, you mostly don't have any trouble. People run into so few listeners that, once encouraged, they go on and on and *on*.

Contrary to what people think, there is no *altruism* in the act of listening. One listens coldbloodedly to (a) endear oneself to the talker (b) pull from him what he knows that you *don't* (is it *exploitive,* I wonder . . . them made to educate and amuse while we sap their very *juices?!*) (c) not ever be thought boring . . . you *can't* be boring if you shut *up,* plus (d) there's a tiny touch of laziness involved here; *they* are doing most of the work. And what do you do if your companion isn't somebody you can *learn* anything from (you run into *those*)? I still can't see opening up like a Marine band and entertaining *them; your* talking doesn't make *them* scintillating. You just get away as soon as you can.

Sometimes you get trapped, of course. A limousine driver recently talked to me the entire trip from O'Hare into Chicago about Floreen's gallbladder ("Had to pick Flo up in the hosp'il myself . . . couldn't arouse anybody else up to do it though I have twenty-eight grands, six sons, eight girl-children and my ol' daddy. Now ol' Daddy had the gallbladder business *hisself* . . .") Drone, drone, drone. Under these circumstances, I do biofeedback, face exercises and think of fifty things you can do with peanut butter. Taxis are less "dangerous" now that partitions have gone up between driver and passenger. I've never ever had the nerve to ask anybody *not* to talk, only recently had the guts to ask that the radio be turned down.

I find listening is a *game.* On airplanes, I have traveled all the way from New York to California, encouraging my seatmate to talk, and, sure enough, as we touch down five hours, three thousand miles later, on the opposite coast, I have yet to be asked one single question about me. Talkers expand like bread dough. On a ride from Memphis to Atlanta, I'll never forget (does one forget *gum* surgery?) a talker talked right through my lunch, my reading the *New York Post,* staring out the window and feigning sleep. Yes, I did encourage him at first, as is my wont, but there are *limits.* Finally, to get away, I pulled out my shorthand book and began to write—poetry, grocery lists, how many different rooms I've exercised in, everything that rhymes with cluster; on he droned. A few months later I got a letter at *Cosmo* (he knew where I worked) asking when I was going to publish all those notes I'd written about *him.* Incredible! None of this should keep you from listening, however. Now for the rules about *how,* starting with the big *Numero uno* to be engraved in your skull.

Whether in Private Conversation or in a Group—
If You Are Doing All the Talking,
You Are *Boring* Somebody!

You may be amusing and articulate, may be the "star" of this particular conversation, may have just had an adventure that *must* be told—but if you think anybody in the world wants to hear *only* from you without his opening his mouth, you are deranged!

Don't misunderstand. Few conversations in life *are* "equal." For whatever reason, one person *is* frequently doing more of the talking in a twosome; in a group, one talker often holds the floor. From somebody *informed* you will learn a lot and, if he is a great raconteur or famous, you may be quite willing to let him babble on, but even *he*—isn't this true?—gets to be tedious and you get restless if you *never* get on.

So, aside from a life crisis during which you may talk to a friend about yourself, even for hours, or you're in a teaching situation, you should check *up* on yourself. If you've been going on quite a while, *stop!* After somebody's twenty-five-minute monologue, it's aggravating to be brought in, finally, with "Well, now, let's talk about *you*" . . . your *talk*-juices may have dried up by then. Better to break the monopoly, I think, with some specific question about his life like "Tell me, whatever happened to those T-shirts you were going to have run up and sell on your vacation?"

But now back to your specialty—listening.

How to Be a Superior Listener

1. Give the storyteller a *chance*. He is telling you about the garage door having slipped its hinges and demolished three bicycles and a Volkswagen. You're apt to lunge in instantly with your *own* garage-door story or, worse, the merits of Volkswagens versus Audis—people slippy-slide so from subject to subject before the storyteller is halfway to his *finish* line! Do let him complete his little story—*everything*—before *you* pitch in. It takes guts not to contribute instantly—"Yes, I was in Cozumel myself" or "My cousin was in his class at Princeton," but the storyteller doesn't *need* your input. Later, when he seems to be winding down, you slip it in.

2. If the talker is temporarily interrupted—the waiter brings a drink, the hostess stops by to chat—get right back to where you *were* and don't let the interruption act as a signal to change subjects. You say, "And so then the IRS people landed in your office," or "So you were at the bottom of the Kimberley Mines" . . . don't even *mention* the interruption.

3. When the story seems to be over, don't think for a moment it is *over*—the teller probably still has a few thousand more words to deliver if you'll let him; almost nobody lets anybody go on *long* enough. Think about the last time somebody let you talk yourself to pieces about your first bicycle or the day you locked yourself out of the apartment in a snowstorm . . . you can talk but who's *listening?!* Let the person really exhaust his subject and I guarantee you are going to be known as one "terrific conversationalist." I've heard that said about me many times and as a longtime, *lethal*, stay-with-them-to-the-death listener, I know it's a way for a mouseburger to endear herself.

4. If you don't quite get the hang of what somebody has said or, frankly, your attention has wandered, ask him to repeat it . . . "Could you explain that to me *again?*" People love to do that—start from the ground up . . . gives them a chance to be even *more* brilliant and you a chance to collect your thoughts.

5. Trust your instincts about subject matter. Sometimes people are dying to tell you about wild unhappiness in their lives . . . the divorce, getting fired, first-degree gout—and other times it's the *last* subject that ought to come up. Don't necessarily not introduce the ugly stuff . . . get the *feel*.

6. Try to *relax* as you listen and just *absorb*. This is difficult when your companion impresses the hell out of you and you want to be brilliant; with somebody like that you almost can't *keep* from thinking ahead to what you're going to say when he stops but if you can absorb what he's saying right down to your *bone* marrow, that's the kind of listening that "gets" them. Of course, if you know you're going to see somebody important or famous, come armed with material to talk about and, yes, complete relaxation is probably out of the question.

7. Be modest. You do what we called in Chapter Two "keeping two sets of books"—the private one in which is recorded *truth*—your real worth—and the public one which is *seemingly* modest—only seemingly. Don't worry, you *get* the good news about you across . . . you just slide it in when *appropriate*. God forbid your friends—and enemies—shouldn't *know* the good stuff, but you

don't bash them on the head ("They *loved* my speech at the USC journalism school" or "Phil and I have never been happier—that man really loves me"). When you sit next to an important man at dinner (you know me, I'm *hooked*), they frequently barely open their *mouths* about what they do . . . you have to *pry* it out. I suppose men in that league *could* feel it beneath them to be questioned by a little sparrow, but I never ran into one who minded.

8. For special people, keep a dossier of what they tell you—names of children, family members, countries visited, committees served on, jobs held—so you don't keep asking the same dumb questions every time you meet. People are happy, if incredulous, when you recall that Sandra Jane, their beloved eldest, wrote a treatise on liturgical music in the twelfth century during her sophomore year at Skidmore or that *his* first job was selling papers for the *Toledo Blade.* How are you possibly going to remember all these (fascinating?!) things about every person you talk to without help? I have notes on about fifty people. Jot them down the minute you get home (or back to the office); consult before next meeting.

Compliment Something He or She Is *Not* Famous for or Good At

The night somebody said to me, "Aren't you Lee Radziwill?" I just said to myself, *Forget Cosmopolitan,* this is for *me!* The short, pudgy man looks "marvelous in that cableknit," the neighborhood grouch is a good dancer, the bookkeeper has a keen sense of humor (does he want to hear he does great bookkeeping?!). You can pay passing obeisance to their "thing," but complimenting their sideline—or their *deficiency*—is more appreciated.

Never underestimate the vanity of a man or woman who is *not* beautiful. You can forget praise for the beauty; they *know.* Tell the pretty girl she is brainy, well-organized or witty but pick the bosom, skin, teeth, hair, feet, eyes, *something* of the less than beautiful and praise *that.* I'm on sure ground here.

Don't Give Away the Store Every Time

You don't have to say what you are *really* thinking to everybody every moment on every subject. You know not to agree with the hostess that the ratatouille was oily or the host looks like a walking sofa in his plaid Bermuda shorts, but do you know enough to hold back your gut beliefs? You have *not* sold out because you don't declare at a *National Review* cocktail party you think the Rosenbergs were framed, or declare for the Monty Python Flying Circus at an opera buffet. You may not *feel* like having it out with machetes and whip chains with these alien folk this particular afternoon and your precious integrity will *not* disintegrate if you keep quiet. On a personal level, I am never for revealing one's gut beliefs, the real me, *all* of me, ever, to an employer, and that rule has served me well all my professional life.

"Listen and Talk" Rules Vary with Participants

No, you are not *always* listening. . . . Yes, you *do* get to talk! Well, there are people you talk to about what *you* want to talk about and those you talk with about what *they* want to talk about. Only a fool chatters away as though all listeners were "equal." In the former category are true friends, and with the best you get equal time. Bosses are in category two. To David's and my genius tax accountant, our *employee*, you might say, we *listen*. If Mr. Meyer is feeling expansive—about the banking of frozen mice embryos, the superiority of paid companions to damsels met in singles bars, neighbors who don't mind their own goddamn business—even though your Krazy Glue is just getting "tacky" and you were all set to get the wastebasket *bottom* stuck back to the *top*, you *listen*.

Cosmo's executive editor, Bobbie Ashley, listens to *me* about 90 percent of the time—sheer indulgence on *her* part, self-indulgence on *mine*. I don't begin to think she is as hypnotized as she seems. She listens because (a) she's one of your industrial strength charmers; (b) I'm her boss; (c) she *cares* for me; (d) the more she hears of my woes and joys, the more power it gives her—information about somebody's troubles, in particular, *is* power, and don't you forget it. But I never kid myself she is having as much genuine fun listening to me as I am having doing all the *talking!* With my close friend Charlotte Kelly I start talking (about myself) the minute she picks up the phone, but she does the same thing with me—we're fifty-fifty. With my close friend Ann Siegel I listen a *bit* more than I talk, but I adore her. My secretaries listen to *me*. May I say if it's important to you that something not get around, don't tell *anybody*—not one other person. If *you* can't shut up and keep a secret that means a lot to you, how can you expect a person once-*removed* from you to be a mummy? That person will tell *somebody*—husband, lover; why then are you astonished when the word gets about? P.S. I've never yet resisted telling some friend or other nearly *all* the news (David hates that) so am never surprised when I get it coming *back* around the mountain.

Telephone Manners

1. Always ask, when you call, if someone is busy, is this a good time to talk. They were obviously doing *something* when you called, or *need* to be doing something. Depending on what they say, you'll know whether to dive right in and expand, to keep the conversation short or call back later. It is the most peculiar thing that even *smart* people figure because *they've* got thirty minutes to kill, you must be free to listen . . . dodos!

2. As the conversation proceeds, voices tell whether they wish you'd get the hell off the phone and not prolong anything or it's going okay. You can't *fail* to get signals without even *asking,* so listen and do what the signals say.

3. If you're getting desperate to get away yourself, try not to say, "Look, I've got a doctor's appointment" or "Harry's waiting for me downstairs." That *instantly* makes the other person feel he was a chattering fool—possibly true, but make a few attempts to finish up with *subtle* pressure: "Cindy, it's been *wonderful* talking to you." "Phil, I loved hearing about Grand Canyon . . . more later?" If the person *still* can't sense your need to finish, then you have to clamp down . . . *way* down with callers who *won't* let go. Jesus, I hope you aren't one of *those.* They pick up the phone and it's *you* and their first thought is, She's a lovely girl but please, God, not *now* . . . I'm busy! I have two friends like that. Wish I had the nerve to say who they are.

4. If you're calling to glean information and the other person is getting restless, it helps to say, "Okay, just these two more ques-

tions and we're through!" They can see light at the end of the tunnel and may continue to talk to you.

5. Do not lie about why you're calling. A noted doctor called recently and said, "Helen, this is a social call . . . I want to know how you are . . . I've missed you." Honestly, he said this. "Well," replied I, flattered to the metatarsal, "I've been following your splendid regime, Doctor, and David too . . . I haven't touched a gram of sugar since last December . . . we're both really great except I came home from Egypt with something I can't seem to shake, blah blah blah. . . ." I was getting ready to do five minutes on the Egyptian blight and at least five more on the Valley of the Kings when he said (I swear), "Listen, Helen, I've finished another book and it's all there but needs pulling together. I thought you might know somebody who could do that." Incredible! A. Anybody I know who could pull a book together is probably working for *Cosmo* so I'd have to take him away from *us*—my livelihood! B. To get me to *do* that, you'd have to be sensitive and *smart;* this friend was neither. It's *okay* to call about your book but better to be direct and honest. "Hello, this is me. I need some help. Is this a good time to ask you? Don't know whether you can do this, but here's the situation." I think you *start* the conversation by explaining almost instantly you need a favor—a writer for your book, a little boost with a boy you've just met, how do you get a relative into dental hygiene school . . . just "throw away" what you really called for (your need) but tell them first you'd like to know how *they* are.

6. Call sometimes when you *don't* want anything. I buy a great deal wholesale and a phone call from me, alas, probably means I *now* need a trench coat, a sweater, a garment bag. *Cosmo* never delivers fashion credits *because* of me—the *editor* picks what she wants—so the only reason I've lasted in my wholesale places is probably that *once* in a while I remember to call just to say their fashion show was beautiful or how's the new grandchild. (You already know by now that I am *sickeningly* careful!)

Show Time

Parties make your apartment or house come alive . . . rooms spruced up, candles gleaming, flowers flowering, records playing, ice clinking, and they move *you* out of sluggish to overdrive. *Guests*, except for crazies like me, *like* parties (I like *little* ones—not more than twenty people). Anyway, they're a known—if somewhat expensive—way for a mouseburger to win and reward friends.

So many books have been written on how to *give* parties, I'll only jot down the tiniest thoughts. I *have* learned how to *give*, even if I don't altogether *enjoy*.

Giving

1. When inviting, think carefully who will work with whom. You love *all* your friends but they won't necessarily love each *other*—or fit together. If somebody is very "fancy," you'd better have a couple of other fancy people for him or her to talk to or at least who live in his world. When I was a bride, Carl Sandburg came to dinner, and the day of the party he must have called five times to say he was bringing still *another* friend. I nearly went mad. How could anybody give a party with add-ons every fifteen minutes and who did he think he *was?* Well, who he was was a living-legend poet and who *I* was was *nobody*. He got there with his five add-ons and it was the most wonderful night of my life. He played his guitar, read his poetry, let all the civilians (*my* friends) read and sing along *with* him. He also drank a fifth of sour-mash whiskey, peed on the front lawn and was memorable in every way. Famous or not, you need to figure out which guests will *probably* be happy with whom. You get better at this as you age. Spend a *lot* of time thinking about it.

2. When you invite, tell people what time is dinner. "Come at seven-thirty—dinner's at eight-thirty" and keep your word. Then they'll know how long to prepare to drink and also not to stroll in forty-five minutes late thinking they're "on *time*." Do you say who else will be at dinner? Many people *don't* but I think it's a good idea.

3. Make the choice—you will be a guest and "have fun at your

own party'' (lots of women claim to do this) or see that *they* have fun. I'm not sure you can do both . . . at least not 100 percent. At a party not long ago we guests all got our food from the buffet, then found places to sit down—normal procedure. I wound up at a coffee table with the hostess' mother, her nineteen-year-old nephew (cute, if not exceedingly bright) and a nuclear scientist. We odd ones got on fine for about forty minutes but then conversation wore a little *thin*. Dessert was finished but we all felt we couldn't *leave* each other because there were no empty seats anywhere at another table to go to—we also knew the other three would be stuck with each *other* and things would have got even *thinner*—guests *do* have a sense of honor. During this thinness, the hostess was at a table with ten ''good'' people having what looked like the time of her life. Now *that's* not a sin—I hate guests who insist on only ''stars'' to sit with—but all this time the hostess paid not one whiff of attention to *our* little quartet, slowly ossifying. She should maybe have been keeping track of us and moved somebody from her table over to ours and vice versa after dessert and coffee:

4. Don't *you* let people get stuck. Rescue anybody who seems to *need* rescuing . . . you can tell when you walk over to them whether they grab you like they were falling out of a tree or seem content to stay put—in which case you *let* them. All evening you have to watchfully move about, chat with the lonely, comfort the stranded, bring guests over to other guests or take them away someplace else. Your duty is in the *trenches*. Watch who talks to whom at cocktails and separate them if they're going to be seated together at dinner.

5. If you're not a great cook, learn to make one perfect little dinner and use it on everybody. You can even serve it to the same people twice—don't you order the same things twice in a good restaurant?

6. You've probably seen this done, but if you're giving a dinner party for more than ten people, some of whom don't know each other, go around the table at dinner and do a little testimonial (say who they are and what they mean to you) to each. People love it. Practice ahead of time.

Going

There is almost no way anybody wants you not to accept an invitation if they've invited you. Never delude yourself they won't really miss you or don't want you there. Even if somebody gives a party for three hundred, he or she keeps track of every little invitee; you are *always* doing them a favor to accept. If you say you will, then *show*. That doesn't mean you have to go to *everything*—you *can't*—but every host/hostess in the world is insecure, and a "no" to the invitation means, inevitably, a rejection; a "yes," and subsequently *attending*, means love. Do you tell the truth when you can't attend? Not necessarily. If you've got a Tiffany reason (i.e.,—one the hostess can *accept*), truth is fine: you've got another date; you'll be out of the city; you're making a speech. But saying you've been out five nights in a row and have *got* to get some sleep before you get mono won't go down well. It's supposed to be dangerous to make *up* something but I prefer that to the old standard recommended, "Sorry, I'm busy"—with no explanation. Too cool. "I've got people coming to dinner," "Paul's family is in town," "We've got theater tickets" sounds fine to *me*. Yes, you can get caught in a lie but probably you *won't*.

When you get to the party—let's say a *big* party, my unfavorite kind—if you are miserable and lonely (we discussed this already) you have to show some guts. As you know by now, I almost don't think you can *be* any lonelier than at a party where everybody but you seems to be connecting, so of course, you have my *total* sympathy. Advice: Find another lady, even a *lonesome* one, to talk to. Females are much underrated as party friends. Do *not* do what I did once in San Francisco—walk into a group of strangers and say, "Will you talk to me? I don't know anybody at this party." They will let you in—what *choice* do they have?—then act as though you'd brought hepatitis *with* you. Don't ask for a handout . . . have the courage just to stand quietly with that group and listen for a minute and see if there is an opening you can jump into. Usually there will be. If people are too rude to welcome you, then you have to move off and try another group.

Think about the shy rules at big gatherings. Everybody is *not* thinking what a nudzh you are—they are not thinking about you *at all*, and it is doubtful you will be alone *all* evening. I've never seen *that* happen even in my worst days, have you? Probably you will

343

be talked to by somebody, however boring, and that brings us to the next rule. Try to *learn* something from the boring one. He or she has got to know *something* you don't. Pull it out.

If you are stuck with one person a long time, these are ways of getting unstuck—I'm sure you know them: "Let's go to the bar and get another drink"; "I have to help the hostess now"; "Excuse me, I'm going to the ladies' room." There's another I find useful . . . "Let's go rescue my husband . . . or rescue that lady *from* my husband . . . they've been talking for half an hour (doesn't have to be true) and they could probably use some new friends." If you cannot find *anybody* to talk to and are really dying, go hide out in the ladies' room for a little while and redo your makeup. I still do that at big charity bashes though about twenty minutes is as long as you should do it before your strength utterly deserts you and you run the risk of *never* coming out. I ran into Lorraine Wallace (Mike Wallace's wife) doing the same thing once at a party.

These are things people have said to me at big parties—coming or going—which made me happy, and which you might want to appropriate: "I learned something from you tonight; you've added to my life." "It cheers me just to see you." (Arlene Francis says this . . . she's dear.) "You made the party worthwhile." "Oh, *you're* here . . . now I know it's going to be a wonderful night."

Getting

May one suggest that you receive presents *graciously?* Open them *immediately* unless the donor doesn't want you to—don't let them languish. Put flowers in water instantly. Write thank-you notes *right away.* As we said, if you write fast, you don't have to write so *good.* There isn't a present-giver alive who isn't *still* waiting to hear whether the wine decanter or luggage tags arrived. I finally *wrote* Phil Donahue to ask if he'd got the antique cuff-link case I sent after doing his show (I thought it was the best show I'd ever done). He *had* got it, wrote a darling letter (he is a nice man) but had to be prodded. Don't ever use one of those printed cards that say "Thank you for your gift" unless you add fifteen handwritten sentences.

So now I'll bet you've absorbed—or rejected—all the advice you could ever want to hear from me for the next hundred years about friends and everything else so let's begin to close down the shop.

Chapter Eleven

MONEY

There's one thing we haven't talked about yet and that is making money. You will *make* money if you follow the tenets of this book, but merely earning a good salary—a *terrific* salary—will never make you rich or even financially secure. To be those things you've got to *save* money from your salary, fees, commissions or business, year after year, and invest it. Seems odd to be talking about money after we've been so *emotional!* You may not get *rich* by saving and investing unless you are a financial wizard—possibly not your area of expertise—and take risks, but if you start early enough to save and invest, you *can* be in good financial shape when you are fifty-five or sixty. Mother *strongly* recommends that you do that.

Forget saving for the moment—I can hear you say that yours isn't a money brain. Your eyes glaze at the mere *mention* of tax-exempts. That is childlike and you know it. You might as well say you don't understand *dentistry* and refuse to brush your teeth! Perhaps you dream that a rich relative or lover will dump a pile of money on you someday—how convenient! But they rarely do, you know. Rich people can be quite chintzy about handing out money to "deserving waifs." . . . That's one reason they're rich! As for sleeping with a man to get it, it's not a bad idea, really, but that takes possibly *more* talent than learning about the stock market—the talent not to fall in *love* with the man because "in love" will louse up your ability to get money from him, plus you have to put your blinders on regarding other attractive (poorer) men, pick a man mostly *for* his money, concentrate on getting some away from him and, when you do *that*, run the risk of screwing up your sexual responses. Go to bed with somebody you're not turned *on* by sexually (so you can keep your brain clear to concentrate on his money), and pretty soon sex has become a little repugnant to you and you're not turned on by *anybody*. Happens. Further, it's not so easy to get money from a wealthy man anyway, even one who's fond of us. Oh, you may be gifted with vacations in St. Croix and some frisky jeans and T-shirts to take along, unlimited Chivas Regal and smoked salmon for your lovers' nest and don't *ask* the number of expensive dinners you'll be taken to (if only you could get your hands on that dinner money one *night* you'd be delighted to fix peanut butter-and-jelly sandwiches for the two of you). *Once* in a while he buys you a trinket, a bracelet or a brooch, but the big stuff usually goes to a wife, which, we will assume, you aren't. No, my dear, getting *keeping* money, stock-portfolio money from a man is, well, *not* easy!

P.S. You also need to be *gorgeous*, not necessarily a mouse-burger credential. Howard Hughes, when pressed by a lady for something substantial, is reputed to have given her a modest bracelet (he had a barrel of them) with a promise to remember her in his will. You remember his will! It was contested for years, but in none of the versions was a girlfriend ever mentioned. Well, you get the picture. . . .

So, to avoid being a destitute old lady some day, or even a *middle*-aged one with the shorts (and possibly some sexual problems!), and, assuming there is no genius man in your life to manage your money or to have made you rich with *his*, then you're probably going to have to make, save and invest money *yourself* in order, one day, to be comfortable. We've already talked about *making* money. Now, let's talk about saving.

Socking It Away

How do you save? Simple. Every payday you march to the bank and deposit *something*, no matter how small. Yes, *you*. I will not listen to you say you can't do it because of recession, inflation or disinflation. Anybody can do it, but it takes guts and a particular mind-set: you have to be *cheap* in the early years and careful to the point of crazyhood about leakage and waste. One of my favorite people in the world—single—decided at forty to buy her apartment when the building went co-op. Wonderful. But when it came time to secure the mortgage, she *couldn't*. Can't you put up assets, a money-smart friend asked, so you won't have to borrow so *much?* Assets . . . *what* assets, asked Alana?! Here is a bright, talented girl who has made money for *years* with her brain who has dribbled away every sou . . . who has never seen the inside of a bus, never *not* eaten well in Northern Italian restaurants, endlessly helped unemployed lovers and friends, treated her *folks* to vacations in Maui. Another close friend—divorced—fifty-two, is vice president of one of *Fortune* magazine's Top 500 corporations and doesn't have one penny in the till or own *anything*. She has changed jobs a few times so there is no money piled in a pension fund; she has some profit-sharing if—*if* she stays with this company another ten years, which she isn't going to do. The Pitiful Rachel stories are *endless*. So are the Good Gladys stories, of course, but I don't think we need to go into those.

I only want to point out it is *not* too late to start being thrifty, and you *must*. Now I could give you a hundred and fifty rules on how to conserve—read other people's newspapers and magazines, sleep in the nude, eat *very* little, bring your lunch, never order *in*, take food home from airplanes and dinner parties, do your own dry cleaning, *walk*, stay off the telephone or call from the office, cut your own hair, wax your own legs, do your own nails, make your own presents—but we haven't got *room*. The only thing you have to remember is DON'T SPEND IT on trifles that are gone in a flash, and that policy must permeate every aspect of your life. Temptations are rampant *and* so are rationalizations: "I *deserve* these three-hundred-dollar boots—I work *hard* at my job; I can't wear anything but pure silk against my skin, genuine leather is *me*. . . . Why *can't* I take myself to lunch with Paula and Vivian at Lutèce? They'll think I'm penurious to say no. Cashmere—I must have cashmere! So what's two hundred and fifty dollars for a briefcase for Pierre's birthday measured against my *love* for him?" *Stop it!* We are trying to build you a little *nest* egg.

Okay, after you have saved—and you *can* do it—here is our little financial plan, masterminded by David, who is a money maven (written up in *Forbes* magazine recently for his investment smarts).

1. Be sure you squirrel away enough cash to tide you over for at least four months of unemployment, six if you're over forty. This money can be in a savings bank or money fund but it must be where it can be converted easily into cash. What *is* a money fund? It is a fund in which your money is pooled with other people's and invested for you by professional managers in Treasury bills, commercial paper, bank certificates of deposit and the like. The kind you want is one that pays a high rate of interest but can be cashed in at any time without penalty or loss of principal. A reputable broker like Merrill Lynch or your bank can help you select one. You can even find one that lets you write checks against your account . . . and still pays interest on what's left.

2. After you have that amount socked away for emergencies (no, not for a mink Eisenhower jacket marked down a third), you must *invest* the next amount of money you manage to save. Study the choices of places to *put* your money . . . it's quite a smorgasbord.

These are some possibilities: Savings bank (with their new money-market certificates replacing the all-savers certificates), stocks, bonds (corporate, federal or local government), certificates of deposit, U.S. Treasury bills, U.S. Treasury notes, money-market funds, mutual funds, etc.

I started to write a little paragraph describing each of these and discovered there is no such *thing* as a little paragraph. Read *Make Your Money Grow*, a Kiplinger Changing Times book (Dell, $3.95), the financial pages of your newspaper and *Standard and Poor's Stock Guide*, available free from any broker who thinks you may open an account. *Barrons*, published weekly by Dow Jones and Company, is a good guide for the small investor. So is *Fact*, the money-management magazine. These are other investment possibilities. Commodities—corn, oil, sugar, wheat, etc.—are *not* recommended for us because "the bottom can fall out" in ten minutes. Investments that *don't* need such hourly attention are probably better. Gold is a commodity and *its* price has been falling *lately* like crazy. Real estate? Possibly, if you have a real feeling, a flair for real estate, you can buy cheap and sell rich, but if you are just buying in order to own your own apartment or house, you don't really have to do that. You can often live just as well in a rental place. Alice Mason, the real-estate baroness of New York, always lives in rentals. Renting doesn't tie up all your money, whereas owning your apartment or house deprives you of interest on your investment. On the other hand, owning an apartment or house can protect you from greedy, rent-raising landlords if the rental market is tight. Whether you buy to have your own home or buy only for investment, remember the poorest property in a good neighborhood is usually better than the best house in a poor or deteriorating neighborhood. Never acquire property far from home—the Azores or New Caledonia. You have to be able to visit your property to have an idea of what's going up—or down.

Collectibles: If you like antiques, silver, porcelain, furniture, prints, paintings, etc., you might consider putting a small amount of money into such purchases. You should have a knowledgeable friend to advise you, probably from an auction house, or a good dealer, but recognize that this type of investment is not liquid. Over a period of years such investments may appreciate, and you have the joy of living with some cherished object, but collecting is not usually the way to get rich.

3. You must learn to move your money *around*. Time was when you could just leave money in a savings bank or "blue chip" stock (American Telephone & Telegraph, General Motors, New Haven Railroad—"widows' and orphans' stocks" they were called) because they were *safe* and let it nest comfortably there and grow. If you do that now, it not only doesn't necessarily grow at a rate to keep up with inflation, but in some cases it can even disappear (the New Haven Railroad went bankrupt). Money can always make money, but you must check continuously what's happening in the *marketplace* and not get trapped. New possibilities keep opening up. Short-term "commercial paper"—lending money to companies at high interest rates for short periods of time—has been a good source of income for the past several years. Ask your broker. Money-market funds that pay high rates of interest are now available for sums as little as one thousand dollars or even less. That means we "civilians" can take our money from a savings bank where we receive 5½ percent interest (at this writing) and put it in a money-market fund which can earn, depending on current interest rates, as much as 13.5 percent. Certificates of deposit are also something new for the not rich. All this may have changed around by the time you read this so *check* your banker, broker, but not

your beau. Men friends—and especially lovers—tend to give bad financial advice. I could tell you real "horror stories" about ladies who took the advice of men they were sure were financially savvy and solvent. Better to seek *impersonal* advisers and keep checking.

Now after you have some of your money stashed away, and keeping in mind the advice just given, here's how David suggests you invest any extra money you might save:

1. Put one third of your *extra* savings in investments that would survive anything but the collapse of the capitalist system or a collision with an extraterrestrial body. That Standard and Poor's monthly booklet you can get free from any broker lists "conservative" stocks; select three or four of these—or (if you have fits over the ups and downs of the stock market even if it is AT&T or IBM) you might try a *bond* of one of these recommended companies and maybe a Treasury bill or note. If you can't afford the "Treasuries"—they come in somewhat large denominations—have a broker recommend a money-market fund consisting only of U.S. government obligations—these are the very safest, of course.

2. The second third of your investment should go into less stuffy stocks (listed in S&P as "aggressive"). They have a chance to rise substantially in value but are still "safe."

3. Your third group should be in more speculative issues. Ask a broker, but specify you don't want *wildly* risky ventures. You want to be reasonably sure that if you do take a chance on less secure stocks or bonds, they may go down but they won't go *out*. If you're lucky, this third of your portfolio is your chance to make a big "score" . . . while the other two thirds of your savings are just that—safe. No oil and gas wells yet—that's for six- and seven-figure incomes, but investing in a business opportunity, carefully checked out, is okay too for this less conservative third of your stake. The point here is to take some chances but not go crazy.

Nobody can forecast what money will be worth in years to come or whether, in fact, our economic system will even survive! One august investment-banker friend—who prefers not to be named in view of his advice—thinks young women (and men, for that matter) are best off saving little and borrowing much to buy whatever they want. (Okay if inflation is high and interest rates low.) They tax *savings* income, he points out, but permit tax *deductions* for borrowing! Still, I think it's best to count on survival of the system and *save* (especially if inflation is down and interest is up). If the worst happens, there's nothing you can do about it—if the worst doesn't happen, you're in beautiful financial shape! The Kiplinger

Changing Times book says *these* are the investment mistakes that keep people from *being* winners—and you'd do well to avoid them.

1. Not having an investment plan or philosophy (such as the one David outlined). You need to know what you're *after*—long-term growth, speculative quick returns, etc.
2. Being optimistic at the top and pessimistic at the bottom. You need to look beyond and away from what's currently going on out there—optimism and bullishness as well as pessimism and bearishness are infectious.
3. Not taking the trouble to be informed.
4. Not getting the best advice.
5. Investing money that should be set aside for another use.
6. Buying on the basis of tips and rumors.
7. Buying low-priced stocks on the theory that they will show the largest percentage gains.
8. Becoming sentimental about a stock or industry.
9. Selling the winners and holding on to the losers.
10. Failing to learn from mistakes.

If you're investing in the stock market, these stock-buying rules given me years ago by my ad tycoon boss, Don Belding, are still valid. Buy stocks in companies that:

1. Pay a 6 percent dividend or more.
2. Have a long record of dividend payments.
3. Have a twenty-year low (market quotation) not less than 25 percent of their twenty-year high.
4. Have crurent assets to current liabilities at least four to one.
5. Have cash and equivalent more than current liabilities.
6. Have no burdensome long-term debt.
7. Have very little, if any, preferred stock.
8. Have modest capitalization of common stock.
9. Have a five-year record of advancing sales or evidence of progress.
10. Have a last report of earnings up.
11. Are impervious to bombing (away from congested centers or have several plants).
12. Are listed on the New York Stock Exchange.

Will a broker brush you off if you come in to invest a few hundred dollars? Possibly yes. "To avoid this," writes Sylvia Auerbach in an article in *Fact*,* the money-management magazine, "send a postcard with your name and address to the New York Stock Exchange, Dept. SF, Public Information Office, 11 Wall Street, New York, NY 10005 and ask for a copy of the *Individual Investors Directory*. In it you'll find the main office of 300 New York Stock Exchange member organizations that *welcome* individual investors. You'll also get a list of the firm's branch in your state."

David suggests you also ask for and read the annual report of a company whose stock you are considering. Look for the list of directors to see if they have other substantial affiliations such as banks or other major companies. Important: Ask whether the management owns stock in its own company. The proxy report—part of the annual report—will tell you.

All this information is to help you *avoid* a penniless middle or old age. *In addition* to what you can *save*, you'll want to do something about retirement benefits. No matter how young—or old—you are, now is not too early—or late—to do some *planning*. Fortunately, the book we've referred to earlier, *Make Your Money Grow*, tells you in Chapter 24 just about everything you need to know to get started. In fact, you ought to read the *whole* book. It's what this chapter is all about—but in sufficient and unboring detail.

Now a word about a mentor . . . somebody smarter than you about money who can give you fabulous advice and thrilling stock tips. Without any question you should talk money and investments with people whose specialty it is. Talk and talk and talk. Just bear in mind that *they* can make abysmal mistakes, too. You need to start with a base of your knowing as much as you possibly can, then conferring with your two or three special money friends. Two or three are better than one. Very rich people usually get diverse advice from their advisers . . . sometimes even contradictory advice. That tells them something. As for one genius mentor who can move you along to the big time, it doesn't happen that *often*. One night at dinner, I sat next to my beloved friend Jules Stein, the late half-a-billionaire founder of Music Corporation of America (I worked there as a secretary, you'll remember), which later bought Universal Pictures—and I asked him about buying MCA stock.

*April, 1982, issue of *Fact*, published at 711 Third Avenue, New York, New York 10017, editor W. Russell Wayne.

"Overpriced," said Jules. "Wait for it to go down a little." MCA stock went on to double, triple and quadruple within a few months—after *Jaws* was released. Fortunately David had bought some. Jules was not usually wrong—he was one of the shrewdest money men ever—but "insiders" sometimes do not put the same value on their stock as less informed outsiders. The big takeover artists who pay premiums to buy companies frequently astound the company heads who have no idea their companies are worth that much.

More on "experts": One day I told a business associate I longed to be rich before I died (this was before David made some money) and the friend took me to lunch with the chief partner of a large and prestigious investment company bearing his name. My "needs" duly noted, the partner recommended their mutual fund. I went home and got the money from David, who was actually doing fine with our investments. Within six months my investment—not that big—was worth eight thousand dollars *less*. I bailed out. They can *all* be so wrong, you see. Then there are the crooks. I remember several people in a beauty salon I went to being cleaned *out* of life savings by a "beloved" client whose husband had a scheme for them to double their money in six weeks. It was so *sad* . . . utter naiveté and greed operating here. I've alluded to this before, but I don't want you to forget: Don't *give* your money to a friend or your brother-in-law or any other crazy person without credentials or even *with* them who presents you with a scheme too good to be true. Yes, social contacts *can* be used to pick up information—somebody working in a major company who knows something—but then you assimilate it and check it out with your advisers. Do *not* be afraid to use your own common sense in investing, or to ask "dumb" questions. Sometimes the "dumbest" questions are the smartest.

Well, pussycat, maybe we've got you *thinking* about not being a money idiot, and determination not to be one will grow.

Chapter Twelve

HAVING IT ALL

I've been handing down pronouncements like Solomon . . . do this, don't do that. . . . Work, love, bend, stretch, endure! What gives *me* the authority? Nothing . . . Nobody. And it's about *time* you asked! Sometimes it seems a little *peculiar,* me sitting here doling out advice. Only the other night I was reading Anne Edwards' biography of Vivien Leigh in which Miss Leigh is described as manic-depressive, frequently paranoid and *indubitably* a crazy lady, and identifying with her like *mad,* especially with the parts about her temper tantrums followed by intense remorse. I checked it out with David at dinner. "I identify with Vivien Leigh a *lot,*" I said. "Do you think *I* am a little disturbed?" "Yes," he said. "I mean not emotionally *stable?*" I embroidered. "I *know* what you mean," he said, "and the answer is yes." "What can I *do?*" I asked. "Just try to keep it under control," he said.

Yes. Right. Keep it under control. Well, do you suppose my way of keeping it under control could be to advise *you?* Jesus! But I *do* tend to think of myself as *your* Evita Perón. Glittering in her jewelry, undulating in her Jacques Fath suits, standing on the balcony of Casa Rosada in Buenos Aires, Eva used to tell the girls, "I am one of you . . . all these beautiful things in *my* life bring glory to us *all!*"

Well, I've got this one good David Webb brooch and ring which I keep in the bank because I'm afraid they'll get stolen and I'm sitting here in my tiger panties at my Royal 440 suggesting via typewriter *not* that whatever *I've* got will bring glory to us all, but that you can *have* whatever I have and probably much, much *more* . . . if you want it. That's all I'm saying but, like Eva, I do feel the need to "share." I got *into* the advice business by accident.

Twenty years ago, when I was writing *Sex and the Single Girl* and doing it all third person—this is what's happening to single women of America, this is how they are coping, blah blah blah— the publisher, Bernard Geis, sent word, Couldn't I be a little more *personal*—maybe even give a few suggestions?! Aha! From that moment on I became a shameless, unblushing, runaway, unmitigated advice giver but careful to say then, as *now,* what I'm advising is just stuff that works or has worked for *me*—or for friends. I've got this simple credo—and that's what I've been writing about for these hundreds of pages: We must fight *back* . . . we must *try!* I feel half of life's challenge is to achieve and accomplish; the other half is to overcome blights so you *can* accomplish. I've always had the blights. There are Saturday twilights *still* when I lie on the couch in David's den covered with my woolly blanket and watch the sun go down . . . David is in California . . . and I am that kind of lonely that has *not* to do with calling a friend up and dragging him/her over to babysit with me but gut-loneliness from not feeling beautiful enough, strong enough, smart enough or "copable" enough just to get *by.* Maybe I will never accomplish another thing as long as I live, I think, including being able to get off this couch and make *dinner.* At that point I identify with every woman in the world in a bathrobe who for that moment in time cannot do a blessed thing but have some more coffee, wolf some more crumb cake, read some more papers, read a magazine if she's out of papers, read the same magazine *over* again if she's already read it but it's the only one she's got, and just wait—wait for an end to come to gloom or to come to *her.* The end of *you doesn't* come, of course, but the end of *it* (the inertia) *does,* and you get back in action again.

The other night on the Merv Griffin show I said I thought of *age* as a disease to be fought back against like cancer, multiple sclerosis, typhoid. The other guest, Rosemary Clooney, whom I've always admired, said she'd had five children, was proud of every stretch mark, didn't believe, as it were, in "having at" yourself, and from that moment on, well, the more I talked, the more the audience loved *her,* hated *me.* Rosey obviously doesn't watch her weight, looks okay, is a beloved person, and I could *feel*—or thought I could—the audience asking, Why are you recommending facelifts and exercise and diet when Rosey Clooney looks as good as you do, maybe better, and she doesn't do *anything?* Well, Rosey is six years younger than I, had better bones to *begin* with, and *I* haven't had a face-lift either. The point is: How would I look if I *didn't* fight back with whatever I've got to fight with? To me *fat* is a ravage of age, and if Rosey wants to be forty pounds overweight, that's *her* style, but it isn't for *me.* Maybe you don't fight *age.* You *can't* stave off birthdays, but you can fight age's *ravages,* can't you? Okay, if not age, you fight *whatever* is having at you and sometimes it's of the *spirit.* Some of us come from *behind* emotionally, and I've been sharing *my* special fears and blights . . . things that plague a mouseburger aside from *looking* mousy, and saying what I do about them. Could I go *on* since we've come so far? I want to say a *few* more things about life—and coping.

You May Not Be Able to Get It (Them) Fixed this Minute

I was getting ready to fuss at a *Cosmo* writer the other day who wanted us to send her to California "to do a movie-star profile for the magazine." Do we *need* her in California? I asked myself (we've got plenty of competent writers there), not having to *ask* whether we needed her at home (we *did*)—but then I withdrew the question. *She* needed her in California. She's married to a criticizing, unsatisfactory mate whom she needs to get away from occasionally and is so valuable to *us* I'm going to help her live with her not-perfect husband until she doesn't want to anymore (they have children). People always urge you to get it fixed *now* (throw Peter *out;* tell your mother to get her own apartment), but it takes time. The thing you *mustn't* postpone, don't *need* to postpone because nobody but *you* is involved, is work on *yourself,* your job. That is what keeps you sane and progressing while you get relationships with imperfect people sorted out, isn't that true?

Everybody Pays

Life is pricey. You can have nearly everything *from* it you want and are a fool if you don't take your share, because hardship and grislies happen to people who *don't* take, so you might as well compensate for them with *success,* but eventually everybody gets handed the tab—a *big* one. You look at some golden people and say *they* only have it *good.* Maybe for *now,* but they just haven't been handed the tab *yet.* As I write this, a certain actress is the golden girl of the hour . . . new baby, adoring husband, Academy Award nomination, *Time* cover and rapturous reviews for her latest picture, etc., etc., etc. But she's *young* . . . check her ten years, twenty years from now. It's not that we wish this luminous actress *harm,* and perhaps she had a rough time getting where she is, but nobody stays golden forever. Some mouseburgers pay *early,* with pain, disappointment, and then later the toll isn't so high. There are *no* people who don't pay. With some there may be no *visible* problem so you think them happy happy happy, but their misery may be of the *spirit.* . . . Some of the most gifted, beautiful, rich and famous people in the world are depressed, work-blocked, alcoholic; they're paying *that* way. Rather than faulting them for being so "silly," we should simply acknowledge that those are *those* people's problems (*their* tab), and we have our own. The reason everybody adores Marilyn Monroe (*now*—we weren't that enthralled when she was alive) is that we learned the sexiest woman of our time—gorgeous, gorgeous, gorgeous—*suffered,* which certainly validates the theory that nobody gets off free! Okay, it really doesn't pay to envy anybody *now* because their scenario isn't yet played *out. Count* on their running into trouble if their good fortune is giving you fits this minute.

Smelling the Flowers

You can rarely grasp how sweet it is, how precious while you're *in* it. . . . That's like being grateful for *air.* I think of my dear, springtime days as a copywriter at Foote, Cone and Belding, living in my mossy-green-shocking-pink-and-white apartment on Bonnie Brae Street, dating, working, doing what young career girls *do* and I could weep *now* for how . . . well . . . how *young* I was! Being okay *today* and having survived, why did I worry so much then that it wouldn't turn out okay . . . why didn't I just *enjoy?* Well, I wrote about my super single life in *Sex and the Single Girl after* I was married and could look back and *see* everything turned out okay! At the time you don't know it's *going* to. So it seems there is almost no way not to waste deep summer nights in your little bed, not realizing at that *moment* how precious life is, how fast you'll be fifty, sixty, and regretful that you didn't gratefully drink it all in . . . guzzle, guzzle, guzzle. What you *can* do to make up for not appreciating it at the time is to *use* everything, accept most offers, the free trip, somebody's house for the weekend, a fur coat loaned for the night, fruit to take home from the party. You should use all your good silver and your good china if you have any, and your good jewelry. . . . Nothing is for boxing and storing and taking out just sometimes. You "use" and see your friends. Your apartment should be used to bring friends *to* and your vagina should be the same way—occupied and bringing pleasure; unused sexual organs may be the biggest waste of all the things you are wasting.

May I offer a whopper cliché? The only things you regret *are* what you didn't do. In my single days I passed up a trip to Bermuda with somebody I wasn't *that* crazy about to stay home on vacation and refinish dining-room chairs. . . . Cop-out! I haven't seen Bermuda *yet.* One day a little groupie from *Life* magazine I was lunching with was going to the track right after lunch with Jack Dreyfus, the investment wizard, to see one of his horses run. . . . The limo was right outside. *I* had to get right back to *Cosmo,* I said, and waved them goodbye at the curb. About five *seconds* later I knew I'd made a mistake and ran after the car but too late!

A younger sob story: As a secretary covering an early-morning radio show for Music Corporation of America, I went right back to the office after checking the AFTRA members' pay scale, etc., and didn't stay for the breakfast party. Even my Simon Legree *boss* thought I was crazed. My point, aside from confessing that *some* mouseburgers don't know when to let up and polish the playful side of themselves (though I have my moments!), is that you can't always feel the sweetness of the scene while it's happening, but you must indulge in what's *there* so it can be poured over you later and the sweetness felt. . . . *Don't miss what's offered.*

You Belong There, *Too*

Sometimes shy or scarred (that's *scarred,* not scared) or apprehensive people are convinced certain kinds of fun are not for them, that if *they* try tennis, dancing, visiting ritzy places, everybody will stand around and die laughing. I felt somewhat that way about discotheques, which only got going after I was fifty. Getting into Studio 54 wasn't a problem, owner Steve Rubell was a friend, but it just seemed to me everybody at Studio 54 was going to be so glitzy, dazzling and *young* . . . hundreds of fifteen-year-old Brooke Shieldses flailing the night away . . . I would feel awful. Well one night I went and, far from everybody being a fifteen-year-old flailer, most of them looked more like Archie and Edith Bunker, and they were all having a very good time, thank you, and *none* were paying any attention to *me*. Listen, there *are* some snooty, glitzy types who might shrivel you if they had a chance, but there aren't enough of them to go *around*. They're spread so thin they can't get *to* all the derision and laughing-at "needed" so it goes unattended. Most of the people who eat at "21," for example—possibly the poshest restaurant in the world, a virtual *club* of power and privilege—are quite ordinary-looking because "21" has to fill up the tables, you see, and there are only so many P. and P. people who could possibly glance askance at *you*. Baby darling, I'm passionate about this! If it intrigues you, challenges you, *haunts* you—the activity *or* the place—then you *must* have a go at it!

We Always Take It Too Seriously

Do you have this problem? We take the *little* stuff as big as the *big* stuff. We get just as upset at the cleaner for losing a dress as we do the airline for losing five pieces of luggage! One summer day I waited in the lobby of the Argonaut Building (my office) over an hour for a limousine to pick me up to go to the airport to fly to Martha's Vineyard to be with David for a weekend during the filming of *Jaws*. I was catching the last plane out that night and the demented car was over an hour late. I couldn't take a taxi because the limousine had presumably picked up my luggage, plus stuff David needed, at the apartment and I *had* to wait. I came close to a *stroke,* very close, and all the time I told myself it was *only* a missed plane, there would be other planes the next day and if, indeed, I couldn't get on one, there would be other weekends, and if not other weekends in Martha's Vineyard (because shooting was nearly finished), there would be other weekends other *places*. I never got *anywhere* with myself! I missed the plane, missed the weekend, and it still hurts! Tell someone *else* to be philosophical!

I *am* trying something new in line with not worrying so much about *silly* stuff. My shrink has advised when you've worried yourself almost to shrieks about something rather trivial (or even *not* so trivial), you finally say to yourself, out loud preferably, just as though you were addressing a recalcitrant child, STOP! Enough, already, STOP! And then you simply *stop*. Do that every time the worry comes back.

We Dread *Everything!*

Woody Allen says, "Early in life I was visited by the bluebird of anxiety." Me, too. Most mornings when I get up and am exercising on the floor, I look forward to a day *filled* with grislies— people at the office angry with me or each other whom I'll have to placate, but whichever one I side with, the other is still going to be unhappy. You buy a blazer that was a mistake and have to try to get the store to take it back, only the ticket clearly says "All Sales Final." You're going to have to spend an hour with a Totally Impossible Person, or break the news to a writer you will *not* be buying the article he thinks is wonderful but you know is *terrible*, or try to track down the painters who left a hole in your wall but they've already been paid. Some days I feel like Thomas Culpepper, who has been caught with Henry VIII's Catherine Howard and is going to be tortured, *then* drawn and quartered and he is lying there in chains with his cellmate and says "I shall know pain before this day is through"—yah! But that's what a *successful* mouseburger *does*. She dreads and then she does it. And when it's all over—all those wretched chores and facing the music—you feel fantastic and proud and good. I've never learned *not* to dread, to take pleasure in the idea that I know I can *do* it. I dread each and every time and feel terrific when it's over.

360

You Hate Yourself Sometimes
(But You Get Over It)

I get it on vacations, even in cities where nobody is chic, or in strange new mirrors. You let yourself *see* once again the hippiness, bulgy tummy, short legs. I had this body structure in my teens, true, but it's aggravating to have it *still* after all those years of self-improving! (To be fair, the structure didn't change but the flesh *has* got firmer and lesser.) I wouldn't call this feeling *depression* (more in a moment) so much as just plain self-*hate* because you aren't and never will be—*beautiful!* Feminist Frances Lear, wife of television tycoon Norman Lear, told me in the airport the other night she thinks young women nowadays *are* confident, are not consumed with self-doubt, believe they deserve to, and *can,* have it all. Frances may be right but I believe this feeling of inadequacy—of not being "good enough" permeates many women—most of us—some of the time. I am staggered anew, racing through New York's wonderful Bloomingdale's, to see that most of the whole bottom floor is cosmetics, miles and miles and *miles* of lipstick, blusher, nail polish, hormones, collagen cream, perfume, the most populated area of the store. What are all these women *doing* here, I ask myself? Don't they *know* none of these things will make them technically more beautiful? They are who they are *forever!*

I *know* the answer, even if Frances Lear thinks I'm wrong. They're all trying, even the young ones, to stamp out the old "inadequacies!"

I got a big case (of feeling inadequate) on the plane (I seem to write a lot about airplanes but things *happen* to me there) on a fourteen-hour trip from Hong Kong to Johannesburg last year. Blessed just to be *going* to all these places, I've told myself for ten days, but the blessing and glamour of it all have worn a bit thin. This particular dawn I am a *mess.* David, in the seat next to me, looks terrible and has been cross as a hedgehog all night. Life is *bleak.* I tot up twelve things that are *wrong* with life at that moment and I don't have to scrounge for number twelve. They're all *easy.* Aside from the twelve *things,* and, granted, one is a little numb from travel, it's the *self*-dislike that seems to pervade this grisly morning. . . . You feel at such times you couldn't chat with a giraffe and hold your own, that your looks would frighten a Royal Saudi Air Force AWAC. Life problems are *always* there but this *self*-not-liking is different—worse than real problems—and is at the heart of my early-morning gloom. And then it happens. It *always* happens, for me at least. *You* don't change. *It* changes—the self-hate goes away. I go to the loo to splash water on my face because we are about to touch down in Mauritius. I look *carefully* at the face—airplane johns have flattering mirrors—and yes, it *has* come through pretty well, the trip, the years. I go back to my seat and begin to like David, who has stopped being a wildebeest now that we are in wildebeest country, and is *himself* beginning to wake up and be caught up in Africa. We are the same two people we were an hour ago, when *one* of us at least was ready to jump out the window, but the gloom, the self-doubt bordering on self-hate have vanished and joy *is* possible after all. Would you call this madness moodiness or vice versa? Yes, I guess so, but I think of moods as something that *show* ("He's moody," you say of a Hamlet type) and this self-not-liking I never visit on anybody else . . . nobody ever *knows,* so I would more accurately call it mouseburger *angst.* Theoretically there shouldn't *be* any self-doubt and self-hate and angst for mouseburgers—only self-acceptance because of one's accomplishments. Well, I can only tell you that for me it's still there sometimes; then it disappears like soapsuds under the cold-water tap. Reason returns. Relief comes in like a fresh breeze off the ocean. Miracle! It's called *life . . . living!*

Rejection Happens to Winners

This morning I called up twelve moguls to ask *their* definition of power for an article in *Cosmo.* Eleven of the twelve—Walter Wriston, Edward Bennett Williams, Alexander Haig, Lane Kirkland, Ted Kennedy, etc., etc., all said, through their secretaries, No quote from *them,* and even the *secretaries* weren't wonderful. Abe Rosenthal of *The New York Times* did send a nice message—I love you but *no* to your request. Only Ted Turner got on the telephone, gave me a power quote and then said, "You're an interesting woman, how old are you . . . forties?" "A little older," I said. "Well, *how* old?" he said. Knowing even *then* I was out of my mind, I said fifty-nine. I could feel the telephone ice over. It was *not* a good morning, but who am *I* not to get rejected? So maybe you and I couldn't sell encylopedias door-to-door for a living, but getting turned down is what you do in life. François Mitterand,

President of France, says, "Everything is a struggle. Everything requires courage and effort." Yah! Hard to remember rejections usually aren't *personal* . . . I may never learn that as long as I live but getting said No to has to happen if you put your head out the *door* in the morning. Rejection is for the President of France, *our* President, *all* presidents—especially for them—and for *us!*

You Can Bear It . . . Yes You *Can!*

I just don't see you/us going berserk under pressure—and disappointment—and blowing our cool and blowing our life. We *know* about people your age who insist life be only love and flowers, friendship and beauty and pleasure, and with the least *pressure* (naughty old society *doing* that to them!) or even disappointment, up go their baby arms to ward off the pain, and they say No no no, I can't be expected to *deal* with this shit and it's off into drugs, booze, hippiedom (though that's pretty much over). Listen, hideousness is right out there ready to take a swat at you at all times and it *does* occasionally . . . it always will—but we've got a tremendous capacity for *absorbing* pain and hurt and, yes, frustration. You can go underground for a day or two or a week—not be quite so foxy as usual—but don't stay down there too long. You won't meet *anybody* you like and I don't want to have to come looking for you!

Now I want to talk to you about a big-deal problem that even a winner, somebody *not* hiding out, can run into.

Depression

People who don't *have* depression of any kind have no sympathy whatever with us "deep feelers" who *do!* They think we can make it go away by saying, "Scat, go away, dumb old depression," and *not* to be doing that is sheer self-indulgence. Hah! A man I work with—an almost *criminally* undepressed type—was clucking disgustedly over his secretary the other day. She'd told him she hadn't slept *any* the night before . . . was "just sort of anxious and worried." "Would you tell me what that girl has to be anxious and worried *about?!*" he demanded. "She has a good job, her husband loves her, they go to Jamaica every summer and ski every winter— pretty terrific trips for kids their age. Together, I'd say they make

363

about forty thousand a year. For God's sake, what has she got to be *unhappy* about?!''

Because this man is a dear friend, I have resisted—with almost *inhuman* effort—saying "Screw you, Mr. ———. One might wish *you* would come down with a tiny bit of depression just *once* and you'd stop being such an ass." We depressed ones really *don't* choose to be depressed any more than a migraine victim chooses a migraine or a person with one arm *prefers* getting dressed by shuffling into his clothes that way! A woman I greatly admired—Sue Kaufman, who wrote *Diary of a Mad Housewife*—was beautiful, rich, successful, beloved by her family, and finally jumped off a roof to end her *monumental* depression. Did she really "want" to jump?

Depression comes in three forms: One: physical malfunction—Asian flu, a cold, anemia, cystitis, low blood sugar, syphilis, recovery from surgery, the curse coming on, haven't eaten for ten hours—all of which can sap your *joie de vivre*. Two: exogenous—an *outside* happening—death, firing, loss of lover, etc.—brings you down. Three: endogenous—though you may find a "reason" and say *that's* what felled you, this kind of depression really has little to do with external causes. Doctors believe endogenous depression (the *bitchiest* kind because it keeps coming back) is caused by a biochemical imbalance—the sufferer has a predilection toward depression, probably hereditary (it can run in families) and there is no way to *explain* its existence any more than you can explain diabetes.

Now, endogenous sufferers often have *real* reasons for the blues so our depression is both endogenous *and* exogenous. Through the years, I have had some fairly horrendous *real* problems—family, health, money. My shrink says that, given the set of problems I had growing up and as a young woman, it's quite astonishing I'm not locked away in a mossy little cell somewhere. I am an absolute living monument, he says, to what one frail little person can do about life! Nevertheless, with all these problems solved—by the mouseburger system—what *else?!*—mild endogenous ("causeless") depression does tend to come back on me. Even now, I wake up *mildly* depressed or anxious about 30 percent of the time—wake *up* that way, mind you, not *stay* that way or go to *sleep* that way.

What to do?

Solution for Depression

Blues caused by illness go away when the illness goes away—so much for them. Exogenous depression, brought on by the big, *real* problems, gets "solved" when the problems get solved. Endogenous depression—*not* connected with outside happenings—might be serious enough to send you to a shrink. Go, by all means (more in a moment). Less *federal* endogenous depression, *my* kind, you simply live with (I went to a shrink for other reasons) and find it's taken care of—at least mine has been—by the same technique that's helped me solve all my other (real) problems and get what I want from life: action, self-discipline. I have never been able to *think* away a depression. Mine goes away not because of hope, faith, wishing, prayer, religious conviction, transcendental meditation, incurable optimism or *any* mental activity, and I would not suggest you try to get rid of *yours* that way either. Mouseburgers get results by *acting*. My early-morning blues evaporate because of getting *on* with whatever I have to *do* that day—which is usually *plenty!* It starts with exercise. All that bending, stretching, reaching, breathing, gasping, groaning, pounding, hurting—physically punishing yourself a bit toward having a better bod—*helps!* Edward Villella, the ballet star, is said to be physically battered when he finishes his daily practice sessions. If you're young (or my age and used to it), it's okay to push your body quite far beyond comfort. So I wake up with the blight, but, after exercising an hour, there is no *way* you don't feel better.

It isn't *just* exercise that perks me up in the early A.M., though that's the *big* helper. (Afraid I'm still babbling about *me!*) I put on my makeup (which I kind of enjoy because I'm *good* at it—lots of practice—and the face responds), get into one of my little outfits which I adore although I'm not on the best-dressed list, and feel better *still.* Breakfast—gucky stuff (Optifast) that tastes like a thick chocolate malt, made in a blender—only eighty calories but twelve grams of protein and *delicious*—while I read *The New York Times.* Out to get the Number 10 Central Park West bus, and *whatever* it's doing out there—snowing, raining, heavenly blue October day, soft, shiny April pink one—I love the look and feel of New York City. On to my office (studying people on the bus), into *my* world, and by the time I start doing the work I'm good at and get paid well for and am rewarded for . . . well, by then, unless the depression

365

is caused by a BIG PROBLEM, I feel *virtually* undepressed. I don't believe there has ever been a time when I have been unable to work—to get *on* with it—and there shouldn't be for you, either. Feeling horrible you can't help. Not getting on with it you *can*. And the blessed thing about fighting depression this way is that you don't need anybody to *help* you—not a soul; it's all within *your* grasp. I guess I've always said to myself, Well, I may not be the smartest or brightest or youngest or most beautiful or talented, but by God *nobody* can self-discipline any better than *I* can! That I can do. And you understand—I've made clear, haven't I?—what is self-discipline? Just doing whatever you're supposed to do that day plus a little *more* if you're really scared and worried!

Shrinkage

If you have severe personal problems—big *real* ones or unpindownable general depression, then I think you go to a shrink for advice and support. I can no more imagine not going to get your hurting head and *heart* taken care of than one would go around the streets with blood spurting out of your throat or broken bones sticking out of your *arm*. The idea that you ought to be strong enough to "handle these things yourself" is so fatheaded, I picture the perpetrator of this idea as somebody clanking around in a suit of armor, eating the still-beating heart of a human enemy he's just slaughtered. Neanderthal! Yes, we've all known people who've been in therapy for twelve years and are just as crazy (crazier?) than the day they went in, but they've undoubtedly got rid of a lot of psychic pain during their years in sessions, and if they're not more stable now than then, it's highly unlikely a shrink "worsened" them. When a person *continues* to stay in therapy through the years, it's not *necessarily* because the shrink is a Svengali and won't let go. . . . It's probably because he's still getting some good out of his therapy and would be *worse* off shrinkless. (Woody Allen checks in with Dr. Erica Freeman every day he's in New York and by phone when he's *out* of the city.) Six *Cosmopolitan* writers—our *best!*—are all patients of Dr. Mildred Newman and Bernard Berkowitz, who wrote *How to Be Your Own Best Friend*.

How do you find a *good* shrink? For indeed, there are many "bad" ones, just as there are plenty of not particularly competent *medical* doctors. Well, you shop. My first *good* shrink, after a few duds, was recommended by another doctor. So was my second and present psychiatrist, Dr. Herbert Walker. You must basically *like* your shrink, even though the sessions can be difficult and you cry a lot.

My first *good* shrink, consulted in my thirties, got me off the Don Juan trail, made me able to love a *lovely* man when he came along (David), got me *married,* said I *could* manage a high-powered ad agency job and steered me through it, contributed ideas for *Sex and the Single Girl.* You see, no matter *how* willing and able you are to do it yourself, a mouseburger needs a *support* system, which may indeed include this person. A few years ago, now living in New York, I had a special problem and found Dr. Walker. He helped—he was wonderful—and I see him now every two weeks usually for one forty-five-minute session (you can get a *lot* done in forty-five minutes). We discuss my business problems, terror of getting older and a few other anxieties. He has never steered me wrong, never. He is the Elizabeth Arden of my *soul* I tell him . . . *insides* need sprucing up, *too!* Shrinks are expensive, God knows, but if you need one, you *manage.*

Crazies Are Out There Who Can't Be Fixed

A man I know visits his long-ago-divorced wife two or three times a year because (1) she is pitiable; (2) he is kind; (3) his children implore him "not to forget Mama." He has been married twice since *that* marriage and is happy with his present wife. During his visit, the first wife keeps a handkerchief in her bra which comes out fairly soon after the visit begins because she will start to cry. This handkerchief-sequestering and subsequent crying during visits have been going on for about fifteen years now. Couldn't they somehow have a calm, friendly visit *without* tears? he asks her . . . could she possibly get herself *not* to cry? No, she says, she *couldn't* get herself not to cry. Something is obviously wrong with the lady. She decided long ago not to grow up, to continue to have "tantrums." Her sadness is deep and primordial and apparently as important to her as oxygen. It's also a way of punishing the man who left her, only he is not a good punishee any longer; she doesn't make him guilty, only sad.

Another divorced friend was harangued by his wife when they split with cries of "Your sons are going to grow up homosexual if you leave!" (She knew how to get *at* him.) Also, "You cannot bring *my* sons into the presence of that *whore!*" (the man's girlfriend—perfectly nice lady). Five years later, she has custody of the children; the man takes his boys to dinner three times a week no matter *what* else is going on in his life, but his wife has never forgiven his leaving her or ceased to make flogging him her principal *raison d'être*.

Crazy ladies, right? You wouldn't be one of *them* for all the mink in Maximilian's—right!—but having chatted with both these men recently, I decided to ask myself the other night (here it comes—this is a *biggie!*). . . .

Am *I* One of the Crazy Ones?

Is there something *I* am doing—or not doing—some idiot behavior hung on to, some idiot friend unparted with who is dragging me down, keeping back happiness, fulfillment? I couldn't find it. And you know I would *tell* you if I could! I would *insist* on telling you! I think I have taken my very average self and now, after mistakes, am not letting very *much* interfere with happiness. So now I'm going to ask *you* a two-part question. First part: Do you not know people who, if they would give *up* some idiotic behavior, let in common sense and reason, would not be infinitely happier and more productive? Examples: the man who is deep into cocaine; the girl who eats to obesity; the mother who harangues her loved ones until they hate her; the boss who brags and belittles; the girlfriend drowning after ten years with her married man. Second part of question: Is there something dopey, crazy, counterproductive *you* are doing that is blighting your life but nobody can get you to stop it? Just asking. If you get a Yes answer, is this maybe the year you want to *fix* it? I'll bet you can. I *know* you can.

You *Do* It!

While I was learning shorthand and typing at Woodbury Business College so I could work (as it turned out, the rest of my life!), my complexion was raging with acne, ruining my life a bit, so every Saturday I would get all dolled up and go to downtown Los Angeles to try on clothes in department stores (I couldn't afford to *buy*), window-shop up and down Broadway, cheer myself up; I was nineteen. One day I decided to go to the Clark Hotel on Hill Street to see if I could find anybody to interview for the school paper. I didn't even *work* on the school paper but was taking a journalism class. Some dear bellman—he didn't get tipped or even seem to *expect* to be—said there was a lady radio commentator in the hotel whom he called up and got to come downstairs. I'd never heard of her. I got out my little notebook and took notes for about an hour, typed up the notes. Well, the school paper wasn't the *least* interested—they'd never heard of her *either*—and the whole exercise was ludicrous really. Nobody asked me to rout out a "celebrity" to interview; nobody needed me to and I was *scared.* I've got to stress how unprepossessing I was and how *lonesome* . . . always all alone on my little projects, but they seemed a way to forget about the acne for the afternoon and maybe "accomplish" something.

"Worthless" or not, the interview was good practice in initiative. You do it when you don't *have* to—think *up* stuff, ridiculous and unasked-for as it is. . . . You do that when you're young and scared to get you shaped up for the *better* stuff later. I'm still at it, older and still scared! Fear never leaves you.

My friend John Clerc-Scott, former West Coast director of Previews, the international real-estate firm, who moved millions of dollars of Malibu beach houses and San Fernando Valley ranches, castles in Ireland and villas in Mexico during his time there, said to me the other day, "The relaxed salesman is not a good salesman. If you go in dreading the pitch, internally in some turmoil, but determined to do the best you can, you are probably going to be terrific. . . . Fear and dread give you a fighting edge. People who seem to be 'born salesmen' are just as apprehensive as the low-key ones. . . . Their fear and dread are turned into positive selling."

Jeffers/Carr Associates, in their book *How to Find a Job: A Woman's Handbook,* say "Feel the fear. . . . And do it anyway." Yah! As you get older, the stuff you go after, the goals you lavish your fear on, become a little "worthier" perhaps.

When we bought our apartment from Mike Nichols five years ago, we asked him to leave the Steinway as part of the deal—it was a buyer's market then and you could get sellers to *do* things—because one day I hoped, prayed, fantasized that Stephen Sondheim would come and *play* on that piano. (I saw *Follies* nine times, every other Sondheim show at least three, am a Sondheim *freak*.) Well, I don't give that many parties—maybe three a year—am not the *bravest* hostess, so it took me four years to get up my courage to ask S.S. because I also had to ask *other* people I didn't know so he'd have somebody to play with. I got *them* first, then sent my letter off to Stephen—all I had was his address, no phone—said how *much* I hoped he'd join us. He said Yes; I whooped with joy and worried four solid weeks before the party that he'd drop out. He didn't. He came . . . and didn't get anywhere *near* the piano except to see what kind it was. On being asked to play, he got his wounded-fawn look, backed away and changed the subject. I *knew* somehow he'd do that though I had hoped otherwise. We haven't become buddies; I admire him as much as ever. My point is that you must *do* things—get them out of your system. I will probably never get to hear my idol play the piano in person but at least I don't have to keep working on *that* project, *that* fantasy . . . I *did* it!

I'm working on *something* like that all the time, and you are *too*, yes? Initiative doesn't cost a *thing* and you don't have to be born with it. Dozens of my projects haven't worked as *well* as Stephen. It doesn't matter. You *try!*

Passion Is One of Your Component Parts

I plucked this out of a magazine, attributed to somebody named Brother Jeremiah: "If I had my life to live over again, I'd try to make more mistakes next time. I would relax. I should be sillier than I have been this trip. I know of a very few things I would take seriously. I would take more trips. I would climb more mountains, swim more rivers and watch more sunsets. I would do more walking and looking, I would eat more ice cream and fewer beans. I would have more actual troubles and fewer imaginary ones. Oh, I've had my moments; and if I had it to do over again, I'd have more of them. In fact, I'd try to have nothing else. Just moments, one after another, instead of living so many years ahead of each day. If I had it to do over again, I would go places, do things, and travel lighter than I have. If I had my life to live over, I would ride on more merry-go-rounds . . . pick more daisies."

Brother dear seems to *me* to be uttering sheer *drivel!* You can't have "moments" if you don't do *everything* with passion. You can't be *selective*. For me, watching sunsets, picking daisies and riding merry-go-rounds only have meaning when contrasted with, yes, achievement—or at least taking out *after* achievement. Passion is not noisy—just quiet and *determined*. Someone dear to me with lots of problems, *not* self-induced, often says she simply can't

370

cope—"I have no coping equipment," she says, and believes sincerely that some vital thing was left out when they got her recipe together.

I could shake her. *Nobody* is born being able to cope. Coping is an outgrowth of motivation. You gotta *wanta*. You learn coping by *wanting* to cope and practicing and trying some things that don't work and discarding them for something better. . . . Yes you do it with *passion*, with *determination*.

In his book *Christ Was an Ad Man*, Bob Pritikin quotes these words of Calvin Coolidge: "Nothing in the world can take the place of persistence. Talent will not; nothing is more common than unsuccessful men with talent. Genius will not; unrewarded genius is almost a proverb. Education will not; the world is full of educated derelicts. Persistence and determination alone are omnipotent!" I call those two things *passion!* And, as my book-publisher friend Howard Kaminsky says, "Life is not a sprint, it's a marathon—you don't do this one crazy thing for a few months or a year and then you've got it all wrapped up—you keep running and after a few *years*—minimum—you begin to get in view of the finish line."

That about *says* it. Author Jill Robinson feels "It's much better to be in the condition of longing . . . getting satisfied turns out not to be everything you want," says Jill. Maybe—longing *is* delicious but so is *getting!* I think you ought to be doing *both* at all times. And I devoutly believe *now* is the best time of all to be alive. I heard some dopey actor say on television the other day, when asked whether he had children, "I wouldn't want to bring a kid *into* this world with what's going on!" My God, it's a *fabulous* world to bring a kid into! When *I* was a kid in Little Rock, black people were getting lynched, white women were in disgrace forever if they gave in to perfectly normal urges, got pregnant out of wedlock and had an illegitimate baby—don't *ask* about the blemished life awaiting the *child!* People died of pneumonia, tuberculosis, childbirth and syphilis. . . . There was barely a labor union. . . . Well, I could go on. Of *course* it's scary and rotten out there in many ways, but read Barbara Tuchman's *A Distant Mirror* about fourteenth-century horror if you want to stop thinking it's so tough and rotten *now*. My dear, you live in a world that is the best it's been *so* far in terms of humanity and opportunity, especially for women, never mind how very far we still have to go. I just thought I'd get in that plug!

* * *

I'm now going to leave you with just these thoughts. First a set of "irrational beliefs," culled from two books by Dr. Albert Ellis (*Guide to Rational Living*—Hollywood-Wilshire, and *Reasons and Emotions in Psychology*—Lyle Stewart); if we could rid ourselves of *these*, we really would come close to emotional maturity.

1. The idea that it is a dire necessity for an adult human being to be loved or approved by virtually every significant other person in his or her community.

2. The idea that one should be thoroughly competent, adequate, and achieving in all possible respects if one is to consider oneself worthwhile.

3. The idea that certain people are bad, wicked, or villainous and that they should be severely blamed and punished for their villainy.

4. The idea that it is awful and catastrophic when things are not the way one would very much like them to be.

5. The idea that human unhappiness is externally caused and that people have little or no ability to control their sorrows and disturbances.

6. The idea that if something is or may be dangerous or fearsome one should be terribly concerned about it and should keep dwelling on the possibility of its occurring.

7. The idea that it is easier to avoid than to face certain life difficulties and self-responsibilities.

8. The idea that one should be dependent on others and needs someone stronger than oneself on whom to rely.

9. The idea that one's past history is an all-important determinant of one's present behavior and that because something once strongly affected one's life, it should indefinitely have a similar effect.

10. The idea that one should become quite upset over other people's problems and disturbances.

11. The idea that there is invariably a right, precise, and perfect solution to human problems and that it is catastrophic if this correct solution is not found.

Aren't those wonderful? And now these final thoughts from me.

1. Happiness isn't *there* every day . . . not the lush, euphoric kind. Every so *often* you get to get on the happiness raft and float around in the sun, spent from swimming, but you did good and you're so happy. But you can't stay on the raft forever and pretty soon you have to get down, paddle back to shore and do what you usually do in life—cope, climb, manage, endure. . . . Then

"summer" comes again and you get to get back on the raft—more happiness! The raft is always there waiting to welcome you.

2. People who only love their family—husband, children, a relative or two, plus maybe a friend—haven't got the hang of love at *all*. You have to go outside to really love.

3. Do not muck around with hate. The most virulent kind should last only about as long as a severe case of cramps. After that you can remember and eventually "get even," but don't stay roiled. Hate keeps you too messed up to get anything done.

4. The only difference between people who get a divorce and those who don't is that the latter just don't *want* to; their aggravation with each other is just as serious; they get just as angry as the divorcers but they stick.

5. There is enough time to do everything *important*. You maybe have to give up shopping, staying at the party until 4 A.M., lunching with girlfriends, suffering fools, stuff like that, but time is ample.

6. If you don't put "something in the mail," you won't get anything back. No use waiting for the letter or phone call if you haven't given anybody a reason to call or write. You have to *initiate*.

7. If you don't consume sugar, salt, caffeine, booze, very much starch or smoke; if you sleep enough, exercise a *lot,* take multi-vitamins, have work you adore and no secret *need* to be sick, you very likely never *will* be—not even a cold.

8. Having work you love is as important as having *somebody* to love—not *more* important but just *as*. Men *know* this; women are learning.

9. When you have to get somebody to do something over or better, don't criticize instantly; say something wonderful about their talent, then suggest the improvement. Nobody can redo work very well who has just been *destroyed*.

10. If you're going to rave to somebody about somebody else's wonderfulness—that person is the smartest, funniest, friendliest—you'd better start off the raving with "except for *you,*" if the raved-to person could remotely be considered in the same competition.

11. Stay away from doctors. They tend to make you sick.

12. Do not fail to know that when you have been doing most of the talking, you are *boring* somebody (this is a repeat rule).

13. Do not put anything rotten in writing. Tell the person to his face (another repeat).

14. Never fail to get *all* the soap out of your hair even if you have to stand in the shower fifteen minutes. The least bit of soap still in will screw up your shampoo—and the rest of your week.

15. When a woman is older, good posture, exercise and real jewelry are the only things that make any difference in her looks.

16. Good posture is the one most important thing anybody can do *now* to look better.

17. The only way to get your weight down is not to eat as much as you have been eating. Satisfied is out of the question. You have to feel slightly uncomfortable and hungry during your weight loss or it probably isn't *happening*.

18. Do not fail to know you can feel as rotten and suicidal about another man as you do *this* one, even though you are sure you will never love anybody but him as long as you live (repeat rule).

19. Do not pick a pimple before its time. If you can wait until "after" its time, you may find there was no time at *all*—false alarm—and save yourself lousing up your face.

20. An orgasm is like vitamin C. Your body can't store it. . . . You have to keep getting a new fix.

21. Always leave for the airport fifteen minutes earlier than you *could*. It will save your valves wearing out.

Oh, darlings, I could go on and on . . . but I've *got* to stop so you can get to your mouseburgering! And I can get back to *mine*.

I'm wishing you all the happiness I can possibly wish you—and this is something to think about—though I don't know who said it: "Do not follow where the path may lead. Go, instead, where there is no path and leave a trail."

I'll bet that's what *you* do.

374